W9-CPX-318

Faith-based Schools and the State
Catholics in America, France and England

Faith-based Schools and the State
Catholics in America, France and England

Harry Judge

Oxford Studies in Comparative Education
Series Editor: David Phillips

SYMPOSIUM
BOOKS

Symposium Books
PO Box 65, Wallingford, Oxford OX10 0YG, United Kingdom

Published in the United Kingdom, 2001

ISBN 1 873927 39 8

This publication is also available on a subscription basis
as Volume 11(2) of *Oxford Studies in Comparative Education*
(ISSN 0961-2149)

© Symposium Books, 2002

All rights reserved. No part of this publication may be reproduced,
stored in a retrieval system or transmitted in any form or by any means,
electronic, mechanical, photocopying, recording or otherwise, without
the prior permission of the publisher.

Typeset in Monotype Plantin by Symposium Books
Printed and bound in the United Kingdom by Cambridge University Press

Contents

Preface

The writing of this book was made possible by a generous grant from The Spencer Foundation of Chicago, for whose encouragement over the years I have good reason to be grateful. The work could not have been completed without the willingness of scores of busy people, in each of the three countries studied, to engage in confidential interviews and arrange visits to schools. I try to explain in the first chapter why it is not possible, for reasons of confidentiality, to identify them here but I hope that they are all aware of my warm appreciation. It is a common, and agreeable, custom to dedicate books of this kind to those who have had to tolerate some of the inconveniences caused by the author. As the book goes entirely in threes, I offer it to my three children with a particular ascription of Morant to Simon, Combes to Hilary, and Ullathorne to Emma. They will be able to work out why.

Harry Judge
Oxford
April 2002

CHAPTER 1

The Tapestry

This volume is peculiar in at least two ways. Since most books sensibly enough begin at the beginning and go through the middle to the end, the design of this volume needs some initial justification. In terms of both time and place, its argument moves about in unconventional directions. There are good reasons for this apparent aberration.

This first brief chapter is the introduction to a case study in one of the classic problems of politics and theology – the relationship of Church and State. It takes as its focus the educational policies of successive governments with regard to Roman Catholic schools in three countries. It must, therefore, seek to be comparative, and not simply expository. At the same time, it needs to be historical as well as comparative, for the good reason that without the history (or rather histories), contemporary problems are unintelligible. A conventional method of interpreting the factual material would therefore explain the situation in each of the countries, taking each of them separately and in turn, and in each case starting at the beginning of the story and building towards the present. Only when that task had been completed three times could a comparative or contrastive style be attempted. The weakness of proceeding in this superficially attractive way is that the single case study quickly dissolves into three quite separate narratives. The reader and the writer ignore or forget, during each phase, the importance of what is happening at precisely the same time in the other two countries. The synchronic is sacrificed to the diachronic.[1] In this book, however, the reader is deliberately encouraged to hold all three countries concurrently and continuously in focus and to remain aware of the multiple similarities and contrasts which they reveal. Therefore, in each of its three principal sections, the book rotates around all three societies: at no point is it in danger of becoming a one-country study.

The second peculiarity of the book relates not to place, but to chronology. Most studies of this kind would start at the earliest point and work to the contemporary. Some might begin with the present and then attempt, with some difficulty, to move backwards. This book does neither. The argument underlying the method adopted is that in all three countries a critical point was reached, and some key issues resolved, at about the year 1900. Thus, the year 1900 becomes a natural pivot for the presentation which follows. For that reason, the presentation begins, in chronological terms, neither at the beginning nor at the end, but in the middle. So, the book opens with a case study within a case study, by exploring the lives, work and prejudices of three contemporaries at the turn of the nineteenth and twentieth centuries. Archbishop John Ireland opens a window into the American case, and Emile Combes and Robert Morant into the French and English respectively.

Each of these biographical studies can, however, make sense only in terms of its antecedents. These antecedents further illuminate both what is common and what is distinctive in the three national cases. The antecedents are explored in the second section of the book through three parallel biographical case studies from an earlier time: Horace Mann for America, François Guizot for France, and Archbishop Ullathorne for England. Running through these six biographical studies, as through the section which immediately follows, are the threads tracing the relationship of Church and State. The shape of this book is better compared with the design of a tapestry, rather than with the logical precisions of a map or an architectural drawing.

After these six biographical studies, the reader should be left with a clear picture of the roots and realities of the situation in all three countries at the very beginning of the twentieth century. The ways in which those conditions have since been, sometimes dramatically, modified are then to be explored in the third section. This is now attempted not through biographies, but by a discussion of the distinctive ways in which each of the three countries addressed the unsolved problems. These distinctive ways of tackling common issues are the 'arenas' of the third part of the book: the Courts become the dominant site for American developments, the Streets and political revolution for France, and the Corridors of Westminster and Whitehall for England.

The fourth section again embraces three countries, this time by describing the present (early twenty-first century) relationship of government and State to the Catholic schools in all three countries. These Catholic schools are not, however, to be viewed in isolation, as they have been chosen as a particular and serviceable example within the larger category of religiously affiliated schools in all three countries. They were chosen to serve as exemplars for an obvious reason: as members of an international grouping of schools, they might be assumed to share at least some characteristics across national boundaries, and are in any case the only group of denominational schools present in all three countries in sufficient numbers to make a comparative approach practicable.

The final chapter of the book aims to identify the most significant comparative threads running through the tapestry of the book, and closes with policy recommendations that might usefully be derived from them. The reader who finds this order of presentation unhelpful can, of course, plot a different path across the book.[2]

The book is based upon an extended study of the sources and commentaries identified in the bibliography. That work was, moreover, supplemented over some four years by scores of interviews and visits to schools in each of the three countries. It must be emphasised that these valuable encounters were not designed systematically to assemble an empirical base for the analysis and conclusions offered here. They were properly described to those agreeing to take part as constituting a reality check. It was necessary to acquire as accurate a sense as possible of the character of the schools, and to satisfy myself of the degree to which practice and policy at school or local levels accurately reflected official policy pronouncements. For that reason, a guarantee of confidentiality was given and I am grateful to all those who gave freely of their time and experience: heads of establishments, administrators, teachers, pupils, government officials, representatives of associations, bishops and politicians. I regret not being able to thank them here by name and accept full responsibility for the conclusions drawn from private discussions with them and of which full records have been preserved.

A few more technical points must be clarified. I have tried, wherever this proved practicable, to group notes and references at the end of chapters and to keep the text itself as uncluttered as possible. Citations have been directly identified in the notes. The study deals only with England rather than the United Kingdom as a whole, although there must obviously be references to both Scotland and Ireland. Wales, for most of the period under review, was politically and administratively assimilated with England.[3] Although the term 'public school' is notoriously ambiguous in England, it is hoped that the context always makes clear which meaning is intended: used as a synonym for one of the well-known independent schools when the reference is purely domestic, it resumes its plain and obvious sense whenever direct comparisons are made with publicly funded and controlled schools in America or in France. There are, similarly, a few occasions when 'Catholic' in England needs to be specified as including at least some Anglicans as well as all Roman Catholics. Normally, however, Catholic and Roman Catholic are employed interchangeably. The author has failed to achieve any consistency in the use of capitals for the two frequently linked terms, Church and State. Taste and context have again been determinant.

The lives of the three contemporaries which now follow – Ireland, Combes and Morant – illuminate the extent to which relations between Catholic schools and the State differed at the beginning of the twentieth century. Their three antecedents – Mann, Guizot and Ullathorne – expose the roots of those differences and similarities. The three arenas – Courts, Streets and Corridors – illustrate three different ways of resolving conflict.

Notes

[1] For the important issues underlying this distinction, see P. Burke (1990).

11

[2] For one who prefers to reflect on each country consecutively (rather than all three concurrently), and to follow a strictly chronological thread, an obvious possibility is: chapters 5, 2, 8, 11 (for America); 6, 3, 9, 12 (for France); 7, 4, 10, 13 (for England). In any case, chapters 1 and 14 keep their natural place.

[3] A fuller and recent account of developments in Northern Ireland and Scotland is to be found in the special number of *Oxford Review of Education*, vol. 27, no. 4, December 2001.

CHAPTER 2

Three Contemporaries: John Ireland

The free school of America! Withered be the hand raised in sign of its destruction!

Those were the long-remembered, if sometimes regretted, words spoken in 1890 by a flamboyantly eloquent archbishop on the unlikely occasion of a meeting of the National Education Association in his Minnesota home town.[1] The National Education Association was, as it still is, one of the most influential organisations in American public life, representing (even more comprehensively than at present) a wide range of those who worked and fought for the interests of public education in America. Its ranks embraced not only teachers but administrators, professors and university presidents. To the surprise of many and the annoyance of some, a Roman Catholic prelate of Irish origin had been invited to address, at 9.00 am on Thursday 10 July 1890, one of the sessions of their annual meeting. Who was that prelate? Why did he say what he did? Why were his remarks contentious? Two years later, on a summer evening, but thousands of miles away in Paris, he made a significant, if less well-reported speech, this time in perfect French. What had this second speech to do with the first? In the answers to these four questions lie many of the clues to unravelling the complicated and highly charged story of the relationship between Catholic schools and the State in America and in France, two of the three countries with which this volume is concerned.

The name of the archbishop was John Ireland, and the whole of his life was deeply marked by the faith and history of the unhappy island from which his Irish father had emigrated in 1849, when John was eleven years old.[2] The family, after a short time in Canada and Vermont, had settled in the small frontier town of St Paul. Already established there, in the modest circumstances appropriate to a missionary enterprise, was a French bishop, educated in the characteristically Gallic traditions of the seminary of St Sulpice in Paris. The dominant threads were already being woven into the life of the young émigré, whose rapid progress at the local Catholic school was noted by the bishop, who, loyal to his own country and traditions, despatched him to a junior seminary at Maximieux, lying on the road between Lyon and Geneva. In that place, John Ireland acquired a mastery of the French language, a deep affection for the culture of what was now his third country, and a permanent taste for the polished oratory of the seventeenth century (and especially of the formidable bishop Bossuet). He was plunged into a changing world dominated by the powerful interactions between politics and religion: as the newly enthroned Emperor of the French, Napoleon III strongly supported the influence over national education exercised by the Catholic Church and its largely anti-republican clergy. Many of the French clergy still regretted the loss of the effective monopoly of education which they had enjoyed until 1789, and remained painfully aware of how much their predecessors had suffered during the years of revolution. They were bitterly aware of the continuing threat to their influence represented by the radical tradition in French life and politics and by the increasing and hostile involvement of the State in the business of educating the young.

After his return to Minnesota, from his senior seminary where he had found life much less enchanting, Ireland served (for a shorter period than the tone of his later recollections implied) as an army chaplain in the War Between the States, relishing the robust mood of those years and the camaraderie of the military life, fiercely proclaiming his patriotism while allegedly leading his flock in the singing of the Marseillaise.[3] In 1870, he paid the first of his many visits to Rome, acting as an adviser in the deliberations of the Vatican Council of that significant year. In 1875, he was appointed coadjutor bishop of St Paul – an assistant bishop with rights of succession – duly becoming the diocesan bishop in 1884. Four years later, he was promoted to the rank of archbishop in his newly created province. The rest of his life was divided between energetic activity in the rapidly emerging West, active participation in the national affairs of the Catholic Church, and an increasing entanglement in the intricate webs of Vatican politics. As an active campaigner for temperance, he was an outspoken enemy of the saloons and became an ally of the railway magnates, with whom he cooperated in establishing new settlements for immigrants, who, in his firmly expressed views, needed to be rescued from the corruptions of the east coast.

In the official eyes of Rome, the United States remained until 1908 a missionary territory and was, moreover, a country in which the true Church was perpetually threatened by the incomprehension or hostility of an overwhelmingly Protestant and often secular majority. The American Catholic bishops, working among the unfaithful, therefore enjoyed considerable powers and exercised a degree of autonomy, the extent of which in the fullness of time caused the curia many headaches. As there was little formal organisation, the bishops were often left to improvise their own policies in circumstances that were largely unprecedented, and often misunderstood by Eurocentrically minded cardinals in the holy city. At their third national meeting in Baltimore in 1884, the American bishops demonstrated their sense of oppression in a largely unsympathetic society, as well as their orthodoxy, by formally restating the principle that Catholic children should, wherever this was practicable, be educated in Catholic schools and that every parish should therefore strive to establish such a school.[4] Such an insistence was, of course, entirely compatible with the doctrines of Rome and with the policy which the Catholic clergy struggled to apply in the widely differing circumstances of European countries. The Catholic cause in Europe had, at least since 1789, been indissolubly linked with that of monarchism and political reaction. Republicanism, on the other hand, was associated with nationalism, hostility to the Papal States, infidelity, freemasonry and a powerful distrust of the clergy. As successive waves of immigrants poured from Europe into the United States, the Catholic school became for many of them at one and the same time the focus for cultural continuity and identity and, paradoxically, the means of integration into the burgeoning new society. For many of them, as for some but not all of their bishops, the national parish (defined by its Polish, German, or Italian population) and its parochial school were the indispensable bulwarks against the perils of being submerged in an Anglo-Saxon, anglophone and overwhelmingly Protestant establishment.

These, however, were not the opinions or prejudices of John Ireland. A dogmatically convinced Catholic, he was at the same time an outspoken American patriot who never tired of emphasising the crucial differences between European and American forms of the republican tradition. There were often ambivalences in his attitudes and statements but, whenever accommodation seemed feasible, he asserted the virtues of the common school for all Americans, as Horace Mann had classically defined them.[5] The Archbishop, as an anglophone Irish-American, had little sympathy with those (especially if they were Germans and challenged his authority in his own diocese) who wished to remain permanently rooted in the world from which they had come, rather than to transplant their lives and families into the pluralist culture of the republic of their adoption. While he of course supported the right of Catholic schools to exist and to preach the faith, he foresaw clearly the potential dangers of segregation and separation. In expressing and seeking to pursue educational and cultural integration, he was consistently and vigorously opposed by the Archbishop of New York, Michael Corrigan. Corrigan and his supporters argued that Roman Catholics had good reason to distrust and separate themselves from a Protestant majority which had successfully dominated the public school system in the metropolis. Ireland was by no means isolated in his defence of a specifically American solution to what he saw as a specifically American problem. His allies included the firm but diplomatic Cardinal Gibbons, Archbishop of Baltimore, as well as the founders of the Catholic University of America (who also had strong views on the distinctiveness of American Catholicism). The volatile Denis O'Connell industriously manoeuvred in the offices and corridors of Rome to represent the views and aspirations of Ireland and his friends.[6]

This informal yet well-organised clerical group pursued a number of closely articulated policies. Their policy towards elementary schools, Catholic and public, has already been identified, and will be further developed later in this chapter. The Catholic University of America was an equally necessary part of their plan to articulate a specifically American form of Catholic higher learning and to raise the profile of their religion in the republic. They wished to remain open to, although never to be confused with, the best of what they nevertheless regarded as an aberrant Protestant tradition. By doing so, they hoped to moderate the dangers of being marginalised in a society whose fundamental values they approved, and which through a united Christian effort they wished to defend against the excesses of materialism and secularism, the deadly enemies of all forms of spirituality. This relative openness was viewed by Rome with sceptical distrust. Several of the more outspoken among the American bishops, aware of their solidarity with the American Catholic working man and anxious to secure justice for him, resisted the conservative Roman tendency to attribute to trade unions (in all countries) malign intentions towards the established order, and enmity towards religion in general and its Catholic form in particular. A legitimate distrust of freemasonry, they objected, should not be extended to justify opposition even to relatively harmless forms of 'secret' societies: Ireland's party therefore argued successfully for a number of years against the threatened condemnation of such broadly moderate organisations as the Knights of Labor, founded in 1879 as a national union open to all workers. For similar reasons, they persisted in supporting the controversial priest, Edward Glynn, an open ally of the radical New York politician, Henry George, in his long struggle against the efforts of the Archbishop of New York to silence him.

Deep differences of opinion running through all these ecclesiastical squabbles bubbled to the surface when Peter Abbelen, an American priest of German origin, resentful of what he denounced as the deliberate and insensitive disregard by Church leaders like Ireland of authentic and distinctive European traditions, in 1886 carried his protests to Rome four short years before Ireland's dramatic speech to the National Education Association. In his memorandum, Abbelen fulminated that: 'The "Americanization" of the German immigrants should ... not be hastened to the detriment of the religion of the Germans, least of all by bishops and priests who are not themselves German'. Any such Americanisation should represent a slow and natural process: '"Americanizatio" Germanorum sit processus lentus naturalis'.[7] Ireland and Gibbons mobilised their troops to refute these unwelcome accusations. Denis O'Connell was indefatigable on their behalf and a somewhat bemused Pope and curia politely brushed aside the protests from disgruntled clerics in a remote and imperfectly understood country. These, they concluded, were American and not European quarrels, and therefore of no great significance. Ireland and the Americanist party, arguing that Catholics in America were Americans and not German or Polish (or even Irish), seemed to be gaining the upper hand. Separate schools for Catholics were, it could now be openly argued, not necessarily a universal virtue in the youthful United States, where monarchy was no longer an issue, and where the republic, in the spirit of its founding fathers, was respectful of traditional religion and Christian virtue. John Ireland was now emboldened to speak his mind in the very citadel of American public education, and to declare himself and (some of) his fellow bishops its friend. Unfortunately, one of the immediate effects of such an unsolicited declaration was a suspicious hardening of attitudes against the Catholic cause.

Ireland's position was developed with some care, not least because he wished to make clear the principles on which he was about to carry forward some bold educational experiments of his own and within his own diocese. He demonstrated yet again that his position was very different from that of the Archbishop of New York and his supporters: 'I am a friend and advocate of the state school. In the circumstances of the present time I uphold the parish school. I sincerely wish the need for it did not exist. I would have all schools for the children of the people to be state schools'.[8] But if that wish were to be realised, certain conditions would first have to be satisfied. Religion should be taught in all schools of all types: how else could irreligion and materialism be resisted, as all the best voices in America argued that it should be? Moreover, there should be appropriate financial support for teaching in denominational schools, including, of course, the Catholic schools. To achieve this just end, Catholic and other schools could be leased by their owners (the churches) to the local school board, which would then assume responsibility for employing the teachers, who would then in effect be paid from the public purse for delivering instruction in the so-called secular subjects. The giving of specifically denominational teaching, for example through the catechism, would therefore continue to be the direct responsibility of the churches, who would as a result of these new and favourable arrangements have the resources and the capacity to discharge these duties. Church teaching would be given on church premises by church teachers, but not at public expense. Such proposals could be made with some confidence at the beginning of a decade when religious instruction of some kind was common in many of the public schools and when students could commonly be withdrawn from those schools for denominational teaching, and when the efforts of the Supreme Court to establish a strict wall of separation between Church and State still lay in a remote and unanticipated future. The Archbishop pointed towards England as a country which had since 1870 succeeded in providing public funds for religious schools at the same time as according an appropriate place to the teaching of religion in all the public schools.

John Ireland, however powerful and persuasive his renowned rhetoric, was rarely content to launch words without actions: within a year of his National Education Association affirmation, he tried to apply the principles of an 'English' solution to the problems of education in his own archdiocese.

In the summer of 1891, he was happy to endorse the arrangements proposed by the parish priests of two communities, carefully designed to secure support from public finances for their economically struggling schools. Despite the fact that they were not without precedent, the arrangements in Faribault and Stillwater immediately attracted hostile national attention. A similar scheme had been in operation since 1873 in, of all places, the archdiocese of New York, at Poughkeepsie.[9] It is not clear why two successive archbishops, both fervent advocates and builders of separate schools for Catholics, chose to ignore this anomaly. In closely similar ways, the Faribault-Stillwater scheme provided for the renting for a nominal sum by the local school board of the Catholic school premises. Instruction in religion was to be given within the school, but outside normal classroom hours. Responsibility for modest payments to the Sisters who continued to teach in the schools was assumed by the school board. What had been quietly accepted in a corner of New York (where indeed the arrangements continued until the end of the century, when they were terminated only by a significant amendment to the State's constitution) would not be allowed to pass unchallenged when openly associated with Ireland's campaign to change the whole framework of relations between Church and State in the field of education, and to do so on the basis of an argument about the specificity of Catholicism in America. Was American Catholicism now to be accepted as being somehow different from Roman Catholicism, more open in its relationships with a democratic republic, more patriotic, more accepting of pluralism in society? Fundamental questions of theology and politics were now deliberately superimposed on what had previously been seen as convenient, and perhaps exceptional, local arrangements.

The depth and complexity of these wider issues, in which the Catholic school question was an essential element, is illuminated by the arguments surrounding the campaigns of Simon Peter Cahensly (1838-1923) and the rise of so-called Cahenslyism.[10] Cahensly, a German Catholic layman, had been for many years deeply concerned about the plight of German and other immigrants arriving in the United States, lamenting that they were often welcomed only by Protestant welfare societies and that their own spiritual and cultural needs were neglected. He established a well-endowed movement and in 1891 (a significant year for Ireland's life and plans) presented a memorial to Pope Leo XIII asserting that over ten million immigrants had been lost to the faith, and that churches and schools were urgently needed to minister in their own languages to the new immigrants. Predictably, the movement secured some support from Michael Corrigan. Ireland and his allies were appalled, and the Archbishop succeeded in having Cahensly denounced in the Senate as a foreigner seeking to 'Germanize' the United States. The Pope took no action beyond referring the matter to the American bishops themselves, but the passions which had been aroused were slow to die.

A barrage of pamphlets exploded in an increasingly violent debate around Ireland's own schemes (fundamentally opposed to those sponsored by Cahensly), and the Archbishop took himself to Rome to defend both himself and the cause of which he was now the acknowledged but unofficial leader. In April 1892, Rome, in the letter *Tolerari Potest*, concluded somewhat unenthusiastically that the Faribault-Stillwater and other similar arrangements, could be 'tolerated'. Both sides could therefore hasten to claim a measure of victory and, unsurprisingly, the quarrel continued. In the event, it was Protestant opposition, both locally to the particular plan and nationally to the whole notion (as it was caricatured in England and Wales a decade later) of 'Rome on the Rates', that soon killed off the scheme. Nevertheless, during the 1890s there was every reason for Ireland to be encouraged in his efforts: powerful interests in Rome had now conveniently discovered in his arguments elements which could be diplomatically useful in strengthening the position of the Church in Europe. American issues were now to be projected on to a European scene. Within a year of Pope Leo XIII's ambivalent judgement on the Faribault-Stillwater plan, the Archbishop of St Paul, Minnesota was to deliver a singularly well-received address to a large audience in Paris, France. He went there with diplomatic encouragement from the Pope to deliver an American message to French Catholics. It was hoped that he might help to persuade those Catholics who were intransigently loyal monarchists to become more accommodating in their attitudes towards the modern State, towards republicanism, and towards public education. In effect, although not, of course, in these terms, he was asking whether an English solution, which was now being experimentally attempted in the United States, might not also be extended to France. If French, like American Catholics, could be both devout and republican, might not their own schools and the teaching of religion in all schools become part of a state subsidised system?

The full significance, in the circumstances prevailing in 1892, of that implied question will be addressed in the next chapter. In the event, the relative optimism of the early 1890s was soon to be exploded by dramatic events leading to a formal rupture between Church and State in France. Meanwhile, a small part of that story must be anticipated here to explain the rise and fall of that 'Americanism' with which John Ireland had associated himself. The fall of Napoleon III (whose accession to power in the 1850s brought much comfort to the seminarians of Maximieux) had led to the inauguration of the Third Republic in 1871 and subsequently, in the early 1880s, to a series of legislative acts introducing a fully developed system of public education. That system excluded religious orders from teaching in the public schools, which were now to be free (that is, gratuitous), compulsory and – above all – secular. The Third Republic deliberately created a system of schools committed to the loyal service of the Republic and the elimination of the pernicious influence of a clergy still nostalgic for authoritarian and pro-Catholic regimes. The reaction of the clergy, and of the Catholic party at large, was understandably frosty. At the same time, the papal establishment in Rome (with the Pope a voluntary prisoner in the Vatican) and the international authority of the Church were under direct threat: Leo XIII desperately needed allies against his own Italian enemies. For how long could the Roman Catholic Church sensibly continue to regard the bourgeois French Republic (hardly a hotbed of revolution) as its sworn and implacable enemy? Leo and his advisers had, therefore, in the early 1890s, moved towards a judicious accommodation, which would at one and the same time attract France into a political alliance and secure a significant place for the Church in French society. Within such a context, something at least of the previous influence of the Church on education in France might be slowly recovered. Operating within this new but ephemeral frame of reference, Rome had therefore encouraged John Ireland to carry his distinctive message to the French. His approach to them was to be part of what was labelled the *Ralliement*, the rallying of French Catholics to the support of the new Republic and the abandonment by them of their monarchist past. The French, like Ireland's (idealised) Americans, could and should be simultaneously and consistently democratic and Catholic.

Ireland delighted all those whom he met during his acclaimed visit to France by his command of the French language and his admiration of the classical traditions of a country to which he owed his own education. His major speech in July 1892 was on the subject of Roman Catholicism in America, but its implied message to the French was clear enough. At least from his own perspective, the possibilities of some accommodation with the State (in France, as in his own country) had rarely looked brighter.[11] Yet, the engagement of the American with the European experience was to have unpredictable and, for Ireland and his friends, deeply unfortunate consequences. The *Ralliement* proved to be short lived: wrecked by the passions of the Dreyfus Affair (for which see the next chapter), it was followed by an interlude of open warfare between Church and State in France. John Ireland was, thereafter, no longer useful to the Roman cause. The European engagement was to prove fatal to the Archbishop's attempts to enlarge the channels of communication between Church and State at home. He had in 1891 written a relatively anodyne preface to a biography by Walter Elliott of Isaac Hecker, the founder of the Paulists who had died three years earlier. Hecker was for many an epitome of what was being characterised, in an increasingly hostile spirit, as Americanism. He had defended a more open attitude towards American society, stressing the importance in an unsympathetic and materialist environment of the evangelising mission of the Church. Hecker also lauded the superiority of the (characteristically American?) active virtues, and developed a doctrine of the Holy Spirit which (in the eyes of critics at least) stressed individual inspiration rather than ecclesiastical authority. Not much more might have been heard of all this if a zealous French priest had not published a translation of the life of Hecker by Walter Elliott, complete with Ireland's preface, in the year 1897. The translator, Félix Klein, in his own approving comments on Hecker and the implications of his ideas, was so imprudent as to suggest that France should indeed emulate the United States.[12]

The enemies of the Archbishop of St Paul now saw the opportunity for which they had been patiently waiting: Rome might contrive to ignore as irrelevant much of a debate in distant America, but not when it now threatened to infect Europe itself and had been translated into a continental European language. The Dreyfus affair was inflaming passions while a pamphlet warfare erupted around the work of Klein. Early in 1899, Rome, in the letter *Testem Benevolentiae*, condemned a number of propositions.[13] The condemnation, without mentioning the term Americanism, was clearly aimed at the kind of theses which John Ireland and the so-called Americanist party had espoused. The underlying orthodox assertion (which Ireland would not and could not disavow) was that Catholicism was by definition always and everywhere the same. Neither American nor French exceptionalism could by direct implication be allowed (even if they refused to die). The opportunity to 'do something different', specifically in the United States, had passed by.

John Ireland, claiming that Rome had condemned beliefs that no sensible person in fact held, lived on to fight other battles, dipped into the high politics of Washington, came close to serious financial troubles through his complicated dealings with the railway barons, and died in 1918 without securing his Cardinal's hat.[14] The importance of his career, epitomised in the two major speeches which have been at the heart of this chapter, was that he hoped that it would be possible to be at one and the same time fully American and fully Catholic. In particular, he resisted attempts (which would themselves become self-validating predictions) to build a separate school system for Roman Catholics, believing that the right place for the members of his own flock – whether they were by the accidents of origin German, Polish, Italian or Irish – was within the American public school. In the event, the distinctive characteristics of the American Catholic immigrant population, and the unwillingness of a Protestant anglophone majority to be open to their influence, ensured that in the last analysis he failed. He visited Europe twice again during his long life: in 1906, he went for the last time to Maximieux. When he next went to France in 1909, that seminary had been closed and the complex links between Church and State in France brutally severed by the Law of 1905. Emile Combes had done his work.

Notes

[1] Ireland, 1890.

[2] For the details of the life of John Ireland, see O'Connell, 1985.

[3] O'Connell, 1985, p. 84.

[4] Ibid., p. 168.

[5] See chapter 5.

[6] Morris, 1997, p. 217; Dolan, 1992, p. 275.

[7] O'Connell, 1985, p. 223.

[8] Ibid., p. 296.

[9] Morris, 1997, p. 99.

[10] Dolan, 1992, p. 298; O'Connell, 1985, p. 315.

[11] O'Connell, 1985, p. 375.

[12] Ibid., p. 439. Dolan, 1992, pp. 235-236.

[13] O'Connell, 1985, p. 461.

[14] Ibid., p. 505.

CHAPTER 3

Three Contemporaries: Emile Combes

[The Catholics] wish to do away with the Republic. ... The first trees of liberty will die if they are sprinkled with holy water.

Like John Ireland of Minnesota, Emile Combes was educated in Roman Catholic seminaries in France. Their lives were in all other ways totally dissimilar, and (as far as I know) they never met or even referred to one another. Nevertheless, their interests overlapped, and at the most fundamental level their passionate commitments collided. Within a few months of the 1892 speech made by the American Archbishop to an appreciative Parisian audience, Emile Combes addressed in very different terms a republican committee in the small town in France in which he had practised medicine and of which he was for many years mayor. He, unlike Ireland, was contemptuous of the *Ralliement*, the short-lived and belated effort initiated by Pope Leo XIII to persuade French Catholics to 'rally' to the support of the French Republic, and in doing so abandon their historic monarchist preferences. In the opinion of the Mayor (who was also a devoted Freemason), priests should address the concerns not of this world but of the next:

> *The Pope has grasped that an attachment to the monarchy is an attachment to a corpse. ... The Church fears for its official position, and for the money which it receives from the Government budget for the support of religions ... At the next elections the Catholics will put on false noses. ... This is only a seeming reconciliation. They wish to do away with the Republic. The clergy and the clerical party are more dangerous than in Gambetta's day, for they are now disguised. This is no imaginary danger: the first trees of liberty will die if they are sprinkled with holy water. ... The clergy exists to fulfil a task that has nothing to do with politics; it exists to speak to mankind of another life and another world, to console it for the miseries of this world, to lift its soul ... This is the mission of the clergy. If they are wise they will limit themselves to this mission.[1]*

This was the uncompromising message of the man who, a decade later and as Prime Minister of France, cut the pervasively complex links which had for centuries bound the civil to the ecclesiastical power in that country. John Ireland, drawing on the experiences of his own very different world, pushed in the opposite direction for a closer alliance between the Church and civil society, while Combes strove for the breaking of a historic partnership between the two.

He had been born on 6 September 1835, a few years before John Ireland, in the rugged countryside of south-west France; his father was the village tailor, and he grew up in very modest circumstances, which he never forgot or disowned. It is an eloquent commentary on the capacity and ambition of his family, as indeed on the success of the French educational system in promoting some forms of social mobility, that two of his brothers also became doctors and one a lawyer. His godfather was a cousin and a priest (although not, it seems, always a contented country *curé*), who encouraged the younger members of his extended family, securing the admission of Emile to the *petit séminaire* (a junior seminary) in nearby Castres. There, at the age of seventeen, he achieved the *baccalauréat* and left his remote province for Paris and higher education at the Ecole des Carmes, in the rue de Vaugirard. In Paris, he was exposed to the influence of the great secular luminaries of the University: the eclectic philosopher Victor Cousin, Michelet (whose optimistic belief in progress was indelibly transferred to the young student), and Edgar Quinet (who argued for the separation of Church and State, and was later to be exiled by Napoleon III). Combes, like many of his contemporaries, was slowly moving away from a traditional (and, for him, not deeply engaging) Catholicism towards a mood – for it was hardly more than that – which contemporaries were happy to describe as *spiritualiste*. This term in this context has no connotations linking it with the apparently identical English term: Combes never became the kind of man to attend a seance, but did share with many of his later political and intellectual allies a belief in the importance of a spiritual dimension in life, and in the necessary subordination of material to more noble considerations. There was no irony in the anticlerical yet other-worldly comments he made, as already quoted, to the audience which forty years later he addressed as Mayor.

He had agreed, before leaving for Paris, that part of the cost of the two years to be spent there would be met by returning to teach, without pay, at Castres. He fulfilled this obligation before moving on to the *grand séminaire* in the dramatically impressive town of Albi, the centre of the great medieval heretical movement to which it gave its name. He was still moving towards ordination as a priest, until his superiors in the seminary concluded that he lacked a genuine vocation, and he left in 1857 at the age of twenty-two, but without at that stage any dramatic break with the Church or with his past. He frequently, if somewhat wryly, commented on an education that gave him an invaluable insight into the working of the clerical Catholic mind. For his many enemies, it was, of course, a proof of his ingratitude and indeed perfidy, just as for them his later policies reflected a bitter resentment against an institution which had rejected him. At this point, he seemed still to be assuming that he would eventually be ordained, and accepted a teaching post at a Catholic establishment in Nîmes, where he remained for two years. In 1860, he moved to a similar appointment in western France, at Pons – the town which was thereafter to remain at the centre of his life and political activity. He completed his two theses for the doctorate (begun at Albi), on Thomas Aquinas and on St Bernard, drifted further away from his clerical anchorage, and married in 1862. His first son, Edgard, who until his tragically early death was to be a devoted collaborator in his father's public life, was born two years later. Emile Combes taught in Pons, with apparent success, for five years. At that point, he determined on a complete change of career, and – under the pressure of considerable financial hardship – took himself back to Paris to prepare for his new life as a medical doctor. In 1868, two years before the collapse of the Second Empire, he returned to his adopted Department (Charente Inférieure) and set up in medical practice in Pons. At the same time, he completed his long journey away from Catholicism, and found in freemasonry what was for him (as for so many like-minded contemporaries) a new religion. Emile Combes was undoubtedly a man who needed to belong. The speech which he made on admission was a diatribe against contemporary Catholicism in general and the ageing Pius IX in particular. Combes argued that by condemning in his *Syllabus of Errors* of 1864 so many modern ideas and scientific progress in general, the Pope had in fact condemned his own church and faith to extinction:

> *Confronted with these immense ruins of which each one of us represents*
> *a fragment, it is impossible to resist a feeling of sadness mingled with*
> *respect. In this debris of beliefs which litter the ground of the nineteenth*
> *century, we recognise the early lessons which our mothers' lips planted in*
> *our young souls; almost half of our intellectual life has crumbled. Yet we*
> *can be comforted by, and indeed rejoice in, the certainty that*
> *Freemasonry is destined to harvest the heritage of Catholicism.* [2]

Here, indeed, are the two Frances confronting one another, with no serious doubt left in the mind of the young doctor about which side in the battle he must now join.

For the next ten years, Combes devoted his considerable energies to building up his medical practice and entrenching himself in the local community. His political power and national position were built on rock solid local foundations: in this important sense he was a typical representative of that characteristically French institution, the *notable*. Like many public figures, then and since – indeed, into the twenty-first century – he accumulated offices, never relinquishing his modest local positions even when called upon to exercise the highest national offices. This same decade witnessed the end of the Second Empire and the uncertain and contested beginnings of the Third Republic. The early years of the new regime were marked by oscillations of power, until the Republic eventually settled itself after 1875 into its classical form. Combes was briefly a member of his municipal council as early as 1870, and then more permanently after 1874. In 1878, he became Mayor of Pons, a position which he carefully protected until his death in 1921. In 1879, he was elected to the General Council of his home Department, and in 1885, to the Senate in Paris. As that was a paid post – always a significant consideration for a citizen with no private means – and one which required long periods of residence in Paris, he then gave up the practice of medicine. Throughout the lifetime of the Republic (and, to some extent, even beyond that), the Senate reflected local interests and loyalties, and claimed to speak for France as a whole (especially rural France) rather than for the metropolitan and commercial elites.

Before his election to the Senate, where he became one of the leaders of a coalition of radical groups, Emile Combes – local doctor, Freemason and Mayor – had already established the clear outlines of his policies. Complementing his powerful local advocacies, for such causes as improved railways and roads, was a commitment to public education, which for much of the nineteenth century existed in blurred and uneasy competition with an extensive network of private schools (mostly Catholic) which enjoyed considerable support from public funds and official patronage. In the context of local disputes, he had already declared himself a supporter of the Ligue d'Enseignement, founded by Jean Macé in1866 to promote the cause of public education. In the speech which he made to the assembled worthies empowered to make the senatorial election in 1885, he identified his own and his party's priorities. As a good and frugal bourgeois, he understood well enough the need for economy in public expenditure. But such economy should not starve the schools of resources, since it could be only through the influence of those schools that the Republic would perpetuate itself, and overcome the resistance of monarchists and the priests who imprudently supported them.[3] His opposition to the influence of the Congregations – the religious orders which controlled most of the instruction given in formally Catholic as well as many other schools – became manifest at this time. As a Senator, he was a predictably eager supporter of the major education laws of the 1880s associated with the name of Jules Ferry: the Law of 1881, which made elementary education free (that is, gratuitous); its complement in 1882, which ruled that such public education should, moreover, be obligatory and *laïque*, or lay (that is, with the Congregations and clergy removed from taking any part in it); and the consolidating Law of 1886, which incorporated these new requirements in a carefully designed and integrated system of educational provision. Hitherto (see chapter 6), public and private – that is Catholic – education had been elaborately intertwined, with many local 'public' schools being staffed and run by the Congregations. In principle, public education would now everywhere be republican and secular, although in practice it would be many years before such geometric clarity could be achieved. Congregations might continue to provide their own schools, but now, of course, without any support from public funds, and only if they were formally authorised to do so by the State – although, once more, legal theory and local practice for many years did not always coincide.

Shuttling regularly between Pons and Paris, Combes was an active and highly visible Senator, playing a significant part in many of the specialised commissions of that august body. In a report on Algeria, he urged (significantly, in opposition to the generally assimilationist tendencies of his day) that Islamic culture and habits should be respectfully preserved. He defended any apparent inconsistency between that recommendation and his secularising policies in France itself on the grounds that the circumstances were entirely different: in Algeria, the prevailing religion was that of the oppressed, whereas in France, Catholicism had become corruptly associated with the dominance of a priestly caste, threatening (always) the integrity of the Republic and the principles of 1789.[4] He attempted, with only limited success, to limit the power of the classical curriculum, arguing that an extensive knowledge of Latin should not be required of all intending doctors, and that subjects other than Latin, Greek and mathematics should be accorded dignity and respect. It was, therefore, not surprising that he should become Minister of Public Instruction in one of the many short-lived ministries of the Third Republic. He exercised his responsibilities only between November 1895 and April 1896 – in a government in which every minister was a Freemason! His son Edgard joined him as the head of his own *cabinet* – that is, in the French tradition, the panel of expert advisers assisting a minister. Among the more permanent servants of the State were Louis Liard for higher education and Ferdinand Buisson, the architect of much of the distinctive elementary school system of the Republic. His period of office was not associated with any dramatic changes, for which in any case there was little enough time. He was, however, also responsible for the Ministère des Cultes, which supervised the complex relationships between the churches and the French State, as they had been defined by Napoleon at the beginning of the century. He refused, prudently no doubt, to respond to the more or less ritual demand of some parliamentarians that the budget of that Ministry should simply be cancelled: such a draconian action would, of course, have precipitated a crisis in the relationships with the Catholic Church. The Government had not been elected on any such programme and the time, the Minister judged, was not ripe for such drastic surgery: but it soon would be.[5]

The Radical critics of the continuing dominance of the Roman Catholic Church in much of French public and private life were not satisfied with the incomplete victory of the Republican cause, as it had been registered in the Ferry laws of the 1880s. This, in the view of that Radical opposition, was by no means the first time that the patriotic will had been frustrated: governments of many different kinds had time and again acted against the power of the Church, and especially of the Congregations, only to find that in practice the old ways persisted. The Ferry laws had not been the first, for example, to require that teaching could be undertaken only by Congregations which had secured from the State formal approval for their existence in France. When Combes became President of the General Council of his Department in 1897, he was shocked to discover that twelve years after the passing of the 1886 Law there were still within that one Department twenty-seven schools being run as public schools by the Congregations, with public funding. It was clear that more radical measures would soon be required. Meanwhile, France was plunged into one of the most celebrated crises in its history as the Dreyfus case burst open in 1898, and ideological battle lines were formed and hardened. The time for implicit, half-concealed compromises was rapidly passing and, by the time Emile Combes achieved the highest political office, had vanished forever.

The circumstances of the Dreyfus trial and of the *affaire* to which it soon led are sufficiently well known, and will be recalled here only in order to relate them more directly to the evolving political career of Emile Combes. Captain Dreyfus was a Jewish officer in the French army, which at the end of the nineteenth century represented (as is now generally acknowledged) a bastion of right-wing views, monarchist sympathies, Roman Catholic loyalties and anti-Semitic prejudice. In 1894, Dreyfus was accused of betraying secrets to the Germans, found guilty by court martial, ceremoniously stripped of his commission and imprisoned on the notorious Devil's Island in French Guiana. Two years later, fresh evidence was uncovered suggesting that the charges against him had been concocted, and were indeed the fruit of a cynical conspiracy. Esterhazy, the officer identified by the champions of Dreyfus as being responsible for this grave miscarriage of justice, was tried but acquitted in 1897. On 13 January 1898, Emile Zola, the renowned author, published in *L'Aurore* – a newspaper owned by Clemenceau, the Radical politician and later Prime Minister – and under the banner headline *J'Accuse*, an open letter to the President which was a ferocious denunciation of the whole conspiracy. In the great affair which now exploded, neutrality was impossible. Tempers flared and families were divided as some of the most raw passions and prejudices in a deeply divided French society were exposed. The scars of 1870, 1848, 1830 and 1789 had not healed. On the one side were the liberals, the freethinkers, the Protestants, the Jewish community, the Freemasons. On the other were ranged the Congregations (notably the Jesuits and the Assumptionists, founded in 1851 in the emotional reaction against recent revolutionary excesses), much of traditionalist Catholic opinion, the political conservatives, the nostalgic monarchists and authoritarians, the defenders of the old order and of the aristocracy, and – above all, of course – the officers of the army, their families and the champions of the Catholic schools which many of them had attended. Old friendships and alliances were ruptured and families split between 'the revisionists', who wanted the Dreyfus trial reopened, and those who were bitterly opposed to any such potentially threatening procedure. Later in the same year, Colonel Henry, who was alleged to have been involved in the frauds underlying the attack on the Jewish officer, committed suicide. In 1899, the new Radical government led by Waldeck-Rousseau pardoned Dreyfus, although it was not until 1906 that the Court of Appeal formally overturned the original conviction. He died in 1935.[6]

One effect of this celebrated affair was the consolidation of left-wing political alliances, leading to a period of relative stability under Radical leadership in the ministries of Waldeck-Rousseau (1899-1902) and then of Emile Combes himself (1902-05). The Third Republic had not previously enjoyed, nor was it ever to witness again, so extended a period of continuous power in which a determined – indeed ferocious – effort could be made to regulate once and for all the relationship in France between Church and State, and notably in the critically important field of education. During the first of these two ministries – the longest surviving of the volatile Third Republic – Combes was influential in promoting the legislative programme. Outstanding at the head of that programme was the great Law of Associations of 1901, which survives to this day as the fundamental definition of the relationship between voluntary associations of all kinds and the framework of public law and administration. Combes presided over the Senate commission charged with reviewing the new Law. The essential and original purpose of that Law was to curtail and control the influence of the Congregations. Waldeck-Rousseau was more cautious, or tactically astute, than his successor would soon prove to be, seeking to represent the new arrangements as being in principle a reaffirmation and consolidation of existing practice. No government of whatever complexion could tolerate the existence of a state within a state, and no ideologically committed Republican government could contemplate with equanimity a resurgence of the kind of hostility to its basic purposes and philosophy which had marked the tumultuous debates of the closing years of the previous century. If a Congregation wished to continue in or now acquire legal existence, it should, therefore (as previous laws had indeed proclaimed, albeit with uneven effects), be formally approved by the State, having made an appropriate application to that end. The presumption appeared to be that Congregations which had under previous dispensations taken such steps would be, at least for the time being, secure in their existing position. Indeed, the Prime Minister assured anxious critics that the Law would not have retrospective effect, a position with which Combes chose not to associate himself. The political intention of the Law, not always easily distinguished from its juridical pronouncements, was to bring into a framework of legal control those Congregations which had, on grounds of principle or through negligence, abstained from making any such application.

The solid impressiveness of the present-day French educational system makes it deceptively easy to underestimate the importance of the schooling provided in the nineteenth century by the Congregations. The relevant considerations are both qualitative and quantitative. Although the statistics for access to positions of power and prestige cannot be satisfactorily reconstructed, loyal Republicans were unshakeably convinced that the Catholic secondary schools – like those in which Emile Combes had himself taught for a while in Nîmes and Pons, as well as the more prestigious establishments associated, for example, with the Oratorians – contributed a disproportionate number of successful entrants to the high quality institutions of higher education (notably the *Grandes Ecoles)*, the major professions, and – above all of course, and as the Dreyfus affair had for them tragically demonstrated – the armed services. Even if it is difficult to provide a quantitative justification for them, such perceptions explain and perhaps justify the conviction of the Radical Republicans that the Church, or more precisely clericalism, was the real enemy. There can certainly be no doubt about the scale of the importance of Catholic educational provision, or the significance to it of the Congregations themselves. By 1877, the Congregations for men had 30,200 members, and those for women no fewer than 127,000: the religious orders in France were, therefore, at that time larger than they had been before the Revolution of 1789.[7] The women significantly outnumbered the men, and it was a recurrent theme of the Republicans that the Church's control of the education of girls represented a particularly insidious threat, as Jules Ferry had memorably insisted (see chapter 6). Whoever controlled the education of girls controlled the minds of women, and therefore the deepest convictions of sons and (even) of husbands. Combes had himself recognised this in the speech already cited which he made on admission as a Freemason, and for this very reason – for as long as women might remain more subject than men to the influence of priests – remained hostile to extending the suffrage to women. (That did not happen in France until 1948.)

In the year after the adoption of the 1901 Law of Associations there were, according to Combes himself, no fewer than 1371 Congregations operating in France, most of them active in the educational field (which is where the controversies were focused), and of that total number, 457 were – still – not authorised. Of the remaining total of 914 authorised Congregations, only 5 were orders of men, but that small number managed a total of 1410 establishments. The 909 authorised female Congregations operated no fewer than 15,915 establishments. For their part, the 457 unauthorised Congregations controlled 1964 male establishments and 1534 female. The total number of establishments controlled by the Congregations (men and women, authorised and not) was therefore 20,823, of which 16,904 were dedicated to teaching. Whatever else Emile Combes and the Radicals were doing, they were certainly not making a polemical mountain out of a statistical molehill. Emile Combes himself was meanwhile, and on his own territory, promoting the cause of an authentically 'Republican' and anticlerical education: a pedagogical, moral and civic initiation that would promote the perennial values of 1789 and of 1875 within the framework of the Ferry laws. In that scheme of things, the *instituteurs*, the elementary school teachers, had the fundamental role to play. It was important that the

Ecole Normale, the training college for those teachers, should become the lay and secular equivalent of the seminaries that Combes knew and suspected, and rigorously train the priests of the new order. Ever the active local politician and *notable*, he promoted the transfer to la Rochelle, the principal city of his Department, of the *Ecole Normale* for boys, and the housing of it in new and appropriate buildings. In doing so, he overcame the opposition of local merchants who would have preferred a barracks in their town, since soldiers spent more money than teachers in training. At the time of the Dreyfus affair, he saluted local *instituteurs* as:

> *the priests of the republican ideal, the ministers of this new religion whose altar is liberty, whose dogmas are the rights and duties of the citizen, whose weapons of propaganda are conscience and human reason. [8]*

This was an extension of the language he had learnt as a young student in Paris from Cousin, Michelet and Quinet. Just as the temple of the Freemasons should replace the parish church, so must the *Ecole Normale* now usurp the seminary.

Although Combes had by now achieved a position of considerable national eminence, he apparently shared the surprise of many of his fellows when President Loubet called on him in 1902 to form an administration. Waldeck-Rousseau, displaying his customary prudence, chose this moment to withdraw (temporarily, as he no doubt intended) from the front line of the thickening battle with the Church. The electoral campaigns of 1902 (the year, as will appear, of the Balfour Act in England) were fought on starkly opposed principles: the anticlericals pitted against the traditionalists. Combes himself, at the age of sixty-seven, was showing his combative spirit, which surprised even his astute predecessor. He now moves into history as characterised by his enemies: 'Little Father Combes' (*le petit Père Combes*) – short of stature, mediocre in quality, provincial and bourgeois, a failed seminarian, mean spirited and nursing old grudges. The ever sharp journalists made sport of the fact that, climbing out of a carriage at the height of the tense discussions always surrounding the construction of any new administration in the Third Republic, he seemed most concerned that he had lost his umbrella. (Umbrellas, as both Louis Philippe and Neville Chamberlain should have noticed, were for some reason symbols of a slightly ridiculous insignificance.) His critics seriously underestimated the new Prime Minister's mastery of his brief and total commitment to pushing the Law of 1901 far beyond the limits envisaged for it by its original promoter. Combes added the Departments of Ecclesiastical Affairs (perhaps the least misleading translation of the Ministère des Cultes) and of the Interior to his bulging portfolio: since he was himself now determined to provoke them, he knew very well where the troubles were about to break. As his Minister of War, he recruited General André, with a clear brief to purge the higher echelons of the army of its reactionary elements. One of his firmest allies was the socialist, Jean Jaurès – a persuasive orator and powerful Deputy who, since his assassination in 1914, has given his name to so many streets in France. Although Jaurès was not a member of the Government, Combes owed his survival in power for thirty feverish months to the principle that his own group would have no enemies on the Left (*pas d'ennemis à gauche*). He would certainly need all the friends he could gather to the support of his contentious cause.

His clearly stated policy was to apply in its full rigour the Law of 1901, which he had, of course, piloted through the Senate, and to repeal the Falloux Law of 1850 (see chapter 6), enacted after the return to France of Louis Napoleon and epitomising a signal and long-lasting victory for the champions of Roman Catholic schooling. These were the dominant themes of his public programme, alongside an equally characteristic insistence on economy in government expenditure and on the importance of strengthening public control of the railways. In public, at least, he remained a conditional if cool supporter of the century-old agreement on Church-State relationships in France, represented by the Concordat concluded between Napoleon and the Pope. Combes insisted that 'The laws derived from the Concordat enclose the priest in the religious domain' – that is, once again, in the affairs of a spiritual and not of a material or political world.[9] In the Chamber of Deputies, one of his more effective allies was the same Ferdinand Buisson who had formerly served as the official responsible for primary education and whose great *Dictionnaire Pédagogique* was the bible of the new secular priesthood of the lay teachers. In the Luxembourg Palace, a powerful but less reliable Senatorial ally was Clemenceau himself, later a Prime Minister of great importance and a Radical who had played a significant part in raising the temperature and the tempers in the great Dreyfus debate.

The new Prime Minister's tactic was effective and subtle: to establish formal categories dividing the Catholic schools, and to pick them off a group at a time. Complete success in this war of attrition was achieved with surprisingly brief delays. There were authorised Congregations which had existed for many years, Congregations which had existed before the 1901 Law and had never sought authorisation, others of this type which had made the necessary application since the new Law came into effect, others which were of more recent creation and had secured authorisation, and others which had not. Although most of the larger Congregations were involved in teaching (and therefore exposed to the Government's hostility), a significant minority were engaged in hospitals and welfare work, and relatively immune from unfriendly criticism. Moreover, a distinction was drawn between Congregations which had received the necessary authorisation and the establishments which they had opened: an authorised Congregation which opened an establishment without first securing specific authorisation for it was also in breach of the law. Obviously, the most vulnerable target was that group of establishments maintained by Congregations which had never been authorised: promptly, in June 1902, 125 were closed, most of them schools for girls. Many of the Congregations which had existed without authorisation before the Waldeck-Rousseau Law protested that they were not subject to that Law, but only to its tamer predecessor of 1886. Their defence was rejected, and the Prime Minister (being also Minister of the Interior and of Ecclesiastical Affairs) simply ordered the Prefects to close them within eight days. Although some had, with more or less haste, already applied for authorisation, they too were to be shut, pending the consideration of their tardy applications.

There were several local disturbances in Paris and Lyon and elsewhere in the provinces – especially in the profoundly Catholic Brittany. The Archbishop of Paris, stepping outside (according to the anticlericals at least) the role assigned to him by the Concordat of 1801 and laws derived from it, wrote an open letter to the President. The next step taken by Combes was to refuse en bloc all the applications currently being made for authorisation. Waldeck-Rousseau dissociated himself from what he saw as injustices (and imprudent). The jaws of the anticlerical vice were remorselessly closing. The 1850 Law which protected the Catholic schools was repealed (or, more precisely, many of its stipulations were reversed although some clauses remained in force to cause another fierce dispute in 1994). The new Law replacing it, hotly debated between December 1903 and March 1904 in and out of the two chambers of the legislature, simply banned the Congregations from taking any part in any kind of educational undertaking in France. Buisson – freethinking, Protestant and 'spiritualist' – was emphatic:

> *Those who abdicate their rights as persons and subject themselves to a religious power have no right to teach. The State has the right to preserve youth from their influence. Monastic society and democratic society are incompatible.*

For his part, the eloquent Jaurès affirmed the superior right of the State as it had been proclaimed in the Revolution of 1789 – 'this right of the State as a teacher, as a secular [laïque] teacher, as a secular and rational teacher, as a revolutionary teacher'. And finally le petit Père himself: 'It is an abuse of logic to claim that the notion of liberty implies the right to destroy it'.[10]

The year 1904 was, therefore, as significant in the long story of the relationship between the State and the Roman Catholic schools as 1801 and 1850 had been – and as 1959, 1984 and 1994 were in their turn later to prove. Of course, Catholic schools did not disappear overnight; but the changes between 1880 and 1910, and especially between 1900 and 1910, were cumulatively dramatic. Most significant of all (as the events of 1905 were to confirm) was the sharp and apparently definitive separation of Catholic from public provision in schooling: the two had, at least since the reforms associated with François Guizot (see chapter 6), been inextricably intertwined: a public school was until the 1880s defined as an establishment which was funded in whole *or in part* from public funds. Many public schools were for that reason maintained by the Congregations, and continued to be so (albeit on a diminishing scale) even after the application of the school laws of the 1880s. The balance of public/lay and Catholic schooling then began to shift. After the 1904 Law, most of the teachers in the schools run by the Congregations were secularised (whatever that meant in practice) and the schools reopened as private Catholic schools with lay teachers. In 1880, before Ferry and his devoted colleagues set to work, 43% of girls in *public* schools were taught by members of the religious orders. For boys, the corresponding figure was a more modest 13%. These pupils were therefore being educated in public schools but taught by the Congregations and on overtly Catholic principles. Even in 1900, more than a decade after the new laws had been applied, the figures for the same categories were 13% for girls and 1.5% for boys: a massive reduction, of course, but still (as Combes protested when he reviewed the facts and figures for his own Department) representing a substantial legal anomaly, and an offence to the conscience of the anticlericals. More significant, in terms of the impact on opinions and loyalties, were the high proportions, when Combes came to power, of pupils being taught by the Congregations in their schools, mostly 'private' but some (as has been shown) still public. In 1902, 20% of boys were being taught by the Congregations and 39.4% of girls. By 1912, those percentages had fallen to 0.6% and 1.5%. Meanwhile, as has been noted, many of the schools previously managed by the Congregations reopened as private schools of a Catholic character, and with lay teachers. Within ten years of 1902, the percentage of girls educated in private (lay) Catholic schools had for that very reason climbed from 2.6% to 23.3% and for boys from 1.6% to 12.2% (in both cases, as percentages of the total relevant population attending school). These figures, somewhat surprisingly, are roughly equivalent (as proportions) to the situation now prevailing in France at the beginning of the twenty-first century. Roman Catholic education had been dismayed but not extinguished. Nevertheless, as a result of the draconian measures taken by Emile Combes, nearly half of the girls who had been educated in Catholic schools no longer would be, and nearly one quarter of the boys. The ideological battles were bound to continue, and Emile Combes had not finished yet. A few months of power remained to him.

His clear ambition was now to complete what he had begun, by liberating the State from the power of the Church, and of course (or so he insisted to sceptical critics) at the same time freeing the Church itself from entanglement with the State – so that it might then address only its true spiritual mission. Within days of the enactment of the 1904 Law, banning the Congregations from taking any part in education, his government issued a circular ordering the removal from courtrooms of crucifixes and other religious symbols. It was noted with some bitterness that the Garde des Sceaux (the Minister for Justice) required that this regulation should be applied on 1 April, which happened to be (of all days) Good Friday.

The movement towards the final separation of Church and State ran in parallel with the assault on the Congregations. The 1801 Concordat between the Pope and Napoleon had always been the source of disagreement in interpretation and application. For the French authorities, of whatever political complexion, it was a treaty between two powers – the Papacy and the Empire (then the monarchy, then the Republic). Papal diplomats, on the other hand, preferred, in most circumstances, to view it as concession made by His Holiness to a secular state. The Roman interpretation was that important matters such as the appointment of bishops should always be subject to a preliminary understanding (the *entente préalable*). Although, subject to that condition, the right of the civil power to nominate to bishoprics was conceded, the formal papal documents then despatched to Paris after 'nominations' had been received often contained the contentious phrase 'nominated *to* us' (*nobis nominavit*). Paris, of course, rejected the offensive *nobis*. And so on. The public protest against the exclusion of the Congregations delivered by the Cardinal Archbishop of Paris in an open letter to the President of France has already been mentioned: Combes was clear that such an initiative represented a clear breach of the Concordat. The offence was compounded when, later in 1902, seventy-four bishops petitioned the President against the action of the Government. The Conseil d'Etat, as the guardian of the constitution, condemned their action: the Concordat did not acknowledge the existence of the bishops of France as a corporate body. As individuals they enjoyed the rights of citizens, as State functionaries they were paid from public funds, but they might in no sense constitute a state within a state. The Government withheld the salaries of five of the offending bishops. Nor would the Conseil d'Etat agree to register the Bulls coming from Rome and instituting bishops whom the French Government had nominated: the Bulls contained the dreaded *nobis*. In December, still in 1902, Rome retaliated by refusing to institute three bishops whose names had been submitted by Emile Combes without the *entente préalable*. In 1903, the Government ordered all bishops to close unauthorised chapels, so applying the Law of 1901, and to exclude from preaching in their cathedrals members of unauthorised Congregations. The Bishop of Nancy flouted the order, compounding the offence and infuriating the anticlericals by inviting a Jesuit to preach: that bishop also lost his government salary. Meanwhile, a parliamentary commission with Aristide Briand as its secretary had been appointed to examine the tortured and tortuous relationships between Church and State: Combes at least was now looking for a quarrel.[11]

Ever since the loss of the Papal States and the 'occupation' of Rome in 1870, the Pope had chosen to regard himself as a prisoner within the Vatican: he could have no dealings with infidels and usurpers. The head of any Catholic State (but not, paradoxically, of a Protestant power) who paid his respects to the King of Italy on a visit to Rome could, therefore, not be subsequently received by His Holiness. The death of Leo XIII in July 1903 was followed by the election of the even more intransigent, and much less subtle, Pius X. In April 1904, when President Loubet of France returned the visit which King Victor-Emmanuel had paid to France in the previous year, he was (somewhat to his embarrassment, for the quarrel was certainly not of his choosing) received with enthusiastic cries of 'Viva Loubet! Viva la Francia anticlericale!' Pius X was not pleased. Even although, earlier in the year, the Bulls instituting two new bishops had dropped the *nobis*, the suspiciously implacable Combes noted that the word had not been omitted or deleted but simply struck out, without any validating signature in the margins. The eloquently influential Jaurès was now pressing hard for Separation – as was Clemenceau, who remarked that if Combes (still showing some caution) did not move decisively forward, all his talk of anticlericalism would simply be 'a load of eyewash'.[12] The Tiger never minced his words.

The skirmishes dragged on, sometimes in conditions which approached the farcical. A few of the bishops, whether from opportunism or conviction, proclaimed themselves to be good Republicans – still hankering after the days of the short-lived *Ralliement*. The bishops of Laval and Dijon had gone further by refusing to sign the petition of the seventy-four. The former bishop had been in the bad books of Rome for some time and had been invited to resign in 1899, partly on the grounds that he made suspiciously long visits to a local convent. The matter was now revived, but Combes would not allow the unhappy bishop to resign quietly: when he set off for Rome without government permission in order to explain himself to his ecclesiastical superiors, his salary was suspended. The bishop of Dijon was accused by his enemies of still more heinous offences: he was said to be a Freemason and, leaving for Rome in response to a papal summons but without formal permission from the Government, he too lost his salary. Combes rejected his resignation too, on the grounds that he still had official duties to perform, and the poor man crept off to retirement in Normandy. It was obviously being made impossible to serve two masters. The pro-Catholic newspaper, *La Croix*, organised a petition with one million signatures to be sent to the Pope. The people would soon take to the streets, as both Pius X and Leo XIII had already warned. Combes introduced the draft of a law to separate Church and State, but his fragile coalition was now crumbling. Some (like the influential Waldeck-Rousseau, who had died in August 1904) thought he had already gone too far. Others, to his left, were impatient he had not yet gone far or fast enough. Vicious accusations were being repeated against his son, Edgard, accusing him of taking bribes to favour some of the Congregations. The zeal of his acolytes, if not of Combes personally, in pursuing a witch hunt against Catholic and anti-Republican army officers, using the Freemason lodges to collect information about them and their religious loyalties, was distasteful to many. General André was obliged to resign, and was followed by the Prime Minister himself in January 1905, with his great project incomplete. His successors in office nevertheless carried it through, and when their efforts finally succeeded in December 1905, Emile Combes wept.[13]

That Law of Separation, while guaranteeing freedom of conscience and of the exercise of religion, roundly declared in Article 2 that:

The Republic neither recognises, nor provides the salaries for, nor subsidises any religion. As a consequence ... in the budgets of the State, the Departments and the Communes all expenses related to religious exercises are suppressed.

By an application of the Law of Associations of 1901, church buildings and properties might be handed over to 'religious associations' (*associations cultuelles*), duly constituted as essentially secular bodies and therefore in law free from direct episcopal control. As part of such legal transfers of property, official inventories of the contents of buildings were to be made under the supervision of the Prefect. The Pope denounced the Law. For several years, many priests and communities refused to form associations, which were repeatedly denounced by the bishops, and on some dramatic occasions actively resisted official efforts to prepare the required inventories. There were scuffles, and more serious riots. In the Basque country, outraged peasants chained bears to the church doors. Yet, life slowly returned to normality, especially after Clemenceau as Minister of the Interior (and later Prime Minister) adopted a relaxed attitude towards the enforcement of the Law, and allowed time for adjustment and accommodation: counting the chandeliers, he characteristically observed, was not worth the life of one Frenchman. The Separation obliged the Church and its leaders to rethink their policies, and their place in French society.

Apart from a brief period in a (largely symbolic and ceremonious) ministerial position during the Great War, Combes was not again to hold national office, although he continued to be active as a Senator. In his own town, he promoted the vigorous application of the recent laws. Since the two religious establishments (a convent and a private college) did not form the required associations, their property was confiscated. Combes was instrumental in sponsoring the establishment, partly from the proceeds of these confiscations, of two *Ecoles Primaires Supérieures* (senior primary schools), one for boys and one for girls. These institutions were important in promoting an authentically republican education for the children of the less affluent classes. He died on 24 May 1921, on the same day that the arrival of a new French ambassador in the Vatican signalled the resumption of normal diplomatic relations between the Third Republic and the Holy See. But the apparent equilibrium remained unsteady: in the same decade, the official requirement that children in French schools should be taught, along with many other civic responsibilities, their 'duties towards God' disappeared from official texts.

Nor had the passions aroused by the life and work of Emile Combes been finally laid to rest: the events of the 1980s and 1990s were to rekindle them in dramatic forms. The world had not heard the last of *le petit Père Combes*. On 28 October 1928, a crowd of *notables* gathered in the main square of Pons for the unveiling of a statue to its most renowned citizen, and to celebrate his contribution to both national and provincial life. Eloquent tributes were paid, in the true French manner, before adjournment for further celebrations in the *Ecole Primaire Supérieure*, to which Combes had been devoted. Meanwhile, gendarmes kept an eye on the statue, and were alerted by the arrival of a crowd of some fifty youths. One of them walked towards the statue, and then took from the bunch of flowers which he was carrying a hammer, with which he smote the nose of the former Mayor and Prime Minister. An anxious policeman fired his gun, and the youth died of his wounds. The Bishop of la Rochelle dissociated himself from the assault on the statue, while observing that the celebration was nevertheless a defiance of God. The two Frances still existed, and Dreyfus was still alive, symbolically as well as literally.

Notes

[1] Merle, 1991, p. 147. This admirable study by Merle is the basis of much of this chapter. See also Visse, 1995.

[2] Merle, 1991, p. 79.

[3] Ibid., p. 121.

[4] Ibid., p. 176.

[5] Ibid., p. 201.

[6] The literature on Dreyfus and the *affaire* which took his name is, of course, vast. For an excellent recent introduction, see Cahm, 1994.

[7] Merle, 1991, p. 249.

[8] Ibid., p. 221.

[9] Ibid., p. 267.

[10] Ibid., pp. 311, 312.

[11] Ibid., p. 323.

[12] Ibid., pp. 327-331.

[13] Ibid., pp. 343 ff.

CHAPTER 4

Three Contemporaries: Robert Morant

In 1892, the Irish born Archbishop of Minneapolis eloquently defended in Paris (and in impeccable French) the advantages of a proper and respectful relationship between the Catholic Church and a secular republic. In the same year, the Mayor of Pons bitterly attacked the Catholic Church for undermining the basic principles of the secular state and for now seeking a rapprochement with it in a cynical and desperate effort to protect the financial and political advantages long enjoyed by Catholics in France. In 1892 also, a young Englishman employed as tutor to the family of the King of Siam was looking forward to a long oriental career as an educator and government adviser. But in the following year, his promising if somewhat exotic career was abruptly terminated. His energy and style had made many enemies, although he himself was disposed to blame his fall from grace on an international squabble involving Britain and France. In spite of the reversal of his fortunes, the young former royal tutor was, within ten years, to receive a laudatory letter from the Cardinal Archbishop of Westminster, leader of the growing Catholic community in England:

> *Now that your ship has entered port, after so much stress of weather, I must write one line of congratulation and of most hearty thanks for all you have done for us – for the tact and determination by which you have brought about the impossible on more than one occasion, and for a Bill that is destined to save Christianity while it is being wrecked by Education in so many lands.[1]*

Cardinal Herbert Alfred Vaughan had been born into an old Catholic family, which had remained loyal to Rome through the dark years when the so-called Recusants were suspected of treasonable disloyalty, vilified annually on Guy Fawkes Day, subjected to occasional bursts of violent anti-Popery, and deprived of most of their civil rights. His birth into a large family (six of his eight brothers became priests, while all six of his sisters entered convents) came only three years after Catholics had acquired the right to vote in parliamentary elections, and twenty years before the restoration of the Catholic hierarchy in England, of which he was head from 1892 until his death in 1903. Like many of his generation, Vaughan completed the Catholic part of his education abroad: his aristocratic Englishness earned him in Belgium the soubriquet of 'Milord Roastbeef'. In a deliberate effort to end the closed introversion of the English Catholic community, he founded a missionary order at Mill Hill and in 1872 became Bishop of Salford in the North of England. As one of the bishops in the restored and initially widely resented hierarchy, he proved to be a vigorous champion of the cause of Catholic schools and of their rights to the enjoyment of state support. He was ready and willing to make strategic alliances with other religious groups, persuading the Pope to abandon his opposition to the attendance of Catholics at the Universities of Oxford and Cambridge, and forming in 1884 the Voluntary Schools Association, dedicated to extracting from the Government a better deal for denominational schools of all kinds. As Archbishop, he began building the magnificent cathedral which was so powerful a symbol of the growing power and confidence of Catholics in England, and was especially zealous in defending the interests of the state-subsidised Catholic schools. In writing a year before his death of the wrecking of education in 'so many lands', he no doubt had especially in mind the iniquities across the Channel of *le petit Père Combes*. But who was the man to whom he wrote so gratefully in 1902, and what had he achieved in one short decade to deserve the praise of a Cardinal Archbishop?[2]

Robert Laurie Morant was born in Hampstead, London, on 7 April 1863 into a comfortable family that was impoverished by the death of his father ten years later. His early life, and to some extent his lifelong attitudes to work and mission, were profoundly affected by the evangelical piety of his mother and the dominant influence of the nearby church, Christ Church Hampstead. With some difficulty, resources were found to support a private (that is to say, classically English 'public school') education at Winchester, where he worked at his books with grim determination. New College Oxford followed in the natural course of things. He worked zealously in some of the poorer local parishes, proceeding to a study of theology since he had long intended to be ordained as a priest in the Church of England. His exposure to the higher criticism that marked much of the theological scholarship of the day eroded his commitment to a clerical career (or indeed to dogmatic religion), although he never lost a powerful sense of commitment to high and noble causes or to the most rigorous standards of work. Shortage of money obliged him to take jobs as a private tutor during the university vacations, and for a year after graduation he taught in a preparatory school for younger boys in Surrey. He was introduced to an Englishman working in the Siamese delegation in London, who was the nephew of the ubiquitous and formidable Florence Nightingale, by whom he was encouraged to take up an appointment to a princely family in Bangkok, with the immediate task of preparing three small boys for their entry to Harrow School. The impressively tall Morant arrived in Siam in January 1887 and soon made a considerable impression on King Chulalongkorn, who obviously appreciated the pedagogical talents of the English. (Morant, however, was not destined to achieve the kind of unlikely fame later enjoyed by Anna Leonewens, on whose memoirs Rodgers and Hammerstein based their 1955 musical extravaganza, *The King and I.*)[3]

Within two years, he was absorbed into the royal household, not only acting as tutor to the Crown Prince but also establishing himself as an educational adviser to the reforming King and his government. Morant's powers of organisation were always formidable, and explained much of his later meteoric rise to power in England: his study in Bangkok housed five separate tables on which different categories of his work were meticulously arranged, with one reserved for government business. He wrote textbooks for use in Siamese schools, quickly mastering the necessary language skills. He made a visit to England in 1891, partly in order to recruit staff for the new schools which were planned for the children of the Siamese aristocracy. His growing influence and unbending manner were understandably resented and aroused jealousies, eagerly exploited in the following year when French imperial ambitions led to an extension of their sphere of influence in Indo-China. The British were reluctant to intervene in defence of the integrity of the Siamese territory, Rosebery as Foreign Secretary somewhat plaintively observing in a letter to his Queen:

> *The behaviour of France has been base, cruel and treacherous. ... But that is not our affair. We cannot afford to be the knight errants for the world, careering about to redress grievances and help the weak.[4]*

After seven years building the foundations of a career which had now been abruptly terminated, Robert Morant at the age of 31 now found himself back in England.

Determined to waste no time, he moved into Toynbee House – a settlement founded by the Reverend Samuel Barnett to carry the light of Oxford to the dark and impoverished East End of London – and began there to address his mind to the educational problems of his own country. In May 1895, he wrote to the Government's Education Department to ask for a job. The Department was then immersed in a series of efforts to bring some coherence into the sprawling and confused national arrangements for schooling, and the latest in a series of major Royal Commissions (Bryce) was nearing the end of its work. An Office of Special Inquiries and Reports had recently been created to carry forward the surveys and research on which any proposed major reforms would be able to draw, and Morant was appointed as assistant to its director, Michael Sadler – soon to establish himself as one of the founding fathers of the serious practice of comparative education.[5]

A little before the signing of the Bryce Report in August 1895, the Conservative leader, Lord Salisbury, had replaced the Liberal Rosebery as Prime Minister. Major reform was now inevitable: it had been repeatedly delayed, and as a result, the voluntary schools (still mostly Anglican, but with an expanding Catholic minority), all of which had for the past sixty years depended heavily on government grants, were in desperate financial straits.

Equally problematical, however, was the lack of any adequate central machinery – of the character which had for a century functioned in France – for the coordination of public education. Moreover, even the local arrangements for such planning and provision – which were strong in the highly decentralised American system – were inadequate and hotly contested. All three problems – the future of the voluntary denominationally based schools, central coordination and local control – interacted in a complex manner, and were deeply entangled with English (and Welsh) political and religious prejudices.[6]

This was the untidy world, more fully explored in chapter 7, into which the orderly and methodical Morant now threw all his energies and ambitions. He would not for long be content to remain as a junior official and adviser. By the time he had worked himself into the centres of administrative and political influence, the structural problem of central coordination had at last been solved: it was the least contentious of the three key issues. The clue to any understanding of the work of Morant lies in the history of elementary education in England. The State, as in the United States but not France, had been deeply reluctant to assume any overall responsibility for schools, and everything had therefore for long been left to voluntary efforts by the churches, and especially by the economically favoured and legally established Church of England. Anglican schools throughout the nineteenth century had dominated the countryside, and from the 1830s received government grants. These grants were administered by a Committee of the Privy Council on Education, whose misleadingly named Vice President was in fact an embryonic Minister of Education, accountable to Parliament for the administration of the public funds made available to the voluntary schools. There were, of course, for many years no other public elementary schools to worry about. Such grants were made to Anglican, Roman Catholic, non-sectarian Christian, and Jewish schools. In time, absolute dependence on state-subsidised voluntary effort ceased to be adequate, and in 1870 local School Boards (not wholly dissimilar to their American predecessors) were established by Act of Parliament in those areas where voluntary provision was demonstrably insufficient to meet local needs. These elected Boards built and financed schools that were essentially secular, although they were allowed (indeed, in effect, generally encouraged) to offer religious instruction of a non-denominational kind, based on the reading of the Authorised Version of the Bible. All elementary schools – whether built and managed by these new Boards or by the churches and other bodies which had established faith-based schools – at first charged modest tuition fees, with a reduction in such payments for the poorest children. Both types of schools also received substantial and specific grants from central government, distributed by the Education Department, acting as the administrative arm of the Committee of Council, a de facto if diminutive Ministry.

This patchwork of arrangements and of funding applied in principle only to elementary education of a basic kind. Secondary education was, for much of the nineteenth century, provided on a private and voluntary basis by the well-established independent schools with a national reputation (the misleadingly so-called Public Schools), supplemented by smaller private establishments of varying quality, and by ancient grammar schools established and endowed as acts of charity to offer some locally based schooling. Growing industrialisation and urbanisation, accelerated and symbolised by the Great Exhibition of 1851, entailed that no government could continue totally to neglect education of a technical and secondary character. Government grants were therefore hesitantly made available to institutions of various kinds, including the schools maintained by the local Boards. These grants were, however, managed by an entirely separate government agency, not responsible to or integrated with the Education Department and operating from its own headquarters in South Kensington.[7]

Elementary and secondary education, at central as at local levels, moved in hermetically sealed universes and under entirely different rules and assumptions. In 1899, a national Board of Education was at last created with its own President (a government minister, and in effect, although not in name, a Minister of Education). At the heart of the national government in London, but there alone, the overall direction of public (Board) elementary schools and voluntary denominationally based elementary schools, and of the grants made for the extension of schooling of a higher or secondary character had therefore by the last year of the nineteenth century all been formally unified. Morant, who had contributed much behind the scenes to securing this degree of architectural order, now had access to the levers of a machine which, if skilfully manipulated, could steer the development of a recognisably national system of education. Such a national order, unless it attempted their abolition, would need either to replace or incorporate Anglican, Catholic and other religious schools. They could certainly not be ignored.

Abolition, even for those who found it ideologically tempting, was never on the agenda of realists like Robert Morant. A powerful contribution towards the campaign for radical reform was made by Sidney Webb in his 1901 Fabian Society pamphlet, *The Education Muddle and the Way Out*:

> *It is politically impossible to abolish these voluntary schools; and*
> *whatever we may think of the theological reasons for their establishment,*
> *their separate and practically individual management does incidentally*
> *offer what ought to be, in any public system of education, most jealously*
> *guarded, namely, variety, and the opportunity of experiment. [8]*

Webb calculated that, although there were in England no fewer than 2527 separate School Boards, more than one-third of the population of the country lived in areas where no such Boards had been established, and where families were therefore dependent for their schooling on the national network of Church of England state-assisted elementary schools. Moreover, there were over ten thousand parishes in which the *only* provision available was controlled by the Church of England: the consequences for families which were Catholic, Nonconformist, or indifferent to religious teaching were often painful, even if the rights of conscience (and therefore of the withdrawal of pupils from religious instruction) had been legally secured for the past thirty years. Of the voluntary schools in receipt of state grants at the end of the century, 11,777 were Anglican, 1079 interdenominational but unambiguously Protestant, 458 Methodist, and 1045 Roman Catholic. These 14,359 voluntary schools were complemented by only 5788 Board schools (that is to say, public schools in the full and obvious sense of the term). Most of the Anglican schools were in country districts, and the Board schools tended to be larger and more generously funded. More significant, therefore, were the proportions of the population served by these very different schools, of which by far the most self-consciously distinctive were the Catholic establishments. Some 53% of all pupils attending schools in receipt of public grants were in the voluntary schools, and 47% in Board schools. Of the 53% of all pupils who attended religious schools, 73% were in Anglican establishments, and only 6% in schools built and provided at considerable cost and sacrifice by the relatively poor Roman Catholic community. Even if it had been thought practicable and desirable to eliminate the flow of government money into these Catholic schools, the very size of an Anglican contribution operating under the same legislation and administrative rules rendered such radical policies politically and financially inaccessible. Morant calculated that it would have cost thirty million pounds to replace 'voluntary' provision on so massive a scale, and the crippling expenses of the Boer War made any such nationalisation totally unrealistic. Moreover, the increase of the Catholic provision over the past thirty years had been so dramatic that it had already advanced from very modest beginnings to form a significant, if not totally integrated, part of an emerging national system. There had been places for 66,066 pupils in state-supported Catholic schools in 1870; at the close of the century that figure stood at 255,036.[9] The Catholic contribution to the elementary education of the poorer classes had quadrupled in size.

Although all denominational schools operated under closely similar regulations, many had nevertheless developed significantly different characteristics. The non-sectarian religious schools (essentially those operating under the aegis of the British and Foreign Schools Society, and embracing a wide range of Nonconformists as well as some Anglicans) had in the thirty years since the passing of the 1870 Act been progressively assimilated with Board Schools. In many cases indeed, they were virtually indistinguishable from them – using the Authorised Version of the Bible and refraining from teaching the doctrines or formularies of any particular Christian sect. Many of them had been surrendered without fuss to the local Boards. The Anglican schools in receipt of state grants – operating under the aegis of the National Society – covered a wider spectrum of distinctiveness and commitment. Most of them had grown naturally as part of the evolution of small communities: alongside the parish church, in principle serving the whole community as it had in the Middle Ages, a small school would evolve – under the supposedly benevolent eye of the local incumbent, associated with the National Society and receiving government grants for building as well a wider range of specific subsidies. There would always be at least a diffused Anglican character about any such school, sometimes reinforced by a commitment to an aggressive denominationalism. Indeed, there was a sense in which the Church of England did not regard itself as a denomination, but as the national church. The reality was, of course, often different from this somewhat bland vision. Especially in those many villages where there was no alternative to the National (Society) School, parents alienated from Anglican practices and beliefs were placed at an obvious and disagreeable disadvantage. At the other end of the spectrum of Anglican establishments, and generally in the larger towns, were to be found the schools associated with churches having a much more assertive, and even partisan, view of what the Church of England represented. Some of these churches and their associated schools would be of a fundamentalist and evangelical character. Many more – and these were the High Church parishes and schools in which Nonconformists would feel most resentful – stood in the traditions of Tractarianism and the Oxford Movement. Most of these were in poorer districts in the inner city, and proclaimed the catholicity of the Church of England. They promoted ritualistic forms of worship, practices and doctrines (of the Mass or of auricular confession) which their critics denounced as Romish.

Anglican schools of this kind were, therefore – in their sense of mission and identity – in important ways closer in spirit to the Roman Catholic schools themselves. Those Catholic schools had been built, steadily from the 1830s but rapidly after 1870, to serve the needs of an emancipated Catholic community, and in particular to secure the loyalties and protect the faith of the Irish immigrants. Anglicans and Protestants of all kinds, as well as the growing numbers of parents generally indifferent to the nuances of religious differentiation, would have absolutely no reason for sending their children to these distinctively Catholic schools. Since there were, of course, no single school areas in which the only school was Catholic, the Protestant conscience could not be directly offended by an assertion of Catholic beliefs and values. A Catholic school in receipt of public grants could for such obvious reasons readily accept the imposition of a conscience clause (allowing parents to withdraw their children from religious instruction), since such children would not be in the school in the first place. For Catholics (as, at an earlier date, for some leading Anglicans), religious instruction could never be relegated to the optional margins of schooling, leaving secular subjects to be taught in an atmosphere of sterile neutrality. Some High Church Anglicans had, understandably, taken a similar view. But by the end of the century, there had emerged a clear division between those who accepted or approved of 'regulated hours' and those who, like the Catholics, insisted on stressing the 'total atmosphere'. For the former, secular subjects (like mathematics, or reading, or geography) could without difficulty be taught to integrated classes of pupils by teachers of any religious affiliation or of none, while religion should be taught only by members of the denomination to which the individual pupil belonged, and at a time of day when withdrawal from such classes could be conveniently arranged.

At the turn of the century, all voluntary schools, in spite of their wide diversity, now shared one common problem: a desperate shortage of funds. The questions of whether and how to rescue them were deeply embedded in contemporary politics. The core of the Conservative Party, led by the Marquess of Salisbury and other members of the Cecil family, tended to favour the Established Church and its schools and had made some tempting promises to them (and inevitably, therefore, to the Catholic schools as well) in the General Election of 1895. Allied to the Conservatives since Gladstone's policies towards Ireland had split the Liberal Party was the Unionist wing of that party, led by Joseph Chamberlain – a formidable champion of the Nonconformist interest and of the cause of the Board schools with which it was increasingly associated. For its part, the main body of the now divided Liberal Party had long enjoyed the support of the Nonconformists and was traditionally and deeply hostile to the vested interests and financial privileges of the Established Church. At the same time, its precarious alliance with Irish members of Parliament required a sensitivity towards the Catholic interest, which at significant points coincided with that of the Anglicans. The Board schools were, for plain reasons, perceived by the voluntary schools as their rivals if not their enemies, enjoying access to copious local funds as well as to the national grants on which the voluntary schools depended. The National Society and its political allies were, however, profoundly uneasy at a possible dependence on the Boards for any substantial part of their funding. Catholics were equally nervous of becoming dependent on local opinion and prejudice for their own finances. Yet, Catholics and Anglicans desperately needed public money, and recognised the advantages of being a securely permanent part of a local system, rather than a vulnerable and centrally funded annex to it. In any case, the state exchequer was now – as a direct result of Chamberlain's expensive and imperialist commitment to fighting the Boer War – itself short of funds. But what if the Boards were now to be abolished, and replaced by more comprehensive and less partisan local channels of public funding and coordination?

The central achievement of Morant was to recognise and exploit the connection (political rather than logical) between the religious issue and the cause to which he had, since his return from Bangkok, become increasingly dedicated. For – alongside the perennial religious question – there was, as has been suggested above, another potent reason for challenging the authority of the Boards. Although some of them were advancing tentatively into the fields of technical and secondary education, they had no legal authority to do so and were being challenged by the youthful all-purpose local authorities (the county councils, and county borough councils in major cities), which had been organised as recently as 1888. Had these new locally elected authorities already existed in 1870, it seems unlikely that the single-purpose School Boards would have been manufactured in the first place. Now, however, they did certainly exist, and were testing their muscle. Many, and notably the London County Council, had solicited and received from South Kensington substantial grants for the encouragement of education beyond the elementary level. For Morant, it made no sense that responsibility for public education should be fragmented in this way. The degree of unity which had been achieved centrally in 1899 with the creation of the Board of Education must now be replicated locally.

In the few years between his return from Siam and the passing of the great Education Act of 1902, Morant skilfully leapfrogged over his superiors in the Education Department.[10] He worked under the general direction of Sadler, contributing studies of the education systems of both France and Switzerland, by the coherence and effectiveness of which he was understandably impressed. He contrived to insert an apparently inoffensive footnote in his Swiss report suggesting (a matter hardly within his research brief) that the activities of the School Boards in spending public money on any form of education other than elementary was illegal. He drew the attention of enemies of the School Boards to this potentially explosive remark, and provoked before the local auditor a successful challenge to the legality of the Boards' actions. The Boards lost that argument, as well as their subsequent appeals to the courts. Morant helped to secure the passing of a bill which authorised such expenditures – but for one year only. A decision on matters of principle could therefore be delayed no longer. His work for the Act establishing a single central government ministry for education had been much appreciated by the difficult and unpredictable minister responsible for securing its passage into law – Sir John Gorst, who distinguished himself by riding to work on a scarlet bicycle. Morant became the minister's personal secretary, and was rewarded by displacing his own superior as the civil service head of the Board of Education in 1902. His remarkable grasp of complex detail, a finely tuned sense of political reality, and commitment to remorseless hard work brought him to the attention of A.J. Balfour, Leader of the House of Commons and nephew of the Prime Minister, Salisbury, whom he was to succeed later in 1902.

Morant first met Balfour at a discreet luncheon in the house of Edward Talbot, the Bishop of Rochester, and formerly the first head of Keble College, Oxford. Talbot was closely identified with the High Church party among the Anglicans, and dedicated to the cause of denominational schooling. Balfour was impressed by Morant and persuaded by his arguments. Morant himself had already recognised the importance to his plans of the religious issue – not just because the voluntary schools would have to be somehow accommodated within any workable and affordable settlement of the national problem, but also because he saw that only the religious issue could 'get up steam' and push reform ahead against opposition from powerful coalitions of Liberals, Nonconformists (who bitterly disliked the idea of any further support for the Catholic and Anglican schools), secularists, and the School Boards themselves. Voluntary schools were now disappearing at the rate of sixty each year: if this continued, Catholic and Anglican anger would mount, while the State would face an insuperable difficulty in struggling to provide alternative accommodation.[11] The temporary relief which the voluntary schools had secured as recently as 1897, and which included an exemption from the payment of local rates, was already exhausted. If the religious problem could not be resolved, the whole cause of reform would be lost. Morant's plan, now adopted by Balfour with as much enthusiasm as he could ever muster, was to commit the responsibility for the whole of local educational provision to the elected councils of the counties and county boroughs (with a few marginal concessions to some smaller local authorities), and to channel all support for the voluntary schools through those same authorities. In this way, a coherent system would at last be established, and the voluntary schools securely embedded within a publicly funded and locally managed educational framework.

The problem was, of course, the predictable and tough opposition of Joseph Chamberlain, and so Morant was despatched to confront him in his Birmingham stronghold. In an interview which Morant regarded as representing the greatest achievement of his life, Chamberlain was persuaded by the force of the arguments deployed, and especially by Morant's insistence that it was Chamberlain's own commitment to fighting an expensive imperialist war which had drained the Treasury and made totally impracticable any further rescue by central government of the beleaguered voluntary schools.[12] But Chamberlain did insist that the new local authorities might be empowered but could not be compelled to support the voluntary schools within their territories: it must be left to them to decide. This condition therefore appeared in the draft bill, alongside a proposal to withdraw the virtual prohibition on the teaching of denominational versions of religion in the public schools themselves, now of course to be transferred from the old Boards to the new local education authorities (LEAs). The Anglicans were unhappy with the first concession to their critics, for it would have made their schools permanently vulnerable to fluctuations of local politics. But they welcomed the concession that denominational religious instruction might be allowed in Board schools. Although the Catholics were, of course, profoundly unhappy with both proposals, they reacted with prudent care.

In the event, amendments in the lengthy House of Commons debates soon eliminated both of these (and, to the systematic Morant, unwelcome) concessions: LEAs would after all be obliged to support the recognised voluntary schools, and so enable them to make a significant contribution to local education. The anger of the enemies of Anglican and Catholic schools now exploded. The fiery Lloyd George, later to be Prime Minister, denounced the Romish plot (for to the Nonconformist Welsh the distinction between a Romanising – and English – High Church and the immemorial Roman Catholic enemy was trivial). This proved to be his great political and parliamentary opportunity, as he declaimed against the plot 'to rivet the clerical chain around the necks of the people'.[13] 'Rome on the Rates!' was adopted as the emotionally effective, if technically inaccurate, rallying cry of public opposition, as memories of the Gunpowder Plot, the Armada and the Protestant martyrs of the reign of Bloody Mary were revived and inflamed. The Baptist leader, Dr John Clifford, orchestrated a national campaign of protest against state subsidies for and official recognition of Catholic and Anglican schools. The tireless pamphleteer, J. Hirst Hollowell, applied his talents to composing battle songs:

> *England rouse thy legions*
> *Ere it be too late*
> *Foes of right and foes of light*
> *Would storm the schoolhouse gate!*

The North, like Wales, was a focus for opposition to the amended bill: sixteen special trains carried protestors to a mass meeting in Leeds, where a procession one mile long was peacefully marshalled.[14]

Nor were the Anglicans universally happy. In its original form, the 1902 bill had proposed that denominational teaching would in effect be tolerated in the former Board schools. This concession to the Established Church was withdrawn during the debates in the Commons in an amendment proposed by Colonel Kenyon-Slaney. A distraught clergyman denounced it as 'the greatest betrayal since the crucifixion', adding implausibly that 'he would rather the Colonel should have seduced his wife rather than come to Parliament with such a proposal'.[15] More moderate Anglicans were concerned by the stipulations that one-third of the managers of the voluntary schools in receipt of public money should by appointed by the new LEAs and that the teaching of religion should be subject to the supervision and control of the managers as a whole, and not of the parish priest. The Catholics, while sharing some of the concerns about the LEA presence on the governing bodies of their schools, were not worried by the formal requirement relating to the control of religious education. They were understandably confident that lay managers would be happy to follow the guidance of their own priest in such matters. Cardinal Vaughan, who died in the year after the passing of the Act, remained in close touch with Morant throughout the negotiations and forcefully reminded the Catholic community of its own vulnerability. He insisted to the Catholic Poor Schools Committee that:

> *We must remember that we are an unpopular and insignificant minority*
> *in this country and must take care lest by seeking to obtain the ideal we*
> *do not lose what we have hitherto gained.[16]*

On 1 November, Morant supplanted his superior, Kekewitch, by becoming Acting Secretary, or chief executive, of the Board of Education: he took over the office formally in the following April, and was never forgiven by colleagues and critics for what they perceived as his Machiavellian intrigues. The deeply controversial bill which he had designed, and which Prime Minister Balfour was now promoting, consumed a record fifty-seven days of the time of the House of Commons. In December, it began an unruffled passage through the Lords, receiving the royal assent a few days before Christmas. Balfour's Act of 1902, by establishing a clearly articulated partnership between a department of central government and the elected local authorities, and by incorporating the voluntary schools within the national system, provided for the rest of the century the essential foundation for educational development in Britain. It also ensured that that development would thereafter be directly linked to the vagaries of national politics and to the power and influence of the churches.

Robert Morant did not, however, make the mistake of supposing that all problems had now been resolved. In spite of his own mild scepticism in such matters, he was fully aware that the religious issue would not simply evaporate: 'Of course at bottom one knows only too well that the ultimate difficulty is for ever and everywhere insoluble'.[17] Certainly, the Nonconformist Welsh, urged on by the rhetoric of Lloyd George, were not going to give up without a struggle. All the major towns in Wales joined in a rates boycott, refusing to levy taxes which might be deployed for the support of religious schools. Morant and Balfour responded in 1904 with a punitive Act which allowed the Government to withhold the payment of grants to such rebellious authorities, and to use the money thereby saved for the support of the voluntary schools threatened by the boycott. Although the revolt had by 1906 faded away, the bitterness remained and Balfour and the Conservative Party were soon to pay the price. Balfour resigned in December 1905 and his Liberal successor, Campbell-Bannerman, promptly called an election. Although the disputes over imperial trade and preferential tariffs were no doubt the main cause of the deep divisions within the Conservative Party and of its shattering defeat, the religious issue was also a factor of considerable importance in arousing public interest in that election. At the previous general election in 1900, the Conservatives had secured 402 seats and the Liberals 184. But the Liberals now commanded an overwhelming majority – 400 seats ranged against a mere 157 for the Conservatives, with 83 seats going to the Irish Nationalists (closely linked to Catholic interests, of course) and 40 to the emerging Labour Party. The new Liberal Government, with Lloyd George entrenched as a powerful minister, now attempted to fulfil its election promises and disentangle itself from the Balfour Act, and in particular from its unacceptable generosity to voluntary schools – be they Anglican, Catholic, interdenominational, Methodist or Jewish. Morant, in the best traditions of a reformed civil service, supported his new masters loyally if unenthusiastically: in 1907, he was knighted for his public services.

Doubtless, he knew better than most how difficult it would be in practice to fulfil the seductive election promises. The first and most creative attempt to resolve the difficulties was made as early as April 1906 by the new President of the Board of Education, Augustine Birrell – a man of scholarly tastes and eirenic disposition. Birrell, the son of a Baptist but lacking the crusading zeal of John Clifford, naturally favoured the cause of the non-denominational or secular public school. But he had seen and admired the work of the voluntary schools in the poorer areas, and especially those maintained by the Catholics and their unacknowledged cousins, the Anglo-Catholics:

> *I have seen the schools belonging to these creeds in Liverpool, London*
> *and elsewhere and had a great admiration for them. [18]*

Birrell made a valiant effort to make legislative and administrative sense of what was doubtless a substantial but elusive distinction between two broad categories of voluntary schools: on the one hand, the schools (notably in the troublesome single school districts) which were moderately Anglican and served the general needs of the local population and, on the other hand, those (notably the Catholic elementary schools but also some of the urban Anglican schools) which laid deliberate stress on their powerfully denominational character, and therefore on the close integration of all teaching within the framework of shared religious belief. All the voluntary schools, however, apart from those which might contract out altogether in return for an imprecise promise of some grants from central government, would be transferred to the control of the elected local authorities. Birrell and his supporters hoped that while the Catholic schools would choose to place themselves in the second category (marked by a stronger 'atmosphere', in the interesting words of the bill), most Anglican schools would slide comfortably into the first category. The twelve Jewish voluntary schools would no doubt align themselves with the Catholics. Such clearly self-defining schools would be allowed 'extended facilities' for religious education, extending over all five days of the week. The other former voluntary schools would be allowed such facilities on two days only, with non-denominational religious education permitted on other days. The newly appointed Anglican Archbishop of Canterbury was openly unhappy with the proposals, and a Church Schools Emergency League was formed. Thirty-two special trains were chartered to transport protestors to a massive demonstration in London. The bill bristled with difficulties: in its original form, it did not require the new LEAs to accept an offer of surrender by a voluntary school, nor did it require them automatically to grant to such a school the 'extended facilities' which all Catholic schools would certainly expect and require. Moreover, four-fifths of the parents would have to request such extended facilities, which in any case could be granted only in towns with a population in excess of five thousand. Catholics wondered how many of their schools, now beginning to prosper under the terms of the Balfour Act, would in the end be accepted as authentically Catholic schools within a reshaped local system. Tim Healy, the

Irish MP who later became the first Governor General of the Irish Free State, spoke for many when he protested:

> *The Catholic convict, the Catholic pauper, the Catholic soldier and*
> *even the Catholic corpse is looked after with extraordinary punctilio by*
> *the great Parliament of England. So I must be either a pauper or a*
> *foundling in order that the rites of my religion may be conserved. [19]*

In these unpromising circumstances, some Catholics would, therefore, even have preferred to return to the state of affairs prevailing before the Balfour Act, disentangling themselves from the politically unpredictable LEAs and becoming once more dependent on the more exiguous but more dependable grants from central government. But that would almost certainly have driven a wedge between the Catholic and the much larger number of other voluntary schools, segregating them in vulnerable isolation and condemning them once more to poverty: in the few years since the passing of the Balfour Act, the salaries of teachers in Catholic schools had quadrupled. The Catholic Education Council (which had in 1904 replaced the Catholic Poor Schools Committee) was itself divided on this issue, but finally decided to concentrate on improving the terms to be offered to their schools, and to any others which attempted to place themselves in the sharper denominational category. In that effort they were now joined by many Anglican spokesmen and campaigners: the better the terms offered to such schools (the so-called Clause Four schools in Birrell's bill), the more likely it became that substantial rather than negligible numbers of Anglican schools would seek admission to that category, and so subvert one of the main intentions of the bill. Birrell, advised by Morant, was anxious to be as accommodating as possible, and eventually an acceptable compromise was hammered out in the House of Commons. The Catholics would in all probability have been content to accept the final solution offered to them, which in many ways anticipated the later solution represented by the great Butler Act of 1944. But the bill was wrecked in the House of Lords, encouraged by the Conservative leader, Balfour, who was anxious to cause the greatest possible embarrassment to the Liberals as well as to conserve the basic elements of his own recent legislation. The Lords' amendments were rejected out of hand by the Government: a great opportunity to resolve the religious problem had been lost and, even more significantly, the two Houses of Parliament had been brought into an open collision. Religious and political issues were now deeply embedded in major constitutional questions and in the polemics of party politics: they were to remain so for at least the rest of the century then beginning.

The Liberal Government was nevertheless obliged, both by its election promises and by the pressure maintained upon it by its Nonconformist allies, to make yet further attempts in the next few years to modify in significant ways the settlement of 1902. At the same time, and although – for as long as it enjoyed a massive majority – this was not especially significant, the Liberals were obliged by the presence in the Commons of a considerable Irish contingent to be attentive to the Catholic interest. Birrell's successor, Reginald McKenna, was not interested in compromise and introduced a bill which would have transferred all the (Anglican) schools in single school districts to the LEAs, and allowed 'facilities' in them and in them alone for the teaching of religion of a denominational character. Other voluntary schools could either surrender themselves to the LEA, or 'contract out' of the local system, becoming thereafter dependent upon central government grants of uncertain size and scope. Catholics, in alliance with Anglicans, angrily defeated this proposal. The third Liberal education minister, Walter (later Viscount) Runciman, proceeded by way of careful but ultimately fruitless negotiation, starting with the Nonconformist and Anglican groups. Although Francis Bourne – Vaughan's successor as the Catholic Archbishop of Westminster – was informed of the outline proposal, he understood well enough that serious discussions about the future of the (still) relatively small number of Catholic schools could not be usefully initiated until some agreement had been reached by Runciman with the Church of England:

> *He knew and I knew perfectly well that until he had squared the*
> *Anglicans it was no use speaking to us, because the whole arrangement*
> *depended upon that.[20]*

Runciman had hoped to square the Anglicans by balancing the compulsory transfer of all their schools in single school areas with the concession that they would be able to provide religious education, with safeguards for the rights of conscience, in all LEA schools. Roman Catholics and all Anglican schools in other districts would either be surrendered to the LEAs or contracted out of the local system, once again becoming dependent on the good will and grants of central government. The teacher unions were angered by what they saw as an attack on professional autonomy and an extension of the career advantages enjoyed by Anglicans. Their opposition, combined with the profound reservations of many Anglicans and the deep resentment of the Catholics at the attempt to sideline and isolate them and their schools, ensured the collapse of the proposals.

The Act with which Sir Robert Morant had been so closely associated therefore survived unscathed if not unchallenged, and political attention turned to even more urgent and divisive matters: the opposition of the House of Lords to the dangerous radicalism of Lloyd George's 'People's Budget' of 1909, the determination of the Liberals to curb drastically the obstructive powers of the upper house, the two bitterly fought general elections of 1910, and the Parliament Act of 1911. Moreover, after those two elections the Liberals became dependent on the support of the Irish members, and therefore of the Catholic interest in England: there were in the new House equal numbers (272) of Conservative and Liberal members, 42 Labour representatives, and 84 Irish Nationalists. But if Morant's legislative and administrative achievement therefore survived, so did the bitterness against him. His enemies took advantage of a relatively minor indiscretion committed in 1911, when – by adding the note 'approved RLM' – he authorised the publication of a report which was arrogantly critical of the LEAs and of the teachers they employed. Runciman was forced to resign, and Morant moved away from the educational limelight to make a massive contribution to the evolution of the new Ministry of Health and of the many schemes of social welfare associated with it, thereby earning from his grateful minister the ambiguous soubriquet of 'that magnificent hustler'. The former tutor to the Crown Prince of Siam had not lost his reforming zeal, nor forgotten what he had learned from Florence Nightingale. Shortly before his death in 1920 at the age of fifty-six, he told the inaugural meeting of the Society of Civil Servants:

> *I always regard men and women who work at all seriously at things as falling into two classes roughly – those who leave absolutely no stone unturned to make the things they are at a success and [here he paused and with a smile continued] those who turn just enough stones to make it just about do.* [21]

It was reported when A.J. Balfour died ten years later he had been 'about to pay his tribute' to Robert Morant. It is a pity that history has been deprived of that statement. By their combined efforts, the statesman and the civil servant had ensured that Church and State were irreversibly committed to cooperation at both national and local levels of government in developing an integrated system of elementary and secondary education within which the voluntary schools would play an important part. In the coming years, the Catholic schools, now rescued by local rates from the penury of the nineteenth century, would in absolute and relative terms become steadily more important within the voluntary sector. These were the schools which were most clear about what they wanted from the State and about the absolute priority of preserving a distinctive identity. The failure of the attempts of Augustine Birrell, whom Morant as the Board's permanent Secretary had also served, nevertheless entailed that the 'non-provided' or voluntary school, for whose building costs no adequate public provision had yet been made, would now find it financially difficult to match the progress made by the LEA 'provided' schools, especially when the expenses of a major reorganisation were involved. In that sense, the voluntary schools became a reluctant brake on educational progress. The work of Balfour and Morant further guaranteed that, in future, the realignment of Church and State relations in education would be negotiated in the corridors of Whitehall and Westminster, through which in their day they had so confidently walked.

Notes

[1] Allen, 1934, pp. 197-198.

[2] Norman, 1984, p. 361.

[3] For Morant, see especially Allen (1934) and Judge (1984a). Wyatt (1969) is of considerable interest on the Siamese phase of his life, and for the surprising connection to musical comedy, see R. Rodgers (1955) Rodgers and Hammerstein's *The King and I*, based upon M. Landon (1973) *Anna and The King of Siam*. Bath: Chivers.

[4] Allen, 1934, p. 86.

[5] Grier, 1952.

[6] Eaglesham, 1967.

[7] Eaglehsam, 1967, p. 24.

[8] Webb, 1901, p. 14.

[9] Cruickshank, 1963, Appendix C.

[10] Grier, 1952.

[11] Allen, 1934, p. 153; Cruickshank, 1963, p. 70.

[12] Ibid., p. 57.

[13] Ibid., p. 176.

[14] Hollowell, 1901. *The Times*, 22 September 1902.

[15] Fitzroy, A.W. (nd) *Memoirs*, vol. I, p. 112. London: Hutchinson.

[16] Public Record Office, Ed 24 (undated) quoted in Cruickshank, 1963, p. 81 and Allen, 1934, p. 196.

[17] Allen, 1934, p. 161.

[18] Birrell, A. (1937) *Things Past Redress*, quoted in Cruickshank, 1963, p. 91.

[19] Cruickshank, 1963, p. 95.

[20] Minutes of Catholic Education Council, 24 November 1908, cited in Cruickshank, 1963, p. 106.

[21] Judge, 1984a, p. 67.

CHAPTER 5

Three Antecedents: Horace Mann

When Archbishop John Ireland raised his fist and proclaimed before the National Education Association his devotion to 'the free school of America', he was paying his own distinctive tribute to the memory of the Massachusetts reformer, Horace Mann, who had died thirty years before. No name has been more closely identified with the characteristically American commitment to the ideals of the common school, open without charge to the children of all classes and creeds. Perhaps the most remarkable thing about Mann is how much he said and how little he did. His role was that of the prophet and the persuader: he controlled no school system and managed no bureaucracy. But he did celebrate and make possible the growth of the American common public school, from which the Roman Catholic community ultimately felt obliged to distance itself. In that sense, neither Ireland nor Mann succeeded in realising the shared ideals of common citizenship, patriotism and civic virtue.

In 1834, Horace Mann was commissioned by the Boston city government to investigate the dramatic and disturbing events of the night of 11 August, when a virulently anti-Catholic mob had attacked the Ursuline convent in Charlestown, which housed a school where the daughters of Protestant as well as Catholic families were welcomed. The convent was burnt after the nuns had been ejected. These events reflected only too well the deep hostility nursed by the less prosperous elements in an increasingly diverse society towards foreigners in general and Catholics in particular.[1] Although Mann was not in good enough health to complete the enquiry, his knowledge of these events and of the irrational passions inflamed by them reinforced his belief that the stability of New England society was at risk, that sectarian strife was an index of the tensions and hostilities inherent in a society that was rapidly moving away from its traditional base in orderly Puritan consensus, and that only a sustained and vigorous campaign to promote education for all children could forestall the dissolution of his familiar world. Like many of his contemporaries, Mann was alert to the challenges to traditional forms of life and thinking represented by the accelerating shift of the economy from an agricultural towards an industrial base and by the enlarging scale of Irish immigration.[2] An education capable of sustaining such a society would need above all to be moral and civic, and – if it were indeed to be a force for unity – non-sectarian. It therefore came to display in the 1840s several of the characteristics of the great republican education movement in the France of the 1880s. But New England was not old France, and its schooling would also of necessity be in some fundamental if cloudy sense religious, while that promoted by Jules Ferry and his allies was emphatically not.

Religion, even or especially when he was struggling against it, played a crucial part in Mann's life and upbringing. He was born in the small township of Franklin in 1796, and grew up on the family farm. The dominant figure of that small community was the minister, Nathanael Emmons, who for over half a century preached to his flock a pure and ferocious version of Calvinism, emphasising the inherent wickedness of man and an uncompromisingly absolute separation of the saved from the damned. The young Horace Mann resisted the pressures to declare his conversion, and – with much pain and difficulty – distanced himself from doctrines which, even in early adolescence, he found increasingly repugnant.

> *I remember the day, the hour, the place and the circumstances, as well as though the event had happened but yesterday, when in an agony of despair, I broke the spell that bound me. From that day, I began to construct the theory of Christian ethics and doctrine respecting virtue and vice, rewards and penalties, time and eternity, God and his providence which ... I still retain.[3]*

The content might change, but for Mann, the format of religious belief (ethics and doctrine, virtue and vice, rewards and penalties, time and eternity, God and his providence) remained constant and made a deep imprint on the ethos of the emerging American public school. Shortly after this break with orthodox Calvinism, Mann's father died (Horace was thirteen years old) and within a year, his elder brother was drowned, while breaking the Sabbath by swimming in a local pond. Emmons preached a predictably brutal sermon. Mann could have no shred of sympathy left for doctrines which divided – American from American, Congregationalists from Baptists, Presbyterians or Episcopalians, the saved from the damned, the native born from the immigrant, the Protestant from the Catholic, the affluent from the poor.

Mann worked hard to secure admission to Brown University, later marrying its President's daughter, whose tragic death at the age of 23 confirmed him in his serious, not to say joyless, view of a world where duty should rule all. Law became his chosen career and in 1827, he was elected to the House of Representatives of the Massachusetts legislature, the General Court. Shortly thereafter, a modest sum of federal money became available for local expenditures: Washington was at last reimbursing the Commonwealth for the expenses of its militia during the 1812 war against the British. Mann was already interesting himself in reform movements of various kinds: the provision of asylums for the mentally ill, and (like John Ireland) temperance and the building of railways. The availability of federal money was used to promote school building, on condition that the local community also taxed itself in the same cause. The provision of schooling in the state was haphazard, and desperately uneven. Schools, where they existed at all, were small, usually open only during the winter, poorly funded, lacking any sense of overall purpose and run by ill-paid and often itinerant teachers. The urgency of making more systematic provision was emphasised by riots and disorders, which alarmed the professional and propertied classes. Schooling as much as temperance was part of an urgent social reform. In 1837, there were ugly scenes when a detachment of the Boston fire brigade collided with an Irish funeral procession. In the same year, the legislature passed a law establishing a State Board of Education, and Mann (who had been elected to the Senate in 1834) became its first full-time Secretary.

The duties of the Board and of its Secretary were carefully and restrictively defined: they were not to control (even if there had been any system to control), but to collect and disseminate information. The provision of schools was and must remain a purely local responsibility, and each school would strive to meet the needs, and doubtless reflect the religious and other preferences, of each community. When he assumed office, Mann claimed no special knowledge of education, and indeed never developed any elaborated theories. He prepared himself for his new duties by a month's reading of educational journals (never a cheering experience) and of a handful of standard works. He was, however, much impressed by Victor Cousin's well-known work on Prussian schools, which he read in translation. Like many reformers, of his day and since, he used comparative studies mainly in order to strengthen his own arguments. What he most admired about the Prussian arrangements was a strong sense of system coupled with the emphasis on the importance of high quality professional teaching. He was not as a general rule a great admirer of European ways and habits, especially when they reflected inequitable and divisive social arrangements. Education above all should save the Americans from the fate that would otherwise soon overtake them. During a later visit to England (when he met James Simpson, Kay-Shuttleworth, Cobden and Brougham), he remarked, 'Oh! If I ever return, how I shall work to save our people from the miseries which are here so abounding'.[4] It is not easy to see how he could ever have worked any harder: fifteen hours a day was his usual ration, and he remarked that 'work has always been to me what water is to fish'.[5] He travelled thousands of miles, usually in great discomfort, to address meetings large and small, collecting impressions as zealously as figures, and distilling comments and recommendations in his twelve successive *Annual Reports*.

He succeeded in opening a small number of Normal Schools for the training of teachers (the first at Lexington as early as 1839) but, lacking any professional staff or financial resources, he relied for the most part on argument and persuasion. He abandoned his successful law practice in order to devote himself to the cause with which his name (like those of Henry Barnard in Connecticut and Rhode Island, Calvin Stowe in Ohio and Calvin Wiley in North Carolina) will always be associated. 'Let the next generation be my client', he declaimed.[6] His opinions were much affected by the influence of the Peabody sisters, Elizabeth and Mary: he married the latter, but never accepted the fully Transcendentalist position of the former. Through her, however, he met the Unitarian, William Ellery Channing. Unitarianism, with its emphasis on reason, progress and virtue, came closest to representing Mann's own beliefs. As a movement, it successfully infiltrated New England religion, taking over a number of existing church buildings and attracting the wrath of orthodox Trinitarian clergy. It appealed to Horace Mann for very obvious reasons: undogmatic in character, taking an optimistic rather than a pessimistic view of human perfectibility, avoiding arid theological debate and highly supportive of practical and achievable reform, in schooling as in so many other areas of social life.

In insisting on what was common to all forms of the Christian (or at least of the American versions of the Protestant) religion, Mann could appeal to the Massachusetts law of 1827 which forbade the teaching of sectarian doctrines in publicly supported schools. He believed profoundly in the teaching of civic virtue, in a simple piety based on scripture. In effect, as the principal means of salvation he substituted the school for the church (which had recently been finally disestablished in Massachusetts), even if that salvation was essentially social and civic. Like Jefferson, he was convinced that no modern society could be at the same time ignorant and free. In the rhetoric of Mann the circuit rider, there could be no mistaking the missionary zeal, the echoes of a revivalist Calvinism which he had painfully rejected, the sound of old evangelical wine being poured into new educational bottles:

> *The common school is the greatest discovery ever made by man. In two grand, characteristic attributes, it is supereminent over all others: – first, in its universality; – for it is capacious enough to receive and cherish in its parental bosom every child that comes into the world; and second, in the timeliness of the aid it proffers; – its early, seasonable supplies of counsel and guidance making security antedate danger. Other social institutions are curative and remedial; this is a preventive and an antidote; they come to heal diseases and wounds; this to make the physical and moral frame invulnerable to them. Let the common school be expanded to its capabilities, let it be worked with the efficiency of which it is susceptible, and nine tenths of the crimes in the penal code would become obsolete; the long catalogue of human ills would be abridged; men would walk more safely by day; every pillow would be more inviolable by night; property, life and character held by strong tenure; all rational hopes respecting the future brightened.[7]*

The purpose of education for Mann, whose ideas became even more appealing and relevant as the rate of immigration accelerated, was to turn all men and women into good Christian republicans, reverent towards the Almighty and as attentive to their moral duties as they were inattentive to the niceties of theological dispute. With such divisive disagreements Mann was openly impatient. Education was dignified by noble purposes, having little to do with earning a living or developing national prosperity:

> *its domain extends over the threefold nature of man;– over his body,*
> *training it by systematic and intelligent observance of those benign laws*
> *which secure health, impart strength and prolong life; over his intellect,*
> *invigorating the mind, replenishing it with knowledge, and cultivating*
> *all those tastes which are allied to virtue; and over his moral and*
> *religious susceptibilities also, dethroning selfishness, enthroning*
> *conscience, leading the affections outwards in good-will towards men,*
> *and upward in reverence to God. [8]*

In his twelfth and final Report, he characterised education as 'the balance wheel of the social machinery'.[9] He then was elected to Congress and took up the anti-slavery cause before finally becoming for a few years, until his death in 1859, the first President of Antioch College.

Horace Mann preached civic virtue and reverence towards the deity, asserting that ethical elitists like himself could lead men to improve human nature and change society. He approved straightforward bible reading in schools, but such lukewarm concessions naturally failed to satisfy the anxious concerns of those who believed that education stripped of allusions to highly specific Christian doctrine was vain and empty. For them, specific and dogmatic (and therefore denominational) teaching was essential, and they protested angrily at Mann's attempts to synthesise, homogenise and dilute. It may be that he overreacted to some of this sustained criticism, either out of resentment that this moral authority should be challenged, or because he wished to raise the stakes in what he indeed saw as a campaign against ignorance and vice as well as against irrational and sectarian prejudice. The hostility of his orthodox Protestant critics diminished over time as their own hegemony was eroded, and as a traditionally American way of life and system of belief appeared to be threatened by immigrant groups who did not speak English, and whose loyalty was represented as being directed towards a foreign leader, the Pope, and an alien tradition. After Mann's death, and as his principles and practices were adapted and softened in an effort to consolidate a non-sectarian but patriotic form of generalised Protestantism, it became increasingly difficult for a Roman Catholic minority to accept the ideology that had for Mann and the advocates of the public school been the necessary precondition of national solidarity and personal virtue. In the event, the Catholic leaders determined instead, whenever and wherever they could, to build schools of their own.

It had by no means always been obvious that they would wish or need to do so. With a sense of mounting urgency which became steadily sharper as between 1837 and 1848 he wrote his twelve successive annual reports,

Horace Mann urged the importance of gathering into one common school system the children of all American citizens. But the time when such an inclusive effort might be expected to prosper was inexorably slipping away. The 1834 attack on the Charlestown Ursuline convent had brutally exposed the irrational strength of the tense hostilities then developing in New England society. Four years later, the appointment of the pugnacious John Hughes as coadjutor bishop of New York initiated a long period of growing controversy in that city, as elsewhere: Catholics wished the public schools to be more welcoming towards them while at the same time insisting on their rights to public support for the growing number of their own parochial schools. The more relaxed and accommodating days of John Carroll, appointed to Baltimore in 1789 as the first Catholic bishop in the States, were rapidly coming to an end. Carroll, educated in French Flanders and consecrated a bishop in an English castle, adhered to the principles of the Declaration of Independence as firmly as to the traditions of Rome. He rejoiced in the separation of Church and State, and believed as steadily as did John Ireland a century later in the necessary existence of a distinctly American form of Catholicism. Carroll referred in approving terms to 'the American way of life', urged the necessity of the election of bishops, approved (unlike John Hughes) of the lay trusteeship of churches rather than rigid clerical control, and commended the use of the vernacular in church services. Such open flexibility was perhaps desirable, or even necessary, for as long as Catholics in America represented only a vulnerable and unthreatening minority, Carroll insisted that:

> *If we have the wisdom and temper to preserve [civil and religious liberty], America may come to exhibit a proof to the world, that general and equal toleration, by giving a free circulation to fair argument, is the most effectual method to bring all denominations of christians to an unity of faith.* [10]

Such words, which would have been welcome music to the ears of Horace Mann, were by 1837 no longer being spoken. Mann, in the interests of encouraging an open, ethical, undogmatic Christianity, was as opposed to the Catholic parochial school as uncompromisingly as he was to the sectarian Protestant academy which had hitherto dominated so much of educational provision in New England. The most outspoken early critics of his efforts were, of course, champions of a dogmatically evangelical faith – such as Charles Hodge of Princeton and the like-minded clerics who disliked the tone of so many of the books Mann and his Board recommended for school libraries in Massachusetts.[11] But, as Catholics began to build their own schools and in an attempt to avoid the even more obviously threatening evils of popery, those same orthodox Protestant critics and their successors chose to rally behind the doctrinally imperfect public school.

No figure more impressively represented to anxious and patriotic Protestants the novel assertiveness of that papist threat than John Hughes, the first Roman Catholic Archbishop of New York. He never minced his words. For him, there should be no secret about the intentions of a growing Catholic power, and no nursing of Protestant susceptibilities. In a famous 1850 sermon, he declaimed that the mistake which Americans made was to underestimate Catholic ambitions:

> *Protestantism pretends to have discovered a great secret. Protestantism startles our eastern borders occasionally on the intention of the Pope with regard to the Valley of the Mississippi and dreams that it has made a wonderful discovery. Not at all. Everybody should know it. Everybody should know that we have for our mission to convert the world – including the inhabitants of the United States, – the people of the cities, and the people of the country, the officers of the navy and the marines, commanders of the army, the Legislatures, the Senate, the Cabinet, and all![12]*

Hughes had been born in Ireland in 1797, and worked as a labourer after emigrating to America at the age of twenty. After ordination, he was despatched to Philadelphia where he became a vocal supporter of the clerical party against the lay trustees who, in John Carroll's scheme of things, had controlled so much of the life of the Church. He became the tough adversary of the nativists, who fought to preserve 'their' America as the natural domain of Anglo-Saxon Protestants. Promoted to be coadjutor bishop of New York in 1838 and succeeding to the see four years later, he rapidly became the leader of the New York Catholics and a popular national spokesman for his Church. A few years after his nomination as the first Archbishop of New York in 1850 and shortly before his death, he laid in Manhattan the foundation stone of that surviving symbol of Catholic confidence, St Patrick's Cathedral. Meanwhile, he had broken more than one lance with the New York Public School Society, a private Protestant foundation which enjoyed (unjustly in his view) considerable support from local taxes.

The circumstances of New York City were unusual, but serve to highlight the tensions inherent in the development of the traditions of the American public school. The population of the city in 1800 was 95% Protestant, but atypically fragmented among a number of competing sects, many of which maintained their own charitable schools: this was, of course, not the situation in most of the New England states. When in 1795 the state legislature first granted public funds for the support of public schooling, it was entirely natural that within the city the available subsidies should be distributed among the growing number of Protestant sectarian establishments. A group of philanthropists, genuinely concerned about the education of the children of the poor and anxious to avoid the divisive fragmentation of efforts, came together to found the Free School Society – which was from the beginning non-sectarian, although (of course) unambiguously Protestant. They were successful in securing a growing share of public funds for the partial support of their schools, although the enlarging power of the Society offended several of the churches, which aspired to maintain their own schools and therefore to increase the public funding they had traditionally enjoyed. Such efforts were successfully resisted by the influential Society (notably in defeating the efforts of the Baptists to secure support for a new school in 1825) and the state legislature decided to delegate the apportioning of funds to the Common Council of the city, which consistently favoured the Free School Society over its denominational rivals. In 1826, that Society significantly renamed itself as the Public School Society, reasserting the principles of non-sectarianism and in effect claiming to be the sole agent in New York for the channelling of funds to the support of a 'public' school system. This attempted (and for a while successful) transition from private philanthropy to public monopoly was dramatically disturbed by the flood of immigration into the city during the 1820s and 1830s. The population of New York, which in 1820 had been 120,000, had by 1840 risen to 300,000. By 1855, fully one-half of the residents of the city had been born abroad, and of these, over one half were Irish, and Catholic. The Public School Society was firmly opposed to any support for sectarian Protestant schools but at the same time fundamentally committed to maintaining a religious (that is to say, Protestant) framework for the schooling which it provided.[13]

Hughes objected that the reading of the King James Bible (a perpetual source of offence to the Catholic community), the singing of Protestant hymns and the crude anti-Catholic propaganda permeating many of the approved textbooks made the public schools inhospitable places for the children of his own diverse and rapidly enlarging flock. His attempts to secure for the many Catholic schools in his diocese a share of the public funds to which his flock contributed through taxation aroused the predictable opposition of Horace Mann. In alliance with Governor William H. Seward, and in the first attempt to mobilise the Catholic vote for candidates pledged to support the Catholic cause, Hughes secured significant concessions and changes in the law. The Public School Society of New York was replaced by a system of conventionally defined public schools, based on the wards of the city. Bible reading became less common in New York schools, as elsewhere on the east coast. Predictably, there was a strong and angry reaction, most spectacularly in 1844 in the Philadelphia which John Hughes knew so well, where there were extensive riots provoked by the concession that the Catholic Douai version of the Bible could be read in the schools. Hughes made it quite clear what would happen if any Catholic church was attacked in his fiefdom: he would turn the city into 'a second Moscow'. Influenced perhaps by this violent popular reaction to the granting of concessions to Catholics, Hughes and his allies chose not to exploit the modest victory won for his cause in New York, concluding rather that 'the benefits of public education are not for us'.[14] He, unlike John Ireland, was fundamentally opposed to the whole notion of common schooling: schools without religion were as offensive as schools where Protestantism prevailed and Catholicism was despised as foreign and superstitious. John Hughes became the archetype of the fund-raising proselytising bishop, determined eventually (although never succeeding) to provide a place in a Catholic school for every Catholic child, even exhorting his people and their pastors 'to build the school-house first, and the church afterwards'.[15] Catholic educational policy therefore developed two priorities: first, to build Catholic schools for the Catholic community, and at the same time to ensure that the public schools themselves were made as non-sectarian, in effect as non-religious, as they could decently be.

The spokesmen for the traditional Protestant cause were, therefore, in their anxiety to forestall the creation of a threatening and alternative Catholic school system, driven into the support of those very policies championed by Horace Mann and which they had themselves angrily attacked in an earlier and more confident time. They slowly rallied to the defence of non-sectarianism, assisted in their transition by the assumption underpinning Mann's faith that the American way of life was somehow at its heart identified with Protestantism. Studies of textbooks indicate the continuing importance throughout much of the nineteenth century of an emphasis on the Bible, of reverence for God, and the identification of sound morality with Christian principles. The index to *The Annotated McGuffey Reader*, which enjoyed an astonishing circulation in the schools, has more references to God than to any other subject; the only indexed subject which challenges it is 'death'. Textbooks abounded in references to the divine inspiration running through American history: the writing of the Constitution itself showed:

> *the finger of that Almighty Hand, which has been so frequently and*
> *signally extended to our religion in the critical stages of the*
> *revolution. [16]*

The National Education Association (which evolved from the National Teachers Association in 1869) remained suspicious of Catholics and of their schools, as also of what it saw as an attempt to minimise the importance of religion in public schools. But the paradox persisted. If common school advocates wished, and for good reason, to incorporate Catholics and especially immigrant Catholics into the public schools, religion would have to be marginalised. In 1855, an Episcopalian bishop urged, at a meeting where some nostalgic delegates were advocating a renewed emphasis on the importance of religious instruction, that what mattered most was not a system of belief but the moral example of the teachers, who:

> *can teach only the ten commandments, the Lord's prayer, the Sermon*
> *on the Mount, and a few other similar passages, before they get over*
> *into the stoney region of polemics; God save the schools from that.[17]*

He later observed that, unless such a firm line was held:

> *affairs might take such a course that in ten years we should find the*
> *Protestants, the Catholics, and the unbelievers, all standing side by side,*

> *shoulder to shoulder, toppling that magnificent system [common schools]*
> *to its base; and if that time shall ever come I verily believe that it will*
> *have been invoked by the excessive zeal and impatience of those wishing*
> *to introduce religious instruction in these schools.*

The presence of the unbelievers alongside the Protestants and the Catholics is an interestingly early indication that secularist as well as incorporationist motives were at work in the modification of the ethos of the American public school. Careful work on school textbooks suggests that the balance between religion and morals shifted, and indeed that their combined importance diminished across the century:

> *the readers used in the colonies prior to 1775 devoted 85% of the space*
> *to religion and 8% to morals; those between 1775 and 1825, 22% to*
> *religion and 28% to morals; those between 1875 and 1915, only 1.5%*
> *to religion and 7% to morals.[18]*

The same researcher argues that by the time of the Civil War there was little in the textbooks designed to give the reader an understanding of the natural theology approved by Mann, still less of Christianity itself. This shift was, of course only partly the result of an attempt to accommodate the Catholics, and reflected wider and deeper changes in intellectual life across the century. The evidence suggests that accompanying and reinforcing the shift from doctrinal religion through general religion towards the teaching of morality was the displacement of moral and spiritual by materialist values in classroom teaching.[19] The assimilationist motive – the wish to moderate the implicit Protestantism of the public school to make it less unacceptable to Catholics – was nevertheless significant, and represented no small sacrifice of principle. As early as 1844, a Congregationalist journal had argued that:

> *It is better that Roman Catholic children should be educated in public*
> *schools in which the Bible is not read, than that they should not be*
> *educated at all, or educated in schools under the absolute control of their*
> *priesthood.[20]*

Could these efforts to incorporate the Catholic community within Horace Mann's comprehensive dream be realised?

How realistic was the hope that Roman Catholic children would all be educated in the public schools, whether or not the Bible was read there? The effort inspired by Horace Mann might have succeeded if immigration had proceeded in a steady trickle, but of course it did not. Between 1820 and 1920, some 33.6 million immigrants settled in the United States: first, of course, the Irish, and then Germans, Italians, Poles, French Canadians, Mexicans, Slovaks, Czechs, Lithuanians, Ukrainians ... 'In 1820, the Catholic church included no more than three foreign-language groups; a century later it was a cosmopolitan church speaking twenty-eight languages.'[21] In the history of American education, the cultural diversity of that immigration was at least as important as its scale. Not all of the new immigrants were, of course, Roman Catholics: many of the Germans remained loyal to their Protestant roots, while even today most of the Americans claiming Irish roots are in fact descended from Protestant immigrants.[22] Nor were all the nominally Catholic immigrants practising members of the church to which they traditionally belonged. In 1850, the Catholics were only the third largest denominational group in the United States: by mid-century, there were probably about 1.6 million of them. Immigrants did not step off the gangplank already committed to living as good Catholics in the country of their adoption; on the contrary, a massive missionary effort was needed to incorporate them in the Catholic life of America. It was as a direct result of that campaign of conversion that they had by 1890 become the largest religious group in America, numbering some seven million souls.[23]

The American Catholic Church experienced great difficulty in absorbing these new arrivals, and not least because it was for many years dominated by an English-speaking Irish hierarchy. Archbishop John Ireland was furious when he was expected to welcome to his diocese a married priest, belonging to one of the Uniate churches – groups in communion with Rome, but practising with papal consent their own liturgy and discipline. Relations broke down, and eventually most of the Uniate Ukrainians joined the more hospitable Eastern Orthodox Church.[24] In the great cities, immigrants tended to cluster in working-class neighbourhoods dominated by a church loyal to the traditions and language of the country from which they had come. The 'national parish' became the characteristically American institution, preserving deep cultural and religious roots. Language was the key to that preservation, which was why members of the Americanist party among the bishops were so uneasy about the fragmentation (and, they feared, the threat to true American patriotism) which it represented. Just as St Patrick's Cathedral in New York survives into the twenty-first century as the symbol of the confidence of a rapidly enlarging church and the power of its Irish hierarchy, so St Stanislas Kostka, founded in 1867, epitomises the robust survival of Polish religion, language and culture in the cosmopolitan city of Chicago. By 1880, many parishes had become national rather than territorial: as late as 1916, half of America's Catholics attended a parish church where a language other than English was sometimes used (for the vernacular sermon, for example) and 21% attended a church where English was never used.[25]

The building of schools and the staffing of them by nuns and members of male religious orders stood at the heart of the missionary efforts of Redemptorists, Paulists and Passionists to perpetuate and, even more importantly, enlarge the distinctive Catholic community. Teaching in the native languages of the immigrants was an essential part of their strategy, and as over the years younger generations acquired a mastery of English, the rich cultural traditions of the homeland were still jealously guarded. The urban Catholic school was as much an agent of integration as of the perpetuation of jealously guarded and ethnically specific traditions. By 1884, when the plenary council of Baltimore proclaimed the desirability of providing a Catholic school for every Catholic child, some 40% of parishes already supported their own parochial school.[26] The effort of building began with the impetus imparted by John Hughes of New York, and by 1890 – the year of John Ireland's speech to the National Education Association – there were 626,496 enrolments in parochial schools.[27] A quarter of a century later, the Bureau of the Census report on religion recorded that:

> *At the end of 1916 there were under the auspices of the Roman Catholic Church in United States [sic] 102 ecclesiastical seminaries, with 6,898 seminarians; 216 colleges for boys with 49,813 students; 676 academies for girls, with 96,194 students; and 5,687 parochial schools, with an attendance of 1,537,644 children.[28]*

This dense and varied network of schools, sustained without any assistance from public funding, was itself part of the building in America of a parallel society in which hospitals, benefit societies and orphanages also played a significant and related part. The nineteenth-century church was a society of and for the immigrants, and its schools enjoyed a great and distinctive vitality, above all in cities like Chicago, where in the Stock Yards district:

> *Within walking distance of each other were three Polish schools, along with an Irish, a German, a Slovak, a Lithuanian, and a Czech school, eight schools in all, as well as a German Lutheran school. These parochial schools enrolled more than twice as many students as the three public schools in the area.[29]*

There were, of course, wide variations in the provision and style of Catholic schools: in Boston, for example, such provision was much less substantial than in Chicago or Philadelphia. The Boston Irish spoke English and dominated much of political and social life, including the control of the public schools. Yet even there, Catholic schools flourished. The aspirations of Horace Mann, as of John Ireland, were frustrated by the missionary efforts of the Catholic Church and by the persistent inhospitality towards the unfamiliar immigrant of the common school they both championed. What would become of the Catholic school as Catholics swam into the mainstream of America society, as the public school itself was increasingly secularised, and as the financial pressures on maintaining a separate school system increased?

Notes

[1] Messerli, 1972, p. 192.

[2] Tyack & Hanson, 1982, p. 59.

[3] Messerli, 1972, p. 20, quoting Mary Peabody Mann (1891) *Life of Horace Mann*, p. 14.

[4] Messerli, 1972, p. 391.

[5] Mary Peabody Mann (1891) *Life of Horace Mann*, p. 11; Messerli, 1972, p. 14; Tyack & Hanson, 1982, p. 56.

[6] Messerli, 1972, p. 279.

[7] Cremin, 1957, p. 137.

[8] Messerli, 1972, p. 443.

[9] Ibid., p. 492.

[10] Dolan, 1992, pp. 109, 111.

[11] Glenn, 1988, p. 150.

[12] Ibid., p. 231.

[13] Ravitch, 1973, pp. 3-76.

[14] Finke & Starke, 1992, p. 140.

[15] Dolan, 1992, p. 263.

[16] Nord, 1995, pp. 67-68.

[17] Glenn, 1988, p. 176.

[18] Ibid., p. 177.

[19] Nord, 1995, p. 61.

[20] Glenn, 1988, p. 230; Nord, 1995, p. 72.

[21] Dolan, 1992, p. 135.

[22] Finke & Starke, 1992, p. 111.

[23] Ibid., pp. 113, 115.

[24] Dolan, 1992, p. 188.

[25] Finke & Starke, 1992, p. 127.

[26] Ibid., p. 134.

[27] Tyack & Hanson, 1982, p. 78.

[28] Vol. 2, p. 652 noted in Finke & Starke, 1992, p. 139.

[29] Dolan, 1992, p. 291.

CHAPTER 6

Three Antecedents: François Guizot

Two years before the great Revolution of 1789, François Guizot was born in Nîmes – the city in which, seventy years later, Emile Combes was to teach for a short while. He was born into one of the many families in that city who were deeply committed to a Calvinist form of Protestantism. His lawyer father was guillotined when François was seven years old, accused of propagating seditious opinions hostile to the centralising ambitions of revolutionary Paris. It is, then, hardly surprising that Guizot should have been throughout his life distanced from Catholicism as well as implacably hostile to all forms of totalitarianism – of the Left as well as of the Right – and to all efforts to centralise power in one monopolistic institution. The Revolution which began dramatically in 1789 swept away all the familiar institutions of the *ancien régime*: monarchy, aristocracy, the Catholic Church, the ancient professions, universities, colleges and schools. Under the old dispensation, the Church, with grudging concessions to Protestants in those remote parts of France where they formed an obstinately significant minority, had enjoyed a virtual monopoly of education and – except where local patriotism had stimulated the creation and maintenance of communal colleges – furnished virtually all the schools and teachers. During his long and active life, Guizot was frequently to observe that, well into the nineteenth century, France had no system of education worthy of the name. In a well-known essay published in 1816, shortly after the final defeat of Napoleon and the restoration of the Bourbon monarchy, Guizot directly attributed the collapse of order in 1789 to the inherent weaknesses of education in France:

> *Let it never be forgotten that it was the establishments of public education which existed at that time, the men who directed them and the methods that then prevailed which formed that unwise and turbulent generation, some members of which made or approved the Revolution, which others of the same generation could neither anticipate nor control. [1]*

A decent primary education, based on religious and moral principles, would have engraved on the minds of the common people the principles of duty, order and discipline and so prevented them from taking to the streets. Nor had that Revolution itself in any sense succeeded in making good these grave deficiencies in education: its leaders had been fertile in ideas and projects, but ineffectual in the building of stable institutions. That constructive effort was left to the autocratic Emperor Napoleon I.

Meanwhile, Guizot was taken by his mother to the safety of Geneva to complete his education. By the time of his return to France, Napoleon had reimposed civil order and embarked on a highly directive reshaping of the French educational world. At is heart was the *Université de France*, not a university in the conventionally modern sense of the term, but a state institution or corporation designed to control in a military fashion the educational officers of the State, to monopolise the granting of degrees and qualifications, and in particular to develop an elite form of secondary education in the *lycées*, the main purpose of which was to train effective servants of the State. The Emperor was content to leave the more basic provision of primary schools largely in the hands of the Church, provided that it proved loyal to him and accepted the formal educational suzerainty of his University. The Church, he assumed, could be relied upon to teach those habits of obedience which would contribute to public order. As a fundamental part of his ambitious programme, Napoleon wished to repair some of the damage which had been inflicted upon Church-State relations by the revolution of 1789. In the wake of that revolution, the lands of the Church had been confiscated, many of the clergy coerced into accepting a form of state-dominated Catholicism, with Catholics themselves bitterly divided by internal schisms, and for a while Christianity itself had been abolished and replaced by the worship of a Supreme Being. Many priests had fled the country, while others nursed bitter thoughts of rebellion and of a royalist restoration. Napoleon reached an understanding with the Pope, recorded in the long-lasting Concordat of 1801. The State would thereafter support the Church financially, recognising Catholicism as the religion not of France but of the majority of Frenchmen, while in return the State would secure the right of nomination to bishoprics. Shortly after the conclusion of these novel arrangements, Napoleon extended similar concessions to the Jewish and Protestant communities, whose loyalty he was also now anxious to secure. The clergy became the employees of the State in an alliance of altar and throne designed to repress rebellion and anarchic dissent. While insisting on the superior authority of the State, the Emperor was content to share educational and other power with a largely docile clergy. He needed a coronation in the cathedral of Notre Dame, but insisted on placing the crown on his head with his own hands. It was within the framework of these agreements that Napoleon accepted a division of power, although not of formal authority, between a Church which kept in its own hands virtually the whole of primary education and a State which dominated secondary education through the monopoly of its University.[2]

The splendidly titled Grand Master of that University (in effect, the Minister of Education) recognised the talents of the youthful Guizot and in

1812 – the year of the disastrous Napoleonic march on Moscow – assigned to him a chair in history at the Sorbonne. There he became a colleague and protégé of the philosopher, Royer-Collard, and his disciple, Victor Cousin, who was later to influence the opinions and career of Emile Combes. Meanwhile, Guizot, with his first wife Pauline de Meulan, had begun to produce the *Annales de l'Education*. In the six volumes extending over the years 1811-14, he made many admiring references to the experience of other European countries, urging the absolute priority of moral and religious education in the inculcation of appropriate social and civic attitudes and insisting on the serious consequences for France of the lack of any systematic provision of education. Guizot became a member of a small group of conservative reformers clustered around the University, rejecting both the possibility of a return to the old order prevailing before the cataclysm of 1789 and (more cautiously) the autocracy represented by the Napoleonic Empire. He was a moderate royalist, hoping for the peaceful return of the Bourbon royal family within the framework of a constitutional monarchy: neither revolution nor autocracy.

After Napoleon's first and temporary exile, to the island of Elba in the Mediterranean, his monopolistic University was dismantled: liberals disliked its autocratic style, while many Roman Catholics resented its ambitious superiority. In its place, seventeen regional universities were speedily manufactured, with vaguely defined powers over local education. Napoleon's triumphal return, for the Hundred Days of his restoration, was followed by a prompt resumption of the centralised educational system he had created in 1808. After his second and definitive banishment, this time to the Atlantic island of St Helena, and the return of Louis XVIII to his throne, the basic structures of this system were left in place. The office of Grand Master was, however, abolished and a Council for Public Instruction replaced (although not for long) the Napoleonic University. The Brothers – the *Frères des Ecoles Chrétiennes* established in the seventeenth century by Jean-Baptiste de la Salle – maintained the privileged position in primary schooling which had been effectively conceded to them by Napoleon. But those privileges, and the power over the minds of the people which they conveyed, were increasingly resented by liberals, who were understandably suspicious, especially in the early and enthusiastic years of the Bourbon restoration, of the ambitions of the Church to regain the dominant position it had once held. On the educational front, the virtual monopoly of primary education by the Catholics was directly challenged by the newly formed Société pour l'Instruction Elémentaire. That society was active, especially in Paris, in founding elementary schools as well as training colleges for teachers, and offended the Brothers by sponsoring new methods of instruction. The Society favoured the so-called 'mutual' method, popularised in England by the followers of Lancaster and Bell and known in that country as the monitorial system. This enabled more senior pupils to undertake many of the routine tasks of teaching large numbers of pupils, and was presented as a preferable alternative to the so-called 'simultaneous' method championed by the Brothers, which grouped pupils at the same level of achievement in smaller classes taught as a group. Although these increasingly bitter struggles were largely confined to the towns and had little direct impact on the countryside, where most of the French population lived, their ideological and political importance in the forming of entrenched attitudes and antipathies was considerable. The battle between the two groups was not only a competition for resources and control, but also a struggle with powerful political and ideological overtones. Zealous members of the Catholic party denounced the mutual schools for emphasising basic instruction in useful subjects at the expense of the inculcation of moral and religious duties, and detected in the monitorial method a dangerous whiff of subversive democracy. The battle lines between Church and State in France were drawn in the years after the fall of Napoleon along contours which persisted for at least two centuries.[3]

François Guizot, although he did become a member of the Society, remained characteristically cautious in his support of its work: as the years went by, he became increasingly doubtful of the contribution made by mutual schools to the maintenance of traditional order and values. For the first part of the reign of Louis XVIII, his career progressed smoothly. In a transition typical not only of the man but also of the relationship of the University to the world of high politics and administration, he worked in the Ministry of the Interior where he prepared his 1816 essay on public instruction in France. This revealing text laid out clearly the lines of policy which, in positions of much greater power, he was later to pursue: the sustained intervention of the State was essential if anything was to be achieved; education at an appropriate level was necessary for all citizens, and not just for a minority; the education system should maintain the barriers between the classes into which society must be divided. His career was jolted by the crisis provoked by the assassination in 1820 of the heir presumptive to the throne: for conservatives this was a direct and inevitable result of the prevailing liberalism of the day, and led to a period of marked right-wing reaction. In the educational field, this reaction was reflected in the resumption of the full title of the University, the restoration of the style and dignities of the Grand Master and the elevation to that office in 1822 of a Catholic bishop. Monseigneur Fraysinnous was quite clear about what was implied by these abrupt changes:

> *His Majesty desires that the youth of his realm should more and more be brought up with religious and monarchical feelings ... Anyone who has the misfortune to live without religion or without being devoted to the ruling family should feel unworthy of being a teacher of the young.[4]*

Guizot was deprived of his government appointment.

In 1824, Louis XVII was succeeded by his brother Charles X, and the lurch towards the right and towards Catholic monarchism accelerated, finding one of its most potent expressions in the ostentatiously elaborate coronation of the new king in the cathedral at Reims. By that time, at least seven of the Rectors (who were responsible for public education within the regional Academies into which France was and is divided) were in holy orders. The more extreme members of the Catholic party, the so-called Ultras, had concluded that, since they could not destroy the University, they would at least dominate it and ensure that it became (however paradoxically) a weapon of ecclesiastical rather than of secular power. This was, of course, a curious inversion of what were becoming the traditional roles of the participants in the perennial debates about the relationship of Church and State in a modern society. When in 1830 the balance of power once again shifted, but this time towards the left, a new but ephemeral group of 'liberal Catholics' emerged, arguing (in the interests of a Church now threatened by an unfriendly government) for the separation of ecclesiastical and civil powers and, most immediately, for educational freedom for the Church. If the State was proving to be (even intermittently) hostile, then the Church must be set free to attend to the needs of the souls of its own people.[5]

François Guizot resumed his academic work and his writing, as he always did whenever the gyrations of French politics forced him out of government. In the dying months of the Bourbon monarchy and as a critic of the authoritarian regime, he was elected as a Deputy. But he was certainly not about to welcome the kind of violent change into which France was propelled by the 'three glorious days' of the revolution of June 1830: indeed, that kind of turbulence sharply reminded him only too vividly of the dangers – of which he had warned in 1816 – presented by an ignorant and illiterate populace pouring onto the streets in mindless protest against a reactionary and clerical regime. He helped to secure a relatively peaceful transition to the Orleanist monarchy, which, in a predominantly liberal climate, reigned rather than ruled in France until the convulsions of 1848 again drove him from the centres of power. But until the tiger could be tamed, it must at least be ridden, and the scholarly Guizot became Commissioner for Public Instruction in the provisional government of August 1830 – for one day! His later tenure of the Ministry of Public Instruction was more secure, although still marked by discontinuity and endemic political instability. He was Minister from October 1832 until November 1834, and again for a few months from November 1835 until the following January, and finally from September 1836 until April 1837. It was during the first hectic months that, in spite of recurring illness, he pressed through Parliament the law which ever since has carried his name, and completed a complementary series of effective reforms which formed the basis of the classically French system. He was assisted in his efforts by Victor Cousin, later himself to become Minister and destined to remain a powerful influence on policy and appointments in the education service, and by Ambrose Rendu, the fervent Catholic who had exercised comparable power in the days of Napoleon. There was, of course, a strong and vocal anticlerical element in the revolution of 1830. The Charter in which the new King Louis Philippe set out his programme seemed to promise 'freedom of instruction' (*liberté d'enseignement*) to Catholics and liberals alike – both equally resentful of the overweening power of the ubiquitous and intrusive University. In the event, however, the 1830s were instead to witness a substantial and irreversible increase in the power of the State, whatever the nature of the regime in power, in all educational matters. The mammoth, as disenchanted critics were later to call it, was starting to grow in earnest.

Guizot, even more clearly than Napoleon and in the same spirit as Jules Ferry in the 1880s, wished to mobilise primary education directly in the service of the State. State education, if necessary in comfortable alliance with a loyal and publicly funded Church, should above all form good citizens, whether to serve an empire, a Bourbon dynasty, an Orleanist monarchy, or a republic. Its principal purpose was social rather than economic: although a sound and universal system of private education would, of course, in the long run contribute to personal and national prosperity, it should above all serve to prevent any repetition of the revolutionary excesses of 1789 and 1830. If, for Guizot, the loyal and devout Protestant, that priority implied granting a predominant place to the clergy in the moral education of the people, then so be it. In introducing his 1833 Law to the Chamber he insisted:

> *Gentlemen, be attentive to a fact which has never been more strikingly evident than in our own time: intellectual development, when it is accompanied by moral and religious development, is excellent; it becomes a principle of order, and of government* [règle]*, while being at the same time a source of prosperity for society. But intellectual development alone, separated from moral and religious development, becomes a principle of pride and insubordination, of egoism, and therefore represents a danger to society.*[6

Religion, always directly linked in the language of Guizot with morality, must therefore be accorded a dominant place in education, even if for his collaborator, Victor Cousin, its historic links to a clerical and divisive establishment must be weakened. 'The less we desire our schools to be ecclesiastical', insisted Victor Cousin in terms which Horace Mann in Massachusetts would happily have endorsed, 'the more ought they to be Christian'.[7] In any case, and for the foreseeable future, it would be a practical impossibility to maintain even the current levels of primary schooling in France without the willing cooperation of the Church, and especially of the Brothers: Guizot was therefore content to encourage them, and also to assist in the development of new fraternities to move into the villages in regions such as Brittany.[8] Paul Lorain, another of the able collaborators of Guizot but one who preferred to work out of the limelight, persuaded the Minister that it would be unwise to give too much encouragement to the mutual schools: their utilitarian emphasis on instruction unconnected with morality and their more open and democratic approach to teaching could lead to precisely that kind of radical disorder which Guizot was always so anxious to avoid.

Guizot, as both scholar and statesman, was increasingly fascinated by the history of England. It exemplified many of his pragmatically conservative and evolutionary preferences: Guizot wished above all to avoid extremes and to discourage commitment to any simple and absolute principles. In presenting his 1833 Law, he identified four such dangerous principles, any one of which pursued in isolation would lead into danger. The first was statist: everything to the State, *le tout-Etat*. The second was private, *le principe de pure industrie*, dependent entirely on private initiative and funding. The third was communal, relying exclusively on the local community without any national direction and control. And the fourth was ecclesiastical, *le tout-Eglise*.[9] The statist principle taken alone was, for Guizot, who never forgot the fate of his father, perverse. The private principle, acceptable in itself, was nevertheless inadequate since it would leave yawning gaps in provision: a citizens' army cannot rely only on volunteers. The communal principle, applied in an exclusive spirit, would lead to unevenness of provision, conflicts of local interest, and unacceptable diversity. The ecclesiastical principle would return France to the dark days before 1789 or to the aberrations of the last years of the restored Bourbons. Guizot's preferred solution was a judicious blend, in which the State led with firm overall direction, the local authorities managed the system on a day-to-day basis and contributed financial resources, while the Church agreed to cooperate at all levels, from the nation to the parish.

Guizot's Law therefore required every commune throughout France to maintain at least one primary school, either for itself alone or in cooperation with a neighbouring community. Although attendance would be neither compulsory nor free, national and local funds were made available for those whose family means were inadequate. Every commune with a population in excess of six thousand was further required to maintain an upper primary school – the *Ecole Primaire Supérieure* which was to play so important a part in the development of popular and accessible forms of education beyond the basic level, by offering a robust alternative to the prestigious Napoleonic *lycées* (now appropriately if impermanently renamed as Royal Colleges). Each Department was further required to maintain an *Ecole Normale*, a teachers' training college designed to provide local leadership and effective instructors, imbued with loyalty to the nation and equipped with the skills necessary for their work.[10] All these institutions, but especially the *Ecole Normale*, were to work within clear and detailed national guidelines prescribing what should be taught and by what methods, and identifying the moral and civic virtues to be cultivated in teachers and pupils alike. The work of the primary schools was to be supervised by local committees operating at two levels, and on which the municipal and local authorities as well as the Church were well represented. The representatives of the State, the Prefect and his subordinate officers, would guarantee uniformity and the scrupulous observance of national norms. State, Church and community were to cooperate in delivering a system that would be unified without claiming any kind of monopoly.

Guizot and his colleagues were tireless in spelling out, in persuasive exhortations and regulatory texts, precisely what these innovations would mean both in theory and in practice. In his letter to teachers, dated 4 July 1833, the *instituteur* was described as one of the 'authorities' of the commune, expected to show deference to the mayor but to regard himself as the equal of the priest as a collaborator.[11] For many years to come the reality was certainly a little different, since the teacher was assured of a salary of only 200 francs a year and was often obliged to assume other paid tasks: as an assistant to the priest in his ecclesiastical duties, as a clerk for the mayor, or even as a village postman – a man of letters in every sense, as one wag observed.[12] The regulations published in 1834 laid down detailed national prescriptions for schools and teachers: the principle of national control was being unambiguously asserted. Religion and morality are yet again stressed: all sessions of the primary school must begin with prayers, and the pupils are to be taken to the parish church on Sundays and feast days. A monthly journal was circulated by the Ministry piling detail upon detail and seeking to establish a uniform style and content for primary education. Moreover, official textbooks were prepared and issued to all schools. For Victor Cousin the civic and social benefits of such uniformity were of paramount importance:

> *Instruction can and should be unified from one end of France to the other and, through the new force that it will bring to national unity, this uniformity will not be the least of the benefits [of the 1833 Law].[13]*

Among the crisp administrative measures taken to promote that unity was the appointment in 1835 of an Inspector to each of the eighty-six Departments into which France was for all administrative purposes geometrically divided. Inspectors, and the hierarchical control which they exercised over the teaching of pupils and the training of teachers, ensured that the mandates of Paris were followed and the traditions of teaching as a public service systematically developed. Many of these Departmental Inspectors had already worked with Guizot and his expert collaborators in assembling a remarkable national review of primary education in all its many forms, completed at speed during the last wintry months of 1833 and promptly published in 1834. Four hundred and ninety members of the enquiry teams were recruited for these tasks and everything was counted and evaluated – sometimes with a precision which might arouse Anglo-Saxon scepticism. At that date in France there were said to be 33,695 schools, of which 15,601 were judged to be 'good'. Of the 36,618 communes – each with its own mayor – which formed the base of French government and social organisation, 26,816 had a school of some sort (which did not necessarily mean proper or permanent buildings, or even a regular teacher). Among the most regular and dependable of these teachers were, of course, the Brothers (among whom the *Frères des Ecoles Chrétiennes* remained the most significant) and teachers in the so-called mutual schools. Although their number was soon to diminish, there were at the time of the review some fifteen hundred of the former and one thousand of the latter. These relatively expert groups were for obvious reasons concentrated in the towns, and constituted only a small minority of the teaching force: there were 33,000 other teachers at work. The Brothers and the secular mutual school teachers were nevertheless significant as the most vocal and accomplished advocates of distinctive and rival approaches to teaching, the one indubitably more traditional and Catholic than the other. Even more important in terms of the intricate relationship between religion and the daily life of the schools was the influence of the *curé* in each village throughout France, but especially in areas of strong traditional Catholic loyalties such as Brittany and parts of the West.[14] The 1833 review served to describe the situation as it had been before the 1833 Law began to take effect: between 1833 and 1840, the number of communes lacking a school of any kind declined from fourteen thousand to four thousand, while the number of students registered at school for at least the winter months rose from 1.9 million to 2.9 million.

The 1833 Law, as had been promised at the initiation of the Orleanist monarchy in 1830, secured freedom in primary education, and small private schools existed alongside public establishments: indeed, the lines between the two were often blurred, with many schools supported with private money supplemented by public funds. Guizot explicitly favoured a mixed system. The 'two Frances' with which Emile Combes and his contemporaries were confronted, and which crystallised in the divisions manifested in the Dreyfus affair, did not yet exist. The parish clergy and their bishops, save in those few areas where there was also a significant Protestant minority, in effect controlled at least the moral and spiritual (if not the pedagogic) life of the primary schools, and helped to consolidate the loyalty of the Catholic populace to the moderate Orleanist regime. Although the promises of 1830 had referred simply to 'freedom of education', without any implied restriction to the primary field alone, it proved much more difficult to resolve the historic tensions in secondary education. Since the establishment of the University by Napoleon, private secondary schools (most of them Catholic) had been more or less grudgingly tolerated by the State. Bonapartist and Orleanist governments were uncertain of their reliability, fearing that they might openly or covertly nurture Bourbon sympathies. The appointment of the directors of such schools was subject to the stated requirements of the University, which itself controlled all examinations and the granting of diplomas and to which a much resented annual tax was paid. Junior seminaries (of the kind attended by both Emile Combes and John Ireland) provided a supplementary form of Catholic secondary education but caused annoyance to the Government and to the University by admitting candidates who had no intention of being prepared for holy orders. Although secondary schools maintained by the municipalities – the communal colleges – might themselves have a more or less strong Catholic flavour (as did, by the standards of the twenty-first century, all the public primary schools), they were – in the sense that Guizot and his contemporaries understood the term – 'public', and generally content to acknowledge the suzerainty of the University. Indeed, many of the teachers in such colleges – again, like Combes himself in Pons – were ambitious eventually to secure an appointment in a more prestigious *Collège Royal* (the rebaptised *lycée*). Guizot wished, without generating controversy, to extend freedom to the (private) Catholic secondary schools on the same general basis as his Law had defined for the primary schools. Anticlerical opposition, and in particular, a persistent suspicion of the Jesuits, made such a concession impossible and, like his ministerial successors in the 1840s, he could make no progress. Only a more authoritarian regime, with (initially at least) a more positively supportive policy towards Catholic secondary schools, would later be able to force through legislation against a bitterly entrenched opposition.

In a long and active life of government interspersed with scholarship, Guizot did not again give his full and undivided attention to questions of educational development. After his fruitful years at the Ministry of Public Instruction, he served, for a few months in 1840, as Ambassador to London, returning to France to be the central figure – although not until the final year formally Prime Minister – in the governments of that decade. He failed to anticipate the scale of the mounting threat to the Orleanist dynasty and to the moderate form of constitutional monarchy which it represented, and failed to make the kind of concession to an increasingly vocal opposition which might have prevented the tumult of 1848. The events of that year were as distressing to him as had been the anarchy of 1830. Louis Philippe went into exile in February 1848, and Guizot returned for a short while to London, before resuming his tranquil life of scholarship and teaching in France, spending much of his time on his country estate in Normandy. The presidential elections of December 1848 registered a 74% vote for Napoleon's nephew, Louis Napoleon. Divisions in France were becoming deeper and more bitter: although the conservatives, as the party of order, won comfortable majorities in the parliamentary elections of 1849, the presence in the Chamber of a significant group of radicals (the Montagnards) made them nervous about the future of an uncertain and vaguely defined yet initially popular regime. What, for example, could the Catholic bishops expect of the new Bonaparte? In December 1851, Bonaparte was elected President for life (the Constitution had forbidden even his re-election for a further four years). In the following month, the Archbishop of Paris made his own position tactlessly clear by solemnly intoning in Notre Dame 'Domine salvum fac Ludovicum Napoleonem'. In December 1852, Bonaparte did indeed become the Emperor of the French, with the title of Napoleon III. No friend to the liberals, Napoleon was nevertheless to prove an unreliable ally of the Church. It was during the two decades of Napoleon's Empire reign that the battle lines between Catholics and anticlericals hardened, and the school wars (*la guerre scolaire*) were prepared in earnest.

One of the earliest consequences of the revolution of 1848, and of the accession of Louis Napoleon Bonaparte to the newly established Presidency, was a resumption of the efforts by and on behalf of Catholics to extend 'freedom' to the secondary schools maintained by the Church. The years of the short-lived Second Republic and the early years of the Empire were distinguished by an attempt, sustained until about 1857, to reinforce the alliance of Church and State and to secure the loyalty to the new regime of priests and Congregations. Guizot and his official successors had, of course, failed to secure a satisfactory settlement for Catholic secondary schools: this was now achieved, or imposed, by the newly appointed Comte de Falloux, who remained in the office of Minister of Public Instruction only until October 1849. The law which bears his name, some parts of which are still applicable in France today, was not in fact passed until the following year. That law extended under fairly relaxed conditions freedom of instruction to Catholic and other secondary schools not directly under the authority of the University. It permitted but did not require local authorities (communes and Departments) to provide funds for capital building projects and other costs for such schools, while limiting the extent of such subsidies to 10% of total relevant expenditure: the Church had no wish to accept sums of money so large that, in the longer run, its own autonomy in educational matters would be eroded. The Falloux Law, accompanied by other initiatives, heralded a golden age for the growth of Catholic education in France, developing in deliberate opposition to the secular alternative epitomised by the University.

The centralised power of the University was trimmed by the abolition of the large and powerful Academies, among which the administration of the whole of the educational system was shared, and their temporary replacement by a larger number (over eighty) of weaker Academies, each associated with an administrative Department and more directly under the eye of its Prefect. Significantly – for the Empire was to prove a fickle ally of the Church – that arrangement lasted for only a few years. Other changes proved more lasting. Immediately after the inauguration of the Second Empire there was a systematic purge of teachers: the more vocally radical and secular of the teachers produced by the Normal Schools favoured by Guizot were purged from the public service. Teachers were required to wear black, the symbol of clerical respectability, and even to remove their beards. Docility and loyalty, with a readiness to teach sound doctrines of obedience and to encourage the common people to vote for the new regime, were the qualities now required for promotion or even survival. The Congregations were encouraged to return to France and to expand: between 1848 and 1863 the number of lay teachers remained fairly constant, while the number belonging to the Congregations increased fivefold. Many of these Sisters, Priests and Brothers taught in schools that were formally 'public', as well as in the separately maintained and enlarging Catholic schools, both secondary and primary.

This permeation of the officially public system, accompanying a parallel growth of the formally private schools, has been insufficiently noted and studied. It explains the growing tension throughout the Second Empire, and into the Third Republic which succeeded it, of the professional and ideological rivalries of the two camps into which France was splitting.

The so-called authoritarian phase of the Empire lasted for a decade: in the field of educational policy, the shift of emphasis thereafter was marked by the arrival at the Ministry of Public Instruction in the rue de Grenelle of the able Victor Duruy, a champion of the University and of the historic cause of national education. Napoleon was rapidly falling out of favour with the clerical party, not least because of the ambivalences of his foreign policy and suspicious attitude towards the Papacy. In 1866, Jean Macé founded the Ligue de l'Enseignement, dedicated to the promotion of public education as Guizot had understood it, and suspicious of the remorselessly enlarging influence of the Church. Throughout these years, Guizot himself remained aloof from politics in general and from the Emperor in particular: only in the final and belatedly liberal months of the doomed Empire did he consent to join a commission on higher education. His writing life was resumed after his return from the brief English exile of 1848, as was his career as a public intellectual. He took a leading part in the affairs of the French Academy, and devoted much time and theological energy to the cause of the Protestant community. His last years were spent away from Paris, in his house at Val-Richer, where between 1856 and 1864 he completed the massive eight volumes of his *Mémoires*, as well as publishing most of his parliamentary speeches. From this safe distance he observed the collapse of the Empire and the convulsions which followed it – for the fourth time in the life of this cautious constitutionalist, a regime had been overturned on the streets of Paris. He died on 12 September 1874, in the early and hesitant years of the Third Republic.

In that same year, Emile Combes was industriously establishing his political base in the town of Pons, and enjoying the kind of company that would strengthen him in his anticlerical views and his determination to break the educational power of the Church. By the time of his election to the Senate in 1885, the celebrated Ferry Laws were making their way onto the statute book. Primary education was thereafter to be both compulsory and free of charge. Teachers in all public schools were now to be exclusively lay and secular and, in theory, members of the Congregations were therefore banned from teaching in them. Private Catholic schools were still to be tolerated, of course, but in principle to depend on private and not on public funds. That at least was the theory: but, as Combes discovered many years later in his own Department, the reality was strikingly different. One more assault by liberals, freethinkers, Freemasons and Protestants would still, so he believed, have to be mounted. Even then, the story would not be ended.

Notes

[1] Nique, 1990a, p. 113.

[2] Basdevant-Gaudemer, 1988.

[3] Nique, 1990a; Johnson, 1963, p. 114.

[4] Nique, 1990a, p. 49.

[5] Chauvin, 1999.

[6] Nique, 1990a, p. 125.

[7] Johnson, 1963, p. 130.

[8] Ibid., p. 130.

[9] Nique, 1990, p. 115.

[10] Judge et al, 1994.

[11] Johnson, 1963, p. 137.

[12] Ibid., p. 139.

[13] Nique, 1990, p. 156.

[14] Ibid., p. 136.

CHAPTER 7

Three Antecedents:
William Bernard Ullathorne

William Bernard Ullathorne was born in 1806 at Pocklington in the East Riding of Yorkshire. His father – a grocer and merchant in that small market town in the far north of England – was a Roman Catholic, whose own grandfather had married a direct descendant of Sir Thomas More, sometime Lord Chancellor of England and executed in 1535 on the orders of Henry VIII. More's unpardonable offence had been to deny the royal supremacy in the Church, and to insist on a superior duty of loyalty to Rome. In sixteenth-century England, loyalty to the Pope was inextricably associated with a rejection of the claims of the Tudor monarchy. Citizenship was legally and emotionally identified with membership of the Church of England, which itself claimed to be the direct lineal descendant of that same church (now purified by the reformers) founded in 597 when Augustine became the first Archbishop of Canterbury. For Anglicans (and with a renewed emphasis for many of Ullathorne's own contemporaries), it was the Papists who had rejected the historic Church in England; for the Romanists (now dismissed as Recusants), it was the Anglicans who had deserted the universal church presided over by the Pope. In a classic text written during the reign of Henry's daughter Elizabeth, it was asserted: 'There is not any man of the Church of England but the same man is also a member of the commonwealth; nor any man a member of the commonwealth which is not also of the Church of England'.[1] Although the last executions for the offence of simply being a Catholic took place in the stormy 1680s, Catholics who denied this identification of the national church with the nation state were until the end of the eighteenth century systematically persecuted. The burning of Protestant heretics (immortalised in Foxe's *Book of Martyrs*), during the brief reign of Elizabeth's half-sister Mary, the excommunication of Elizabeth by the Pope in 1570 and the release of her Catholic subjects from the ties of loyalty to their usurping monarch, the attempted invasion of England by the forces of Catholic Spain in 1588, the Gunpowder Plot of 1604, the short-lived attempt at the end of that century to restore orthodox Catholicism in the reign of James II all served to embed in the Protestant English consciousness a deep hatred and a fear of Rome and all its ways. The violence of the Gordon Riots in 1780 was a forcible reminder that popular passions against Popery had not been extinguished by the supposed reasonableness of the eighteenth century: those passions survived well into the century through which William Ullathorne lived, and politicians (as during a critical period of Ullathorne's life) stood ready to exploit them.[2]

When the Ullathornes were united by marriage with the well born descendants of a Lord Chancellor, they joined the ranks of the 'Old Catholics' in England. Such Catholics had, of course, been deprived of many of the rights of citizenship. The modest extension of official toleration to Protestant dissenters granted in 1689 did not yet include them. The days of harsh persecution may have passed, but Christians faithful to Rome and its teachings certainly did not enjoy the normal privileges of membership of English society. They could not attend either of the universities, they were technically forbidden to conduct their own schools, and – until a period of relaxation began with a 1778 Act of Parliament granting them some modest relief (concessions which then provoked the notorious riots in London two years later) – their religious services could not be held in public chapels. Their faith was kept alive in the private chapels belonging to the nobility and gentry, or in the London embassies of foreign Catholic powers. They could not hold any official positions and, above all, could not sit in the House of Commons. Their social and political power was severely circumscribed. The survival of Catholicism therefore depended on implicit tolerance by the local authorities, and notably by the local magistrates, and on the willingness of the more affluent families to welcome itinerant priests to say Mass for the local inhabitants and to provide the barest rudiments of instruction in the faith. That survival depended above all on the peaceful discretion of the Old Catholics themselves, on their remaining scrupulously loyal to and respectful of the civil power, on their willingness to live (in the evocative phrase of Adrian Hastings) like 'mice in the woodwork'.[3] The family into which William's grandfather married soon came to appreciate the force of these simple lessons: their support of the Jacobite and Catholic cause against the Hanoverian King in the rebellion of 1745 cost them their Yorkshire estates. The Ullathorne family was now obliged to go into trade, and moved to Pocklington, where (legally since 1778) there was a small and inconspicuous Catholic chapel.

The anticlerical enthusiasms of the early stages of the 1789 revolution had driven from France many Catholic priests, one of whom – the Abbé Fidèle – served that small Yorkshire chapel now attended by the young William Ullathorne. According to William's autobiography, colourful in both content and title (*From Cabin-Boy to Archbishop*), the good abbé had only four sermons, which, once the first words had been uttered, the congregation could recite by heart.[4] When in 1815 the family moved to Scarborough on the coast, the small Catholic congregation there received a visit from a priest only once every six weeks. On the intervening Sundays, members of the congregation conducted simple services and read from the widely circulated *Garden of the Soul* by Bishop Challoner. This text, which also influenced the

Catholic spirit in eighteenth-century America, typified the unostentatious piety of the Catholic community, and proved to have little in common with the more assertive and elaborate style of later Catholicism in both these English-speaking countries. Ullathorne reports that, during his youth, he never saw a bishop: England was then regarded by Rome as a distant and difficult missionary country, under the direct authority of the Roman Propaganda (The Congregation for the Propagation of the Faith). The four Vicars Apostolic, as bishops with exotic titles *in partibus infidelium*, exercised their authority in the four unglamorously named Districts: Northern, Central, London and Western. In fact, most of the responsibility for the conduct of affairs rested with laymen, who generally owned the premises used for Catholic purposes and looked after the scarce resources. The parallel with the contemporary situation in the United States is immediately striking. In both countries there would soon be disputes between the champions of a traditionally lay control of local church affairs and an increasingly confident and assertive clergy.[5]

William attended – in the manner of the day, somewhat unsystematically – local schools of a generally Protestant character, where he appears to have behaved like a good Catholic mouse and where his own opinions and faith were left undisturbed. Reading *Robinson Crusoe* encouraged his restless spirit and his compliant, if reluctant, parents allowed him to go to sea as a cabin boy in a ship with a friendly captain (who had the added recommendation of being accompanied on his voyages by his wife). Towards the end of an early voyage, he visited relatives in London, and was taken to St Mary's Moorfields (the pro-Cathedral which had been completed in 1820), where he first enjoyed a glimpse of what a Catholic church and Catholic rituals might represent. The days of the mice in the woodwork were slowly passing.

The events of the French Revolution had effects on English Catholicism as powerful as they were unintended. The cluster of English educational institutions in exile in northern France around Douai was now scattered, and as a direct consequence, new establishments took firm root in England. The English Benedictine monks fled from Douai in 1795 and in 1814 established themselves permanently at Downside in Somerset. They opened a school, to which Ullathorne went nine years later. The total enrolment was of twenty boys. The Old Catholic observed that until this point in his life he 'had never seen a cope'.[6] He resolved to join the Order, but was destined to spend very little of his long and active life in the cloister: there was too much new and demanding work to be done, and Ullathorne was swept along in the major revival and expansion of an English Catholicism that was now destined to enter the mainstream of English public life. Of central importance in that evolution was the passing in 1829, after long hesitations and bitter disputes, of the Catholic Emancipation Act. Roman Catholics, while still suffering from a multitude of legal disabilities, were now allowed to sit as Members of Parliament. Such a relaxation of the laws against the Catholics, deeply contested and leading to a split in the Tory party, had been rendered virtually inevitable by the Act of Union with Ireland in 1801. Although in that year the Irish lost their own Parliament in Dublin, members of the Catholic majority in that island were now allowed to seek election to the London Parliament. Growing numbers of Catholics secured election to the House of Commons, mostly because of the support of the Irish vote.

Three years after Catholic emancipation, William Ullathorne was despatched on a long mission to Australia, where he spent most of the decade of the 1830s. His principal concern was with the convicts and ex-convicts who had been transported to that inhospitable shore as a punishment for offences (in many cases of a political character). Soon after his arrival, he met the leading Catholics in the colony, 'all of Irish origin'. He was appalled by the conditions in which the convicts lived: 'Anything more demoralising than this system of treating men worse than dogs cannot be imagined'.[7] He inveighed against the evils of drink, and wrote a sermon on that social theme which enjoyed growing fame. During these years of exceptional difficulty and hardship, Ullathorne acquired a strong sense of the injustice of prevailing systems, and a profound sympathy for the poor. Such concerns were to be a marked characteristic of his own life, and indeed of most members of the new Catholic leadership in England. He argued powerfully before a parliamentary committee in England against the vices of the system of transportation. As Vicar General in the colony, he enjoyed good relations with the Governor and his officials, who – as in many of the British colonies – were anxious to enlist the support of the Catholic clergy in containing the massive social problems with which they were confronted.[8] It was during Ullathorne's missionary years in the colony that, as a direct consequence of the Emancipation Act, a Roman Catholic admitted to high office under the Crown was – after some brief equivocations – allowed to take the new Catholic form of the oath of allegiance. Fortunately, a declaration against the doctrine of transubstantiation was no longer imposed. Although Ullathorne was successful in securing financial support for Catholic schools and other institutions, he displayed an acute awareness of the dangers as well as the advantages of entering into partnerships of that kind with the State. He quoted with approval the comment made in 1836 by the Governor that such grants should be made only on one occasion and in order to build schools, but that thereafter such institutions 'would roll off state support like saturated leeches'.[9] When within ten years Catholic schools in England also for the first time sought and received support from public funds, Ullathorne proved to be outspoken in emphasising the dangers he believed to be inseparable from such innovative arrangements. In 1836 and 1837, Ullathorne visited Europe, arguing in London against transportation and reporting to the authorities in Rome on the work for which he was then responsible on the other side of the world. In Rome, he met the Rectors of the English and of the Irish Colleges, Nicholas Wiseman and Paul Cullen, who were destined to become the leaders of the Catholic revival in their respective countries.

Nicholas Wiseman, with whom Ullathorne was later to disagree on the thorny subject of government funding for Catholic schools, had been born in Seville in 1802, the son of an Irish merchant whose father had settled in Spain.[10] His mother returned to Ireland after his father's death a few years later, and in 1810 the young Nicholas entered the Catholic school recently established near Durham at Ushaw – another of the institutions refounded in England after the dispersal of the English educational communities in exile around Douai. At the age of sixteen, he was admitted to the Venerable English College in Rome, a seminary for the training of priests. He continued there as a teacher, earning a high reputation for scholarship (notably by his work *Horae Syriacae* in 1827) and in 1828 he became Rector. By the time of Ullathorne's visit to Rome, Wiseman was well established as a significant figure in ecclesiastical politics and was the agent in Rome of the English Vicars Apostolic. He was impressed by distinguished visitors from France – Lammenais, Lacordaire and Montalambert all visited Rome in 1831 – although anxious to distance himself from the political philosophy of the controversial Lammenais, who asserted the superiority of the universal Church to the local State: like the English Apostolic Vicars whom he represented, he was careful to assert his patriotic loyalty to the British Crown. In 1835, he began a long visit to England during which he delivered his famous course of lectures at the London church which had so impressed the seafaring Ullathorne – St Mary's Moorfields. These lectures were unprecedented in being designed for an audience which included non-Catholics, and reflected Wiseman's determination to make Catholic thinking an integral part of the public debate on intellectual issues. He was especially anxious to interest and attract Anglicans now coming under the influence of the revival of traditional belief and learning initiated by the youthful Oxford Movement.

Ullathorne returned to Australia for a further spell of arduous duty before what was to prove his final return to Europe in 1840. In an effort to recruit missionaries for Australia, he first undertook a tour of Ireland, earning a compliment from Father Matthew, the Apostle of Temperance. Although he appears not to have commented directly on educational matters, he must have been made aware of the recent developments in Ireland, and of the significant differences between them and the situation of which he was about to have direct experience in the English Midlands. The British Government had, for many years but not without causing considerable controversy at home, been anxious to secure the loyalty of the Irish Catholics and, in particular, the support of their clergy: it was for this reason that it had founded the college at Maynooth for the training of priests, and made regular grants for its support (to which the young Gladstone at that time objected). Securing the loyalties of the large Catholic community in Ireland became even more essential after the 1829 Act, and it was, therefore, a matter of concern that the public money which had since 1816 been granted to a voluntary society for the support of elementary schools (the Kildare Place Society) had been applied predominantly to the support of Protestant schools. In 1831, the British Government therefore established a Board of Commissioners of National Education, on which the Catholic and Protestant Archbishops sat alongside the leader of the Presbyterian community. Public funds were allocated through this national agency to schools admitting children from families of all denominations. Religious instruction of a specifically denominational character could be given at any time on any one agreed day of the week, as well as at the beginning or end of normal sessions on other days. Instruction in all secular subjects was given in unsegregated classes, although (more surprisingly, and under a later agreement) some religious instruction based on the Bible could also be given to such mixed classes, making use, however, of specially agreed translations of selected parts of that text. Although these arrangements were deeply resented and resisted, especially by some Protestant groups, they survived the barrage of criticisms. The separation of religious and secular subjects, on which the Irish settlement depended and which allowed public grants to be made, was nevertheless in England warmly resisted throughout the century by Catholics and Anglicans alike, who vigorously defended the integrated interdependence of the two.[11]

The country and the Catholic community to which Ullathorne returned in 1841, and within which he was to spend the rest of his long life, were undergoing profound change. He first assumed responsibility for the Catholic mission in Coventry, a rapidly growing centre for the new industries that were now drawing immigrants both from the English countryside and from Ireland, from which unhappy country grinding poverty and the famines of the 1840s were driving ever growing numbers to seek a new life in America or England. The majority of these new immigrants were, with widely varying degrees of commitment, Catholic and their arrival changed for ever the demographic and cultural shape of Roman Catholicism in England, as indeed in America. When he arrived in his Midland town, William Ullathorne found himself responsible for a congregation of some one thousand souls.[12] In the census of that year, it emerged that the Irish-born population of England (alone) amounted to 284,198, and formed 1.9% of the total population of that country.[13] This was only a beginning: in the second half of the nineteenth century, the Irish made up some 80% of the Catholic population of Britain as a whole.[14] The Old Catholics had been submerged, and the emerging community could no longer be swept under the carpet. Its leading members now began to make a strong and public case for the validity of their distinctive beliefs: the London lectures given by the future Cardinal Wiseman had recently made a marked impression, and he was similarly active in launching and encouraging new Catholic journals.[15] When the new church in Coventry was opened in 1845, it was consecrated by Wiseman – since 1840 a bishop in an England that was still treated as a missionary country –

and Ullathorne, in spite of worried warnings from some of his more cautious co-religionists, wore his Benedictine habit: a demonstration which was, until as late as 1926, technically forbidden in public places. 'It was a new thing', he later wrote, 'to see a Catholic church with all its Catholic appointments, just like the old churches as they were furnished in the Middle Ages. ... Much of the old timidity of the persecuting days was still to be found in England, but in the colonies we had learned greater freedom.'[16] But there were still limits to what it seemed safe or prudent to attempt: although the growth of the Catholic population in England had persuaded Rome in 1840 to double the number of Vicars Apostolic, proposals to remove the kingdom from the supervision of Propaganda and (as in other European countries, and, of course, Ireland) to establish a permanent hierarchy of archbishop and bishops were at that time successfully resisted.

In Coventry itself Ullathorne organised public missions and openly sought converts. Religious communities, and especially the teaching orders of nuns that were making so large (if controversial) a contribution to the work of the Church in France and America, were founded. In Mother Mary Hallahan, he found an indispensable ally in the educational and social work of his mission. Many new schools were built, financed entirely from the funds collected from the faithful. The tasks now faced by the bishops in providing schools for the growing populations of young Catholics were massively daunting, and pressure grew to secure some measure of government relief. During the six years which Ullathorne spent in Coventry, the number of priests in England as a whole grew from 530 to 714, and of chapels from 446 to 540. Although in England as many as 30,000 children were receiving free or highly subsidised schooling, such figures represented only a fraction of what needed to be achieved if the Irish Catholics were to be absorbed peacefully into English society and preserved as loyal members of their church. In 1836, the bishops had argued for the urgent necessity of some such relief, appealing directly to the Irish example: 'To improve the feelings, the conduct, the morals and the loyalty of the Irish Roman Catholic poor in this country, it would be necessary that the Government should, at least, extend the same assistance for education as is granted to them in Ireland'.[17] Although central government professed itself powerless to act, in Liverpool the municipal corporation supported in that same year two schools in which the basic elements of the Irish solution were applied: the schools were open to the children of all religious denominations, with secular subjects taught to them all in common classrooms. Religious education would, however, be provided, on agreed terms, by the clergy of the respective denominations, with some such instruction given in unsegregated classes. Representatives of the more rigorous Protestant groups protested loudly against such subsidies to support Roman superstition, and against the insult offered to the Authorised Version of the Bible (the King James version of 1611), which was totally unacceptable to Catholics, in England as in America. For the Catholics, already uneasily consulting Rome about the acceptability – even as a temporary measure – of the Irish solution, schools of their own for their own children may always have been preferable, but how were they to be funded by poor communities? In any case, some of the most active providers of such schools objected vehemently to any entanglement with the State: Ullathorne's own principal collaborator, Mother Mary Hallahan, soon to found a successful teaching order, angrily dismissed such arrangements as 'a deep laid scheme of the devil'.[18] Ullathorne himself generally took a more moderate view, but never overcame his suspicion of the compromises inseparable from accepting public funds. Attempts to extend the Liverpool and Irish solution more widely had already been defeated, and in 1842 the Liverpool experiment was itself terminated by the insistence of the Corporation that only the Authorised Version of the Bible could be used in its schools. The local priests then led a procession of nine hundred children from the public schools into a new Catholic school, the opening of which had been delayed for ten years by the difficulty of raising the required funds. Catholic policy was now hardening: Catholic children should attend only Catholic schools, with or without some public funding, but always without sacrificing the essential confessional character of such schools.

The search for such funding can only be understood against the background of the history of the making of such government grants for other schools in England: Ullathorne himself was later to emphasise that the problem of securing grants and guaranteeing acceptable terms was in no sense peculiar to his church. The State in Britain was exceptionally slow in accepting any formal responsibility for the provision of schooling, which was generally, although by no means universally, regarded as a matter for private or philanthropic effort: citizens should help themselves, and good ones should help one another. Moreover, the complex links between the Church and education had never been formally severed, as for example they had been in France. In the sixteenth century, the established national church ceased to be Roman Catholic and became Anglican, with the monarch as its Supreme Governor and the bishops as its civil servants. However much circumstances changed, notably with the legalised growth of nonconformity and the reluctant inclusion of Roman Catholicism, there would always be strong voices arguing in effect for a traditional and ecclesiastical monopoly. Erosions of that clerical monopoly, typified in the 1829 Act and the extension of the franchise to larger numbers of non-Anglicans in the Reform Act of 1832, led directly to an ecclesiastical revival within the Church of England and a dogmatic reassertion of its superior claims. The creation in 1811 of the National Society for the Promotion of the Education of the Poor in the Principles of the Church of England provided a framework to the encouragement of voluntary effort by the Anglicans. It was in part a response to the formation a few years earlier of the British and Foreign Schools Society, an interdenominational and largely Nonconformist group. Although both these societies stressed the necessity of a religious basis to all education, they differed profoundly in the application of their principles. The British

Schools advertised themselves as being open to the children of all denominations, and promoted a form of the Christian religion that was avowedly unsectarian but unambiguously Protestant. The National Schools, on the other hand, advertised the unity of religious and secular education and were explicitly linked to the established Church of England, to its parishes, and to its clergy. Both societies enjoyed in the early nineteenth century a period of rapidly growing enrolments, made possible in part by the adoption of the monitorial method of teaching which enabled a small number of teachers to instruct large numbers of pupils.[19]

The Reform Act of 1832, by extending the franchise to a larger number of voters, strengthened both the Protestant Nonconformist and the Roman Catholic voices in Parliament. The crucial question now was whether, or to what extent, a national and universal system of elementary education could be developed in England. In the following year, a Radical Member of Parliament, pointing towards the encouraging examples of France and the State of New York, introduced a Bill which would have initiated just such a process, in which all denominations would be treated equally. But the established interests of the two societies, and a suspicion of the enlarging powers of government, guaranteed vigorous opposition to such a development. The making of grants in support of the two existing societies was then accepted as a modest and probably temporary experiment. Such grants could be made only to the nationally established societies for distribution as they saw fit, and not to individual schools. Grants could be made only to supplement voluntary contributions. Consciously or not, the choice was now being made for parallel national systems of elementary education, based on current religious divisions. The money now granted, which could be applied only to the provision of buildings and not to any of the expenses of providing teaching, amounted in the first year to £11,000 for the 690 schools associated with the National Society, and £9000 for the 190 linked to the British Society. By the end of the first decade of the operation of these arrangements, however, 80% of the public resources had in fact gone to the National Society and, of course, none to the Catholics. Lord John Russell, a principal architect of the Reform Act of 1832 and an advocate of Catholic emancipation, looked favourably as Home Secretary on the Liverpool experiment of these years but appreciated the force of the national opposition to its extension. Nevertheless, in 1839, he proposed the creation of a non-denominational training college for teachers, with a model school attached to it, in which the principles of the Irish settlement would in fact be applied. This modest proposal generated furious opposition, and led *The Times* to inveigh against arrangements which would have obliged good Protestants 'to herd with the leprous brood of Papists, Socinians, Freethinkers and fanatics'.[20] The proposals were withdrawn.

Immediately thereafter, measures were taken to secure greater public control over and scrutiny of the expenditures involved in the grants to the two recognised societies. A special committee of the Privy Council was created, all its members being laymen and belonging to the government of the day. Over the coming years, the Minutes of this Committee defined the principles governing the distribution of public money and, to a growing extent, the ways in which such money was spent. Such intervention was viewed with predictable suspicion, and not least by the Tractarians – the High Church party within the Church of England initiated by John Keble's Oxford sermon in 1833 and committed to resisting the growing secularisation of society. By insisting on the catholic character of the Anglican Church, it added a further complication to the current debates: for Nonconformists and secularists there was now a double danger, represented not only by the Roman Catholics but also by Anglicans who were introducing Romish practices and beliefs into the Established Church. Critics like G.A. Denison, for fifty years the High Anglican Vicar of East Brent in London, was as outspoken in his criticisms of state interference as were the most determined defendants of the rights of the Church of Rome. In 1840, a fragile and incomplete agreement was concluded between the new government Committee and the Established Church. The supervision of Her Majesty's Inspectors of Schools (now created for this very purpose) was accepted, but only on condition that the inspector of any Church of England school must be an Anglican approved by the relevant bishop and subject to removal. Anglican spokesmen attached so much importance to the full integration of the teaching of secular and religious subjects that they insisted that this HMI should therefore inspect both. It was a continuing condition that only the Authorised Version of the Bible could be used in any school receiving a government grant. Catholics were, therefore, still excluded from these arrangements, and their schools remained dependent on such fees as could be afforded and on the raising of funds from an impoverished community.[21] The pressure on that community, and the urgency of providing a basic education for its children, grew as the worsening conditions in Ireland in the 1840s added to the flood of immigrants: during this decade, 400,000 new immigrants arrived and clustered in a number of major cities. By the end of the 1840s, there were 100,000 Irish in Liverpool alone. Although in 1851 the Catholic population of the whole country amounted to some 680,000, schools had been provided for a mere 41,382.[22]

Just as Catholics in Ireland had been willing to accept some of the worrying ambiguities of the settlement there, so the lay leaders of the Catholic community in England tended to prefer an imperfect government funded solution for their problems to the alternative of leaving multitudes of Irish Catholic children to roam the streets. The Catholic Institute, a philanthropic body led by such Old Catholic grandees as the Earl of Shrewsbury, was for that reason prepared to tolerate the Factory Bill of 1843, which – even though the religious instruction would be of an Anglican character – would have offered some basic schooling for children working in factories.[23] Wiseman and his fellow Vicars Apostolic were for their part profoundly disturbed by this apparent victory for 'the mediaeval party' of

Denison and the (still) Anglo-Catholic Henry Edward Manning. They determined to exercise a tighter measure of control over their flock. In 1847, Wiseman himself, as a member of the education committee of the Catholic Institute, seconded a resolution which reflected the growing anxieties and the more insistent tone of an episcopate which was now beginning to feel its own strength:

> *THAT this meeting, deeply impressed with the outrage offered to the rights of conscience by the declaration of her Majesty's present government that Catholics are to be excluded from participation in a grant of £100000 to be voted by Parliament for all other religious communions call upon all classes of their fellow Catholics to unite in one cry of indignant reprobation at this insulting exception from a public grant.[24]*

Wiseman, unlike some of his intransigent colleagues, was willing to accept government grants for Catholic schools, but only on terms that in no way threatened their independence. Ullathorne, promoted from Coventry in 1846 to become a bishop and Vicar Apostolic for the Western District, was even more alert to the dangers of sacrificing liberty in return for government money.

Official government policy towards the Catholics was now inevitably softening: in 1845, the Conservative ministry of Sir Robert Peel placed the Maynooth grant on a permanent footing – an event which led Gladstone to resign on the unusual grounds that, although he now supported it, he had earlier been openly opposed to such a concession. The new Whig Prime Minister, Lord John Russell, had hinted that further concessions to the Catholics in England might soon be made. Meanwhile, and most significantly, the grants to the two Protestant societies had been increasing in both scale and scope, and now included substantial sums for the training of teachers and for extra payments to well-qualified teachers. All this entailed a greater control by the agencies of government and a closer inspection of the voluntary schools – developments naturally resisted with vehemence by the Anglican High Church party, whose power within the National Society was, to the consternation of Nonconformists and evangelical Anglicans, being systematically consolidated. The Catholic bishops now took the decisive step of creating the Catholic Poor Schools Committee to act as the single agency appointed on their authority to negotiate with the Government, and to receive and distribute all grants made for the support of Catholic schools in England and Wales.[25] Its chairman for the next twenty years was Charles Langdale, who had previously been influential in the counsels of the Catholic Institute, and who was admired by Wiseman as:

> *a man equally venerated by Catholics, respected by Protestants, and listened to with deference by the first ministers of State; ... who had renounced a life of ease at his country seat to live in the metropolis ... and work for the poor.[26]*

By 1850, five hundred elementary schools were associated with the new CPSC, although it was some time before considerable sums of money began to flow. It was agreed that a Roman Catholic inspector would have to be appointed for the schools in receipt of any grant, but (since the concept of any control of religious instruction by a government official, even if he were a Catholic, was anathema) his mandate would be restricted to secular subjects only. In 1852, the bishops appointed their own inspectors for religious instruction. This policy, paradoxically but understandably, contrasted with that of the Established Church, which laid emphasis – as in principle, of course, did the Catholics themselves – on the coherent integration of the whole curriculum, and rejected any formal distinction between the sacred and the profane. The dispute about trust deeds and the management clauses for schools was even more protracted. The Privy Council committee wished to ensure a predominance of lay members on the committees managing the schools (Catholic or Anglican) as well as lay rather than clerical control over the teaching of secular subjects. Denison, in language which (and not least in the use of the word 'catholic') reveals the complexity of the Church/State debate, insisted:

> *I will fight till I die for the Catholic Church of England. I will not move*
> *one finger for a Church which negotiates with the House of Commons,*
> *or any of its creatures, about the means of discharging the trust*
> *committed to her by God.*[27]

Ullathorne, however much he may have demurred at the description of the Anglican Church as 'the Catholic Church of England', could not have made the point more clearly. The discussion of the management clauses was for the moment overtaken by the great ecclesiastical and political storm of the year 1850, generated by the long delayed agreement of Rome to restore (or establish) in England and Wales the Roman Catholic hierarchy of archbishop and bishops.

This was the critical decision for which Ullathorne and Wiseman had argued during their mission to Rome in the year after the foundation of the Catholic Poor Schools Committee, and which fundamentally transformed the position of the Roman Catholics in England, the prospects for their schools, and their relationships with the English government of the day. Ullathorne, as one of the Vicars Apostolic, had joined Wiseman, already arguing the case in Rome, in order to urge that England was now ready to be promoted from its status as a missionary country and to take its place as a fully integrated part of Catholic Europe, with established territorial bishops of its own. His conservative temperament was shocked by the disorderly scenes he observed in 1848 on his journey through Paris. Life was little calmer in revolutionary Rome, where after many weeks of patient negotiation agreement in principle was secured that the hierarchy of archbishop and twelve bishops would now be established for England and Wales. Ullathorne and Wiseman argued that the United States already had their hierarchy, and that the English Vicars Apostolic were more loyal to papal causes than were their republican colleagues across the Atlantic. On the night that Ullathorne left Rome, revolution erupted and the Pope fled from the city: the final announcement of the restoration was therefore delayed for two further years. Even then, the final discussions were complex and obscure: at one point a tearful Wiseman was convinced that Ullathorne would be appointed as the new archbishop, while he would have to be satisfied with being a Curial cardinal. In the event, Nicholas Wiseman was duly proclaimed as the first Archbishop of Westminster, while Ullathorne returned to the Midlands as the first Bishop of Birmingham.

These territorial titles, and the manner of their promulgation, were to provoke an outburst of anti-Catholic passion in England. It was understandable but imprudent that Wiseman should have adopted a triumphalist tone in assuming his new titles. In his first pastoral letter, written in Rome itself and grandly entitled *From Without the Flaminian Gate*, his language invited misinterpretation and resentment: the Cardinal Archbishop asserted that 'we govern the counties of Middlesex, Hertford and Essex as Ordinary thereof'. A few days later, driving in his carriage through Vienna on his way back to England, Wiseman was dismayed to read in *The Times* of 14 October a denunciation of such effrontery. The Prime Minister, Lord John Russell, seized this opportunity of making rich political capital and damaging the cause of the Tractarians within the Church of England. The cry of 'No Popery' was once more raised. The monarch enquired, 'Am I Queen of England, or am I not?'[28] Guy Fawkes Day was approaching, and represented the closest English approximation to a national day: for French and American patriots, 4 July and 14 July might celebrate the defeat of monarchical power, but 5 November recalled the most glorious moments when the English rejected forever the authority of a foreign prelate. Up and down the country, the Pope and the Archbishop who had presumed to take a revered and very English title were burnt in effigy, while early in the new year the Government introduced a law (never in fact enforced) prohibiting the unauthorised assumption of English territorial titles. In London, Wiseman drove in his carriage with his heraldic arms prominently displayed, and certainly enjoyed the pomp and glory of his office as well as the company of the great of this world. Catholics were no longer going to hide. He moved confidently through society, although hardly deserving the portrait of him as an epicure in the thin disguise of Browning's Bishop Blougram. F.W. Faber more sharply if characteristically observed that 'The Cardinal has a lobster salad side as well as a spiritual side' and that 'When in full tog he looked like some Japanese God'.[29] On landing in England, Wiseman did what he could to calm the storm, and wrote a persuasive *Appeal to the Reason and Good Sense of the English People*. The restoration of the hierarchy was 'not as a matter of triumph or a measure of aggression' but a legitimate fulfilment of the process initiated by Catholic emancipation in 1829. It would have been undignified to choose a title (such as Islington) less prestigious than that of

Westminster, rich in echoes of English history and authority. Nor was there any wish to offend the interests of the present Anglican tenants of the ancient Abbey:

> *For there is another part which stands in frightful contrast, though in immediate contact, with this magnificence …. Close under the Abbey of Westminster there lie concealed labyrinths of lanes and courts, and alleys and slums, nests of ignorance, vice, depravity, and crime … in which swarms a huge and almost countless population, in great measure, nominally at least, Catholic … This is the part of Westminster which alone I covet.[30]*

Nothing would therefore be more important for the bishops than to rescue the children of these poor Catholics, and to build schools for them: 'In one district alone we have 5000 children to educate and accommodation for only 400', Wiseman wrote in the year when he and Ullathorne first assumed their new responsibilities.[31] At their first synod, the bishops established unambiguous priorities by asserting:

> *wherever there may seem to be an opening for a new mission, we should prefer the erection of a school, so arranged as to serve temporarily for a chapel, to that of a church without one.[32]*

The spirited internal debate on whether and on what terms to accept government support for such schools, overshadowed by the drama of 1850, was now resumed. For as long as these discussions continued, little money had in fact been granted to the Catholics for their schools. The matter became more urgent as grants to other denominational bodies continued to enlarge in scale and scope, and as the rudiments of a national system of denominational education supported by public funds began to evolve: with the appointment in 1856 of a Vice President of the Committee of the Privy Council dealing with these grants, an embryonic Minister of Education emerged from the mists. The House of Commons wished to have some control of the distribution of ever enlarging public grants to voluntary schools. In the following year, Ullathorne insisted yet again on the dangers of agreeing to any modifications in the trust deeds of Catholic schools which might have the effect of exposing them further to the creeping risks of government control. Annual grants presented a more acceptable risk, for they could always be rejected if the conditions attached to them ever became intolerable. But grants for buildings carried massive risks. In an important pamphlet, Ullathorne – permanently impressed by his experiences in Australia – acknowledged the difficulty of providing from voluntary contributions for the education of the poor, especially as the Irish themselves were more willing to give money for building churches than for schools. But the Roman Catholic HMIs were already trespassing on the rights of the bishops by interfering with religious instruction. Vigilance must be maintained, since:

After ages of exclusion, as Catholics, from the funds at the command of
the State, we are beginning to receive its aid towards educating the poor
of the Church. And in return for that aid, as a matter of course, we are
giving up something of that absolute freedom and independence of
action which, whatever else we have suffered, has been our greatest
earthly blessing, and has outbalanced even much of our suffering.[33]

But Ullathorne, like other voluntaryists, was now losing the battle. The *Tablet*
disagreed with him, and when he responded by making an even stronger case
for maintaining a safe distance from government, Wiseman himself
intervened somewhat crossly on the other side.[34] But the Catholic
difficulties were no more than a part of a larger problem, as both Ullathorne
and Wiseman readily acknowledged. Most of the schools receiving aid were
still Anglican, and many of them were in places where there was no other
provision. In such 'single school districts', Nonconformists, secularists and
Catholics had no choice and no way of insulating themselves from the
doctrines and control of the Established Church. But Denison and his allies
fiercely resisted any attempt to introduce into the conditions of grant a
conscience clause, allowing parents who stated an objection to withdraw their
children from the religious instruction offered by the schools. Surprisingly
perhaps, the Catholics were prepared to accept such a clause (applied only to
catechetical instruction however) for their own schools, on the sensible
grounds that non-Catholics would be most unlikely in the first place to
choose to attend them. In 1860, the Government imposed such a condition
on grants for the building of new schools: in all other cases the problem
persisted for another decade.

It was for such reasons implausible that a purely voluntary and
segmented denominational system, reinforced by public subsidies, would
indefinitely meet the needs of a growing industrial nation. It was just as
unlikely, given the surviving power of the Anglican establishment and the
vigilance of its champions, that the deeply rooted semi-public
denominational system would somehow be swept away. But the pressure for
change mounted: in the year of Wiseman's dramatic if embarrassed return to
England, a national Public Schools Association was founded in order to press
the arguments for the creation of a national system which would be
independent of control by any religious bodies. A majority on the Newcastle
commission on elementary education, appointed in 1858 and reporting in
1861, recommended that subsidies for the voluntary schools should in future
be raised and distributed locally. A vocal minority took the traditional
voluntarist line by arguing that the voluntary schools should remain
independent, in financial and all other terms.[35] As the financial problems
of such independent schools for the poor became every year more acute,
traditional Nonconformist opinion began to shift towards the support of a
publicly funded school system as the only realistic alternative to an Anglican
predominance supplemented by an equally offensive, if smaller, Roman
Catholic system enjoying a measure of public funding. Such a public system

would be overtly non-sectarian, in the clear sense given to that term by Horace Mann. In the event, the Government did not accept the proposal that funds for the support of denominational schools should be administered locally in the light of local circumstances, and instead chose the path of greater centralisation and control. Annual grants were henceforth, by what became the notorious system of 'payment by results', to be distributed with direct reference to the success of the pupils in examinations administered by Her Majesty's Inspectors. Moreover, such tests were to be of secular subjects only, so that grants paid to the schools (and especially the Anglican establishments) were uncoupled from accountable success in the teaching of religion. The Catholics, of course, had never conceded the right of any government agent to inspect or control religious instruction in their own schools. But on other matters, and notably, of course, the management clauses, they were prepared to yield. The willingness of the Catholic leadership to bend a little to the will of the Government, so consistently lamented by Ullathorne, certainly produced results: Wiseman estimated that by 1862 their schools had received £295,757 from the national treasury.[36]

Wiseman's archiepiscopal rule from 1850 to his death in 1865 therefore represented a crucial turning point in the history of Catholicism in England, and of its schools. He was determined that his Church should become a central and permanent part of the intellectual life of the country, that it should engage its critics on open and equal terms, that the converts from the Oxford Movement should be welcomed and properly employed. Indeed, he was realistic enough to acknowledge as early as 1841 (as would Ullathorne, in whose large diocese Oxford itself was situated) that 'if the Oxford divines entered the Church, we must be ready to fall into the shade'.[37] After Newman, welcomed as a new convert by Wiseman at Oscott in 1845, the best known of those former Anglicans was Henry Edward Manning. He had been, as the Westminster Cathedral chancellor, the most effective supporter of the often inefficient Wiseman in the last years of his life, and it was Manning who was summoned from Rome to the Cardinal's deathbed in 1865. Wiseman's funeral procession along the long route from St Mary's Moorfield to Kensal Green cemetery was marked by a remarkable display of public emotion. *The Times* seemed to have forgotten its caustic anger of fifteen years before, commenting that nothing comparable had been seen in London since the death of the Duke of Wellington.[38] Only six years earlier the service for the celebration of 5 November had been removed from the Book of Common Prayer, together with its petition to be delivered 'from the secret contrivance and hellish malice of Popish conspirators'.

Ullathorne's name had been one of three on the *terna*, the list submitted by his fellow bishops for consideration as the next archbishop. But Manning, whose name had not been included, was in the event to succeed Wiseman, and to continue with the outspoken Ullathorne the long disagreement on the relationship of Catholic schools to the State. Manning was born in 1807 and educated at Oxford, where he became a friend of Gladstone, with whom he corresponded for many years and to whose eldest child he was godfather. He became a country clergyman and married, but his wife died in 1837. Three years later, he was promoted to be Archdeacon of Chichester, and soon established himself as a champion of the rights of the Church of England and a defender of the interests of the poor. As an Anglo-Catholic, he was an ardent advocate for the schools of the National Society. Shocked by what he saw as the subservience of the Church in matters of doctrine to an increasingly unsympathetic State, in 1851 he became a Roman Catholic, just after the enthronement of Wiseman in Westminster. As Wiseman's invaluable agent, he supported cooperation whenever possible with the government of the day, in the hope of obtaining 'a share in the treatment of questions which may affect us'.[39] The buildings and development of Catholic schools in London was to be one of the most striking achievements of Manning's episcopate. At the outset, he brusquely offended the wealthy Catholic laymen who had raised money for the building of a grand new cathedral by speaking up for the more urgent interests of the London poor. He observed in his journal:

> *But could I leave twenty thousand children without education, and drain my friends and my flock to pile up stones and bricks? ... My successor may begin to build a cathedral. [40]*

His first pastoral letter was devoted to the same theme, and within a year he had created a diocesan fund for the building of schools. Within three years each of the English dioceses had its own Education Council, although few were as vigorous in raising funds as was Manning in London. Between 1850 and 1870, the number of places available in Catholic schools in England and Wales had nevertheless more than doubled. By 1870, 350 schools were receiving government grants. The fees paid in such schools were on average half of those charged in the schools of the National Society and the British and Foreign Schools Society.[41]

As preparations advanced in the late 1860s for the drafting of a new Education Bill, Ullathorne kept up the pressure for preserving a safe distance between the Catholic schools and the Government as one of their paymasters. Although he showed no personal resentment, he clearly did not find Manning an especially congenial colleague. He apparently referred to him as 'that Manning' and, in a blunt Yorkshire manner and as an old Catholic who had known the hard days, unsurprisingly resented the confident style of a convert whom he found overenthusiastic about Roman and foreign ways:

> *My dear sir, allow me to say that I was teaching the catechism with a mitre on my 'ead while you were still an 'eretic. [42]*

Their relationship had never fully recovered from their bruising encounters in Rome when Ullathorne was representing the interests of the English bishops against Manning, who was arguing the cause of Wiseman. In their correspondence during 1869 and 1870, Ullathorne repeatedly urged the importance of keeping free from the Government. At a well-reported public meeting in Birmingham Town Hall in November 1869, he argued against the proposed abolition of the Roman Catholic HMIs: this was being offered by the Catholics as a concession to be made in return for a promise of higher grants. The further extension of the parliamentary franchise in 1867 rendered even more urgent a major structural reform of the patterns of educational provision and funding: Robert Lowe was not alone in thinking that it was now necessary 'to compel our future masters to learn their letters'.[43] Gladstone's electoral victory in 1868 encouraged those who bitterly resented the near monopoly in educational provision enjoyed by the Church of England, which was still receiving annually three-quarters of the total of all government aid to schools. The hated Church rates were abolished in 1868, and the Irish Church disestablished in the following year. The battle lines were now being more clearly drawn. On the one hand was the National Education League, arguing alongside Joseph Chamberlain for a national and non-sectarian system now acceptable to most Nonconformists and all secularists; on the other side were the serried ranks of the National Education Union. The Union mobilised the forces of the Church of England and of the Roman Catholics: one of the speakers at its inaugural meeting was Thomas Allies, the long-serving secretary of the Catholic Poor Schools Committee. As Vice President of the Committee of Council, the Government's education spokesman was W.E. Forster, a Quaker until he married the daughter of Thomas Arnold. Forster knew that neither the League nor the Union could expect to win an unconditional victory. The debates surrounding Forster's Education Act (1870) were often confused and the issues unclear. Gladstone himself was much preoccupied with Ireland, and although the spokesmen for the Church of England were very much to the forefront, all the Catholic bishops were away in Rome for the meeting of the Vatican Council.

At the heart of the new law in its final form was the recognition, for the first time in England, that elementary schooling for the people could not simply be left to the churches and their voluntary organisations. Local School Boards were therefore to be established 'to fill up gaps' in all places where the existing voluntary provision was demonstrably inadequate.[44] These Boards were to be directly elected, with each qualified voter having a number of votes corresponding to the total number of candidates. This made possible the practice of 'plumping', so that members of minorities like the Catholics could give all their votes to one candidate. Their interests were therefore better represented on the Boards, which had the right to levy a rate for the support of the secular non-sectarian schools directly provided and managed by them. By securing such representation and being moderately cooperative the representatives of the Churches hoped to keep within more modest limits the expenditure of local money on the Board schools, and so to limit the threatening competition which they offered. Building grants from central government to voluntary schools were to cease after a six month period of grace, during which the voluntary societies could mobilise as many bids as they believed they could justify – in terms both of a local need for such new provision, and of their own capacity to raise through voluntary contributions the required matching funds. Annual grants for the routine support of the existing and of the newly built schools would, however, continue indefinitely. The original proposal that the Boards should themselves also make such annual grants was firmly resisted both by the National Society and, of course, by the Catholics. Both groups feared that the Boards would not be impartial in making such grants and would favour their own non-sectarian elementary schools. Manning wrote to Gladstone urging that central government should be responsible for distributing these grants, basing his argument on the necessity of providing equal treatment for all groups:

> Let us all start fair in this race. Let every sect, even the Huxleyites, have their grant if they fulfil the conditions. [45]

Grants to voluntary denominational schools were now to be only for the teaching of secular subjects. Although appropriate religious instruction would, of course, continue to be provided, a conscience clause was now mandatory. The denominational HMIs were abolished, since in future HMIs could be concerned only with the teaching of secular subjects – on the examination of which grants would largely depend. In voluntary schools, the State would henceforth help to fund secular instruction while continuing to sanction the denominational teaching of religion but also insisting that this should never again be compulsory for all pupils in the schools. In the Board schools, on the other hand, religious instruction was to be non-sectarian, in the formal sense that they might not teach a 'religious catechism or religious formulary which is distinctive of any particular denomination'.[46] This requirement, the so-called Cowper-Temple clause, was in the event incorrectly but universally interpreted as imposing a broad prohibition of the affirmation by any individual teacher of any distinctive doctrine or point of view. The rights of conscience were to be legally protected in Board schools as well.

1870 therefore represents the most significant date in the evolution of a national system of elementary education in England. Hitherto, there had been no 'public schools', in the American or French sense of that term. There had, of course, for some forty years been public financial support for elementary education, but the schools themselves were owned, built and governed by religious organisations. Among those, the most substantial was, of course, the established Church of England. Nonconformists, who received financial support on the same terms as did the Church of England, had from the beginning enjoyed a smaller share of those funds, while Roman Catholics were at first excluded. Nonconformists reluctantly came to prefer a non-sectarian and national system, and resented the scale of the grants made to Anglican schools, especially in areas where there was no alternative to such schools. After 1870, an explicitly public system existed alongside these semi-public arrangements, which had from the earliest days been subject to monitoring and control by the agents of government, Her Majesty's Inspectors. Uncomfortably alongside such schools there were now created new School Boards, funded from locally levied rates and controlled by elected members. A dual system therefore became, and remains, an apparently stable element in the English educational system.

However, the two sectors of the dual system originally differed not only in terms of religious affiliation and loyalty, but in structurally important ways as well: the denominational system depended on central funding to supplement private contribution whereas the secular system depended on support from local property taxes, similarly supplemented by substantial grants from central government. The rivalry between the two sectors, for the rest of the century exacerbated and complicated by this difference, was in the intervening years often been bitter and intense. Within the voluntary denominational sector, the Church of England for long remained the predominant partner, as the so-called British schools were gradually absorbed into the fully public sector. But the Anglican schools, as an integral part of the Establishment, claimed to be historically public and in many areas there was no alternative to them. Inevitably, therefore, their purely denominational character was diluted, especially as the law now obliged them to respect the freedom of conscience of the non-Anglican parents whose children often had no choice but to attend such schools. By contrast, the Catholic schools – now fully integrated within the same legal and political framework as other voluntary schools – preserved a very definite and distinctive character of their own. Freedom of conscience had by law to be respected, but why would non-Catholics choose to attend Catholic schools? They were the schools provided for a minority whose leaders were determined to preserve a specific character, and most members of that minority were poor and lived in the new urban areas. Catholics would cooperate with Anglicans in defending the voluntary sector, and were often prepared to seek election to the local School Boards, if only in an attempt to limit the competition offered by the new public schools, whose access to public funds seemed virtually unlimited. Anglicans and Catholics alike looked for support to central government, rather than to the locally elected bodies which were in many cases unsympathetic if not hostile towards them.

A mighty effort was made, as soon as the Act was passed, to raise the matching voluntary contributions needed if the denominational schools were to take advantage of the public funding now on offer, for a limited period, to subsidise the building of new Catholic schools. Although the bids had to be formally initiated within six months, the process of allocating funds took much longer and the last government grants for buildings were not made until 1881. The crisis fund now inaugurated by the Catholic bishops made possible the provision of 75,818 new places. This was the principal achievement of the long episcopate of Henry Manning (made a Cardinal in 1875). By the end of the century, the number of pupils in Catholic schools had more than quadrupled as the number of schools grew from 350 to

1045.[47] This growth was assisted by an increase in the number of teaching nuns, reinforced by the flight to England of considerable numbers after the introduction in France of the Ferry laws. The 1870 Law had authorised the School Boards to employ a part of their revenues to reduce the fees paid for poor pupils in voluntary schools (as also, of course, in Board Schools where fees were also normally charged): the two Churches resented this control by their rivals, and responsibility for such payments to voluntary schools was therefore in 1876 transferred to the administrators of the poor laws. The Catholic schools maintained their commitment to the service of the poor: in 1884, 13.1% of pupils in the Catholic schools paid no fees, compared with only 2.6% in Anglican and 4.2% in the Board schools. The Catholics made heroic fund-raising efforts to ensure that they kept and enlarged their own schools: between 1870 and 1902, some fifteen hundred voluntary schools abandoned their independence to become Board schools, but not one of them was Catholic.[48] Many of them, of course, were the old inter-denominational British schools: the Church of England remained the dominant provider, and even by the end of the century, when many new Board schools had been successfully established, the Anglicans still controlled about one-half of the total number of places in elementary education.

Cardinal Manning, as concerned as Wiseman to represent his Church in the mainstream of English life, urged the fullest possible cooperation with the Government and indeed with the Board schools. He proved to be the dominant figure on the Cross Commission, established in 1886 to review the working of the relatively new arrangements for elementary schools. Four years earlier he had cooperated with Bishop Vaughan of Salford (later to succeed him at Westminster) in founding the Voluntary Schools Association, to mobilise the efforts of all the voluntary societies. The first meeting was held in his own house, and its main initial purpose was to press for the appointment of a national commission.[49] A significant victory was achieved in the legislation of 1891, which abolished the payment of fees in Board schools and authorised a government grant of ten shillings for each pupil in those voluntary schools in which such fees were also no longer to be charged. As the fees charged in Catholic schools were significantly lower than elsewhere, this measure was of particular and immediate advantage to them. But these schools experienced great difficulty in recruiting and retaining competent teachers, many of whom left to teach in Board schools after being trained in Catholic colleges. As early as 1875, the Bishops attempted, without great success, to impose ecclesiastical sanctions on those who, as they saw it, deserted the cause. In 1892, the Catholic teachers formed their own association to defend their professional interests.[50]

But William Ullathorne remained intransigent, wary of accepting government money with its attached strings and suspicious of the sinister intentions of the School Boards and of those who controlled them. Of those Boards, he wrote to Manning in September 1876:

> *Their constitution, object and aim is to establish and maintain schools*
> *and propagate a system of education wholly in antagonism with*
> *Catholic education, and with all definite religious education.[51]*

But Manning and economic necessity together prevailed against Ullathorne's persistent warnings: by the end of the century, 255,036 pupils were attending Catholic schools in receipt of public funds: this substantial number represented 10% of the whole voluntary sector (still, therefore, predominantly Anglican). The number of pupils attending these voluntary schools marginally exceeded the number enrolled in the Board schools. In Ullathorne's own populous diocese, great progress was made under his vigorous leadership: 100 new schools were provided, 67 new churches built, 44 new missions established, while the number of priests increased from 86 to 100 and of convents from 7 to 36. Unlike Manning, whose most famous public intervention was in the London dockers' strike of 1889, Ullathorne never became a civic figure.[52] After the appointment of an auxiliary bishop in 1880, he virtually withdrew to Oscott. On his final retirement eight years later, Pope Leo XIII honoured him with the title of Archbishop of Cabasa. The cabin boy who became an archbishop died on 21 March 1889, recalling that 'the last of the Vicars Apostolic is passing'. He was buried in the convent at Stone, the principal house of the Dominican order founded by Mother Mary Hallahan. Newman died in the following year, and Manning in 1892.

Notes

[1] Hooker, 1981, p. 319 (VIII.i.2).

[2] Paz, 1992.

[3] Hastings, 1991, p. 26.

[4] Ullathorne, 1995.

[5] Bossy, 1975.

[6] Ullathorne, 1995.

[7] Ibid., p. 66.

[8] Hastings, 1991, p. 38.

[9] Ullathorne, 1995, p. 110.

[10] Schiefen, 1984; Ward, 1897.

[11] Murphy, 1972, pp. 11-15.

[12] Butler, 1926, p. 117.

[13] McLelland & Hodgetts, 1999, p. 3.

[14] Tallett & Atkin, 1996.

[15] Holland, 1987.

[16] Ullathorne, 1941, pp. 270-272; Fothergill, 1963, p. 42.

[17] Hornsby-Smith, 1999, p. 184.

[18] Norman, 1984, p. 160.

[19] Murphy, 1972, p. 16.

[20] 18 May and 3 June 1839.

[21] Murphy, 1972, p. 31.

[22] Beck, 1950, pp. 42-45.

[23] Holland, 1987, p. 11; Schiefen, 1984, pp. 125, 136.

[24] Schiefen, 1984, p. 172.

[25] Murphy, 1972, p. 33; Cruickshank, 1963, p. 8; Norman, 1984, p. 160.

[26] Ward, 1897, II, p. 452.

[27] Quoted in Cruickshank, 1963, p. 9.

[28] Norman, 1984, p. 56; Fothergill, 1963, p. 161.

[29] Fothergill, 1963, p. 102 and Chapman, 1961, p. 249.

[30] Wiseman, 1850, p. 30.

[31] Ward, 1897, I, p. 517.

[32] Arthur, 1995a, p. 15.

[33] Ullathorne, 1857, p. 7.

[34] Holland, 1987, p. 260; Schiefen, 1984, p. 265.

[35] Murphy, 1972, p. 43; Cruickshank, 1963.

[36] Ward, 1897, II, p. 450.

[37] Fothergill, 1984, p. 102.

[38] Ibid., p. 201.

[39] Butler, 1926, p. 146.

[40] Manning's Journal, in Manning Papers 1878-1882, in McLelland, 1962, p. 32.

[41] McLelland, 1962, p. 38; Norman, 1984, p. 170; Beales, 1950, p. 370; Cruickshank, 1963, p. 190.

[42] Ullathorne, 1995, p. xii.

[43] Murphy, 1971, p. 48; Butler, 1926, p. 146; Arthur, 1995a, p. 17.

[44] Murphy, 1972, p. 39.

[45] Morley, 1908, I, p. 705; Cruickshank, 1963, p. 36.

[46] Murphy, 1972, p. 61.

[47] Cruickshank, 1963, p. 190.

[48] Evennett, 1944, p. 21.

[49] McLelland, 1962, p. 83.

[50] Arthur, 1995a, p. 21.

[51] Norman, 1984, p. 173.

[52] Butler, 1926, pp. 193, 249.

CHAPTER 8

Three Arenas: the Courts

I

Government and Religious Schools in America

Within four years of the death in 1918 of John Ireland, Archbishop of St Paul, a west coast leader of the Ku Klux Klan warned his listeners that they needed to confront 'the ultimate perpetuation or destruction of free institutions, based on the perpetuation or destruction of the public schools'. For the Klan, inflamed by hostility to Catholics, Jews and Blacks, the survival of that public school to which the Archbishop had memorably pledged his own allegiance required nothing less than the destruction of the Catholic schools, and indeed of all the non-public schools, of America. Although he would not have welcomed support from such a source, Horace Mann would have been obliged to accept some at least of the arguments of the white-hooded King Kleagle. For each of this unlikely pair, the common school represented the great integrating force of American society, the nursery of true citizenship and patriotism. The Klan and its many allies carried that doctrine to its ruthless extreme by insisting that the children of Oregon should therefore be compelled to attend the public schools of that state, and none other. This determined and well-orchestrated attempt to establish an absolute monopoly continued and enlarged a long tradition of hostility, in many of the states, to private education in all its forms – but especially when it was associated with the threat to true American culture posed by foreign immigration.[1]

Many of the states, legalising what in most cases had already been informally achieved, had introduced laws requiring parents to send their children to school, although it was assumed that parents had a right to choose such a school for themselves, and to pay for tuition if they chose. A coalition of Oregon interests succeeded in getting a compulsory attendance law on the ballot in 1922, and won. The startling originality of the law was that it required all children between the ages of eight and sixteen to attend public schools, and no others. Oregon might seem a curious state to choose for such a threatening initiative, which was, of course, aimed principally against what were perceived as the dangerously separatist tendencies of immigrants, many of whom were Catholics. Only 8% of the Oregon population was Catholic, and only 7% of all the children of the state attended private schools of any kind. A similar initiative had recently failed in Michigan, but – as a predominantly white, Anglo-Saxon and Protestant state – Oregon might prove to be more receptive (as indeed it did, returning a comfortable majority of votes for the proposed legislation). Attacks on Catholics and their 'Dago pope' reached an appreciative audience. Catholics refused to accept this outlawing of their schools and carried their complaints, with support from Lutherans and Seventh Day Adventists, to the courts, which were to become the principal battleground for a long struggle that was now entering a new and more bitter phase. The legal disputes recalled, in very different circumstances, many of the arguments which John Ireland and his contemporaries had also employed. Some defenders of the virtues of the religious schools, for example, insisted that private schools were more successful in achieving the Americanisation of immigrants simply because their teachers spoke the same foreign language as their students, and could therefore more effectively introduce them to the ways and customs of their newly adopted country. Although the Oregon courts ruled in favour of the private schools, Governor Pierce carried the case on appeal to the Supreme Court, which agreed to hear it (Pierce v. Society of Sisters, 1925). The complex arguments swirling around the relationships between Church and State were being transplanted to Washington and into the thorny field of jurisprudence.

The Supreme Court upheld the decisions of the lower courts, declaring the Oregon law unconstitutional. It was constitutionally unacceptable on the grounds that it violated the rights of the owners of the schools, who were being unjustly deprived of their property. The Court endorsed the rights of parents to make a choice of school for their children, while acknowledging that a state could legitimately regulate the conditions under which private schooling might be delivered. The right to exist had been secured for Catholic as for other private schools, but the limits of their freedom and, more especially, their relationship to public authority and public financing remained unclear. Was there, in education as in other important fields of public policy and action, a wall of separation between Church and State? Undoubtedly, such a wall had existed in France since (at the latest) 1905, but has not existed since 1959. Undoubtedly, no such wall existed then or exists now in Britain. Why was the American situation fundamentally unclear and why is it to this day contested?

The United States, generally acknowledged to be the most religiously observant of Western societies, enjoys a legally complicated relationship with the Almighty. Sittings of the Supreme Court itself, which has done much to define and redefine (and sometimes to obscure) that relationship, open with the words 'God save the United States and this honorable court'. The recitation of the pledge of allegiance contains a reference, included only since 1954, to 'one nation under God': a highly evocative phrase, culled from

Lincoln's speech at Gettysburg. Coins and treasury notes (the latter only since the Korean War) bear the motto 'In God We Trust'. Both houses of Congress appoint official salaried chaplains and begin their sessions with prayer; a Roman Catholic chaplain was appointed to the House of Representatives for the first time in 2000.[2] Yet, at the beginning of the twenty-first century, prayers at the beginning of school football matches, and periods of silence during the school day (during which private prayers might or might not be 'said') were challenged as unconstitutional. The United Kingdom has no written constitution, but the Act of Supremacy (1559) established the head of state as being at the same time Supreme Governor of the Church (of England). The Constitution of the Fifth, as of the Fourth, Republic in France explicitly declares that republic to be secular (if that word can be provisionally accepted as a translation of *laïc*), but on such matters the American Constitution itself in its pristine form is silent: there is in it no reference to religion, either. There is, of course, such a reference, of profound significance, in the First Amendment to the Constitution, incorporated in 1791 in the Bill of Rights. The interpretation of the wording of that amendment, by the Supreme Court itself as well as by scholars and advocates of all kinds, lies at the heart of the continuing debate about the relationship between religion and public life in America. It reads:

> *Congress shall make no law respecting an establishment of religion, or prohibiting the free exercise thereof; or abridging the freedom of speech, or of the press, or the right of the people peaceably to assemble, and to petition the Government for a redress of grievances.*

The first prohibition in the opening phrase is known as the Establishment Clause, and the second as the Free Exercise Clause.

The exegesis over the past two hundred years of these laconically brief clauses, and especially of the first, has generated a mountain of scholarship obscured by a forest of controversy. What matters to the argument of this book is the interpretation which has been validated at any one time by the Supreme Court, and the implications for Catholic (and other private) schools of that reading. Much of the continuing argument has turned around the correct understanding of the original intent of the Framers (of the Constitution and its first ten amendments) and therefore of the circumstances in which they negotiated their important work of drafting. During the colonial period, several of the colonies did indeed have established churches, in the conventional and European sense – whether they were Anglican (as in Virginia and other parts of the south) or Congregationalist (as typically in New England) or a varied and complex mixture, determined by local preferences. After the achievement of independence, however, in most of those states which continued such arrangements, the 'establishments' were multiple, in the sense that material aid and official recognition were given to more than one denomination. There could, therefore, be local variation within a state (as in New York), depending on the loyalties of each township or community. In practice, this inevitably meant that the established religion was Protestant, in some broad sense, and that the terms Protestant and Christian therefore became interchangeable in constitutional language. State assistance, that is, financial aid directly by taxes levied or approved by each of the constituent states of the federation, and official recognition (through the use of buildings, and on civic occasions) could be and were given to local churches, to their activities and to the schools which they founded or supported. Schools in the colonial period were (of course) Christian schools, of whatever Protestant denomination, and the Roman Catholic and other minority communities (such as the Jews) might accommodate themselves as well as they could. This was the historical background taken for granted in the early years of the Republic, when the early amendments to the Constitution were being drafted. It was assumed that states and local communities would continue to support religious activities (including education), and if they wished, preserve various entrenched forms of establishment.[3]

The Framers would certainly have been surprised by the uses to which the First Amendment was much later to be put. The core of their intention must have been to insulate the Federal Government from being unacceptably influenced by religious partisanship, or even – in the sprit of Roger Williams – to protect religion from political interference by a central government the very existence of which was viewed with some apprehension.[4] Most of the disputed questions which were later referred to the Supreme Court in fact arose not because of some alleged transgression by central government in Washington but from the direct or indirect actions of states. It would, however, require the upheaval of a civil war before, in the name of the First Amendment, any such restriction on the powers of the *Federal* Government would or could be applied to the states themselves. That Federal Government could, of course, itself exercise only those powers which had been formally and specifically committed to it by the states, acting collectively. These were the so-called 'enumerated' powers detailed in the Constitution, and plainly, matters of religion were not included among them. Religion lay exclusively within the powers of the states. The original intentions underlying the establishment clause of the First Amendment therefore related only to laws which Congress might pass. The amendment was not designed to prescribe or limit the policies of the various states, which would be certain to differ in matters related to such locally sensitive issues as religious observance and official involvement in it. Most of the states incorporated in their constitutions provisions which directly address such questions and, at least until the 1830s, various forms of establishment continued to be sanctioned by them.

This originally clear distinction between the powers of the states and the rights and duties of the federal authority was blurred by Section 1 of the Fourteenth Amendment, finally ratified in 1868 in the aftermath of the Civil War. That amendment was broadly intended to extend to citizens of all the states, and especially those which had espoused slavery, the rights enjoyed by all American citizens by virtue of their being American. Such rights could no longer be limited by any of the states. It was therefore stipulated that:

No State shall make or enforce any law which shall abridge the privileges or immunities of citizens of the United States; nor shall any State deprive any person of life, liberty, or property, without due process of law; nor deny to any person within its jurisdiction the equal protection of the laws.

Whatever the implications of this for the establishment clause, it was apparent that the rights conferred on all citizens by the free exercise clause must in principle extend to embrace religious activities throughout the United States, whatever state laws or constitutions might have to say on the matter. Over time, various rights enumerated in the Constitution and its amendments and in federal legislation were extended to apply to the states as well (notably, of course, in matters not included within the enumerated powers of the central government). The First Amendment's protection of free speech was first so extended in 1925 to embrace legislation and actions by the states. The free exercise clause of that same First Amendment was subsequently so incorporated by a ruling of the Supreme Court in 1940, in terms which, moreover, assumed, without arguing the matter, a parallel restraint on the powers of the states in matters relating to the slippery notion of 'establishment'.[5] That assumption was to prove of fundamental importance when the Supreme Court in 1947 turned its attention to that very question, and produced a landmark judgment.

The notion of establishment may properly be described as slippery for a number of good reasons. It has been powerfully argued that the Framers (and not only Jefferson, who was in any case in Paris at the time of the debates on the wording of the First Amendment) must have had in mind a broad and relatively open definition of the meaning of the term. Their experience of establishment, since the declaration of independence from Britain, had included its plural as well as its singular form, as has been claimed above. Although this was not a distinction of central importance in the early Court cases dealing with relations between Church and State in the field of education, and did not directly arise in the 1947 case to which reference has already been made, it was to be a substantial bone of contention as adjustments of all kinds were made to the theory and practice of the separation of Church and State in America. Accommodationists insisted, and insist, that the First Amendment had been designed only to prohibit the monopolistic form of establishment and that, in that case, all kinds of other accommodations between diverse churches and different states are legitimate, and indeed desirable (as in the public financing of hospitals or welfare agencies with a distinctive religious character). Such critics (who have included several members of a frequently divided Supreme Court) take a narrow view of what the First Amendment – progressively extended by the

Fourteenth Amendment to apply to actions by the states – was meant to mean, and now means. They can therefore argue that the original intention of the amendment was to forbid only the preference by Congress of any religion over and above any other, in spite of the fact that the 'establishment' of which those same draftsmen had experience was in many cases already multiple. It was therefore argued that only this narrow and exclusive form of establishment was forbidden (at first to the Federal Government, and later, of course, by extension, to all the states). Such accommodationists are therefore often described, with equal inelegance, as nonpreferentialists.

Everson versus Ewing Township – the fundamentally important case argued in 1947 before the Supreme Court – lies at the heart of all subsequent interpretations of what the Constitution permitted or forbade in terms of the relationship between Church and State in America. The judgment then handed down was, from the beginning, controversial and not least because for most scholars and historians it concealed deep, and to this day unresolved, ambiguities. Its more immediate effect was to heighten the emerging tensions between Catholics and the advocates of public education, and therefore to delay for twenty years any major extension of federal support for education. At the end of World War II, education was not in any substantial sense a primary concern of the Federal Government: its provision and supervision were, as they essentially remain at the beginning of the twenty-first century, a responsibility of each of the states. The national government did, of course, from time to time and when national interests were deemed to be at stake, assist those states in promoting various kinds of education. As early as 1785, in the Northwest Ordinance, the Confederation provided for a section of land to be set aside to furnish financial support for the provision of a public school in each township. In 1862, the Morrill Act similarly provided federal land to fund the creation in each state of colleges specialising in the agricultural and mechanical arts. But these were categorical provisions for the support of local efforts in promoting public institutions.

The situation changed dramatically after World War II when the states needed (even if they resented that necessity and the conditions and control inseparable from it) support from Washington in building up an adequate national system of education. The GI Bill, which doubled the size of the university population in the states, was a massive intervention of this kind: the support for war veterans was delivered directly to them as students, and not, of course, to the state treasuries or to the institutions – public and private – receiving these newly funded students. Nevertheless, these grants represented a massive, even if formally indirect, federal subsidy to the educational system as a whole. Other forms of assistance from Washington had been made available for many years, especially under a range of welfare programmes. Free lunches were provided for poor children attending school, regardless of whether the school attended was public or private. The entitlement was exercised on behalf of the child, not the institution. The same principle was invoked by the Supreme Court as early as 1930, when it applied this same 'child benefit' doctrine to justify the purchase of textbooks for children attending sectarian schools. This theory was to play an essential part in demonstrating the permeability of the allegedly secure watertight wall of separation between Church and State. Payments could be made to Catholics because they were American children, with the same rights and entitlements as all other young citizens, just as they could be made to veterans of World War II to pursue their higher education regardless of their religious affiliations. But payments could not, separationists urged, be made directly to denominationally based elementary or secondary schools, for even if more than one denomination were allowed to benefit from such support this would constitute an 'establishment of religion'.

Between 1937 and 1941, a bitter struggle unfolded in the New Jersey legislature. A proposed new law, supported by Catholics and other groups which maintained their own schools for their own members, would allow school districts to pay for the transport of students to denominational as well as to public schools. Such a measure was strongly and predictably opposed by the National Education Association and by all those groups which resented any effort to divert, as they saw it, public funds from public to private schools. When the law was finally passed, the battle moved from the legislature to the courts. Everson, acting on behalf of and supported by a number of sympathetic groups, complained that the township of Ewing was using tax dollars contributed by him and others for an improper purpose. The New Jersey Supreme Court (which, in spite of its name, was not the highest court of the state) ruled that the new law must be struck down, on the grounds that it violated the state's own constitution. That constitution, in common with those of many of the states, included a clause designed to fortify the wall of separation between Church and State. Many such clauses were closely modelled on the wording of the so-called Blaine amendment, which had begun life as an attempt (finally abandoned in 1875) to modify the federal Constitution itself. It became a useful template for states which did want to entrench separation, and after 1876 Congress required all new states seeking admission to the Union to include some such provision in their constitutions. The first New Jersey court decision was, nevertheless, overturned by a higher state court in May 1945. *Everson* was set on its course towards the mainstream of the American debate.

Public attention was now focused on what had been a local issue. The Church and State question now became a matter of national concern and arbitration, as it had long been in most European countries, and notably in France and England. The Catholic side therefore enlisted the support of their national organisations as well as the authoritative counsel of the Jesuit scholar, John Courtney Murray, whose writings were to have significant impact on the evolution over the years of the national debate, and who later had a profound influence on the development of Catholic policy on Church-State matters at the Second Vatican Council. The National Education

115

Association and the American Civil Liberties Union were similarly engaged on the other side of the argument. The Supreme Court ruled that the New Jersey law was indeed constitutional, but did so by the narrowest of margins (voting five to four) and employing arguments which, in the longer term, confused rather than resolved the basic issues. In particular, Justice Hugo L. Black, in speaking for the majority, placed the ruling of the Court against a background of strong separationist language, incorporating the establishment clause of the First within the context of the Fourteenth Amendment. He declared:

> The 'establishment of religion' clause of the First Amendment means at least this: Neither a state nor the Federal Government can set up a church. Neither can pass laws which aid one religion, aid all religions, or prefer one religion over another. ... No tax in any amount, large or small, can be levied to support any religious activities or institutions, whatever they may be called, or whatever forms they may adopt to teach or practice religion. Neither a state nor the Federal Government can, openly or secretly, participate in the affairs of any religious organizations or groups and vice versa. In the words of Jefferson, the clause against establishment of religion by laws was intended to erect a 'wall of separation between Church and State'.[6]

Nevertheless, the judicial majority held that the New Jersey law did not in fact breach this formidable wall, since no taxes were by that law diverted to a religious organisation: the money went to the families of the children who benefited, to enable them to enjoy the same rights (of free travel to the chosen school) as all other children of the community. Although the Court did not, of course, formally contradict itself, it did appear to deploy one set of arguments to elevate a wall of separation, and another to circumvent it. Moreover, an *obiter dictum* of the Court (*Cantwell, 1940*) on the applicability of the Fourteenth Amendment to the establishment (and not just the free exercise) clause of the First Amendment had now become a formal holding of that Court. A Jeffersonian definition of the wall of separation (to which there was, of course, no reference in any of the foundational texts, and which appeared in a letter written by him in 1802 to the Danbury Baptist Association) now seemed to enjoy the blessing of the Supreme Court, the ultimate arbiter of the Constitution. But at the same time, and after a long and noisy public struggle, public money was in fact to be used to transport Catholic children to Catholic schools. The built-in tensions of the judgment, and the contradicting opinions expressed by a dissenting minority which had been only narrowly defeated, ensured that the fight would long continue. John Courtney Murray sagely remarked, 'We have won on bussing, but lost on the First Amendment'.[7]

'Now will Protestants Awake?' was the question thrown at its readers in February 1947 by the *Christian Century*, a paper of centrist and moderately liberal persuasions. Its editor, referring to the recent outcome of the *Everson* case, warned that Catholics were using such apparently insignificant matters as bus fares 'as the thin edge of the wedge which would ultimately crack open the Constitution and give the Church the privileged position in the United States which it professedly seeks'. The 'ultimate character of American culture' was at risk.[8] The foundation of the powerful and watchful association of Protestants and other Americans United for the Separation of Church and State was a direct response to the *Everson* judgment. The association, having since tactfully dropped the first three words of its original title, remains actively influential to this day. In the course of the following months, Paul Blanshard wrote a series of articles, which when published in book form in 1948 became a best seller, going through twenty-six printings. With the unambiguous title, *American Freedom and Catholic Power*, it attacked the Church for being undemocratic and for seeking to impose its views on divorce and many other matters. Catholic establishments were denounced as 'a system of segregated schools under costumed religious teachers'. He concluded, in terms that Archbishop John Ireland would have understood only too well, that the 'struggle between American democracy and the Catholic hierarchy depends upon the survival and expansion of the public school'.[9] Although Francis Cardinal Spellman, the Cardinal Archbishop of New York, and the most nationally prominent and respected of the Catholic clergy, rejected any such crude definition of the conflict, he too soon found himself at the heart of the battle.

The temperature was further raised when, in the following year, the Supreme Court declared unconstitutional the widely observed practice of allowing Catholic priests and ministers of other denominations to visit schools in order to give religious instruction. The Supreme Court ruled, in a case related to the practice in Champaign, Illinois, that such activities breached the separation requirements of the First Amendment. Justice Frankfurter wrote: 'Designed to serve as perhaps the most powerful agency for promoting cohesion among a heterogeneous democratic people, the public schools must keep scrupulously free from entanglement in the strife of sects'. The preservation of that society therefore required 'strict confinement of the State to instruction other than religious, leaving to the individual's church and home, indoctrination in the faith of his choice'. This was strong language indeed, and a far cry from the prevailing assumptions of the nineteenth, and indeed the first half of the twentieth, century. Four years later, the Court softened its position, but only slightly, by agreeing that students could be 'released' for such religious instruction provided that it was given away from the public school premises and at the end of the regular school day. This represented a small kink in the serpentine wall of separation, but allowed Justice William O. Douglas, in delivering the judgment of the six member majority of the Court, to use language significantly different in tone from that of Justice Frankfurter and frequently quoted with approval by those who take an accommodationist position. The prohibition of the establishment clause he described as absolute, but immediately observed that this does not mean 'that in every and all respects there shall be a separation of church and state'. Otherwise, how could the Court itself begin its session with the petition, 'God save the United States and this Honorable Court'? 'We are a religious people whose institutions presuppose a Supreme Being ... we find no constitutional requirement which makes it necessary for a government to be hostile to religion and to throw its weight against efforts to widen the effective scope of religious influence'.[10]

In 1948, the year after *Everson*, President Truman was elected and at the same time his Democratic Party secured a majority in Congress. Yet, all his efforts to pass legislation to provide financial support for schools failed: the National Education Association and its many allies would not support any such legislation if it included any form of support for Catholic schools; the Catholic lobby would equally oppose any legislation which excluded their schools from any intended benefits. They understood well enough that if considerable federal funds went to the public schools, and none to their own hard-pressed establishments, they could not long survive as a significant educational and social force. Eleanor Roosevelt, the widow of the former President and a passionate advocate of the public school cause, became embroiled in a newspaper exchange with Cardinal Spellman, who accused her of writing 'documents of discrimination unworthy of an American mother'.[11] He later apologised for his language, but not his sentiments. The situation was deadlocked throughout the 1950s, and the efforts of Republican President Eisenhower were frustrated, just as those of his Democratic predecessor had been. Southern politicians, who understood well enough that federal aid would be delivered only with conditions requiring their constituents to desegregate their schools, joined forces with many conservatives. The persistence of the Church/State problem assisted them in resisting all new proposals for federal aid to schools. The Eisenhower administration was, however, able to make some limited progress. As a result of the cold war, communist Russia replaced papist Rome as the bogeyman of the popular American imagination. Who could show greater zeal for passionate patriotism than the Roman Catholic Senator McCarthy in his campaign against Communists? The successful launching of *Sputnik* was perceived as a direct threat to America and generated a mood of panic. The National Defense Education Act (a revealing title) allowed grants to be made, through the states of course, for the teaching of science, mathematics and modern languages. Grants of this kind could be paid for the teaching of students in non-public, predominantly Catholic, schools as well as to those attending public schools. This obviously represented a significant extension, directly into the field of instruction, of the 'child benefit' theory, as it had previously been applied to transport and welfare payments. Would the 1960 victory of John Fitzgerald Kennedy, the first Roman Catholic to reach the White House, make it possible to extend still further the reach of this doctrine? Would a national interest in raising educational standards enable the President and his allies in Congress to extend federal assistance to local schools of all kinds, Catholic as well as public?

Kennedy needed to make it clear from the beginning that he would be neither a puppet of the Catholic hierarchy nor a servant of any sectarian interests. Speaking against any direct funding of Catholic schools at his press conference on 1 March 1961, the newly installed President asserted, 'It is prohibited by the Constitution and the Supreme Court has made that very clear'.[12] Cardinal Spellman, who had forgotten none of the old battles, remained unyielding in his opposition to any federal proposals which would give aid only to public schools and, in the tragically short months before the assassination of the President in 1963, very little progress was made. Not all the bishops supported the Spellman line, while most of the Protestant and Jewish groups supported Kennedy's proposals, fearing the consequences of an entanglement of religious with political issues. Cardinal Cushing of Boston warned Kennedy in prescient terms that, if the Catholics secured the kinds of subsidies that Spellman and others were demanding, many other religious groups would claim equal treatment by the State: 'If this should happen we believe that our American democracy would be impaired by the increasing fragmentation of education with its inevitable result of cultural fragmentation'.[13] Five national Jewish organisations proudly proclaimed, 'We deem the maintenance and furtherance of the Jewish religion to be the responsibility of the Jewish community, a responsibility which we have no desire to impose upon the American taxpayer'.[14] Such sentiments recalled the language used long before by Benjamin Franklin: 'When a religion is good, I conceive it will support itself; when it does not support itself, and God does not take care to support it so that its professors are obliged to call for help from the civil power, 'tis a sign, I apprehend, of its being a bad one'.[15]

The presidential and legislative elections of November 1964 strengthened the determination and capacity of Lyndon Johnson to press ahead with his proposals for federal aid to education, and to extend to the Catholics and other religious groups at least some of the federal benefits to be enjoyed by the public schools. Such proposals were made more palatable by being directly linked to the President's war on poverty, and the legislation was successfully pushed forward, in spite of the persistent doubts and anxieties of some Catholics (for whom not enough was conceded) and of public school advocates (in whose eyes the wall of separation was being made ever more permeable). The Catholic school system was in many senses more buoyant than it had ever been, and enrolments reached a peak in the 1960s. At the same time, financial pressures were growing even faster, exacerbated by the decline in religious vocations and the consequent disappearance from the schools of a large and inexpensive workforce. Although aid by the states had grown steadily, it could never be sufficient, and was restrained and constantly challenged by legal appeals based upon the varying constitutions of each of those states. In the 1960s, twenty-five states were granting aid in some form or other to Catholic education. Twenty-three provided, under various limiting conditions, free transport. Eight furnished textbooks for students in Catholic schools. Three supplemented the salaries of teachers in those schools to subsidise instruction in secular subjects only (although, as will appear, this practice was soon to be challenged and outlawed by the Supreme Court), while one indirectly supported the payment of tuition fees by a tuition tax credit applied to state income tax. The Catholic authorities, who correctly saw themselves as offering in some cities (such as Chicago) an indispensable and substantial supplement to public education, insisted on the need for much more help in delivering what was, they argued, essentially a public service.

The Elementary and Secondary Education Act of 1965, duly reauthorised at regular intervals until it finally expired in 2000, was the largest and most significant piece of federal legislation on education ever introduced. Whereas the National Defense Education Act had provided categorical aid designed to strengthen American society against the military and technological threats of the Soviets, the 1965 Act was aimed specifically at the reduction of poverty and inequity in the United States. That obviously made it less vulnerable to attack from a separationist position, and it sat firmly in the noble tradition of the Civil Rights Act of the previous year. Under Title I of the new Act, federal funds were distributed under carefully regulated conditions by the states to assist students who were disadvantaged or underprivileged. Handicap could be physical, economic, social, or emotional in nature, and complex measures were developed to identify as objectively as possible the level of financial assistance which school districts should be entitled to receive. It was the statutory responsibility of the school district, and therefore of the school board and superintendent, to ensure that such entitlements to aid were available to students in all schools, private and parochial as well as public. This federal insistence on the involvement of the district, and indeed the state, offered some reassurance to those who were concerned about the possible long-term consequences of legislative and financial changes which might, intentionally or not, serve to undermine the public system itself. The aid granted lay within the enlarging and flexible rubric of 'child benefit', and could be available for 'shared time' arrangements. Students from Catholic and other schools could under such arrangements attend for instruction on public school premises by public school teachers, or public school teachers could be paid to teach (for secular subjects only, of course) students on Catholic school premises. In 1947, *Everson* permitted public funds to be used to bus students to Catholic schools. The 1965 Act was drafted to allow such funds (in this case federal) to be used to pay for the teaching by public school teachers of secular subjects to Catholic students in Catholic schools. These significant concessions were to be the source of major controversy in interpretation and application, for at least the rest of the century. Title II made provision, within the same administrative framework, for the use of federal funds to purchase textbooks for students in schools of all kinds. Title III made similar provision for supplementary teaching and support in specially designated centres. The level of federal support for Catholic schools, or more correctly, of course, for students in Catholic schools, was thus raised to new heights, while at the same time the principle of separation of Church and State as celebrated in the general statements of the *Everson* court was, in formal terms at least, scrupulously maintained.

The 'Catholic school question' was now embedded more deeply than ever in national politics and in the manoeuvres of Washington where, for the time being at least, the focus of conflict and its resolution shifted from the Supreme Court to the two houses of Congress. The American Church and State question now began, therefore, to look a little more like its remote French and English cousins. President Nixon was an open advocate not only of tuition tax credits (which had never been available at the federal level) but also of vouchers, promoted to assist families wishing to purchase education in private schools of their choice. Over one hundred bills to promote such policies during his controversial administration failed. Under President Carter, one such bill was eventually passed in the House of Representatives – only to be defeated in the Senate: the President had in any case warned that he would have used his veto against it. The extension of financial aid to private schools became a sharp dividing line between the two parties. Presidents Reagan and Bush were outspoken in their defence of the voucher principle, but enjoyed no more success than had Nixon. William Bennett, the vehemently conservative Secretary for Education in Washington, spoke his mind at a meeting of the National Catholic Education Association in April 1989, praising the virtues of the Catholic schools, and articulating the hope that they might secure financial support.[16] In the previous year, he had suggested that the Catholic schools were so successful in dealing with the least privileged and most difficult students that they should be encouraged and funded to admit from the public sector between 5 and 10% of their own intake.[17] But the advocates of the public school were resolutely unwilling to allow the wall to be pushed back (or forward) any further, and the close ties between the National Education Association and the Democratic Party ensured that the political deadlock would continue. President Clinton, throughout his presidency from 1993 to 2001, proved to be a consistent and determined opponent of vouchers and their use to subsidise Catholic schools. The main arena for the national debate now shifted back through the states to the courts, and therefore ultimately to the Supreme Court itself.

Among the states that had used their own tax funds to pay supplements to the salaries of teachers in Catholic schools, on the understanding (surely not easy to verify) that these extra sums were for the teaching of secular and not religious subjects, were Pennsylvania and Rhode Island. The case of *Lemon v. Kurtzman* (1971), arising from an effort to challenge this practice in those states, made its way to the Supreme Court where the Justices ruled that it was unconstitutional to make payments of this kind. The National Catholic

Education Association had entered an *amicus curiae* petition in this case, hoping to loosen the grip on practice of a strict *Everson* interpretation of the law, but the argument was lost. The Court, by a substantial majority, ruled that the practice of paying such supplementary salaries was unlawful on the grounds that it involved the Government in 'excessive entanglement' in the affairs of a religious denomination, and so violated the establishment clause of the First Amendment. The Justices took the opportunity of enlarging on this ruling, and in effect manufactured what came to be known as 'the Lemon test', which came to occupy a significant place in the development of First Amendment jurisprudence. This was a triple test, in which the two first elements had already been made explicit. The first part requires that an act has a secular purpose (and on this point the paying of supplementary salaries for the teaching of secular subjects appeared to be in principle acceptable). The second part requires that the act must have a principal or primary effect that neither advances nor inhibits religion. The majority ruled that the contested arrangements did in effect advance religion. The third – and newly articulated – element in the test further requires that no such act should excessively entangle government in regulating the affairs of a religion. It was held that since the necessary monitoring of the complex arrangements did require such activity and on a considerable scale, the arrangements would fall foul of the First Amendment as the Court now interpreted it. Chief Justice Warren Burger, speaking for the Court, declared religion to be 'a private matter for the individual, the family, and the institutions of private choice', and not for government. A Justice speaking for the minority drew attention to the paradox generated by such a ruling: the State cannot finance secular instruction if it allows religion to be taught in the same classroom; but if it prohibits such a mixing of the secular and the religious, it of necessity becomes – as the regulatory power – excessively entangled in the affairs of a religion, and that is not permissible either. This, to a European, sounds a little like Morton's Fork, with a third prong added for good measure.[18]

Three years later, the Court disallowed tuition tax credits, and in 1985 an even more strict reading of the Lemon test was applied in *Aguilar v. Felton*. The specific cases raised before the Court arose from litigation in New York City and Grand Rapids, Michigan. Since 1966 these two districts, in common with many others, had made use of Title I funds under the Elementary and Secondary Education Act of the previous year in order to provide remedial teaching in parochial schools. The instruction was delivered by public school teachers, not by any employees of the Catholic system, care was taken to ensure that religious symbols were removed from any room in which such government funded teaching was taking place, and elaborate arrangements were enforced to ensure that all these regulations were scrupulously observed. The paradox embedded in the *Lemon* judgment was exposed, and once again the Court was itself divided. Justice William Brennan, speaking for the majority and at that time the only Roman Catholic on the bench, emphasised the 'excessive entanglement' inevitably required by the necessary monitoring. Chief Justice Warren Burger was with the minority and, abandoning judicial civility, detected in the conclusions of his brethren attitudes bordering on 'paranoia'. It was, he protested, wrong to see the Pope lurking behind such programmes. The judgments of his own Court revealed 'nothing less than hostility toward religion and the children who attend church-sponsored schools'.[19] Justices O'Connor, White and Rehnquist voted with the Chief Justice. With divisions as open and deep as this, it is not surprising that the public regarded the fundamental issues as continuing to be contentious and unresolved. A heavy price continued to be paid for the ambiguities of *Everson*, and when in the 1990s further voucher schemes and experiments were launched by some states, the issues became even more difficult and uncertain.

In 1993, some modest encouragement was given to those who argued for justice, as they understood it, for children in Catholic and other non-public schools: in the *Zobrest* case, the Court tempered some of its own rigour. Once again ruling by the narrowest of majorities (5:4), the Justices allowed public funding for a sign language interpreter for a deaf child attending a non-public school. The majority argued with some ingenuity that in this specific case there was no risk of public funds being used for any form of religious indoctrination: a signer was not the same as a teacher, since her only function was to translate accurately what was said in the class, whether that teaching was religious or not. The Catholic establishment again entered an *amicus curiae* brief. In this case, unlike *Aguilar*, the child benefit theory was applied. This was one of three such cases in the 1990s in which the Court was divided 5:4. Chief Justice Warren Burger had previously remarked, noting the history of narrow margins in critical cases before the Court, that 'five votes can do anything round here'.[20] Justice Sandra Day O'Connor observed that the case before them revealed the conflict between the two bedrock principles, as she called them, of 'no aid' and non-discrimination. In 1994, the Court heard a more complicated case affecting a Jewish Hasidic community. Although this community had established its own distinctive and privately funded school district, there was no provision for special educational needs. In theory, therefore, students with such needs from within the community were expected to leave the enclosure and attend one of the New York public schools. This opportunity was, for obvious reasons, refused by many families and the City of New York therefore proposed that a separate school district be established, exclusively to provide special education for the children of the Hasidic Jewish community, known as Kiryas Joel. There were, of course, challenges, and the United States Catholic Conference, recognising the importance of the principles at stake, again entered an *amicus curiae* brief before the Supreme Court. In the case of *Grumet* (1994), a divided Supreme Court ruled against the public funding of what was in effect a pervasively sectarian school district, albeit one manufactured for special purposes. Although the circumstances were, of course, significantly different, the fact remains that in *Zobrest* the Court weakened the wall of separation whereas in *Grumet* it reinforced it. The complexity and persistence of such divisions among the justices moved the Court towards the exceptional step of agreeing to reopen a file, in this case that of *Aguilar*. This was agreed in 1997 after requests from the administrations of President Clinton and of New York City.

No fewer than five of the Justices in *Grumet* had already suggested that the *Aguilar* judgment should be reviewed. The prohibition of the employment, under any conditions, of government employees in sectarian schools was no longer appropriate, and went beyond a proper reading of the implicit and explicit requirements of the First Amendment, as reinterpreted by the Lemon threefold test. In *Agostini*, and yet again by the narrowest and least convincing of a 5:4 majority (O'Connor, Rehnquist, Scalia, Kennedy and Thomas against the dissenting Souter, Stevens, Ginsburg and Breyer), the Court in June 1997 reversed its own *Aguilar* judgment. More recent cases decided by the Court had quite obviously undermined that original and apparently absolute ruling against the presence of government employees in sectarian schools. Such a presence did not of and by itself serve to advance religion, as *Zobrest* had shown. Moreover, the Court had previously erred in discerning excessive entanglement of the Government and religion in the arrangements made in New York City. Monitoring and control were always and necessarily involved in the expenditure of any Title I funds, and there was in this sense no significant difference between the procedures adopted for the expenditure of such funds on students in public and students in parochial schools. The Lemon test had therefore not been failed. The expenses of applying the rules of *Aguilar* had indeed been high: they were estimated at $100m incurred since the 1983 ruling, and since those costs had to be deducted from and not added to the federal grant, the result had been that Title I services had been withdrawn from 35% of the students who would otherwise have received them. The heavy costs had included the expenses of purchasing and maintaining vans – provided in order that Title I instruction could be given outside the gates of parochial schools – and computers, which could legally be bought with public funds and then installed in parochial schools. The majority therefore concluded that the arrangements in force before 1983 could now be restored on the grounds that under them 'No Title I funds ever reach the coffers of religious schools'.[21]

Speaking for the minority, Souter objected that the result of this mistaken ruling was 'to repudiate the very reasonable line drawn in *Aguilar* and *Ball*, and to authorize direct state aid to religious institutions on an unparalleled scale, in violation of the Establishment Clause's central prohibition against religious subsidies by the government. I respectfully dissent'. The minority further argued that the procedures of the Court had been erroneous: it should not have taken the exceptional (and, on the grounds as alleged, unprecedented) step of rehearing a case which had already been settled. Rather, it should (as in the past) have waited for the arrival of another case to come before it, which would raise closely similar issues, and then deliver what would in effect be a new ruling. Several such cases were – indeed always were – on their way to the Supreme Court. Only if the facts of the case had changed (and they had not) should the Court have agreed to rehear an old case, and to reverse itself. Moreover, the majority had ignored the distinction on which *Zobrest* had been based: namely, that a signer was not a teacher. No such claim was made for the publicly employed teachers who could now constitutionally give instruction in parochial schools. A 'flat ban', Souter argued, should be maintained on subsidisation. He appealed to the experience of other countries as well the history of his own to justify this fundamental prohibition:

> *This rule expresses the hard lesson learned over and over again in the American past and in the experiences of the countries from which we have come, that religions supported by government are compromised just as surely as the religious freedom of dissenters is burdened when the government supports religion.*

Even the nine justices of the Supreme Court, for all their prestige and accumulated wisdom, could not agree that American history and comparative studies did in fact demonstrate that government should not support religion. Nor could the Court arrive at a clear and definitive ruling on the place of religion in American schools of all kinds. The one principle on which judges at all levels did seem to be unanimous was that the courts remained the right place in which to explore and determine such fundamental questions. Courts would determine whether religious schools should be publicly supported, and whether religion should have any acknowledged place in the public schools as well.

II

Religion, Public Schools, and Public Life

No one could accuse the citizens of the United States of not being deeply serious about religion. Nor could it be claimed that they agreed with one another about what that religion should be, or on how it should be related to the various manifestations of the civil power. The largest American denomination, the Roman Catholic, had during the nineteenth and twentieth centuries established a formidable system of separate schooling, stretching from the early years of childhood to the most advanced levels of university graduate work. For some parts of this effort, and under carefully regulated and warmly contested conditions, the Catholics received considerable support from tax dollars, provided that the purposes to which those funds were applied were not deemed to be 'pervasively sectarian'. But the maintenance of a supposedly Jeffersonian wall of separation between Church and State apparently required that no funds should go directly to those schools (or, to be more precise, to elementary and secondary schools). The

Roman Catholic motives for maintaining a largely separate school system, in parallel with the smaller systems established by other groups, originally reflected a deep unease with the inherently and essentially Protestant character of the American public schools. Those Catholic motives changed significantly as the public schools themselves became steadily less pious and more secularised, in something like the French sense of proclaiming formal neutrality. Catholics then objected, with demonstrably good reason, that while the public schools may indeed have ceased to be Protestant, they had in that process become detached from or even hostile towards all that was represented by religion and a religious culture. The logic of the Supreme Court required that this should be so: a logical corollary of the refusal of public funding for or endorsement of sectarian education was the judicial insistence that public schools themselves become strictly neutral – neutral not only between one religion and another but equally between religion and non-religion. Its rulings had the effect of making most schools even less religious than they had once been, and therefore motivating a smaller but nevertheless considerable number of private and parochial schools to become more clearly identified with a powerful and distinctive religious tradition. Deep tensions were therefore generated, complicated by the growth, mostly representing a determined reaction against the growing secularisation of the public school, of new 'Christian' schools. Such schools reflected an ideology very different from that associated with the Catholic tradition in American education, and marked by an emphasis on fundamentalist and evangelical values. They nevertheless shared with the longer established Catholic tradition an interest in securing some official financial support, provided always that this could be won without any sacrifice of their religious integrity. The issue was further complicated by anxieties, more evident in the Christian than in the Catholic schools, about the school curriculum, about the relationship between Darwinian and biblical understandings of the creation of the universe, and (with increasing sharpness) about the values underlying much of the teaching in the dominant public schools.

The 1947 *Everson* judgment stands at the source of a stream of judicial decisions which, for many members of a deeply religious nation, had the effect of severing the public school from its roots in the religion of the Founders, and in the nation-building efforts of Horace Mann and his nineteenth-century sympathisers. The reasoning of the Supreme Court, although not, of course, its conclusion in that particular case, raised and strengthened the wall of separation. Within a few years, as has been shown above, ministers of religion lost the privilege of relatively free access to the public schools where they had been allowed to offer religious instruction to members of their own congregations. Determined rebels against an implicitly prevailing American Protestant orthodoxy soon recognised a golden opportunity to challenge what was for them the continuing indoctrination of young Americans in a faith or ideology of which they profoundly disapproved. The American Civil Liberties Union was on hand to assist in the framing of legal actions. In 1963, the Supreme Court ruled that Bible reading and the recitation in public schools of the Lord's Prayer were both unconstitutional, although Justice Brennan opined that silent prayer would probably not fall under such a ban. About half of the states subsequently adopted laws requiring or allowing such periods of silence. Others had already attempted to avoid legal or constitutional difficulties by embracing in some broad and non-sectarian formulary the essence of a traditional if undemanding form of religious belief. The Regents of the State of New York, exercising an overall responsibility for education in that state, had devised such a prayer: 'Almighty God, we acknowledge our dependence upon Thee, and we beg Thy blessings upon us, our parents, our teachers and our Country'. But the Supreme Court would have none of it, and Justice Black wrote for the majority that:

> We think that the constitutional prohibition against laws respecting an establishment of religion must at least mean that in this country it is no part of the business of government to compose official prayers for any group of the American people to recite as part of a religious program carried on by government. It is a matter of history that this very practice of establishing governmentally composed prayers for religious services was one of the reasons which caused many of our early colonists to leave England and seek religious freedom in America.

The Court's reading of history may be dubious, but its ruling was clear.[22] Sponsored prayer now became an offence against the establishment clause of the First Amendment.

The Supreme Court of the 1960s represented for many vocal critics all that was most dangerous and corrosive in American society. After the *Engel* decision against school prayer, Senator Robert C. Byrd of West Virginia intoned, 'Can it be that we, too, are ready to embrace the foul concept of atheism? ... Somebody is tampering with America's soul. I leave it to you who that somebody is'. Representative George W. Andrews of Alabama with one broad sweep attacked the Court both for its landmark decision on desegregation and for its prevailing policy towards religion: 'They put the Negroes in the schools, and now they've driven God out'.[23] More surprising, perhaps, was the reaction of Catholics, who had in the past repeatedly objected to such 'non-denominational' practices as the reading of the Protestant version of the Lord's Prayer or the use of the King James Bible. Cardinal Spellman, nearing the end of his long reign in New York, now lamented:

> I am shocked and frightened that the Supreme Court has declared unconstitutional a simple and voluntary declaration of belief in God by public school children. The decision strikes at the heart of the Godly tradition in which America's children have for so long been raised.[24]

These were most definitely the accents of John Ireland rather than of Bernard McQuaid or John Hughes, the Cardinal's own predecessors in New York.

Throughout the closing decades of the twentieth century, America nevertheless continued to be a country marked by a uniquely high degree of religious practice and belief. In the 1980s, nine out of ten Americans claimed that they had never doubted the existence of God. Eight out of ten said they believed that they would be called before God on Judgment Day to answer for their sins. Some 40% of the American population attended church in a typical week, compared with 14% in Great Britain and 12% in France.[25] Such striking differences persist into the twenty-first century and, of course, profoundly affect Church-State policies and public attitudes towards them. The paradox is that the importance of religion in private life grew even as its place in public life was attenuated by judicial decisions. Meanwhile, the disputes surrounding school prayer, in all its many forms, continue unabated, with the establishment and free exercise clauses of the First Amendment often being pitted against each other. In 1985, the Supreme Court struck down an Alabama statute authorising a moment of silence in public schools, while adding (unusually) that the law would have met the tests of constitutionality if it had been differently drafted. The case before the Supreme Court involved three Alabama statutes: one which specified prayer as the overt purpose of the silence was for that reason and by a direct application of the *Engel* principle held to be unacceptable; one which referred to meditation as being the purpose of the silence was, however, acceptable since it did not favour (or disfavour) religion; and one which offered the alternatives of meditation or 'voluntary prayer' was also unacceptable since it failed the first prong of the Lemon test.[26] Moments of silence, if neutrally defined, therefore appeared to be constitutionally acceptable: provided that they had no specifically religious purpose or effect. Twenty-three of the fifty states now have such legislation, in some cases amended after the 1985 ruling.

For those citizens and activists who were fearful of the insidious advance of secularism and who urged the importance of spiritual values in personal life and the public life of the nation, these were small concessions indeed. To some it seemed that the combined effect of the two opening phrases of the First Amendment was to place religion at a peculiar disadvantage: an amendment intended to protect it was in fact being turned against it by an unsympathetic Supreme Court. The Court also began, in its consideration of matters related to religion, to pay more attention to the free speech, as distinct from the free exercise, clauses of the Amendment. This, again, seemed a mixed blessing since it implied that religion was no different from any other human activity or voluntary association, and no longer publicly recognised as unique and distinctive. It will be recalled that the full text of the Amendment is:

> *Congress shall make no law respecting an establishment of religion, or prohibiting the free exercise thereof; or abridging the freedom of speech, or of the press, or the right of the people peaceably to assemble, and to petition the Government for a redress of grievances.*

In 1981, the Court ruled – albeit in the context of a university – that religious groups may not be discriminated against by having facilities for voluntary activities denied to them, simply on the grounds that they are religious. The issue was defined within First Amendment terms as one of free speech, and not of free exercise. Congress, responding to pressures from conservative religious groups and succeeding for once in intervening in the conflictual field of religion, required in the Equal Access Act of 1984 that the same principle of access to facilities generally available in a 'limited public forum' (such as a college or a school) should be extended to high school students. In 1990, the Court concurred by ruling that such a law was indeed constitutional.[27] But at the same time, in interpreting the opening clauses of the Amendment, it continued to lean upon the establishment rather than the free exercise clause, and to appeal to the Lemon test. In 1992, the Court declared unconstitutional the reading of a prayer at high school graduations. The skirmishes continued, surfacing in surprising places: in June 2000, the Supreme Court ruled (this time by six to three) that a prayer recited over the public address system before a university football match in Texas was also unconstitutional.[28]

The temperature of the debate on the relationship between religion and public life (and by implication on the place in that life of religiously affiliated schools) was steeply raised in the preliminaries to the presidential election of 1988. On no previous occasion had religious issues and passions dominated so much of the political argument. Two of the candidates for nomination (Jesse Jackson and Pat Robertson) were ordained ministers. George Bush, as the successful candidate for the Republican nomination, sought to make serviceable alliances with the television evangelists, Jim and Tammy Bakker. Passionate arguments about declaring unconstitutional the burning of the American flag (itself a quasi-religious symbol, associated with the daily recitation in schools of the Pledge) were not understood by the coolly rational Michael Dukakis – the Democratic candidate, who as a Catholic was less politically successful than John F. Kennedy had been in distinguishing between his civic and his religious duties of obedience.[29] The lines of battle were now being redrawn, as the bitter dispute in 1987 about the nomination to the Supreme Court of the controversial Robert Bork had already suggested. (Bork was in the event rejected after the usual Senate hearings intended to confirm the appointment.) The Church-State conflict was now less frequently perceived as being fought between Rome as an alien power and a foreign church on the one hand, and Protestant and patriotic America on the other. The deeper emerging conflict was now between the religious right, as it learned to exercise its new power, and the forces which it blamed for the corruption of America by secular humanism and materialism. Inevitably, however, the Catholic interest would be deeply affected by the outcome of this struggle, as was to appear, for example, in the long debate about vouchers and their potential availability to support the funding of students attending religiously affiliated schools.

Pressures mounted to shift debate and decisions from the judicial to the legislative branch: Congress, after all, was democratically elected, whereas the Supreme Court was not. Yet, it was by nine Justices divided in their opinions that decisions were being taken in circumstances never anticipated by the Framers of the Constitution and the Bill of Rights. This populist urge towards the settlement of religious issues by an elected legislature became even more manifest after the landslide victory of the Republicans in the Congressional elections of 1994, two years into the Clinton presidency. Newt Gingrich and the many enthusiastically new members of the House were determined to correct the drift towards irreligion and old style liberalism. One of their chosen weapons, and perhaps the only one which could in the end outflank even the Supreme Court, was a projected new amendment to the Constitution itself. In 1994, Senator Jesse Helms expressed himself with his usual clarity when he recalled the 1963 *Schemp* judgment, in recalling the name of the woman who had been so effective in bringing the whole issue of school prayer to the Supreme Court:

> *I think it is possible to pinpoint when the decline of this country really began. It began when Madalyn Hunter O'Hair ... conspired with communist attorneys who came to her home to orchestrate the lawsuit that resulted in the first Supreme Court decision banning prayer. [30]*

A 1996 law made all social service activities undertaken by religious organisations eligible for public funding on the same terms as secular providers. Why should a similar pluralist generosity not now be extended to educational activities as well? But the tenacity of the Supreme Court in holding to its interpretations of the First Amendment suggested that this could only be achieved by a new amendment to the Constitution. Several versions of such an amendment were proposed, but the one which came nearest to succeeding read:

> *In order to secure the right of the people to acknowledge and serve God according to the dictates of consciences, neither the United States nor any State shall deny any person equal access to a benefit, or otherwise discriminate against any person, on account of religious belief, expression or exercise. This amendment does not authorize government to coerce or inhibit religious belief, expression, or exercise. [31]*

It was openly argued that, under the protection of such an amendment – whatever its precise relationship to the First Amendment might eventually prove to be – full aid, including, of course, the undisputed use of vouchers, could be extended to Catholic parochial schools as well as to those other sectarian private schools which were by now flourishing. None of the proposed amendments to the Constitution secured the necessary preliminary majorities: the determination of policy therefore remains the prerogative of the Supreme Court.

The push and pull between the legislative and judicial branches of government nevertheless continued, reaching another climax in 1997. The relationship between religion and regulated public life was, as has already appeared, affected by no less than three distinct clauses of the First Amendment: the establishment clause (by which Catholic and other faith-based schools appeared to be most immediately affected), the free speech clause (which had been moderately deployed to secure for religious groups in public schools those same rights enjoyed by all other groups), and the free exercise clause (which specifically protected the rights of religious exercise). In many of its judgments the Court had deployed the free speech (rather than the free exercise) clause – for example, to allow access by religiously affiliated groups to the 'limited public forum' offered within the public school. Free exercise was indeed something quite different from the more general right to free speech (as asserted by Congress in the Equal Access Act and validated by the Supreme Court itself), since it plainly implied that religious rights were of their very nature different from, and presumably superior to, undifferentiated rights of a general kind. The implication of such a doctrine is clear: religion is indeed *sui generis*, and as such to be treated by the law with unique respect. Even at a time when an explicitly religious basis for American society was taken for granted, the Court had, of course, never held that any action whatsoever could, simply on the grounds that it was 'religious', therefore be automatically justified. In the nineteenth century, for example, it had proscribed polygamy on the same grounds that it would have forbidden child sacrifice, as being 'odious' and a threat to society.[32] A significant concession was, however, made to the religious rights of the Amish when, in 1972, they were allowed some exemption from laws of compulsory schooling.[33] Other rulings affected employment laws, and by an application of the free exercise principle Seventh Day Adventists were granted protection from penalties when they refused to accept employment which would have forced them, if they obeyed the laws of their own religion, to break the Sabbath.[34]

The Court had, therefore, accepted what came to be known as a 'balancing' test: rights protected by the free exercise clause (as always to be sharply distinguished from its free speech neighbour) were substantive, and needed to be balanced against more general public interests. If laws had the effect of discriminating against religious interests (whatever the intentions of the legislators), they had to be assessed in the light of the free exercise clause. This remained accepted doctrine until 1990, when the Court startled a wide range of opinion by abandoning it. In this case, it refused to support the claims of two Oregon employees who had been dismissed from their public appointments for using peyote (a prohibited substance) in a sacramental ceremony of the Native American Church.[35] Such a judgment obviously raised doubts about what a similarly disposed Court would have made of the comparable exemption granted to mainline Christian churches during the time of Prohibition. The Court, in denying the appropriateness of any consideration of a 'balancing' kind, appeared to its critics to be demoting religion to the status of any other opinion or practice. It suggested that

American society was becoming more openly irreligious and secular, magnified the anxieties of those who feared the remorseless advance of humanism and atheism in the public schools, and strengthened the resolve of religious groups to provide their own schools and, in the fullness of time, to secure appropriate public funding for them. This 1990 judgment of the Supreme Court presented further ammunition to those who now resumed their ill-fated efforts to secure a new religious freedom amendment of the Constitution, to which reference has already been made.[36]

Its more immediate effect was to stimulate a vigorous campaign to undo the perceived damage which had been inflicted on the exercise of religious liberty. The judgment of the Court had been made yet again by the narrowest of margins, five to four. The four dissenting justices openly expressed their concerns, and a diverse but powerful coalition of interests emerged, ranging from the American Civil Liberties Union to the fundamentalists of the religious right, and including strong Roman Catholic groups. The result was the passing by Congress in 1993 of the Religious Freedom Restoration Act, which in effect re-established the status quo as it had been before the Oregon case of 1990. This was not, however, to be the end of the story. In 1997, when considering a very different case affecting planning regulations as they applied to Catholic church buildings, the Supreme Court overturned the 1993 Act, declaring (this time by a majority of six to three) that Congress had overstepped its powers.[37] For the moment at least, the Supreme Court, flexing its muscles for a sustained campaign against the imperialism of a federal power which it suspected of infringing the rights of states, remained the high place where the final decisions were taken. Those decisions had, for the most part, not been favourable to the cause of the public funding of Catholic and other religious schools, and had not been supportive of the maintenance in the public schools of traditional religious practice (Bible reading and minimal prayer), as Horace Mann at least had understood it and as Cardinal Spellman had defended it. Critics of the Court found little encouragement in its record in an equally contested domain, that of the school curriculum and of the values which it and the teachers reflected. If, as a result of *Everson*, subsidies could not with any confidences be assigned to religiously affiliated schools; if, because of *Schemp*, simple Christian practice was to be banned in the public schools and 'secular humanism' now to be taught there, then how could support be expected for those faith-based schools which many citizens of a pervasively religious country so obviously wanted for their own children?

Throughout the twentieth century, the tensions between an increasingly secular school system on the one hand and, on the other, an actively religious yet divided and diverse society became more acute. The position of the Catholic schools within that enlarging society was directly affected by these tensions, which inevitably led to a sweeping re-evaluation of what those Catholic schools were for, and how they should be supported. Catholic schools, at least in the form that John Hughes rather than John Ireland understood them, had flourished in America as an alternative to, and indeed, an abiding protest against, the common public school. If the nature and ethos of that public school changed, what then? The growth of Evangelical discontent with the public schools provoked at one and the same time the dramatic enlargement of private schools with an assertively Protestant character and, even more immediately, a mood of religious discontent with everything that the schools of Horace Mann had come to represent. At first, much of this discontent focused on questions of teaching and of the curriculum, and in particular on the conflict (as many saw it) between evolutionary theory and a fundamentalist reading of the scriptures, and especially of the Old Testament.

The conflict was and is essentially between those who assert the absolute supremacy on matters of fact of the Bible, and those who believe that scientific method and discovery should lead to a more or less subtle reinterpretation of holy writ. Although it never represented a fully articulated view of the relationship of revealed to scientific truth, 'fundamentalism' (a term which became increasingly common after the publication of an influential book on the subject in 1910) was commonly marked by a staunch belief in the inerrancy of the Bible. From the beginning, therefore, it represented a challenge to Darwinian views of the origins of the universe and of the nature of man.[38] Arguments about the curriculum, about what should be taught in schools and about the relationship between revealed and empirical truth had a long history in the United States. In an effort to preserve traditional orthodoxy, the Tennessee legislature had in 1925 passed a law forbidding the teaching of evolution in the schools of that state. This was the opportunity for both the embattled sides in the debate to make this an issue of central importance for public opinion and national politics. A former presidential candidate, William Jennings Bryan, represented the prosecution in the case against John T. Scopes, who stood formally accused of teaching the forbidden theories. On the side of this somewhat reluctant victim stood the American Civil Liberties Union, which had in effect provoked the prosecution, and Clarence Darrow, the famous advocate. The American Civil Liberties Union had been founded in 1920, and this was to be its first opportunity to become a major player on the national scene. The so-called 'monkey trial' was splashed each day across the front page of the *New York Times*, and reputations were made and lost. Bryan himself died soon after the trial, in which Scopes was found guilty. The American Civil Liberties Union was pleased, sniffing an opportunity to carry an appeal all the way to the Supreme Court. Unfortunately for them, the judgment was soon cancelled by an appeals court, but only on a technicality. As a consequence, nothing had been resolved and the teaching of evolution became the central and defining issue in the long and still unfinished battle between irreconcilably opposed ideological camps. The old consensus, on which the American public school had reposed, was shattered.[39]

The width and depth of the gap which now opened – between fundamentalists and modernisers, between parents with conventional religious views and an apparently unsympathetic and secular educational establishment – did not become apparent until the Supreme Court turned its attention in the 1960s to school prayer and Bible reading. Meanwhile, prudent teachers and administrators quietly ignored the matter, and avoided teaching views which might be offensive. The result was an implicit neglect of much of the science curriculum. It was not until the Soviets successfully launched their sputnik into space in 1957 that an alarmed public insisted upon an increased emphasis on the teaching of science in the schools. Lenin, for the moment at least, came to represent a greater threat than Darwin. In 1966, Arkansas nevertheless passed a law which, by forbidding the teaching of evolution in its schools, raised the old passions that had swirled around the Scopes trial. This time, however, the matter did find its way to the Supreme Court, which two years later declared the Arkansas law unconstitutional, as a clear violation of the establishment clause of the First Amendment.[40]

A battle may have been won, but the war rumbled on as the ideological cracks widened. The powerful and unprecedented intervention of Washington in matters of educational policy, prompted, of course, by the threat of foreign competition or attack, stimulated a long series of educational and curricular reforms – not for the last time in the last century. Outstanding among them were the efforts directed by Jerome Bruner, the distinguished Harvard psychologist. His new programme for schoolchildren (MACOS – 'Man: A Course of Study') might have been wittingly designed to outrage those still nursing the 1968 rebuke of the Supreme Court. Its very title smacked of humanism, its moral values were suspect and deeply relativist, and it came from Massachusetts. In 1975, Senator Jesse Helms secured the cancelling of all federal funds deployed to support it.[41] The Creationists regrouped their forces, now trying to secure equal treatment in the schools for their views alongside the opposing evolutionary interpretations of human origins and development. Arkansas passed such a law in 1981, and on the same day the American Civil Liberties Union filed suit – and won. But the decisive legal response did not come until 1987, when the Supreme Court itself struck down as unconstitutional a similar Louisiana law, also passed in 1981.[42] Just as Catholics had kept their children away from the nineteenth-century public schools where they would have been exposed to the King James Bible, so a century later many fundamentalist Protestants began to withdraw their children from schools which they now perceived as hostile to their own deepest convictions. Like the Catholics before them, however, they also hoped and worked furiously to turn those tainted schools into places where their own children could one day be safe. The Church and State frontier was again changing its shape.

Questions of the content of teaching were now embedded in the political and religious agenda. The old alliance of Evangelicals and Progressives – united in an effort to build a democratic and consensually

Protestant America, and distrustful of Catholic attempts to preserve their own identity – had collapsed. These significant changes were reflected in the 1987 controversy surrounding President Reagan's failed attempt to nominate Robert Bork to the Supreme Court (still the effective arbiter of Church-State relationships). This was also the year of the highly controversial ruling in Alabama by Judge Brevard Hand, who (in response to a composite suit in the name of over six hundred offended fundamentalist parents) condemned forty-four textbooks for promoting the religion of 'secular humanism'. This surprising judgment was promptly overruled by a federal appeals court, which invoked the Lemon test and declared that secular humanism (whatever precisely that may be) was not in itself a religion. It was also the year of the publication of Allan Bloom's *The Closing of the American Mind*, a powerful jeremiad against the degeneration of modern American culture education which reinforced the pessimism that permeated the official report four years before in *A Nation at Risk*. In the following year, as has already been noted, religious issues were salient in the preliminary skirmishes surrounding the presidential election.

The religious attack on a liberal/secular/humanist establishment was, without abandoning the assault on evolution, now being pressed on a much wider front. Teaching methods, it was repeatedly asserted, had themselves become permissive and undermined traditional discipline. Whole language teaching rather than teaching based on facts led to a decline of standards. Scepticism about established values threatened the sanctity of the family and the influence of religion. Patriotic commitments were being corroded, and the classroom left open to infiltration by communist principles. John Dewey was pilloried as the evil genius who inspired such offspring of his subversive ideas as the American Civil Liberties Union, the American Library Association, the National Council for the Teaching of English, the National Education Association itself, and new upstarts formed to resist the advance of the religious right, such as People for the American Way, founded in 1980. Worst of all, many textbooks and classroom practices promoted a heretical affection for New Age religion, tinged with magical beliefs of pagan origin. The success of the Harry Potter books for children in the year 2000 provoked a wave of angry reaction and prohibition. The organisation created by Mel and Norma Gabler scrutinised textbooks, in the hunt for pernicious errors. The Eagle Form was founded in 1972 to defend fundamentalist values. Pat Robertson's Christian Coalition mobilised a wide-ranging effort in the same causes. In the year 1993-94, according to one estimate, there were 462 challenges to textbook adoptions in forty-six states.[43] The adoption of the History Standards, as part of the official educational programme being pursued under the banner of *Goals 2000* provoked a furious row.

The determined critics intended to do much more than change the nature of schoolbooks or restrain the false liberalism of individual teachers. Moreover, some of the battles moved away once more from the courts and into local political arenas. There was, therefore, a drive to take over or, in the terms used by the protagonists, to reclaim the control of the public school system and to restore it to its true and original, fundamentally Protestant, purposes. Ralph Reed, the skilful executive director of the Christian Coalition, made no attempt to conceal such purposes:

> *I honestly believe that in my lifetime we will see a country once again governed by Christians. What Christians have got to do is to take back this country, one precinct at a time, one neighbourhood at a time, and one state at a time.* [44]

Citizens for Excellence in Education, a group affiliated to the National Association of Christian Education, produced a sophisticated 'Public School Awareness' kit, which gave advice on how to secure elections to local School Boards. On one estimate, in 1993 alone this organisation helped to elect 7153 such members. The implications of such an orchestrated effort to reclaim the public school are plain and unambiguous. This effort was, and is, bound to change the ecology of both public and private schools in the United States. Equally important for the private school sector was the dramatic growth of home schooling, and of the so-called 'Christian Schools' openly dedicated to those very sectarian principles which Horace Mann had struggled so hard to resist. It has been estimated that in the late 1970s, some 13,000 children were being educated at home, by their parents and other supporters; by 1988, that modest total had exploded to 225,000 and to an estimated 400,000 in 1993. This growth, of course, reflected more than one tendency: some parents reacted against the bureaucracy of public schooling in the spirit of John Holt, Jonathan Kozol and Ivan Illich. Many more, however, were disenchanted with the public school because of its perceived secular humanism and hostility to religion. Home schooling became something of a movement in its own right, with national organisations to support it and its own journal. Many of the materials used for instruction were shared with the Christian Day Schools, the number of which increased at a similarly dramatic rate. Recent estimates suggest that over one million students are now enrolled in these schools, most of which are distinguished by a reaction against the secular tendencies of the public school system. They have powerful regional and national coordinating agencies, and their growing share of the private school market ensures that questions of public support and funding for Catholic schools can no longer be treated in isolation from wider questions of policy and purpose. [45]

The religious right, as it came to be labelled in the later decades of the last century, defines itself as the most conspicuous guardian of 'cultural conservatism', the power of which politicians learned to neglect at their peril. One observer characterised cultural conservatism as advocating:

> *creation over evolution, private school choice, teaching (or technically, teaching about) religion, implacable hostility to government-imposed standards, the virtues of home schooling, phonics instead of whole*

language, no academic add-ons, emphasis on the basics, and the rest.[46]

Education was central to its message and mission, and remains so. Reference has already been made to the sustained campaign to capture School Boards, and at a time when it was usual for only some 5% of eligible citizens to turn up to vote, their influence often outstripped even the weight of their growing numbers. Towards the end of the 1990s there was some evidence that their power was beginning to wane, and some of their own leaders did indeed appear to turn away from direct political activism, or to lament that the famed 'moral majority' in fact no longer existed in America.[47] Both the National Association of Christian Educators and the Citizens for Excellence in Education were in financial trouble, and the liberal Institute for First Amendment Studies, based in Massachusetts, noted with some satisfaction a decline in the influence of its adversaries. Yet, the troops remained ready to mobilise, in local or national causes, and lost no opportunity of weakening the wall of separation between Church and State. In the last year of the old century, and in the wake of the tragedy at Columbine High School in Colorado, where two students massacred many of their classmates and teachers, there was a flurry of public and political concern. Although efforts in Congress to strengthen the gun laws failed, a powerful coalition did succeed in pressing through amendments to a juvenile justice bill which empowered the states to require the display of the Ten Commandments in public places such as schools. Although challenges in the courts to such requirements can, of course, be anticipated, the legislation itself and the anxious mood it accurately reflects make it more likely that continuing efforts to promote prayer and other religious practices in school will meet with some success. The wall of separation erected by the courts is again shown to be insecure, and the change in the political climate after the bitterly contested presidential election of November-December 2000 (in which the Supreme Court itself played an important part) guaranteed that no questions regarding the relationship between Church and State, especially in matters related to the support of religious schooling in its many forms, can be regarded as definitively settled. This is why the experience of other countries in such disputed areas may be especially illuminating as America makes its own choices. Those choices will, however, continue to be governed in large measure by the judgments of courts of law, and of the Supreme Court in particular.

Notes

[1] Tyack, 1987, p. 177. The following account draws on this work.

[2] Doerr & Menendez, 1991, p. 38; Levy, 1994, p. 122.

[3] Levy, 1994; Howe, 1965.

[4] Howe, 1965.

[5] Levy, 1994, p. 165.

[6] Levy, 1994, p. 123; Formicola & Morken, 1997, p. 15.

[7] Formicola & Morken, 1997, p. 86.

[8] Ravitch, 1973, p. 30.

[9] Ibid., p. 32.

[10] For the SC cases of *McCollum* (1948) and *Zorach* (1952), see Levy, 1994, p. 144.

[11] Ravitch, 1973, p. 37.

[12] Doerr & Menendez, 1991, p. 33.

[13] *Church and State*, 14 May 1961; Doerr & Menendez, 1991, p. 92.

[14] Doerr & Menendez, 1991, p. 90.

[15] Ibid., p. 133.

[16] Hunt & Carper, 1992, p. 178.

[17] *San Francisco Chronicle*, 8 April 1988.

[18] Levy, 1994, pp. 130 ff.; Formicola & Morken, 1997, pp. 89, 109.

[19] Levy, 1994, p. 141; Formicola & Morken, 1997, p. 226.

[20] *The Economist*, 8 July 1995.

[21] SC: *Agostini et al v. Felton et al*, No. 96-552, decided June 23, 1997.

[22] SC: *Abington Township vs Schemp* 1963, *Engel vs Vitale* 1962. Formicola & Morken, 1997, p. 150; Nord, 1995, p. 115.

[23] Both these telling quotations are from the *New York Times*, 1 July 1962.

[24] Senate Committee on the Judiciary, *Hearings on Prayer in Public Schools*, 87th Cong., 2nd sess., 56. Cited in Formicola & Morken, 1997, p. 195.

[25] Gallup & Castelli, 1989, p. 4.

[26] SC: *Wallace v. Jaffree* 1985, in Formicola & Morken, 1997, pp. 149, 152, 202.

[27] SC: *Widmer* 1981, *Mergens* 1990, in Wills, 1990, p. 84; Formicola & Morken, 1997, p. 111.

[28] *Kappan*, October 2000, p. 175.

[29] Wills, 1990, pp. 62, 69.

[30] Nord, 1995, p. 259.

[31] Formicola & Morken, 1997, p. 115.

[32] SC: *Reynolds* 1879.

[33] SC: *Yoder* 1972.

[34] SC: *Sherbert* 1981.

[35] SC: *Smith* 1990.

[36] Nord, 1995, pp. 111, 114.

[37] SC: *City of Boerne v. Flores* 1997.

[38] Gaddy et al, 1996, p. 31.

[39] See Cherny, 1985; Larson, 1985.

[40] SC: *Epperson* 1968. Nord, 1995, p. 293.

[41] Wills, 1990, p. 118.

[42] SC: *Aguillard* 1987.

[43] Gaddy et al, 1996; Diamond, 1989.

[44] Gaddy et al, 1996, p. 61.

[45] Carper & Hunt, 1993, pp. 318, 245, 250, 318; Stevens, 2002.

[46] George R. Kaplan, in *Kappan*, November 2000, K3-K12.

[47] Ibid.

CHAPTER 9

Three Arenas: the streets

The Minister of Education who in 1928 presided at the inauguration in Pons of the statue of Emile Combes was himself no stranger to municipal or national politics, or to the long battle between the two rival ideological educational traditions which dominated so much of French public life. A former Prime Minister, he had since 1926 presided over the educational fortunes of France but was to remain in office for only a few more days. The career of Edouard Herriot, a pillar of the Third Republic and the acknowledged leader of the Radical Party, began in the aftermath of the Dreyfus affair. His long life ended in the last months of the Fourth Republic and only two years before the passing of the law (the *loi Debré*) which reshaped in fundamental ways the relationships between the State and Catholic schools in France. Herriot had graduated from the prestigious *Ecole Normale Supérieure* in the rue d'Ulm at the head of the list of the *agrégés* of letters, and was drawn into public life by the polemics swirling around the Dreyfus affair, becoming Mayor of Lyon in 1905. In what remains the characteristic style of French *notables*, he held that great city as his personal fief until ejected by the Vichy Government in 1940. He was then imprisoned and in 1944 deported to Germany, resuming in the following year his mayoral dignities, and enjoying them until his death in 1957. For most of his life, first as a Senator and then as a Deputy, he represented his own district in Parliament. Herriot was three times Prime Minister (albeit on the second occasion only for three days and never for longer than ten months) and had been Minister of Public Instruction since 1926.[1]

His 1924-25 ministry, made up of Radicals enjoying office with the insecure support of the Socialists, had witnessed one of the last serious attempts by the anticlericals of the Third Republic to press still further the victory they had won in 1905 with the constitutional separation of Church and State. Since then, and largely as a result of a decline in anti-Catholic feeling and the unifying effects of the First World War, a tacit consensus had been established. Indeed, after 1914, even the laws excluding the Congregations from educational activity had for all practical purposes lapsed. Catholic schools, albeit without any support from public funds, flourished: replacing them totally would never have been a simple or inexpensive matter, especially since the Church by the mid-1920s was providing about one-fifth of all primary education, and more than one-third of secondary. The anticlericals therefore found it more appealing to turn their attention to consolidating the victories they had already won. By a curious anomaly, which survives into the twenty-first century, the 1905 Combes Law did not apply to the 'lost' provinces of Alsace and Lorraine. These contested territories, seized by France in the seventeenth century, had been sacrificed to Germany after the humiliating defeat of 1871 and were restored to France only in 1918: at the time of the 1905 Law of Separation they were, therefore, not part of the French Republic and Napoleon's Concordat remained in force, a perpetually irritating anomaly for the anticlerical parties. Herriot's efforts to repair this gap in the walls of secular orthodoxy inflamed not only a threatening opposition in the provinces directly affected but, more generally, a fierce revival of Catholic opinion throughout France.[2]

The cardinals and archbishops of France now abandoned the tactical caution that they had usually shown in recent years, and formally reiterated their unconditional condemnation of the anticlerical laws of the Third Republic. In 1929, Pope Pius XI, whatever his reservations about the wisdom shown by the French episcopate in this delicate matter, reaffirmed the formal position of the Church in a long encyclical (*Divini Illius Magistri*): parents had a plain duty to secure a good religious education for their children (and this, of course, meant more than religious instruction); the role of the State was 'subsidiary' and should in no circumstances constitute a monopoly.[3] Such Roman interventions limited the effectiveness of those Catholic groups which, in the spirit of the *Ralliement*, continued to seek ways of cooperating with the Republic, and of bringing a Christian perspective to bear on a national system of education which, while it doubtless must preserve neutrality, need not be in itself hostile to the Catholic conscience or to the Church's commitment to pursue the good of society as a whole. The papal condemnation of the right-wing nostalgia of the *Action Française*, led by the monarchist yet agnostic Charles Maurras, and the growth of the various movements associated with the socially liberal *Action Catholique* both in different ways reflected this very different and more open tradition within French, and indeed international, Catholicism.

Catholic teachers within the state system had for many years organised themselves informally and encouraged one another in such an enterprise, reflected in the evolution after 1922 of the *Paroisse Universitaire*, and the foundation and growth under the editorship of Emmanuel Mousnier of the influential journal, *Esprit*.[4] The Paroisse was consistently active and vocal in insisting on the distinctive contribution which Catholic teachers could and should make to the state funded and controlled schools and universities. After the ill-judged attempts of Edouard Herriot to revive the anticlerical fervour of earlier decades, a mood of cohabitation generally prevailed. The Catholic schools enjoyed a period of relative prosperity, and their share of secondary schooling rose from 39% in 1925 to 44.5% in the last year of peace before the Second World War. Most of the schools were economically viable only because much of the teaching was provided by members of the (formally proscribed) Congregations, but in many of them financial problems were nevertheless acute. Pressure to secure state subsidies rose, and predictably revived all the deep-seated opposition of the Radical Party, of the teachers' unions, and of all those professing loyalty to the historic principles of Jules Ferry and Emile Combes. Parents with children in Catholic schools began to organise themselves, and to create organisations which were to have great influence when their successors in the 1980s took to the streets in defence of state funding for distinctively Catholic schools. Local associations, the APEL – L'Association des Parents de l'Ecole Libre – were founded in the 1930s and formed a powerful national union (the UNAPEL) in 1933. In 1939, Pope Pius XI formally endorsed the demands of French Catholics for state support for their schools. Inevitably, tensions and rivalries surfaced from time to time, and not least because a fall in the birth rate – always a cause of profound alarm in France – inevitably led to sharpened competition between the two sectors of schooling. Those tensions were sharpened and the rivalries embittered by the policies and even more by the overt prejudices of the Vichy regime. The reactions of some of the bishops and clergy to the great crisis of 1940 confirmed the doubts and fears of many anticlericals, and undermined the hopes of many more liberal Catholics that the passions of the 1890s might be forgotten, and Catholic schools somehow accommodated within the framework of a nationally funded pattern of schooling.

The dark and bitter years of the German occupation of France left a permanent mark on the tangled history of the relationships between the French State and the Catholic Church, and not least in the field of education. The first reactions of many, but by no means all, Church leaders to the devastating defeat of 1940 were marked by shock, resentment and repentance for the sins of the nation. Many now hoped for a removal of the many injustices which, in their eyes, had been heaped on loyal Catholics since the beginning of the Third Republic, and notably since the unforgotten iniquities of *le petit Père Combes*. Marshal Pétain, the venerable hero of Verdun, was promising to regenerate a humiliated France, rededicating it to its inherently Catholic traditions, obliterating the shame of 1789, rescuing its vulnerable young from the pernicious influence of Communists and Freemasons masquerading as teachers. This curious mood of euphoria and revenge, unsurprisingly evident among the leadership and the ranks of the clergy, did not long survive the realities of the early 1940s. The anticipated National Revolution, based not on the triple principles of 'Liberty, Equality, Fraternity' but on those of 'Work, Family, Homeland', remained a nostalgic dream. Gerlier, the Primate of the Gauls and Cardinal Archbishop of Lyon (where Herriot was, of course, Mayor), spoke for most of the hierarchy when he proclaimed, 'Had we been victorious, we would probably have remained in the prison of our errors. By being secularised [*laïcisée*], France was in danger of dying'.[5] Within two weeks of the fall of France, the Archbishops of Lyon and Paris, in meetings with the new leaders of a truncated France in

Paris and Vichy, were urging that immediate subsidies should be paid to Catholic schools so that they might contribute to the work of saving the nation. One of Cardinal Gerlier's incautious phrases ('Pétain, c'est la France, et la France aujourd'hui, c'est Pétain') was incorporated in the song which the boys in all schools in France were now taught to sing:

> *All children who love you and venerate your age*
> *To your supreme appeal have answered 'Present!'*
> *Marshal, here we are before you, the saviour of France.*
> *We swear to you, we are your men,*
> *To serve you and follow In your footsteps ...*
> *... For Pétain is France, and France is Pétain.[6]*

The new government, within which ministers of education rapidly rotated, lost no time in attacking what it recognised as the citadels of the entrenched power of the secular educational system. At the very heart of that system stood the *Ecole Normale*, as developed by Guizot and extended by Ferry, the residential training college for teachers replicating (albeit in the service of a very different cause) so many of the characteristics of the clerical seminary, inculcating a Durkheimian morality, anticlerical prejudices and – more recently – left-wing and pacifist preferences. They were all unceremoniously closed: for the future (which did not last long), intending teachers would first be prepared for the traditional and discipline-based baccalaureate before receiving a sharply focused professional training in specially designated centres.[7] The schools were 'purged' of Jews and Freemasons: 1328 Freemasons had lost their jobs by the autumn of 1941, and a thousand of the more vocal and politically committed union leaders were also summarily dismissed.[8] The unions themselves, long associated with left-wing causes and the aggressive promotion of the secular school, were dissolved and replaced by more docile bodies. The upper elementary school was replaced by the college, more firmly rooted in the attitudes and culture of the traditional secondary school and less open, it was hoped, to pernicious influences. The crucifix was restored to the walls of the schoolroom – although it seems that in many parts of France, whatever the laws of Paris had decreed, it had in fact never been removed. The endlessly contested 'duties towards God' (*devoirs envers Dieu*) reappeared in the official school programmes of study, even though (again) it is not clear whether they had ever been conclusively removed in the first place: since the 1880s they had been chased in and out of the circular rabbit warrens of bureaucratic regulation, and would very soon – in the interests of calming tempers – officially disappear yet again (for the last time?). Comparably deceptive mists had shrouded the role of members of the religious orders in Catholic schools: formally excluded since the beginning of the century by the laws against the Congregations, they had in reality been allowed to teach undisturbed since 1914. But a formal recognition of their role was now demanded and conceded: the laws against them were formally annulled in 1940. Public funds for the support of children from poor families were now made available for the first time to pupils attending Catholic as well as public schools, and local communes were allowed (but not required) to make financial contributions for the support of Catholic schools. The Minister introduced regulations (annulled soon after his abrupt departure) allowing religious instruction to be given on the premises of public elementary schools, and within the normal daily timetable. Many of these drastic changes were accomplished very quickly between September 1940 and February 1941 during the brief seventy-two day tenure of Jacques Chevalier as Minister of Education. Chevalier, a zealous Catholic, the son of an army officer and a godson of Pétain, had been educated at the *Ecole Normale Supérieure* and (less successfully) at Oxford.

Chevalier's tenure of office coincided with the months when the supporters of *Action Française* enjoyed most influence in Vichy and over the Marshal. The rapidity and zealotry which marked the actions of Chevalier were not universally approved, even by the initial supporters of the regime: some, including Chevalier's own successor, predicted that his haste and heavy-handedness would provoke an anti-Catholic backlash, while the German authorities in Paris (and notably the ambassador) and their Parisian collaborationist allies had no wish to see the authority or autonomy of the French episcopate strengthened. The honeymoon could not last for long. The Minister was moved sideways into another office, to be succeeded by a more moderate and pragmatic academic. Chevalier was tried and disgraced after the Liberation, and died in 1962. The new Minister, Jérôme Carcopino insisted that he had made it a condition of accepting office that he should be allowed to restore an adequate measure of religious neutrality and moderate some of the excesses associated with his predecessor. He was minister from February 1941 until April 1942, the months during which the true nature of Nazi Germany's intentions for France and for Europe and the severe limitations on the power of Vichy became steadily more evident. The growth both of internal resistance and of the external authority of de Gaulle had the obvious effect of making steadily more dubious the longer-term survival of the regime of the Marshal. Such shifts in perception and expectation were, of course, accelerated by the entry of the United States into the War in 1942. With one significant exception, most of the successes in re-establishing something of the power of the Church in education had, for what they were worth, already been accomplished. Carcopino enjoyed impeccable academic credentials, as an ancient historian and as an administrator. He had been Director of the French School in Rome and of the *Ecole Normale Supérieure* (a post to which he returned), and for a brief period Rector of the Paris Academy. As has already been reported, the *devoirs envers Dieu*, always of more symbolic than practical importance in the texts, again did their disappearing trick. Religious instruction for public school pupils, although still acceptable as a voluntary subject on the timetable, could no longer be given on the school premises (again, a largely symbolic statement). More substantive, and of more significance for the future, were the attempts to deal with the problems raised by the financing of the Catholic schools.

The problems raised by the funding of the many Catholic schools were severe, for the Vichy regime as for the Church itself. The contribution which these schools were making to the provision of education throughout the country was, of course, massive in scale. The severe economic problems they experienced throughout the 1930s had been exacerbated by the damage inflicted on the fabric of the schools by the invasion, and the disruption caused by large movements of the population. This was, of course, a problem, for the communal as much as for the Catholic schools themselves, and the sympathies of administrators were divided. Some half-hearted attempts had been made to require the communes themselves to make some contribution to rising costs but, as always in French history, such efforts from the centre were deeply resented by the local authorities, especially by the many with left-wing sympathies. Pétain eventually decided that the national interest, and the pursuit of the moral regeneration of France, required that direct assistance should now be given to Catholic schools. His minister, Carcopino, did his best to resist such pressures, and (by his own account) at one point threatened to resign if the religious peace which he valued were to be threatened by an attempt to subsidise Catholic schooling. He did nevertheless grudgingly make the necessary minimum of concessions: by the law passed in November 1941, aid was limited to the primary schools and characterised as 'exceptional' in character, destined only to meet extraordinary circumstances.[9] Moreover, the aid was to be distributed by the Ministry of the Interior and not of Education and could be granted only to schools already in existence and producing evidence of financial embarrassment. The subventions which had recently been made by some, although never all, of the communes were now to be discontinued while unwelcome inspection was to be imposed on the schools receiving aid.

These measures caused much bitterness, and – in traditionally Catholic areas such as Brittany and the West – soon led to accusations that unacceptable pressure was brought to bear on parents to send their children to the local Catholic rather than to the public school. At the same time the UNAPEL, as the established advocate of the interests of committed Catholic families, made clear its own dissatisfaction with the new and inadequate arrangements. The public subventions did, nevertheless, lead to a marked increase in the scale of Roman Catholic schooling, although the impact of the new measure varied from one part of the country to another. This variation had long been, and was to continue to be, a marked feature of schooling in France. Between 1939 and 1945, the proportion of pupils in private (mostly Catholic, of course) elementary education rose from 17.7 to 22.6%. But in the department of Loire-Inférieure, it rose from 52.4% to an overwhelming 71.1% (whereas in the Creuse it was only 4.3%).[10] Carcopino, however reluctantly, had now identified the provision of state aid for Catholic schools even more closely with the cause of right-wing anti-Republicanism. The relative consensus on Church-State relations which had prevailed in the late 1930s would not be restored after the Liberation.

Carcopino, unlike his successor, honourably survived the restoration of the Republic, not least because of the substantial and generally welcomed reforms which he managed to introduce in the general educational system. His notorious successor, Abel Bonnard, said a great deal but in fact achieved very little (except to deepen the gulf between the Catholic schools and the rest). A man of no religious convictions and with close connections to the collaborationists in Paris, he epitomised all that was most reactionary and decadent in the fading regime: Pétain called him 'Gestapette', an amalgam of Gestapo and an unflattering slang term for a homosexual.[11]

In the dramatic and painful recriminations of 1944 and 1945, the Catholic lobby argued – with little hope of immediate success – for the maintenance of the subsidies which their schools had been receiving, estimated by critics as likely in the current year to cost over 716 million francs. But in March 1945, the Consultative Assembly – convened to build the foundations of the Fourth Republic on the ruins of the Third – rejected by 128 votes to 48 a motion to preserve state support for the schools.[12] There was no reference to freedom of education (liberté d'enseignement) in the new constitution as drafted in 1945: on the contrary. The French Republic was, for the first time in so solemn and basic a text, formally described as laïque, as well as 'indivisible, democratic and social'.[13] Given the scale of provision already made by the Church, and the penury of the restored Republic, it was doubtless inevitable that in practical terms the Catholic schools would continue to exercise that freedom to provide a distinctive form of schooling which they had in everyday terms enjoyed since 1914 – but without the subsidies which the UNAPEL and its allies had since the 1930s been seeking and which, doubtless to their longer-term disadvantage, they had in fact received under the tainted regime of Vichy. Any attempt to restore that financially favourable position would be perceived by the anticlerical groups (led by the powerful teachers' unions, and especially the now dominant Fédération de l'Education Nationale) as an attack on the cause of National Education and an attempt to restore the dominance which the Church had enjoyed for much of the previous century. In 1951, the formation of a Parliamentary Association for the Freedom of Education (the APLE) was promptly countered by the mobilisation of the CNAL (Comité National d'Action Laïque). Two well-organised and highly politicised groups now confronted one another, and the deadlock would not be broken for as long as the Fourth Republic survived.

The political crisis in Algeria, and its profound consequences within France, led to the collapse of the short-lived Fourth Republic, and the return to power of de Gaulle. The new President – in secure possession of enhanced constitutional powers and, for the moment, enjoying wide public support – was fully aware of the dangers of reopening the ancient quarrels. Although he entertained strong reservations about increasing the powers and influence of the Church, he was bound to recognise that as a matter of practical necessity the State would, for the foreseeable future, depend on the active cooperation of the Church and of its schools if the reforms to which he was committed were to be effective. The rising birth rate brought extra pressures to bear on the national provision of schools, as did the tendency for students to stay longer at school. The minimum school leaving age was raised to sixteen by the Berthoin Law of 1959. Some modest concessions to the Catholic schools had already been made during the 1950s: in 1951, the Barangé Law (so named because that was the name of the first Deputy to appear on the alphabetical list of signatories, all members of the new parliamentary association) made official state support available for families with children in schools both public and private. For the public schools, these subsidies were channelled through a departmental agency, but for Catholic schools, similar funds were administered through the local APEL. The growing influence of these well-organised groups of parents was therefore consolidated.[14] In the same year, the Marie Law (named for the Minister then in power) made available some scholarships for pupils in Catholic schools on the same terms as for those in public schools. The same decade witnessed the failure of complex attempts by the French archbishops and cardinals to negotiate a new concordat, intended to regulate many aspects of the relationship between the Church and the State.

The President and his close ally, the Prime Minister Michel Debré, preferred a more limited approach to the school problem, and favoured a solution which would consistently deploy the language and machinery of 'the contract'. The State, fulfilling its responsibility to provide an articulated system of national education, could therefore choose to enter into specific contractual arrangements with particular schools and teachers. These contracts would enable the necessary controls to be exercised and the fundamental principles of the Republic to be observed. Mgr Descamps, who had since 1945 been responsible to the episcopate for developing the Church's educational policy, was drawn into discussions with the Prime Minister and with Boulloche, the Socialist Minister of Education – soon to be sacrificed to the President's determination to secure a prompt and workable settlement. The suspicions of the watchful CNAL were aroused, and the Government realised that any solution would have to be rapidly developed and enforced before the mood of national urgency evaporated. There were demonstrations against the proposed arrangements in Nantes and on the streets of Paris. The CNAL organised a massive petition, for which it claimed 10,813,697 signatures, as well as a demonstration in the Bois de Vincennes in June 1960 at which an estimated 400,000 demonstrators swore:

> to manifest in all circumstances and in all places our irreducible
> opposition to this law which is contrary to the historic evolution of the
> nation; to fight without truce and without weakening until it is repealed;
> and to ensure that the educational effort of the republic is solely reserved
> to the school of the Nation, the hope of our youth.[15]

Debré was not to be deterred, insisting when introducing his 1959 law on the principle that 'Private education participates in a task of general utility'. He was, however, opposed both to outright nationalisation and, with equal firmness, to a solution which would legitimate a parallel system: a *université bis*.[16] The contracts made by the State, and signed on its behalf by the Prefect, should be specific and limited, and observe general Republican principles, as well as embodying the detailed regulations on which the State would insist before extending financial support. This contractual approach is still, at the beginning of the twenty-first century, the basis of all discussion in France of the relationship between Church and State in the educational field. Among the key principles enshrined in the Law is that of non-discrimination: admission to schools (Catholic and other) under contract to the State must be open to all, selection or exclusion may not be determined on grounds of religion, and freedom of conscience is to be respected. In return, the State respects the *caractère propre* (the special character, the identity) of the school. This, unsurprisingly, was a phrase that proved simpler to accept than to define.

The contracts authorised by the *loi Debré* were of two kinds, of which the first was expected to be temporary and transitional. Under this *contrat simple*, a school (unless it was in a newly developed area) must already have functioned for five years and employ only properly qualified teachers. A school under this contract is the employer of those teachers, for which, nevertheless, the State pays. Other charges fall on the establishment itself – for example, the costs of extending, maintaining, furnishing and operating the building and of providing all teaching materials – unless the commune itself chooses (as by law it now might) to make a contribution. The school must have regard to (*se référer à*) the national programmes formally defining the content of instruction. The *contrat d'association*, on the other hand, represents a closer contractual partnership, and is therefore both more generous in its financial support and more demanding of acceptance of the national norms. A school seeking and securing such a contract must observe all the basic conditions already outlined, and in addition demonstrate that it meets a known educational need. This issue of the *besoin scolaire*, intended to ensure that national resources were not inequitably wasted where there was no proven need for additional school places, was to prove one of the most contentious of the many issues which arose in the application of the terms of the new contracts. Although teachers in schools under the *contrat d'association* were paid directly by the State, they were not (of course) civil servants (*fonctionnaires*). Their legal status was that of a 'public agent' (*agent public*). Many of the privileges of the civil service could not, therefore, be automatically extended to them: this was a complex issue which irritated teachers' unions and caused divisions among the teachers in the Catholic schools. Other public contributions to the funding of the schools, notably for equipment and running expenses, were subject to complex rules. In principle, the *forfait d'externat* was to be a sum equivalent to comparable costs in the public schools, paid in part by the State and in part by the local authorities. The rules differed for primary and secondary schools.[17] The 1959 Law was supplemented by a flood of decrees and other regulations, each of them anxiously scrutinised by friends as well as enemies of these new and extensive arrangements. President Pompidou (1969-74) further entrenched the contractual system in the national scheme by making permanent the status of the simple contract, and by allowing further public investments in Catholic schools through weakening the requirements for demonstrating a clear educational need whenever additional provision was planned. His Prime Minister, Jacques Chaban-Delmas, was unenthusiastic about such provocations and the CNAL was not amused. The APLE, the Parliamentary Association, was now becoming more overtly partisan and strengthening its links with the official agencies of the Enseignement Catholique, which now provided in the rue St Jacques a secretariat for its parliamentary allies. Even with a considerable measure of state support, however, and although the number of pupils enrolled in schools nationally continued to rise, the Catholic schools had great difficulty in maintaining their position relative to the public schools. As many as 39.7% of all students within the secondary sector attended Catholic colleges and *lycées* in 1949, but that proportion had dropped to 26.9% in 1959 and to 22.6% by 1969. If the State had not in 1959 assumed responsibility for the full payment of teachers' salaries in the schools under contract, the fall would have been precipitous: in 1962, the 57.1% of the teachers in Catholic schools who were members of religious orders had by 1974 shrunk to a mere 11%, with obvious financial consequences.[18]

The two rival lobbies – reflecting old and unhealed divisions going back to Dreyfus and beyond – were becoming better organised, and more professional in their efforts to enlist public support. The *laïque* group was, of course, coordinated by the CNAL, which drew many of its ideological principles from such well-established pressure groups as the Ligue de l'Enseignement. Its big battalions were recruited from the the Fédération de l'Education Nationale (FEN), and the Fédération des Conseils de Parents d'Elèves des Ecoles Publics (FCPE) – the aggressively anticlerical association of parents led from 1956 until 1980 by Jean Cornec. Cornec, an eloquent lawyer, was the son of Breton primary school teachers who had, in his view, been persecuted for their secular beliefs.[19] Opinions and priorities on the Catholic side were less uniform. The local APELs, and their national federation, the UNAPEL, were highly assertive, capturing the enthusiasm and often the anger of parents who resented what was for them a system of double taxation. The bishops, organised since the Second Vatican Council as a national conference with an elected president, were often more cautious. Some among them doubted the necessity or the wisdom of continuing to make expensive provision for a separate schooling system, and feared (with good reason) the dangers of becoming too closely associated with a political cause, or even a political party. In 1969, the French bishops – responding to the pronouncements of Vatican II and especially to the encyclical *Gravissimum Educationis* – for the first time recognised the validity of the contribution made by the public school to the good of French society. But they also strengthened the central organisation of the Enseignement Catholique to enable it to act as a more powerful advocate of the cause of the Catholic schools throughout France.[20] Several of them were, however, openly sympathetic to the opinions of those clergy and lay people who believed that the Church would be better employed encouraging good Catholics to work as teachers within the mainstream of the national education system. They looked kindly on the traditions of the (now declining) Paroisse Universitaire and the influential teachers' union, the Syndicat Général de l'Education Nationale (SGEN), which opposed the dogmatism of the more powerful FEN and was affiliated to the Confédération Français et Démocratique du Travail (CFDT). It took a frontal attack on the Catholic schools in the next decade to bring the bishops unambiguously into battle as the allies of UNAPEL. In the shadow of the great church of the Val de Grâce, in the rue St Jacques, were the headquarters not only of the UNAPEL itself (ably led by Pierre Daniel) but also of l'Enseignement Catholique, the official body which represented the many separate interests within Catholic education, and had the task of coordinating their responses to changes in government policy. Since 1972, it had been directed by Canon Guiberteau, with the vigorous and often controversial assistance of Nicole Fontaine.

In spite of the prudent reservations of the two successive right-wing Prime Ministers, Jacques Chirac and Raymond Barre (another long-serving Mayor of Lyon), the presidency of Giscard d'Estaing (1974-81) was marked by significant gains for the Catholic schools. The professional position of the teachers in those schools was improved by the government decision to extend full funding for their in-service training. The CNAL, the FEN and their allies were deeply opposed to the policies of René Haby. They resented the symbolic change represented by his change of title: he was Minister of Education and not of National Education, with all that the latter style implied about the school of Ferry and the Republic one and indivisible. Haby and his successor, Beullac, were the first Ministers openly to criticise the educational system over which they presided. The Haby Law of 1975 offended many of the ingrained prejudices of the FEN (but not its smaller rival, the SGEN) and violated the principles of the Debré Law by speaking of Catholic schools not as discrete establishments being accepted into a contractual arrangement by the State, but as a system – *l'enseignement privé sous contrat* – operating nationally alongside the public system.[21] Haby needed the cooperation and resources of the Catholic schools to carry his own extensive reforms into practice, and more financial assistance from the Government would therefore be required. The Guermeur Law of 1977 was rightly perceived by friends and enemies as effectively consolidating a dual system and represented, for the twentieth century, the high water mark of the success of the Catholic schools in consolidating their own position in society, and in the affections of many citizens who had no particular interest in denominational education as such. The publicly funded Catholic system was now coming to be appreciated as an attractive alternative or supplement to a state system which, for all its considerable power and prestige, was more widely perceived as bureaucratic, cumbersome and unresponsive. Parents were behaving less like good Catholics, or indeed good *laïques*, and more like consumers, often making use selectively of the two systems, and in an attempt to secure what they perceived as being in the best interests of their own families.[22] Although the Catholic 'share' of publicly funded schooling declined between 1960 and 1975 from 18.1 to 16.3%, many families were content to switch their children in and out of the two parallel systems. A third of all the pupils in an age group had, by the time their studies were completed, spent at least one year in a Catholic school. This growing entanglement of the schools in patterns of local provision, and the choices which it offered to parents, partly explains why the UNAPEL seemed often more zealous in defence of the schools than were the bishops themselves. Guermeur, a deputy representing the Catholic district of Finistère and one of the more zealous leaders of the Parliamentary Association, was, therefore, able to extract from the Government many concessions – an achievement for which he was never forgiven by the left-wing parties, and by their active allies in the CNAL.

His success was not, however, total: the volume of financial support for new or extended buildings which might be granted by the appropriate authorities (until the decentralising laws of the 1980s, the State for secondary and the communes for the primary schools) remained subject to the restrictive limits first imposed in the Loi Falloux of 1850. But the position of the teachers – for example, in access to retirement and other social benefits – was once again improved. More significant were the efforts to ensure that the controversial *caractère propre* of the Catholic schools should be protected. The head of such a school (the *chef d'établissement*) now acquired the right to nominate teachers to the Recteur for appointment in the school for which he or she was responsible: hitherto, the formal initiative in making such appointments had rested with the Rectorate itself, albeit acting in concert with the establishment affected. For the FEN, this was a direct assault on the cherished doctrine that all teachers paid by the State were part of a national and undivided public service. This concession, at a time when the members of the teaching orders had effectively disappeared from Catholic schools and their religious character was therefore in some doubt, had great practical importance, tending – in ways of which Debré could not have approved – to establish within France a second and separate educational system, with a distinctive character of its own. The financial position of the schools was further consolidated by the (new) legal requirement that the local authorities should be obliged to make an appropriately calculated payment – the *forfait d'externat* – to subsidise the running expenses of Catholic primary schools operating under contract. This unwelcome imposition was resented, and, of course, ingeniously resisted, by many left-wing municipalities. The parliamentary opposition challenged the constitutionality of the new law, which was, however, duly upheld by the supreme arbiter in such matters, the *Conseil Constitutionnel.* The Socialist leader, François Mitterrand, then committed himself to the repeal of this obnoxious law: the inauguration of a great Public Service of Unified and Lay National Education (the SPULEN) became a central if sketchily defined plank of his programme in the presidential elections of 1981.

On 10 May 1981, Mitterrand was duly elected as the first Socialist President of the Fifth Republic: he would now exercise those quasi-monarchical powers which he had so bitterly attacked when they had been assumed by General de Gaulle. He used that authority to dissolve Parliament, and in the ensuing elections the Socialists were unsurprisingly victorious. Mitterrand named the Mayor of Lille, Pierre Mauroy, as his Prime Minister and the skilful and gracious Alain Savary was installed in the rue de Grenelle: allies and enemies alike had expected that the educational portfolio was destined for the more aggressive *laïciste,* Louis Mexandreau.[23] What would the rhetoric of the SPULEN now mean, and how would the President and his ministers respond to the pressures of the hard left, and to the insistence of the CNAL, the FEN and their many political allies that the offensive errors of 1959 and, more recently, 1977 should be eliminated from the Republic? Did not the transitional settlement of 1959, cobbled together in the aftermath of the disgrace of Vichy, now require the irreversibly final absorption of the publicly funded Catholic schools into the national system? Another good socialist, Guy Mollet, had in the year 1959 predicted:

> *All those establishments and all those teachers who solicit public funds*
> *will be considered, by that very act, to have affirmed their vocation to*
> *enter into the public service. And this is what shall be done.[24]*

But not without a battle and not before the rival armies descended into the streets.

François Mitterrand chose to be invested in the Pantheon, where the unambiguously secular ceremonies were orchestrated by Jack Lang, the new Minister of Culture. In the national imagination, the Pantheon represented the triumph of reason over religion, of patriotism over Romanism, of the Left over the Right, of the *instituteur* over the *curé.* A few steps away are the unobtrusive headquarters of Libre Pensée, where a plaque records the outrage of righteous Republicans when, in 1980, the President of the Republic had dared to welcome Pope John Paul II on an official visit to France. Just before the Revolution of 1789 and after long delays, the building of the Pantheon had been completed on one of the traditional holy places of Paris, the hill named after St Geneviève. During that Revolution it was dedicated to new and more appropriate purposes, receiving the ashes of

Voltaire and Rousseau. Napoleon restored it as a church; under Louis Philippe it again became a necropolis; Napoleon III turned it back into a church again. The Third Republic took its revenge in 1885 when once again it became a *temple laïque*: the cross was removed from the roof on the day before the great ceremony when the ashes of Victor Hugo were ceremonially transferred there. More recently, de Gaulle had ordered that the ashes of Jean Moulin, the hero of the resistance to Vichy, should be received there under the legend *Aux Grands Hommes de la France La Patrie Reconnaissante*. In choosing this building for his installation as President, Mitterrand was therefore making a public declaration of his sympathies. His manoeuvres as a politician struggling to reconcile extremists on both sides of the religious and political debate were, however, a good deal more complex.[25]

The Catholic school question was now being drawn into the centre of the political battle – inevitably so, perhaps, given the substantial advances made by the Catholic cause during the previous presidency, most notably in the Guermeur Law of 1977. Confronted with this dangerous polarisation of opinion, the bishops were understandably anxious. The more ardent defenders of Catholic schools, and specifically of their continued and extended funding by the State, resented the cool hesitation of their official leaders. The UNAPEL, under the skilful leadership of its new president, Pierre Daniel, was anxious to show its muscle. Honoré, the bishop with a national responsibility for educational policy, sought to restrain the embarrassing enthusiasms of Nicole Fontaine, the assistant general secretary of the Enseignement Catholique who had impolitically agreed to appear on Giscard's partisan list of candidates for the forthcoming European elections. The bishops remembered only too well the consequences of the partisan enthusiasm some of their predecessors had shown under the Vichy regime. At the opposite end of the long spectrum of opinion stood Michel Bouchareissas, just appointed as the fiery general secretary of the CNAL and determined that the new government should be firmly held to the clear commitments it had made before the election. The *antilaïque* laws of Debré, Pompidou and Guermeur must therefore be swept away without any delay. Bouchareissas was a committed union leader, *laïque* to the core and a graduate of the *Ecole Normale* of Limoges, the 'red city'.

Bouchareissas and Daniel were both new to their posts, although not to the causes they would now be required to defend. In the same year of 1981, Cardinal Marty was succeeded as Archbishop of Paris by Jean-Marie Lustiger. Lustiger soon proved to be more outspoken and uncompromising on public issues than his predecessors, or than many of his brother prelates. A convert from Judaism and a friend of the Polish Pope, as an intellectual he sought to engage the Church in open debate about the future of a vulnerable society, and recognised in the Catholic school one of the most effective weapons for preserving the national and Catholic heritage. Although as Archbishop of Paris he enjoyed no formal superiority over the other prelates, his moral authority was considerable. Both his influence and his visibility were increased by being close to the media and the journalists of the capital, as well as to the levers of power in a centralised state. Another newcomer to the national scene was Canon Guiberteau, the general secretary of the Enseignement Catholique, who had since 1967 been the diocesan director of schools in the Catholic stronghold of Nantes. These were to be the principal figures in the tortuous dance of negotiation which the new Minister, Alain Savary, now formally opened. Alain Savary was well qualified by experience and temperament to reconcile divergent views. He had been an early and public opponent of Vichy and all that it represented, and joined the opposition in London even before 18 June 1940. He led the campaign to liberate the remote islands of Saint-Pierre-et-Miquelon, lying off the coast of Newfoundland, and was their Governor for two years. He had held ministerial office in the 1950s, before the long exile of the Socialists from political power, and after the electoral victory of Mitterrand rapidly showed himself to be a Minister with a large portfolio of intended reforms. France appeared, yet again, to be the exceptional nation. Thatcher and Reagan may have become the dominant figures on the world stage, but in the early euphoric years of the first Socialist Presidency of the Fifth Republic, everything seemed for a while possible: Savary appointed committees to reform the *collèges* (the lower secondary schools) and the *lycées*, as well as the arrangements for the preparation of teachers and other officials within the national educational system. His ambition was to introduce a greater suppleness into the mighty engines of the school system, and to do so within a general framework of the decentralisation of power and the granting of greater autonomy to local government and to local institutions. This would be the context for redefining the relationship of the state to the Catholic schools.[26]

The interests to be reconciled were complex and contradictory. On the Catholic side, the bishops (organised since the conciliar reforms of Pope John XXIII in an official Conference with its own administrative machinery) were preoccupied by multiple agendas, still uncertain about the role of the Church in the enlarging national effort to extend education more widely, concerned to avoid confrontation and the risks of exploitation by partisan political interests. The Parliamentary Association (for Liberté d'Enseignement) was drawn exclusively from the adherents of what was now the opposition: Guermeur in particular would lose no opportunity of pressing home the advantages his initiatives had already won. The bishops' Commission on education (*le Monde Scolaire*) was more supportive of the cause of Catholic schools than their Conference as a whole had so far proved to be, but anxious that the more zealous professional members of the Enseignement Catholique might compromise their cause, and alienate the ruling powers. The UNAPEL, as a strong national alliance of parents closely involved in the financing and administration of the Catholic schools, was the most apprehensive of the Catholic bodies, and anxious for action before it was all too late. It distributed some 800,000 copies of its monthly journal, *La Famille*

Educatrice. The teachers themselves were also divided: some 40% of them belonged to the Syndicat National de l'Enseignement Chrétien (SNEC), affiliated to the Confédération Français de Travailleurs Chrétiens (CFTC), and opposed absorption into the state system. The 30% who were members of the Fédération de l'Enseignement Privé (FEP) (affiliated to the CFDT, of which the SGEN was also a constituent part) were more sympathetic to Savary's proposals.[27] Cardinal Lustiger, although anxious to avoid the risks of an overtly political entanglement, would prove to be a force in his own right. Nor was the situation on the political Left very much simpler. The largest group of Socialist Deputies was made up of teachers, many of them close to the FEN but some more sympathetic to the more eirenic policies of the SGEN. The CNAL, as an effective grouping of a range of predominantly anti-Catholic agencies, remained well organised and vigilant. Even within the enlisted ranks of Government, more than one voice was heard as the negotiations dragged on and became more convoluted. The Elysée, Matignon, and the rue de Grenelle all had educational experts and advisers, among whom harmony was not always perfect.

Negotiation and controversy focused almost entirely on the Catholic schools. Although the contracts concluded under the 1959 Law were, of course, open to other religious and indeed non-religious groups, the history of the previous two centuries ensured that only the well-entrenched Catholic schools presented a serious political problem, or aroused the old passions which had for so long divided France. The Protestants had been content after the Ferry laws of the 1880s to hand over to the State most of the schools they had founded, and their surviving schools now enrolled only about 3000 students: the sympathies of the Calvinist and Lutheran minorities were on the whole with the public system and with the principles of *laïcité* in which it was grounded. Edgar Quinet, Ferdinand Buisson and many other icons of the nineteenth-century educational reforms had themselves been Protestants of a liberal disposition. The Jewish schools were more significant: several had been founded after the arrival in France in the 1960s of Sephardic Jewish minorities from North Africa, and took advantage of the provisions of the Debré Law. Their schools operating under contract enrolled some 10,000 students, but were careful to accommodate themselves as inconspicuously as possible with the prevailing school system, to which they posed no threat. Whereas Catholic schools attracted large numbers of students on grounds other than religious, and simply because they provided a confessionally undemanding alternative to the public schools, Jewish, and indeed Protestant, schools (although technically open, of course, to students of other faiths) were intended to serve more sharply defined and limited interests. Moreover, the Jewish schools had for many years worked closely with the formal organisations of the Catholic Church, generally happy to enjoy the support offered by such an alliance; for example, in negotiations with the Government. Jews and Protestants were nevertheless ready to take to the streets when the settlement of 1959, as enlarged in the 1970s, was directly threatened.[28]

The daunting challenge confronted by Alain Savary was to preserve a mood of negotiation and adjustment, at a time when the CNAL and the FEN and the Socialist majority in Parliament were all demanding measures against the Catholic schools and the prompt fulfilment of the promises which Mitterrand had made before the May 1981 election. Moreover, 1982 was the centenary of the passing of one of the most important of the Ferry laws, establishing the secular school system. Most of the frictions since 1959 had arisen at the local level, where the elected members of the local authorities (and especially in the larger municipalities) obstinately persisted in finding ways of avoiding or limiting their obligations under the laws passed in Paris. The issue of the payments to be made for the subsidising of the expenses – other than teachers' salaries, of course – of Catholic schools (the so-called *forfait d'externat*) was a perpetual source of irritation. The State (until the introduction of the decentralisation laws in the early years of the new presidency) was largely responsible for these payments to secondary schools, but the local communes for similar payments to the much larger number of primary schools. Many of those communes delighted in refusing to meet their obligations, and the Prefects had therefore been repeatedly instructed by Paris to add these charges to the local budgets without any further consultation in all cases where they had been improperly omitted. In September 1981, Paris ordered the Prefects to abandon that practice, to the annoyance of the *laïque* party. Savary was at this stage in his ministry naturally doing his best to appease the Catholic school lobby, and on 25 January 1982 he met Guiberteau and a large delegation to open negotiations in earnest: by 19 May, the patient Minister had met forty-eight delegations representing the interests of the Catholic schools. At the first meeting, Guiberteau underlined the contribution which Catholic schools were currently making to the welfare of the nation, by educating two million students and employing 150,000 teachers. Savary was well aware of the costs that would be involved in any immediate and straightforward absorption of this enterprise into public education. The Catholics declared themselves happy to see the State as the guarantor but not as the ruler (*garant* but not *gérant*) of the education of the nation, and insisted on the absolute importance of the preservation of the *caractère propre* of their schools. Two days later, the leaders of the FEN in turn made their way to the rue de Grenelle and (as though that were needed) restated their own very different position:

> We remain faithful to the terms of the propositions of the CNAL. Public funds for the public school; private funds for the private school. This is a question of national unity. Education should be the same for all children, without segregation.

157

In February, the supreme authority in defining administrative law, the Conseil d'Etat, ruled that the communes must pay the *forfait*, although how much they should pay and when remained a source of fruitful disputes. In December 1982, a major demonstration in Nantes, with the marchers carrying candles and reciting the Lord's Prayer, was mounted as a protest against the continuing refusal of that municipality to meet its financial obligations to the Catholic schools. Mobilisation was beginning in earnest.[29]

In the same month, Savary elaborated his proposals. He chose to develop them within the context of a wholesale reform of the French educational system, and indeed of the traditionally centralised French State. That did not endear him to the FEN, or to the many groups with an orthodox Jacobin view of the Republic as one and indivisible (and, needless to say, *laïque)*. But without a strong dose of decentralisation, the proposals for the Catholic schools themselves made little sense, and the Minister was in fact asking the bishops and the defenders of those Catholic schools to gamble on the success of a now weakening government in pressing through unpopular changes. Savary genuinely wished to import greater flexibility and responsiveness into a vast and, in his view, dangerously overcentralised system. He naturally saw the Catholic part of a newly articulated system as a useful lever in carrying through the whole range of reforms: there was an important sense in which he wished to see every school in the country enjoying greater autonomy and developing its own *caractère propre*. In that, perhaps superficial, sense he preferred to see public schools become more like Catholic schools, rather than the other way round. But the risks and costs for the Catholic schools were vast and proved unacceptable. Savary proposed the creation of a new (and, for a foreigner at least, somewhat mysterious institution) the Etablissement d'Intérêt Public – an 'Establishment of Public Interest' or EIP, within which the personnel of the partner institutions (schools public and 'private', local authorities, the State) would cooperate in the delivery of a local educational service. Each institution would define its own 'project', which might for Catholic schools incorporate the *caractère propre*, even although that phrase did not appear in the texts. The teachers and other personnel in the private schools under contract would be progressively absorbed into the public service, initially at least on a voluntary basis. While there would, of course, be diversification within the EIP, national norms would be clarified and observed. Honoré and Guiberteau were uneasy at the arrangements proposed for nominating the head of a (Catholic) institution within an EIP: this should be 'concerted, with the intervention of the council of the institution concerned, with the council of administration of the EIP, with the Rector and the lists of aptitude'. The Enseignement Catholique could find no reason to prefer these vague and potentially threatening arrangements to the perpetuation of a contractual status. Savary may have hoped that a measure of vagueness would encourage the parties concerned to take the negotiations forward, especially as he realised that many of the Catholic schools were in financial difficulty. The Catholic leadership was not persuaded, and fully aware of the FEN's implacable hostility – to decentralisation as a policy, as well as to allowing private schools a place of their own within a public system.

Throughout 1983, the tortuous discussions continued, against a background of a deteriorating economic climate for France and of growing tensions within the Socialist parliamentary majority. The UNAPEL, ever suspicious of the risks of a betrayal by unreliable bishops, maintained a watchful opposition. Guermeur captured public attention as the advocate of the rights of families, rather than of the institutional interests of the Church. The identification of the struggle for the survival of the private schools with the political ambitions of the opposition became steadily more obvious and more dangerous. In October, and once again in Nantes, there was another major demonstration, supported by some 100,000 local protesters. In November and in the same city, the CNAL replied with 80,000 demonstrators of their own. These, however, were drawn not just from the immediate region: the CNAL depended for much of its support upon the teachers' unions, and appeared to lack the popular base now being successfully mobilised by the UNAPEL – 1983 was not 1959, and still less 1945, when the *laïque* cause rested on a much wider basis of support. Consumerism was displacing ideology. Savary's revised proposals, made at the beginning of 1984, contained more concessions, but the EIP (now somewhat weakened) survived, as did the proposals for the progressive absorption of the private school teachers – the *titularisation* which would effectively have made them civil servants, a change that would for financial and professional reasons have been welcomed by some but by no means all. But 1984 was above all the year of taking the argument to the streets.

Five major *manifestations* were planned: at Bordeaux in January, followed by Lyon, Rennes and Lille in February, and culminating with the massive gathering in Versailles on 4 March. In Bordeaux, the former Prime Minister Chaban-Delmas remarked that he had 'seen nothing like this since de Gaulle. It is *la France profonde* which is here expressing itself'.[30] The demonstration included Jews and Protestants and was led by Cloupet, the diocesan director of education who was later to become General Secretary of the Enseignement Catholique. The event in Lyon was marked by the singing in the place Bellecourt of the slaves' chorus from Verdi's opera, *Nabucco*, the refrain which, since Nantes in the previous October, had marked so many of the street demonstrations. An estimated 400,000 marched on the streets of Lille. Pierre Mauroy, mayor of that city until 2000 and for the moment Prime Minister, expressed his irritation with the old-fashioned *laïques* who were proving so unhelpfully inflexible. This unprecedented display of popular power on the streets reached its climax at Versailles. Lustiger and several bishops attended, as did a galaxy of politicians including Debré himself, Chirac, Tiberi, Alain Peyrefitte, Juppé, Toubon and Pasqua. Le Pen was there leading a delegation from the National Front, in spite of the efforts of the organisers to keep him at a safe distance from the centre of events. Pierre Daniel declared his assent to decentralisation (which was by now unlikely to be achieved on the scale that the Government had originally wished) and total opposition to the absorption of the Catholic teachers into the serried ranks of National Education. Pressure was mounting for a massive demonstration in Paris itself, but (encouraged by the continuing willingness of Savary to listen and to compromise) the leaders of the Catholic movements struggled to avoid deploying what they regarded as their ultimate weapon. Critics of the leadership argued that, if it was to be effective and law abiding, opposition must be mobilised before the passing of a law: the Church must never again (as after the laws of the 1880s and of 1905) be seen as an overt enemy of the Republic and its institutions.

April was marked by the publication of the twenty-five draft articles of the proposed law. The EIP had survived, but the contractual arrangement by the State was to be directly with the individual establishment: a relatively minor concession which nevertheless represented a return to one of the principles of 1959. The *caractère propre*, on the other hand, had disappeared. The authority of the school principal (the *chef d'établissement*) in nominating teachers to an establishment was to be significantly weaker than in the Guermeur Law of 1977. In an attempt to balance these concessions to the CNAL and its parliamentary allies, the obligation of the relevant authorities to pay the *forfait* was reaffirmed and strengthened. The *titularisation* of teachers was to be achieved progressively, in successive budgets and on a purely voluntary basis. These articles represent the closest that Savary would ever get to an achievable compromise. Pierre Daniel assured the President that 'provided that the text is left alone, there will not be a national demonstration'. Cardinal Lustiger was encouraged by his meeting with President Mitterrand, whose support for his own Government was now wavering: 'What a joy to work with this man!', the Archbishop observed.[31] On the following day, in an article in *Le Monde*, he unequivocally rejected the possibility of any conversion of Catholic teachers into civil servants (*la fonctionnarisation*), or – more precisely – to any such steps which would endanger the identity of the Catholic school.[32] The carefully assembled compromise was already crumbling: the parliamentary commission appointed under the presidency of André Laignel to examine the law began its work in May 1984 and, against the wishes and advice of Savary, accepted thirty Socialist amendments, all of them deeply resented by their political enemies and by all shades of opinion on the Catholic side. In the same month and against the explicit advice of Pierre Daniel, a remarkable convoy of vehicles moved from Nantes to Paris, to build a school in the Place Montparnasse.[33] It remained in place until the end of the month, a focus of opposition and testimony to the impotence of authority. The President himself was coming to doubt the good sense of pressing ahead with an unpopular reform, which threatened to split the party which had swept him to power in the first place. He had therefore concluded that, since nothing was now going to satisfy the Church, the Socialist amendments might as well be accepted. The Prime Minister, believing that he still had Mitterrand's support, objected (a little inconsistently for a Socialist) at the continuing attempts to replace constitutional by insurrectional power: 'The rule in a democracy is that Parliament should decide, and not the street'.[34]

The great demonstration in Paris finally took place on Sunday 24 June. Lustiger had already denounced the Prime Minister and his policies in *Le Monde* on 5 June: 'It is too late to imitate 1905'. On 17 June, the Socialist Party suffered a crushing defeat in the European elections, and the economic policies of the Government were widely regarded as an abysmal failure. The processions on 24 June converged on the Place de la Bastille, arriving from the main railway stations of Paris where 150 special trains had deposited them. The long and orderly processions lasted all day. Some 570,000 citizens arrived by train alone, and the total number participating was estimated at two million. For the moment and in public, the President stood firm but on 14 July in his Bastille Day address he announced on television that a new law would be introduced, later confirming that the Savary project had indeed been withdrawn. Neither the Prime Minister nor his Minister of Education had been consulted or informed in advance, and both resigned on 16 July.

The Catholic schools, it seemed, had now become an immovable part of French society. The long effort of a left-wing government to incorporate them more fully within a national system and to complete the work of Ferry and Combes had therefore failed. But the advocates of the pure school of the Republic had not surrendered and when, under a right-wing government an attempt was made to improve further the position of the private schools within a public system, they were ready once more to take up the old quarrel. Although the compromise of 1959 might just survive, any attempt to adjust it seems still to be doomed to failure.

Notes

[1] Nique, 1990b, p. 270. *Le Monde de l'Education*, February 2002, pp. 70-72.

[2] Wright, 1987, pp. 329, 331.

[3] Dabousville, 1979, p. 36.

[4] Visse, 1995, p. 237.

[5] Cholvy & Hilaire, 1986, p. 73.

[6] Halls, 1981, p. 14; Cholvy & Hilaire, 1986, p. 74.

[7] Atkin, 1991, p. 140; Halls, 1981, p. 109; Judge et al, 1994, p. 63.

[8] Atkin, 1991, p. 137.

[9] Ibid., p. 177.

[10] Halls, 1981, pp. 408-410.

[11] Ibid., p. 35.

[12] Ibid., p. 102.

[13] Duhamel, 1997, p. 391.

[14] Visse, 1995, p. 41.

[15] Ibid., p. 60.

[16] Leclerc, 1995, p. 7.

[17] Ibid., p. 70; Battut et al, 1995, p. 26.

[18] Visse, 1995, pp. 57, 77, 79.

[19] Battut et al, 1995, p. 153.

[20] Ibid., p. 33.

[21] Visse, 1995, pp. 95, 290, 291.

[22] Ballion, 1982.

[23] Battut et al, 1995, p. 14.

[24] Leclerc, 1995, p. 82; Visse, 1995, p. 63.

[25] Leclerc, 1995, p. 85.

[26] Savary, 1985.

[27] Battut et al, 1995, p. 137. See p. 152.

[28] Ibid., p. 172; Visse, 1995, p. 35; Leclerc, 1995, p. 216.

[29] Ibid., pp. 135-138; Savary, 1985; Battut et al, 1995, p. 53.

[30] Leclerc, 1995, p. 205.

[31] Battut et al, 1995, pp. 88 and 173.

[32] Visse, 1995, p. 424.

[33] Battut et al, 1995, p. 90.

[34] Leclerc, 1995, p. 267.

CHAPTER 10

Three Arenas: the corridors

Even if their complexity and contradictions eventually defeated him, nobody could have been better prepared than C.P Trevelyan to manoeuvre his way around the corridors of power, partisanship and influence in which the key issues affecting the relationships between church schools in England and the British State were tortuously resolved. Charles Philips Trevelyan was the eldest son of George Otto Trevelyan, scholar and statesman and baronet. George Otto was himself the nephew of the historian and man of affairs, Thomas Babington Macaulay. Charles Philips, like his father before him, was duly educated at Harrow and Trinity College, Cambridge, where his younger brother (the distinguished historian, G.M. Trevelyan) later became Master. He had been born in the auspicious year 1870, when his father was a member of the Liberal Government led by W.E. Gladstone. George Otto was, however, very critical of Forster's Education Act, passed in that same year, since he was convinced that it would serve to encourage the survival and growth of denominational schools, and specifically those of the Anglican and Catholic variety. Naturally enough, the young Charles absorbed the Liberal sympathies of his family, flavouring them with a youthful (yet persistent) romantic attachment to the hazily egalitarian and progressive theories represented for many of his generation by the idealism of John Ruskin. He became friendly with the Webbs and associated with the Fabians, sharing their commitment to reform – provided always that improvement was achieved without violence or revolution. In 1892, he became a member of the London School Board, taking a passionate interest in establishing in the capital an effective network of public elementary schools, free from the pressures of denominational loyalties. In the last year of the century, family influence helped him to secure a parliamentary seat in the constituency of Elland in the West Riding of Yorkshire. In the House of Commons, he joined his recently elected friend, Walter Runciman. Three years later, the critically important Balfour Act was placed on the statute book, and shortly thereafter Robert Morant wrote to his Prime Minister:

> *I agree with you that voluntary managers will find it a much more*
> *expensive business than they at present realise to bring and keep their*
> *buildings up to the increasingly heightened standards of the local*

> *authority. And possibly there will be some twenty years hence another
> 'intolerable strain' in that respect.[1]*

After just such a lapse of time, and as President of the Board of Education in a Labour government, Charles Trevelyan struggled to deal with that very problem – albeit with less success than Morant and Balfour had earlier enjoyed.[2]

The once mighty Liberal Party to which Trevelyan belonged was now in profound disarray, and had indeed been so ever since Gladstone's heroic attempts to resolve the Irish problem had so bitterly divided it. Its troops were heavily outnumbered by those massed on the Conservative benches. The ferocious debates, in and out of Parliament, which swirled around the 1902 Act and – even more decisively – the divisions within the Conservative Party provoked by the issue of protectionism and imperial preference nevertheless presented the battered Liberals with an unexpected opportunity of returning to power. Lloyd George had, of course, skilfully exploited the religious issue and stirred resentment against priests, whether Catholic or Anglican:

> *The ship of state is making its way through the midst of the rocks, and
> what is the Government's proposal? To put the chaplain on the
> bridge.[3]*

The General Election of 1906, in which Trevelyan himself handsomely increased his own majority while vigorously attacking the Education Act and its offensive concessions to church schools, inverted the fortunes of the two main parties: the Conservative muster fell from 402 to 157, while the Liberals advanced from 184 to 400. Of greater significance in the longer term was the novel presence of thirty Labour members – in 1900 there had been only two.[4] In 1908, Trevelyan was invited to become Under Secretary at the Board of Education, then presided over by his friend Runciman in the newly reconstituted Liberal Government led by Asquith. This experience at the Board during the years before the outbreak of war was no doubt a valuable preparation for the tasks he was himself later to face. Yet, it is surprising that this opportunity of closely observing the problems which Runciman encountered in tackling the thorny issue of state support for church schools did not make Trevelyan more fully aware of the tangled complexities in which that question was enveloped. The issue was, however, temporarily submerged as Parliament and the country were plunged into the great battle between Lords and Commons and into a succession of feverish general elections. In the first 1910 election, the comfortable Liberal majority was sacrificed; in the second, the two main parties achieved a draw (each with 272 seats). The balance of power was held by the forty Labour and eighty-two Irish Nationalist members. After the emasculation of the House of Lords by the Parliament Act of 1911, home rule for Ireland, or at least its southern part, could not now be long deferred. Meanwhile, of course, nothing could be done to offend the Irish Catholic vote, on which the very survival of the Government depended, and therefore nothing attempted which might threaten Catholic schools in England. But the Catholic vote, as will appear, was also important within England itself and especially to the emergent Labour Party in cities with significant numbers of immigrant Irish Catholic workers. The future of Catholic schools in England, like that of their Anglican cousins, depended to a remarkable degree on the vagaries of electoral politics. In England at least, Westminster corridors were more influential than pulpits, or courts, or streets.

Trevelyan's frustration with the party to which he belonged and the Government of which he was a member disposed him to work more closely with the growing Labour Party, and its leader, Ramsay MacDonald. Although he was not yet ready to break his ancestral party loyalties, deep commitment to the cause of peace and hatred of what he regarded as a wholly unnecessary war finally led in 1914 to his resignation from Asquith's team. For the moment, he was therefore expelled to the margins of public life, predictably losing the support of his constituency during the war years and (running as an Independent) suffering a humiliating defeat in the 1918 general election. In that election, fought in the overheated euphoric atmosphere generated by the ending of the War, Lloyd George secured a big majority for his coalition Government and for the tasks of reconstruction. Charles Trevelyan was, therefore, little more than a spectator of the efforts to revivify the educational system in the years immediately after the War, and of the delayed recognition by those in power that nothing fundamental could in fact be achieved without the willing cooperation of the church schools and a serious attempt to resolve their ever escalating financial problems. The pain and dislocation of war not infrequently release a burst of enthusiastic commitment to the rebuilding of social systems, and especially of education.[5] Many critics were convinced that the early victories of Germany were correctly attributable to its clear superiority in technical skills and intellectual leadership, and that the problems of Britain (as indeed of France) arose in large measure from obstinate backwardness in educational reform. The War also generated a powerful sense of the waste of talent associated with a narrow and socially exclusive educational system, and heightened an idealistic commitment to equality of opportunity. Moreover, the years of destruction and the inevitable neglect of buildings at home had produced an intimidating backlog of urgent repairs and improvements for schools.

Lloyd George, as leader from 1916 of the wartime coalition Government, had in any case already resolved that urgent attention should be given to educational development, and resources made available for it. He had, therefore, broken with tradition by bringing into his Government a scholar and administrator who was neither a politician nor a professional educationist. The historian, H.A.L. Fisher, was born a few years before Trevelyan and was almost as well connected: among his cousins he numbered Virginia Woolf, and his father had been private secretary to the

Prince of Wales (later King Edward VII). He had completed an education conventional for his class (Winchester and New College, Oxford) by pursuing advanced studies in Germany and France, whose standards of professional scholarship he admired. After an Oxford Fellowship, he became for a short while Vice-Chancellor of Sheffield University, from which, much to his surprise, he was summoned by Lloyd George to assume in 1916 responsibility for a series of educational reforms. A convenient House of Commons seat was soon found for him. Fisher's enduring achievements included the introduction of national salary scales and superannuation arrangements for teachers, the rationalising and extension of grants from central government to support the educational work of the local authorities, the coordination of the secondary school examination system and the invention of the University Grants Committee, which secured for many years the flow of public funds towards British universities without the imposition of political control upon them. His name is more commonly associated with the Education Act of 1918, many of the noble intentions of which were frustrated by the economic difficulties of the post-war years.[6] The principal innovations of that Act included the raising to fourteen of the minimum school-leaving age, the abolition of part-time schooling, the grouping of older elementary school pupils in establishments designed for more advanced study, and the introduction of plans to introduce (sadly, never implemented) day continuation schools for those who left school at the earliest permitted age.

With the prudence, or perhaps the innocence, of the professional historian, Fisher at first chose to deal with the religious difficulty by simply ignoring it, observing optimistically in his unfinished autobiography (he died in 1940):

For the first time in our national history education was a popular
subject and discussed in an atmosphere cleared of religious animosity. [7]

That may indeed have seemed at first to be true, but the hard fact was that the extensive reorganisation and rebuilding of schools that the serious application of the Fisher Act obviously required would never be accomplished without the active cooperation of the churches. Either public funds would have to be found for those schools – and that could not be achieved without rekindling the controversies that remained fresh in the minds of many – or the Catholics and the Anglicans would be excluded from further developments, and their existing schools would wither or (supposing that acceptable terms could ever be devised) be surrendered to the public authorities. But Fisher hoped to carry through his visionary reforms without in any way disturbing the delicate but increasingly vulnerable balance established by the Balfour Act. In the immediate aftermath of that Act, the voluntary bodies were in reality educating more children than the fully public schools: 3,097,067 pupils in the voluntary schools against the 2,870,213 in the Council (formerly Board) schools.[8] Even if the number of Anglican (although certainly not of Catholic) schools continued to decline, a logistic and ideological problem of these proportions would not simply evaporate. The loss of their distinctive schools would never be acceptable to Catholic voters: indeed, some Catholics wished to establish their own day continuation schools as well.[9]

Fisher's first and highly reasonable response to this quandary was to look north of the border at the settlement of the religious issue which had already been incorporated in the Education (Scotland) Act of 1918. Although that important piece of legislation – demonstrating yet again how fundamentally different the Scottish experience was and is from the English situation – had been actively promoted by the Apostolic Visitor himself, it required the surrender of all voluntary schools to the local authorities. The Catholics had struggled hard to provide for an enlarging immigrant population: the number of schools increased by some 75% between 1880 and 1910. The local authorities were under the new law to bear (as they still do today) all the costs of providing and running the schools, conceding to the religious authorities the right of veto over teacher appointments in them. But such a solution would never be accepted in England. In Scotland, the total voluntary provision still amounted to only 10% of publicly supported schooling, and of the 286 voluntary schools, no fewer than 220 were Catholic. Moreover, the Cowper-Temple clause had never been operative in Scotland, and denominational schooling could therefore be freely offered in schools of all types. In practice (as Catholics in similar circumstances across the Atlantic had long objected), the mainstream public schools had become Protestant in character, and there had been little demand for separate provision – except, of course, by the Roman Catholics. Moreover, the Catholic and Protestant populations had usually congregated in geographically separate communities. The Scottish solution nevertheless continued to haunt the English Catholic imagination, and was from time to time openly envied by the Roman hierarchy. But the objections to it were overwhelming – not least because of the consequences of such a solution for the freedom of teachers in public schools from clerical control.[10]

Fisher was, therefore, driven back into multilateral and overlapping negotiations, hoping (like his predecessors and successors) to square the Anglicans and Nonconformists before tackling the less tractable Catholics. His problem was that any concession to one side was certain to inflame the suspicions and hostility of at least one other, while further alienating those who (like Trevelyan's father) disliked the whole notion of wasting public funds on private schools. Nevertheless, the President of the Board convened a series of conferences during 1919 and took care to explain to the public the details of his own proposals. In a widely reported speech in April 1920, he began by paying a tribute to the memory of Robert Morant, who had just died. But of the dual system itself, he mildly observed that 'we pay an educational price for religious differences'. He had avoided raising the issue while his major reforms were being developed in the previous year because of the risk of 'rekindling the controversy'. He proposed that the voluntary bodies should now be invited (since they could obviously not be required) to transfer the control and effectively the ownership of their buildings to the local education authorities, who would thereafter control all the teacher appointments in them. Religious instruction would be provided not by visiting representatives of the denominations but by these regular teachers themselves, whose rights of conscience were to be safeguarded. Religious education would for the first time be required by law in all schools, whatever their previous status, and such instruction could (if parents so wished) be of a denominational character. Much of this had a Scottish flavour, but in undiluted form it could never be acceptable to English Catholics – who had much more to lose and for whom special arrangements had therefore to be devised. Some schools would therefore be allowed to 'stand out' (that is, contract out of the more general arrangements proposed) while continuing to receive some undefined measure of support from public funds. But, in an attempt to placate those Anglicans who sided with Bishop Knox, Fisher also insisted that in such cases the same terms should apply to all denominations. Knox himself, who had previously walked out of Fisher's carefully orchestrated conferences, was somewhat placated; Dr Clifford on the other hand, who had performed a similar exit, was not. For Trevelyan, in temporary political exile and reflecting on his experience as Runciman's lieutenant, all this must have sounded disconcertingly familiar. In July 1920, the chairman of the education committee of the Congregational Union wrote to Fisher rejecting the proposals on the grounds that they unduly favoured the Catholic and Anglican interests. The National Society appeared to be 'marking time', seeing real advantage in trading off the burden of maintaining their own sprawling school system against the advantages of enjoying wide access to pupils in all schools. The Catholics, of course, saw no advantage in dissipating their current efforts to maintain the loyalty of their flock if it were dispersed across a multitude of schools, and were firmly committed to maintaining the distinctly Catholic atmosphere of their own schools. The Nonconformist interest hoped that simply by doing nothing a well-disposed Government could preside over the peaceful disappearance of Anglican schools crippled with increasing costs and debt. Fisher failed to disabuse them, even when he pointed out that at the present rate of contraction it would take one hundred and five years for the Anglican schools to wither away.[11]

Two years later, the Conservatives finally withdrew their support from the Lloyd George administration, which promptly collapsed and the six years of coalition government came to an abrupt end. So, too, did the Liberal Party. Fisher shortly after withdrew from political life, to assume instead the burdens of the headship of an Oxford college, to muse in conversation on the world he had lost, and to prepare his major *History of Europe*. He died in London in a road accident in the blackout of 1940. In the year of Fisher's own departure from high office, Charles Trevelyan came back to the House of Commons in the general election of November 1922, this time as the Labour member for Newcastle Central.[12]

The Conservatives comfortably won this general election, but the landscape of British politics had been permanently changed. Although since the creation in the previous year of the Irish Free State there were, of course, no longer any Irish Nationalist members, the democratisation of the franchise (by the Reform Act of 1918) greatly increased the electoral weight of the working-class Irish Catholic vote in English industrial constituencies – like Newcastle itself, which Trevelyan now represented. The irreversible decline of the old Liberal Party was now matched by the rising power of the Labour Party, to which the domestic Catholic vote was to be of growing significance. Moreover, Labour had now supplanted the Liberals as the principal party of opposition, and its access to power was not to be long delayed. In the general election called by the (temporarily) insecure Conservatives for December 1923, Labour collected 191 seats and the Liberals 159, while the Conservatives themselves dropped back to a modest 258. The two-party system seemed to be dissolving, and the Liberals prudently decided to nudge an unreluctant Labour Party into office. In these inauspicious circumstances, as Ramsay MacDonald moved into 10 Downing Street for a first brief sojourn there, C.P. Trevelyan entered the new and inexperienced cabinet as President of the Board of Education. His father, on whose death in 1928 Charles succeeded to the baronetcy and the Northumbrian family estate, was pleased, even if he could never reconcile himself to his son's betrayal of the old Liberal Party. Trevelyan was to be President of the Board on two occasions – for a turbulent ten months in 1924, and once again from 1929 to 1931.[13] On assuming high office for the second time, twenty-seven years after Morant had confided to Balfour his suspicion that at about that time an 'intolerable strain' would once more be placed upon the position of the church schools, Trevelyan observed that:

> the two big jobs ahead are raising the school age and a denominational settlement. The first will come off, the second may not come off.
> (Emphasis in the original)[14]

That neither 'came off' is largely explained by Trevelyan's own failure (repeating that of Fisher) to recognise early enough that there was simply no hope of achieving the one without the other.

The problem of the relationship of church schools to the State had changed fundamentally during the first two decades of the twentieth century. Although money and buildings had always been at the heart of the problem (and always would be), the crisis of the 1890s concerned only elementary schooling. Elementary schooling, for Catholics as for Anglicans, was conducted largely on a parochial basis and was relatively inexpensive. The Balfour Act inevitably raised issues about the engagement of the principal churches in the business of secondary education as well, issues that had been sharpened by the progressive intentions of the Fisher Act. Of particular significance for Trevelyan and his contemporaries, however, were the rising aspirations within the ranks of the trade union and Labour movements for the extension of secondary education. In 1922, the year of the collapse of the Lloyd George coalition, R.H. Tawney (whose persuasive talents Trevelyan was later to co-opt) wrote one of the most influential educational pamphlets of the last century, *Secondary Education for All*. He argued that a genuine secondary education, albeit of a different character for different types of pupil, should be made available to all children from the age of eleven and, as a consequence, that the minimum school-leaving age should be raised. This would require new schools – 'central' schools of a secondary character in which older pupils from a number of elementary schools could be efficiently collected, and (at the very least) the provision of extra facilities for the older pupils retained for the present within the elementary schools themselves. If such a wholesale renewal were to be achieved, either the church schools would have to be ignored and therefore sidelined, or they would need to be drawn into an enlarging partnership with the State. In either case, all the old controversies would inevitably be exacerbated, since what was now at issue was no longer simply the maintenance with some State support of existing voluntary schools but the planned provision of a whole series of new denominational schools. But on what terms? To make matters yet more complicated, even the existing church elementary schools were woefully inadequate: on the notorious 1926 Black List of poor buildings there were twice as many voluntary as Board schools.[15] The principles of Tawney's argument were endorsed by the official 1926 report on the education of the adolescent (the Hadow Report) – which is hardly surprising as Tawney was himself a key member of the committee. Even if the Conservative Government of the day predictably rejected these proposals, Trevelyan on his return to office in 1929 was delighted to accept them wholeheartedly. Yet, in these new circumstances the settlement of 1902 had no relevance, since it made no provision for the state funding of new voluntary schools. Impasse seemed inevitable, and so indeed it proved.

The new emphasis on 'secondary education for all' therefore changed the landscape of the relationships between the State and all church schools. Of equal importance were the mutations of attitude, and in the demographic balance of power, within and between the principal churches. If the Catholic 'problem' had not existed, it seems likely that by the late 1920s the Established Church would with reasonable comfort have adapted itself to the principles unsuccessfully promoted by Fisher. Many Anglicans had indeed welcomed Fisher's suggestions in 1920, on the pragmatic grounds that they would increase rather than diminish their influence on the national educational system as a whole. They were, therefore, not unduly alarmed by the prospect of Anglican children (with varying degrees of denominational commitment) attending existing church elementary schools, but then proceeding to local authority secondary or central schools where an acceptable form of religious instruction would be provided. In 1919, the *Church Times* had proclaimed that:

> *the old sectarian strife must be forgotten, for the issue has changed. In bygone days it was whether one or another form of Christianity would get the best of the bargain. Now, the issue is whether Christianity or secularism shall be the future creed of England.[16]*

But the Church of England never finds it easy to agree with itself. In 1926, the Church Assembly moved into a more rigid position, demanding more denominational schooling. In the following year, the National Society nevertheless seemed content with the proposal that 'facilities' should be provided in public secondary schools. Then, in 1929, the Church Assembly managed to produce two contradictory reports.[17] Anglican attitudes were directly affected by the Roman Catholic position, which was consistently more intransigent. It is in that sense that the Catholics rendered the problem insoluble: their objections could not, for sound electoral reasons, be ignored even by a determined government, while any concession made specifically to them would inevitably agitate the Anglicans and incite them to seek the same deal for themselves as well. Concessions on that scale could not be afforded and would in any case anger Nonconformists and secularists.

The Catholic position, the principles of which varied little across these years, was reaffirmed by the English bishops in the spring of 1929. In essence, their statement was little more than a restatement of earlier declarations, and was entirely consonant with the papal encyclical, published later in the same year.[18] The teacher always acts as the agent of the parent, never of the State and whereas it is no part of the 'normal' business of the State to teach, it should encourage every form of sound educational endeavour. It is, moreover, the duty of the State to furnish the necessary means from general taxation to enable those parents whose own financial means are inadequate to fulfil their own duties. In the Catholic perspective, it made no sense to separate instruction in religion from the whole atmosphere of the school and from the rest of the curriculum: a good education could therefore be delivered for Catholics only in a Catholic school and by Catholic teachers. Allowances and dispensations would necessarily be made, but throughout the last century the hierarchy never wavered in insisting on these basic principles, and in challenging concessions which created little difficulty for Nonconformists and most Anglicans. Sufficient reference has already been made to the importance, and not least to Labour MPs, of the Catholic vote. This was dramatically emphasised by the brief campaign in Liverpool to establish for local government elections an openly Catholic party, dissolved in 1928 by a new archbishop wisely apprehensive of the possible ill effects of so close an entanglement of his church with party political interests.[19]

By the 1920s, the Catholic schools therefore no longer represented, as they had in the middle years of the previous century, a weak and politically unrepresented community of immigrants, drawing a modest financial advantage from access to state funding which had at first been enjoyed only by the very differently placed Church of England. Catholics had become more confident about their schools, more assertive in their claims for them, more clear than any other denomination about the purposes to be served by denominational schools, more determined to preserve favourable funding for them without any concomitant sacrifice of independence or integrity. The message of William Ullathorne had been well learned. The Catholic schools therefore became central, as they had not previously been, in any attempted redefinition of Church-State relations in England. This shift of focus is reflected in the raw figures of attendance at schools of various kinds. Although, for complex demographic reasons, between 1903 and 1938 the total number of children attending elementary schools somewhat surprisingly declined, the balance of numbers within that total recorded the shifting balance not only between the local authority sector and the voluntary sector but also the proportions within the voluntary sector. In 1903, the total number of pupils in local authority elementary schools was just under 3 million, whereas the voluntary schools enrolled just over 3 million. By 1938, however, the crude voluntary total had fallen steeply to about 1.5 million while the corresponding figure within the local authority sector had nudged up to 3.5 million. However, within the voluntary sector itself, the total for the Anglicans had in the same years declined from 2.3 to 1.1 million while the number of Roman Catholic places grew from 337,000 to 377,000. At the earlier date, therefore, the Anglican outnumbered the Catholic places by seven to one, but at the later date by only three to one. The greater clarity of the Catholics about the purposes and character of their schools and the more focused concerns of Catholic voters ensured that the policies of the hierarchy would now become the major influence in this field of state policy. This tendency was further accelerated by the very heavy concentration of Catholics and of Catholic schools in certain key areas: in Lancashire in the mid-1920s, no fewer than four-fifths of the elementary school places were voluntary, and many of them predictably Catholic.[20]

In 1924 and once again between 1929 and 1931, Trevelyan was critically hampered in what he might achieve by the electoral insecurity of the Labour Party and by the financial crises of the time. But in the course of 1924 he did manage to relax the conditions on which government grants could be paid to local authorities for educational development and made more free places available in secondary schools. Although the raising of the school-leaving age, which would in any case have exacerbated the problem of the voluntary schools, survived as a treasured objective, it could simply not be afforded. Even although in the general election of October 1924 the Conservatives secured less than half of the popular vote, the vagaries of the British electoral system delivered to them two-thirds of the seats in the House of Commons. Labour was left with 151 seats, while the Liberals declined to 40.[21] Lord Eustace Percy (Lord Useless Percy, according to Trevelyan) enjoyed a secure but unadventurous five years at the Board of Education, effectively inhibited in any case by Churchill's opposition to anything which sounded like educational reform. Churchill's apparent distaste for education as Chancellor of the Exchequer anticipated his later coolness as Prime Minister and provoked an unusually acid comment from Lord Eustace:

> *To tell the truth, Churchill's feelings about education have often reminded me, then and since, of Porson's famous comment on Gibbon's attitude to Christianity; he seemed to 'hate it so cordially that he might seem to revenge some personal injury'.[22]*

Nor were Churchill and his colleagues prepared to run the risk of rekindling the sectarian strife of earlier years. An attempt to defuse the sectarian issues by proposing legislation allowing local authorities to make their own arrangements with voluntary schools came to nothing. Although in the general election of May 1929 the raising of the school-leaving age was indeed a dominant issue, politicians somehow managed to skate around the denominational difficulties which such a reform would inevitably raise. In the general election of May 1929, Labour won 288 seats against 260 for the Conservatives. As the Liberals secured 59 seats, Labour never enjoyed a secure majority in the House. By now, for reasons explored above, the Anglicans and the Nonconformists were prepared to give a little on the voluntary school question. The Roman Catholics were now much more influential than they had ever been and, although no more amenable in principle, compelled by their poverty to take seriously any proposals to improve their position with further state grants. Bertrand Russell anxiously enquired of the new President of the Board of Education:

> *Is it likely that Labour ... will give more public money than hitherto to the non-provided schools, and in particular is it proposed to spend public money on the fabric of the schools? This, I know, is the policy of the Conservative party, but I shall be deeply disappointed if the Labour party also adopts a measure which as everybody knows is against educational efficiency and has no argument in its favour except the hope of getting the Catholic vote.*

Trevelyan robustly replied that:

> *I am absolutely determined that the Labour party shall not get into the hands of any religion, least of all the Catholic. I represent a constituency swarming with Irish Catholics. I would rather lose the seat than give the priesthood a bigger power in the schools.[23]*

Trevelyan was plainly unsympathetic to the Catholic and Anglican causes, and viewed most religious differences and preferences with mild amusement. In his own election addresses he was airily dismissive of outworn creeds, and during the great 1927 debates on the reform of the Anglican Prayer Book had written to his wife:

I hate chasubles and ritual ... But I am near Protestantism as the earth is near the sun from which came the original heat of life. Catholicism is some far off star, infinitely remote. [24]

Trevelyan made three determined attempts to secure a new law, enlisting the persuasive skills of both Tawney and Fisher in mounting an assault on public opinion, but was frustrated by what he denounced as the obsessive caution of Ramsay MacDonald, his Prime Minister. Some Labour members were understandably worried by the lack of any clear provision for the voluntary sector in the expensive business of raising the leaving age and reorganising schools, and the Labour Catholic lobby was restless. A half-hearted attempt to bring the religious groups together in a conference in January 1931 predictably failed: every effort by Trevelyan to concede a little to the Catholics failed to satisfy them, while provoking the disapproval of the Nonconformists. John Scurr, a Labour MP who was also a Catholic, therefore produced a wrecking amendment to postpone the operation of the proposed Act, and the Government was then defeated by an unholy alliance of Labour Catholics and Conservatives. The Lords then threw out what was left of the Bill, and MacDonald had already lost what little nerve he had. Trevelyan resigned from the Government in March 1931, and in August, MacDonald, in alliance with the Conservatives and Liberals, formed a National Government.[25] In the general election in October, Charles Trevelyan ran as an independent and lost his Newcastle seat. He retired to the countryside, enjoyed being Lord Lieutenant of Northumberland, and died in 1958. A trade union MP had made the position only to clear too Trevelyan, in writing to him after his resignation:

Our Party ... has allowed itself to be made a nest for the Catholic party. It's an evil bird that fouls its own nest, which is what the Catholic section did when it defeated the government ... The Catholics will have to be fought by Socialists one day and it is as well that someone has made a start however ineffective it may appear at first. [26]

The anticipated battle between socialists and the Catholics has, however, yet to take place.

In the year of Trevelyan's disillusionment and resignation, the youthful R.A. Butler first attained political office in the new National Government. Rab Butler (as he was always to be known) belonged to an academic and political dynasty to rival that of Trevelyan himself. A distinguished ancestor had at the end of the eighteenth century been headmaster of Harrow, where one of his sons followed him, before going on to become Master of Trinity College, Cambridge (an office later enjoyed by Rab Butler himself). Another son became headmaster of yet another famous public school (in the perverse English sense of that term), while yet another became a canon of Winchester: his wife (Josephine Butler) was one of the foremost social reformers of the century. The remaining son of the dynasty's founder was the grandfather of Rab Butler. Rab's own father had deserted a promising academic career after coming top in the examination for the Indian Civil Service, later becoming Governor of the Central Provinces and finally in his turn head of a Cambridge college. Richard Austen Butler was born in the month when Balfour's Act appeared on the statute book and was educated at Marlborough and Cambridge, where he secured a Fellowship. He had the good fortune and the good sense to marry a daughter of the rich and enlightened industrialist, Samuel Courtauld, an alliance which helped him to secure at the age of twenty-two a safe Conservative seat in the House of Commons. This was in 1929, the year in which Trevelyan became for the second time President of the Board. He was therefore well placed to take a post as a junior minister in the India Office in 1931. Butler was an admirer of Baldwin and of his successor, Chamberlain and, in spite of difficulties with Churchill and his policies, remained in office continuously until the Labour victory of 1945. He represented the same constituency in the House of Commons from 1929 until 1965, on several occasions occupying key cabinet positions and twice coming within reach of the premiership. In 1965 (like another Butler before him), he became Master of Trinity. He died in 1982.[27]

Butler became Chairman of the Conservative Education Committee in 1937, the year after Oliver Stanley as President of the Board had (at last) succeeded in pressing through a significant variation in the terms of the Balfour Act and at the same time, with much less fuss, carrying through some of the reforms unsuccessfully propelled by Trevelyan – including the raising of the school-leaving age, even if that had in the event to be postponed until the end of Word War II. The 1936 Act was carried through as the National Government (now led by Baldwin, after MacDonald's resignation in the previous year) enjoyed a comfortable majority, insulated from electoral shocks. The Act was of great importance in establishing the principle that state grants might once again be applied to the costs of new buildings for voluntary schools. It therefore prepared a navigable path towards the major reforms to be negotiated during the War by Butler himself. The Act empowered, yet did not require, local education authorities to make grants of between 50 and 75% of the total of building works made necessary by the projected raising of the school-leaving age. Such grants were to be made only during a three-year period and only for the specific purposes stated. Teachers in schools so built or rebuilt (later classified as Special Agreement schools) were to be appointed by the local authorities, after consultation with the relevant church body, and a certain number of them were to be 'reserved' to secure instruction in the relevant denominational religion. The Church of England responded coolly to these proposals, and various sections of it were becoming daily more sympathetic to an emphasis on securing Christian teaching in schools of all types. The newly appointed Cardinal Hinsley gave the Act a cautious welcome as a step in the right direction. Some 519 new proposals were duly presented before the outbreak of war and of these, no fewer than 289 were made by the Catholics, in spite of the relatively small size of their own total and their continuing financial difficulties. Politicians and officials at the Board were disconcerted by the bitterness which in some sensitive areas arose from attempts to apply the provisions of the Act. In Liverpool, which had already witnessed some classic disputes as well as the formation of a specifically Catholic political party, the intransigent Archbishop Downey ruled his enlarging flock, paying little attention to the cautious leadership of the Cardinal. The Liverpool local education authority refused to release any of the new grants to Catholic schools – an act of defiance of the will of Parliament which led first to a cut in the amount of government grant paid to it, and then to a special Act enabling that local authority itself to build new schools where they were most needed, and then lease them back to the church. The publication of the Spens Report in 1938, drawing out still further the implications of the Hadow Report, pointed unambiguously towards the creation of a whole new structure of secondary education, with more grammar school places for the academically disposed pupils and a network of (expensive) modern and technical schools for all other pupils over the age of eleven. A financial and therefore a sectarian crisis now appeared to be imminent, and even the outbreak of war in September 1939 would not long delay the introduction of major reforms and a major rewriting of the now obsolete settlement of the Balfour Act.[28]

Meanwhile, R.A. Butler had moved to a junior ministerial post under Halifax at the Foreign Office, where he applauded the Munich agreement and regarded entry into the European war as both undesirable and avoidable. Butler had, moreover, already crossed swords with the implacable Churchill over the India Bill. He had been a consistently enthusiastic supporter of Neville Chamberlain and in when in May 1940 Churchill replaced Chamberlain as Prime Minister, Butler spent five anxious days of uncertainty about his political future. Then he was received by Churchill, 'looking very flushed and with gleaming eyes holding the remains of a very wet cigar half bitten through'. He told Butler:

> *I wish you to go on with your delicate manner of answering*
> *Parliamentary Questions without giving anything away.[29]*

Just over a year later, Butler was again summoned to the presence and wrote this account of the meeting:

> *The PM saw me after his afternoon nap and was audibly purring like a great tiger. He said: 'I want you to go to the Board of Education. I think you can leave your mark there. It is true that this will be outside the mainstream of the war but you will be independent. Besides,' he said with rising fervour, 'you will be in the war. You will move poor children from here to there' – and he lifted up imaginary children from one side of his writing pad to the other – 'and this will be very difficult.' Then he said, 'I am too old now to think you can improve people's natures. ... I should not object if you could introduce a note of patriotism into the schools. Tell the children that Wolfe won Quebec'.[30]*

Obviously, Churchill had no intention whatsoever of encouraging or even allowing Butler to undertake major structural reform, and made this very clear a few months later when the President seemed, for once, to be rushing his fences:

> *It would be the greatest mistake to raise the 1902 controversy during the war, and I certainly cannot contemplate a new Education Bill. ... Your main task at present is to get the schools working as well as possible under all the difficulties of air attack, evacuation, etc. If you can add to this industrial and technical training, enabling men not required for the Army to take their places promptly in munitions, industry or radio work, this would be most useful. We cannot have any party politics in war time. ... Meanwhile you have good scope as an administrator.[31]*

Butler, first inspired with the possibilities of what he might achieve in education by the encouragement of the American ambassador, had other plans. In any case, the process of reviewing the whole educational system had already been quietly begun and it seems likely that the extent of Butler's own contribution to creating a new sense of momentum has generally been exaggerated. His civil servants, some of them in wartime exile in Bournemouth, had already been at work alongside Chuter Ede, the Labour MP and Under Secretary at the Board. Chuter Ede remained at his post with the new President, and made a powerful and expert contribution to the work that now moved steadily forward. He recalled clearly the problems which both Fisher and Trevelyan had found insuperable in tackling the denominational question.

That the resilient settlement of 1902 had lasted so long was due less to its perfection than to its growing inadequacies. Since it represented a vulnerable and uneasy compromise, any attempt to adjust it led to the predictable protests which Churchill, especially in wartime, was resolved to avoid. Yet, by 1941, when Butler assumed office, all the principal partners in the educational enterprise had good reason to seek some further, and preferably definitive, adjustment. The reorganisation of the school system, to include adequate provision for secondary education, was urgently required and public opinion was now supportive of reform and of the necessary expenditure. The all-consuming demands of war lengthened the backlog of necessary building. But the major reorganisation could not be achieved without the cooperation of the churches. The Catholics in particular were understandably protective of their own schools and proud of the investment that they had recently made in them. But their need of public funds was, as always, balanced by anxiety about preserving a necessary independence. The local education authorities, as the heirs of the School Boards of 1870, had by now become the major partners in educational provision – schooling over 3.5 million children alongside the 1.1 million in Anglican and 0.3 million in Catholic schools.[32] Although in many areas the relations between the elected authorities and the churches were friendly enough, in others (notably in the north) there was great tension. The history of Liverpool had epitomised this only too well. Half-hearted efforts by the National Government to permit locally negotiated settlements had foundered, partly because of uncertainty about the financial arrangements and the degree of independence to be ceded. Senior civil servants were anxious for reform, and sympathetic to the aspirations and frustrations of the local authorities: before Butler assumed office, they had drafted with Chuter Ede a first version of the new arrangements. Nevertheless, a strong political impetus would be essential if the inertia in the system was now to be overcome.[33]

Teachers, mobilised in their increasingly confident and powerful union, were deeply resentful of many aspects of the dual system. The residual power of the clergy was offensive to their professional pride and autonomy, and they objected that, in voluntary schools where teachers' salaries were paid by the State, a requirement to teach a particular form of the Christian religion discriminated against those of other faiths, or of none. They were indignant at being in effect excluded from the headships of some ten thousand schools scattered across the country. Although they were in principle less immediately affronted by the existence of the smaller number of Catholic schools serving the Catholic community, they understood well enough that the principled intransigence of the Catholics impeded any necessary concessions by the Anglicans: 'Unless you Catholics are careful in what you say, you will cause such a wave of feeling in this country that all your non-provided schools will be swept away altogether'.[34] The teachers shared with the Nonconformists a strong distaste for the single school districts, of which some four thousand persisted and in which there could be no choice of school. Although with the decline of the Liberal Party, with which they had enjoyed a traditional alliance, the Nonconformists had lost much of their political muscle, doughty champions like the venerable Scott Lidgett (who had fought the good fight as long ago as 1902) kept up their opposition to denominational schooling. Now acknowledging that religious teaching could in an increasingly secular world no longer safely be left (as they had once insisted) to the home and the Sunday school, they worshipped at the shrine of Cowper-Temple: Christian teaching there must be, but never of a denominational character. The Nonconformists were the natural allies of the local education authorities, and implacably opposed to any further concessions to either Catholics or Anglicans.

For the Church of England, the schools question was of fundamental importance. Since the Reformation of the sixteenth century, its privileged position as the Established Church had entailed an engagement with all levels of educational work. It had been early in the field in providing elementary schools for the poor, alongside smaller groups of Protestant Nonconformists. The State, for many years unwilling to take any initiative in these matters, had provided the churches with financial assistance, under different terms at different times. Even if leading politicians had been so inclined, they were simply not free to ignore the contributions made by the Church. The declining importance of the Church of England (in common with most other churches, except, of course, the Roman Catholics) made its spokesmen deeply sensitive to any further loss of influence. Already disestablished in Ireland (1869) and in Wales (1920), it was rapidly losing active membership in England itself. The financial burden had long been intolerable, many buildings were sadly dilapidated, little state assistance was available (to either Anglicans or Catholics) for any new school which may be required, and (above all) no funds were available to establish a genuine system of secondary education. Yet, there would be resistance from many quarters if any increase in public funding were to be proposed without a corresponding concession of control by the State and the local education authorities. For most of the century the school question had consumed much of the energy and tactical skill of Anglican leaders: in the long reign as Archbishop of Canterbury of the astute Randall Davidson, only the contested 1928 reform of the Prayer Book had filled more boxes of correspondence than the debates about the abortive legislation of 1906-08.[35] Although some fiercely committed Anglicans were resolved to maintain their own system of schools, owned by and impregnated with the spirit of the national church, most had come to accept that it was now more important to secure the teaching of the Christian religion to all pupils in all schools. This was the underlying argument of the Archbishops' letter to *The Times* in February 1941, incorporating the so-called Five Points.[36] The Catholic position was and always had been fundamentally different in its emphasis, and inseparable from the extension of denominational schooling. And if the Catholics successfully insisted on improved financial arrangements, Anglican advocates would, of course, at once demand the same. Much of the argument in 1942 and 1943 rotated around these shifting points. Of profound significance in the evolution of these exchanges was the succession in 1942 of William Temple to the leadership of the Anglican communion. Temple, deeply distrusted by Conservative politicians and indeed at first by Butler himself, was the former (if unhappy) headmaster of a public school and, less typically for a future bishop, President of the Workers' Educational Association. A deeply committed Christian socialist, he had officiated at the wedding of R.H. Tawney, by whom he was profoundly influenced. The entente which he rapidly developed with Butler was of crucial significance in the evolution of a new settlement. Temple shifted the emphasis on the role of the Church (of England) away from preserving its own domestic system towards serving the needs of the nation in an open and progressive manner:

> *Above all, let us not give the impression that our concern as church people is only with the adjustment of the dual system: we ought as Christians to be concerned about the whole of the educational progress. I am quite sure that the raising of the school leaving age will of itself do more to make permanent the religious influence of the schools than anything that can be done with directly denominational purpose.[37]*

179

Such unfamiliar sentiments were to disconcert some of his own troops, especially those who kept a wary eye on their Catholic brethren.

Even their most unfriendly critics could not deny the logic of the Catholic position: promulgated in 1929 in *Divini Illius Magistri*, it had been consistently defended, with more or less tact, by the English hierarchy: Catholic schools with Catholic teachers for Catholic children. Catholic spokesmen were not impressed by the offer of instruction in the Catholic religion in a school open to all faiths: what mattered was the totally Catholic atmosphere of the whole school and of every aspect of its life and learning. There could, moreover, be no such thing as interdenominational religious instruction: doctrine which was not explicitly Catholic was Protestant (or worse). The bluntly outspoken Cardinal Hinsley, a Yorkshireman who became famous for his patriotic broadcasts during the War, gave no hostages to fortune:

> *Denominationalism is a bogus slogan. The undenominational teaching in the provided schools is Protestant and the Agreed Syllabuses are Protestant and so denominational.*[38]

At the same time, the Roman Catholics were not especially interested in the question of the ownership of buildings: what mattered was not ownership but control. This, of course, is precisely why English Catholics hankered after the Scottish solution of 1918, which achieved precisely that result. Life would have been simpler for politicians and administrators (as well as cardinals) if the Roman Catholics could somehow have been quietly ignored for a while, or at least bought off with a special settlement confined to them. But this, of course, is precisely what could not happen. Butler had vainly hoped that the Catholics could somehow be sidelined at least until the major questions of the Anglican schools had been resolved, and delivered an early warning to 'the Catholics that this particular settlement was not their pigeon'.[39] In retrospect, it seems remarkable that the Catholics could have been excluded, as they were, from all the early discussions to which representatives of the Church of England and of the Nonconformists were regularly invited. Although in the minds of Butler and his advisers this may have been an attempt to rule by dividing, it would not have been a plausible tactic but for the widespread conviction that Catholics were somehow different, Irish, and not at all English. In 1939, Herbert Hensley Henson, the provocative Anglican Bishop of Durham, could write that:

> *Neither Roman Catholics nor Jews can be brought into any general system of general teaching, for both are minorities so largely alien in race and creed as to be properly accorded distinctive treatment. ... Roman Catholic and Jewish schools are genuinely denominational institutions, for they are only provided where there is a definite denominational demand to be satisfied, and their sharply distinctive character renders them unattractive to the general body of the English people.*[40]

Yet, in spite of the apparent sharpness of the Catholic case, Butler found its exponents infuriatingly elusive, and complained of a succession of representatives taking somewhat different lines. Although this difficulty has been attributed to a deliberate nebulousness on the part of the Catholics [41], it was more probably a result of the weaknesses and ambiguities in the structure of the governance of the Catholic community in England.

His experience of negotiating in the India and Foreign Offices had doubtless prepared Butler for the intricacies of the tasks which he inherited in the summer of 1941. His indispensable ally was his political assistant in the coalition government, Chuter Ede, who enjoyed the multiple advantages of being a Labour MP, a Nonconformist in close touch with sensitivities on that front, a former teacher and member of Surrey County Council. The President of the Board was perhaps at first more at sea than he later chose to remember, or as some of his more enthusiastic admirers were encouraged to suppose. According to Chuter Ede, he came away from an early meeting with church representatives enquiring, 'What is an elementary school?'[42] Of Chuter Ede's dedication to his task, as of his expertise, there could be no doubt: he successfully resisted Churchill's attempts to promote him to another department.[43] Butler's own position was at first dangerously weak. The Prime Minister wanted little done (apart from moving children from here to there), and the previous President of the Board had indeed been disposed of precisely because he too had hoped to achieve something significant. Eden, from whom Butler had sharply differed over Munich, was irreconcilably hostile to 'the appeaser' and may well have manoeuvred him into what was intended to be a backwater.[44] Nevertheless, the Act which Butler eventually steered on to the statute book, and which thereafter bore his own name, was the foundation of post-war education in Britain. It introduced universal secondary education, raised the school-leaving age, strengthened and simplified the powers of the local education authorities, and abolished fees for secondary education. None of these things could have been achieved without a durable settlement of the religious problem. But Rab Butler was preoccupied by this central problem not simply, and not primarily, because dealing with it was a precondition for all the other radical and secular changes. For Butler, the religious issue stood at the very heart of the matter because he believed that denominational schooling should as a matter of sound Conservative principle be preserved. He was equally convinced that, for the first time, the teaching of the Christian religion should be universal in all schools maintained by local education authorities.[45] But how were all these things to be achieved?

The meandering discussions (as already noted) had begun with the publication in the spring of 1941 of the Government's Green Book, shortly before Butler assumed office. On 15 August – the occasion after which the President apparently posed his question about elementary schools – there was an inconclusive meeting with church representatives, naturally not including Roman Catholics. But nothing was apparently said about the voluntary schools (perhaps because the main parties were pleased by their recent agreement about the Five Points) and the emphasis was on teaching Christianity in all schools. The terms in which Archbishop Lang took for granted the exclusion of the Catholics are themselves remarkable:

> *For the first time in the history of English education, the deputation,*
> *instead of representing division among Christian Churches in England*
> *and Wales, represented their unity. ... This measure of unity was the*
> *result of long conferences with Free Church leaders, under Scott Lidgett,*
> *and held under the auspices of the National Society. It reflected the new*
> *attitude forced on people by evidences of widespread ignorance of the*
> *Christian Faith and the challenge of Nazi Germany to any sort of*
> *Christian civilisation. ... I ought to add another quite unprecedented*
> *fact: at the end the President asked me to offer prayers for guidance.[46]*

When in 1942 Lang (the first Archbishop of Canterbury ever to do so) retired, he was succeeded by William Temple, who himself lived for only another two years. Perhaps the most important of all the encounters of these years was between Temple and Butler on 5 June 1942 when, according to the President, the Archbishop was won over to the cause of major structural change by the impressive and depressing account of the number of Anglican schools on the official Black List: even bringing the present embarrassingly inadequate provision up to scratch was obviously beyond the resources of the Church, never mind the raising of the school-leaving age and the realisation of Tawney's dream of secondary education for all, to which Temple himself attached so much importance. Temple, and not only because he needed to reassure his more traditional critics (of whom there were many), mounted at the same time a vigorous defence of the voluntary school principle in an address on 3 June, arguing that the very duality of the educational system helped to avoid the dangers of totalitarianism and concluding that:

> *We cannot agree to anything that constituted the wholesale surrender of*
> *our Church schools.[47]*

Temple and Butler agreed that there should be religious instruction and Christian worship in all schools, while the voluntary schools should be given a choice of status. Those which were content to pass under effectively public control should be fully funded, while those which elected to preserve a larger measure of denominational freedom would have their recurrent costs paid by the State and receive a 50% grant towards the costs of building repairs and improvements. This slowly emerging consensus was rudely shattered in October 1942 by a letter to *The Times* in which Cardinal Hinsley, running true to form, denounced the possibility of any compromise. Churchill, with ill-concealed glee, jumped on this proof that he had been right all along. According to Butler's own (later and questionable) account, the Prime Minister had this letter cut out, stuck on a piece of cardboard and sent to Butler with the discouraging message, 'There you are, fixed, old cock'. More sober and contemporary accounts suggest only that he telephoned the message, or carried it around in his pocket for several days.[48] Butler now wisely searched more urgently for a Catholic representative with whom he could pursue serious negotiations, but with indifferent success. Hinsley had soon discovered, on his return to England in 1935 after a long absence in Rome and Africa, that as Archbishop he enjoyed little direct authority over the other members of the hierarchy – some of whom impolitely objected when he presumed on his own initiative to consult the Catholic Education Council. Butler himself endured a frosty reception in November 1942 when he went to consult the aged Peter Amigo, auxiliary bishop of Southwark (but a titular archbishop) and a hardened veteran of the school wars for whom the Balfour Act (said Butler) was something which had happened in his comparative old age:

> *after much sounding of the bell a sad-looking, rather blue -faced Chaplain let me in and we climbed a massive palace stair to the first floor where the Archbishop was sitting, fully robed, in a small room overlooking the ruins of Southwark Cathedral. His window was open on his left hand so that he could at once take in the tragic picture of the ruins and inhale the chilly morning air. The Archbishop asked immediately we had sat down what I had come to see him for. I obliged by informing him; but it was not an auspicious beginning. He said that a 50% grant was not sufficient and that he saw no chance of agreement with politicians. He said that if I had belonged to his community he would have suggested that we should pray. I said I would be very ready to do so as I was also a churchman.*

> *The interview indicated the nature of the head-on collision with the Roman Catholic Church.[49]*

In March 1943, Hinsley died and there was a delay of nine months before Bernard Griffin migrated from Birmingham to be enthroned as his successor. Meanwhile, the negotiations were conducted fitfully by a committee led by the ageing Archbishop Downey of Liverpool. Unfortunately, the Archbishop had recently adopted a drastic weight reducing regime and was for most of the year recuperating in Ireland, where according to Rab, he 'had been encouraged in his militancy'.[50] A prominent Anglican complained that Downey – whom he dismissed airily as being not highly regarded in 'the spheres of learning and devotion' – had constituted himself as 'the exponent and fighting chief in England of Popish educational policy'.[51] Downey had been profoundly affected by the bitter sectarian attitude in his adopted Liverpool, which he reflected in a speech at the Liverpool Stadium in October 1943.[52] The grandees among the old Catholic nobility neither respected nor trusted the tactless Archbishop, and Butler recorded how the eighty-eight year-old (and deaf) Lord FitzAlan, uncle of the sixteenth Duke of Norfolk and last Viceroy of Ireland:

> *staggered into my room and drawing himself to within an inch of my*
> *nose, said that he greatly distrusted Archbishop Downey and could not*
> *hear what I said. I endeavoured to indicate that I agreed with him. We*
> *both then shook hands and said that although those were our feelings, it*
> *would be unwise to say so.[53]*

The Nonconformist backlash provoked by the insistent public demands of Downey as the Catholic spokesman for most of 1943 was as predictable as it was disturbing: it would not take much to dissolve the agreement that Butler and Temple had already effectively achieved. As late as March 1943 (when Hinsley died), Churchill continued to be a major problem for Butler: at a meeting at Chequers, he made it clear that he had still not made up his mind and was as reluctant as ever to stir up the hornets' nest of educational reform and religious loyalties. He and other leading Conservatives were finally persuaded that educational reform would at least be the lesser of two evils. The implementation of the Beveridge Report on social security, now being vigorously promoted by its controversial author, would have been vastly more expensive and would have meant throwing money 'down the sink'.[54]

The White Paper on which legislation was subsequently to be based was, therefore, finally published in July 1943, but with the Catholics still unsatisfied and anxious. Alongside the major proposals for the development of the national system as a whole were two fundamental changes affecting the relationships of Church and State. The first endorsed the proposal, circulating since 1941, that each day in every school should begin with an act of worship and that religious instruction should, with appropriate safeguards for those who objected on grounds of conscience, be an obligatory part of the school curriculum. Such instruction must be in accordance with an Agreed Syllabus, negotiated locally to ensure that it would be acceptable to most Protestant groups. As for the voluntary schools, they were to be given a clear choice between two future paths. A school could be funded entirely by the State, with the buildings remaining formally the property of the Church, and the teachers appointed and paid by the local education authority. Religious instruction would then be in accordance with the Agreed Syllabus, although denominational instruction could also be provided if parents requested it. Such instruction might, if problems arose, be delivered by 'reserved' teachers, who would have to be in sympathy with the principles of the relevant denomination. Butler and Temple anticipated that this path – that of voluntary controlled status – would be followed by a large majority of the Anglican schools. They proved to be mistaken, although not in the parallel conclusion that all Roman Catholic schools would choose the option of greater autonomy represented by the category of voluntary aided school. The skilful achievement of Butler and Temple during their 1942 conversations had been to divide the category of voluntary school into two sets, believing that both options should be open to both major denominations (so that there could be no suspicion of favoured treatment for the Catholics). The voluntary aided school would remain unambiguously denominational, with religious instruction in the appropriate faith and teachers appointed by the managers or governors of the school itself. Teachers' salaries would be paid by the local education authorities, as would virtually all the running costs of the school. A 50% grant would be made towards the costs of (external) building repairs and improvements, although no provision was formally made for the building of new schools. Butler did, however, agree to reopen the list for Special Agreement schools (under the 1936 Act) where new building was made necessary by the reorganisation of the local system (now into primary and secondary schools, of course) and made other concessions where buildings needed to be redeployed or redeveloped in order to meet local needs.[55]

Although the debate on the White Paper in the Commons was calm, the Lords naturally gave more trouble. Even William Temple seemed unhappy, perhaps once again needing to reassure his own critics that the cause of the Anglican voluntary schools had not been abandoned. He now asked for a 75% grant, but later withdrew, provoking the gibe that 'Temple and Cowper-Temple have kissed each other'.[56] But for the Catholics, for whom voluntary aided status was the only remotely acceptable solution, the financial problem was not so easily brushed aside: they calculated that the costs would be enormous, that 50% was not enough, that vague half-promises of future help with new buildings were not enough. Butler tried to persuade them to be patient, and not to risk everything by pressing too hard at this delicate moment. He was not helped by the intervention of the Apostolic Delegate, William Godfrey, who accused him of paying too much attention to local education authorities and teachers, 'these unimportant persons', grumbling that the Government seemed quite prepared to pay 100% grants for 'atheists' (presumably in the council schools). The Pope sent an aggressive public message, revealing that the subtleties of the English scene were not well understood at Rome and causing Rab 'a certain element of nausea'.[57] In September 1943, Butler the Anglican and Chuter Ede the Unitarian agreed to attend a meeting of the northern Bishops at the imposing Ushaw College near Durham, where the intention seems to have been to overawe the ministers:

> *We were greeted by the Bishop of Hexham, in full robes, and taken almost at once into the evening meal, which, in the tradition of the younger Pitt, was served at about 6 o'clock. There was a large gigot and tolerable quantities of red wine. Immediately this feast was over we were taken to see the chapel, and a magnificent ivory figure was taken down from the High Altar for our benefit. We were all filled with a certain awe, which was no doubt intentionally administered. Chuter Ede told me he thought he was going to faint.[58]*

One bishop, unimpressed by the self-sacrifice (or cowardice) of the Church of England, protested that the Roman Catholics would not advance 'with the smell of the blood of the Anglican victims on the altar in front of them'.[59]

The Education Bill was, nevertheless, introduced in the House of Commons in December 1943. Fortunately, Butler was about to be once again rescued from further acrimony by the arrival of a new archbishop: the translation of Bernard Griffin to Westminster in January was as important to the success of his plans as had been the translation of William Temple to Canterbury two years before. Griffin speedily calmed the fears of his fellow bishops, serving them with celebratory drinks, and uniting the Irish and English as well as the northern and southern factions.[60] He decided to trust Butler and to accept his assurances that generous help would be given in providing on favourable terms loans to assist with the costs of new building, that regulations would be interpreted flexibly, and that once all the fuss was over the clouds would break and further concessions might then be expected. At the second reading of the Bill in January 1944, Butler noticed the new Archbishop in the gallery of the House of Commons and, glancing upwards, recited a verse from a well-known hymn:

> *Ye fearful saints fresh courage take,*
> *The clouds ye so much dread.*
> *Are big with mercy, and shall break*
> *In blessings on your head.*

On the following day, having in mind the coincidence of surname, Griffin sent to Butler a copy of Alban Butler's *Lives of the Saints*.[61] The Roman Catholic schools now seemed a secure part of the English establishment, protected by a benevolent State. Neither the Archbishop nor the President seemed to recall that the first line of the hymn which for them heralded the dawn of this new era was 'God moves in a mysterious way'.

Notes

[1] Allen, 1934, p. 161.

[2] This chapter draws extensively on the lives of Trevelyan by Morris (1972) and of Butler by Howard (1987).

[3] Murphy, 1971, p. 51.

[4] Butler & Butler, 2000, pp. 233-234.

[5] Winter, 1974.

[6] Fisher, 1940; Ogg, 1947.

[7] Fisher, 1940, p. 94.

[8] Fisher, 1918, p. 30; Cruickshank, 1963, p. 191.

[9] Andrews, 1976, p. 48.

[10] Conroy, 2001; Tropp, 1957; Murphy, 1971, p. 103.

[11] *Times Educational Supplement*, 1 April, 8 July and 19 August 1920.

[12] Trevelyan, 1921.

[13] Butler & Butler, 2000, p. 234; Morris, 1972, p. 156; Barker, 1972.

[14] Morris, 1972, p. 173.

[15] Cruickshank, 1963, p. 126.

[16] 12 December 1919.

[17] Cruickshank, 1963, p. 126.

[18] *Divini Illius Magistri*; Arthur, 1995a, pp. 25-27.

[19] Murphy, 1971, p. 107.

[20] *Education*, 21 August 1925.

[21] Butler & Butler, 2000, p. 235.

[22] Percy, 1958, p. 96.

[23] Morris, 1972, p. 176.

[24] Ibid., p. 179.

[25] Simon, 1974, p. 107.

[26] Morris, 1972, p. 181.

[27] For Butler, see Howard, 1987.

[28] Cruickshank, 1963, pp. 131-135.

[29] Howard, 1987, p. 95.

[30] Ibid., pp. 109-110.

[31] Ibid., p. 115.

[32] Cruickshank, 1963, p. 191.

[33] Arthur, 1995a, p. 172; Jeffereys, 1987, p. 415.

[34] *Catholic Herald*, 6 April 1943.

[35] Bell, 1938/1952, p. 510.

[36] *The Times*, 13 February 1941.

[37] Temple, 1942, p. 573.

[38] Heenan, 1944, p. 148.

[39] Green, 2000, p. 150.

[40] Henson, 1939, p. 201.

[41] Barber, 1994, p. 47.

[42] Howard, 1987, p. 113.

[43] Jeffereys, 1984, p. 423.

[44] Green, 2000, p. 154.

[45] Ibid., pp. 153, 157.

[46] Lockhart, 1949, p. 368.

[47] Gosden, 1976, p. 281.

[48] Butler, 1971, p. 159; Jeffereys, 1984, p. 424.

[49] Moloney, 1985, p. 164.

[50] Davies, 1994, p. 233.

[51] Ibid., p. 242.

[52] *The Times*, 16 October 1943.

[53] Davies, 1994, p. 244.

[54] Howard, 1987, p. 133; Timmins, 1995.

[55] *Educational Reconstruction* Cmd 6458.

[56] *Church Times*, 30 July 1943.

[57] Davies, 1994, p. 237.

[58] Butler, 1971, p. 106.

[59] Davies, 1994, p. 240.

[60] Warlock, 1997, p. 133.

[61] Davies, 1994, p. 248.

CHAPTER 11

Three Countries:
Catholic schools in America today

The contemporary relationship of Catholic schools to the State in America is, as has been repeatedly demonstrated in earlier chapters, determined by a unique historical development and by a set of distinctive assumptions and dogmas about the place of religion in private and public life. Underpinning these beliefs are a deep and underlying sense of personal piety and widespread habits of religious observance, uneasily coexisting with a theoretical commitment to maintaining the separation between Church and State. The United States are in a special sense at one and the same time religious and secular. There is an obvious, and not simply mythological, sense in which the origins of the nation were and are rooted in religious traditions and enthusiasms. Many of the earliest European immigrants crossed the Atlantic in an effort to escape from the oppressive corruptions of the Old World, and in a mission to create new settlements where true religion (but not necessarily the toleration of alternatives) could be freely practised. The new commonwealth was to be built as 'a city on a hill', radiating light to the surrounding darkness. Religion in its Protestant or Puritan forms, therefore, lay at the very heart of the colonial enterprise, especially in New England. In most of the colonies there was, therefore, a close association, even a theocratic assimilation, of Church and State, and various forms of establishment were commonplace.

Within two centuries, that pious tradition was to be complemented – and in some respects contested – by the principles and insights of the Enlightenment, by rationality celebrated as the modern foe of superstition, by an emphasis on the civic rather than the ecclesiastical. But the men of the American Enlightenment tended to speak and write more respectfully of the Deity than did their European contemporaries. Nor did they have any reason to share the strong anti-Catholic emotions nourished by their French cousins. Successive European Popes, as John Ireland learned only too well, failed to appreciate such subtle distinctions or to understand that the American Revolution was as profoundly different from its contemporary French counterpart as were the two national versions of republicanism. It was, nevertheless, essential that the American Republic should be able to accommodate a rich variety of sects and denominations and that no kind of national religion should be imposed or preferred. The special circumstances of the American Revolution ensured that the Constitution of the United States, and specifically, of course, in the language of the First Amendment, enshrined a fundamental principle – however controversial its interpretation and application later proved to be – which imposed a separation of Church and State, and in consequence an explicit rejection of any establishment of religion. But that, of course, by no means entailed that religion ceased to be of crucial importance in American private or public life. De Tocqueville, that most percipient of observers, argued that the withdrawal of overt public support for any kind of religious establishment in fact stimulated the vigorous growth of self-reliant faiths and of religious diversity.

This deeply ingrained public and private engagement in religion, until recently in essence identified with the Christian faith (and indeed with typically Protestant versions of it), was for many decades characteristic of the American public school movement, as epitomised in the career of Horace Mann in Massachusetts. This was the frame of reference within which, whatever the patriotic reservations of John Ireland and his allies, Catholic schools were developed: it delimited the context in which those schools, like the ethnic parishes with which many of them were associated, preserved Catholic identity in an inhospitable and predominantly Protestant and Anglo-Saxon world. Catholic schools flourished in the nineteenth and for much of the twentieth centuries as a result of the persistence of the inherently religious and essentially Protestant character of the allegedly neutral and non-sectarian public schools. As those schools themselves became, in the eyes of their critics, less pious and progressively more secular, humanist, rationalist and liberal in their sympathies, so the justification for schools with a strong religious orientation was sharpened and generalised. Not only Roman Catholics but fundamentalist Protestants as well now became more persuaded of the need to maintain 'their own schools' as islands of faith in a secular sea. The debate about the appropriate demarcations between public and private, within which the relationship between Church and State is, of course, one classical element, began to mutate as new alliances were formed. In a strongly 'religious' country, Catholic schools discovered new friends, anxious to preserve American traditions of theological commitment and orthodoxy.

Any discussion of the role of Catholic schools in contemporary American society must for these reasons be conditioned by prevailing national attitudes towards religion in all its forms and towards its relationship to the authority of the State. In this respect, the current American experience has little or nothing in common with the parallel situations in France or in England. Religious leaders in both those countries have for many decades lamented the decline of religious belief and observance and the advance of 'dechristianisation'. But in the United States, declared religious loyalties are, if anything, even stronger now than they were at some points in the twentieth century. The proportion of those surveyed who claimed to have attended a place of worship at least once during the previous week had been 37% in the 1930s; in the 1990s it had risen to 42%. There was, unsurprisingly perhaps, a surge of interest in and support for religion after 1945 and some decline in the 1960s and 1970s. But that decline was emphatically checked in the last decade of the century. In the middle of the last century, 95% of a carefully chosen sample reported themselves as believing in God, compared with 96% at the end of the same century. No less than 87% then considered themselves to be Christians, while over 90% believed (and presumably still do) in God, and 75% in hell. There was a powerful and widely noted religious dimension in the collective responses in New York to the tragic events of 11 September 2001, when the World Trade Center was destroyed by terrorists and thousands of lives were lost. It might therefore have been expected that such a benign climate of opinion would have resulted in a massive endorsement of religiously affiliated schools (however defined) and, indeed, of support for them drawn from public coffers. But things are not as simple as that. Doubtless, any attempt to restrict the rights of parents to have their own children educated in private schools of their own choice would be warmly resisted – and in some cases by those very same groups that, in the name of defending civil liberties, still jealously preserve the wall of separation between Church and State. Private schooling is one thing, but generalised support for the public funding of it quite another.[1] In yet another Gallup poll conducted in the first year of this century, 56% of those surveyed declared themselves opposed to experiments designed to channel public funds towards religiously affiliated schools. The corresponding figure for 1998 had been 50%, suggesting, perhaps, that support for such developments (commonplace as they were in England and France) had in fact already peaked. Moreover, a large proportion of those consulted believed that private schools receiving such subsidies should be accountable on much the same basis as were the public schools themselves: a strong expression of opinion likely to occasion some concern in the minds of those who support private schools precisely because they are at present free from such dangerous restraints.[2]

Opinion in the United States clearly, therefore, remains deeply divided between those who are prepared to promote extensive aid to religious schools, and those who continue to reject such a possibility. Such historic divisions continue to be reflected in the judgments of the Supreme Court, of which the case of *Mitchell v. Helms* in June 2000 was a neat example. In hearing this case, the Court upheld by a majority of six to three that federal grants to religiously affiliated schools for the purchase of books, computers and other equipment were indeed lawful. Such a ruling, unimaginable if the Court had not already reversed its own judgment as embodied in *Aguilar*, was to some extent innovative in articulating the principle that such subsidies would become unconstitutional only if it could be shown that government aid was being applied to specifically religious purposes. Justice Clarence Thomas, while predictably concurring in this judgment, seized the opportunity to deliver a much more sweeping opinion making virtually any form of aid to religious schools constitutional – provided that it was not intended to serve specifically religious purposes, and was available equally to non-religious schools. Although six of the nine Justices supported the ruling itself, five of them rejected this enlarged interpretation of the judgment, demonstrating yet again the precarious balance of opinion within the Court, which continued in the year 2000 to deliver uncertain messages. In June, it heard a case arising from the objections raised five years earlier by a Roman Catholic and a Mormon student against the practice in the Santa Fé school district of authorising a 'non-sectarian, non-proselytising prayer' before football matches. The Court, by a majority of six to three, found the practice unconstitutional. Justice John Paul Stevens opined that the effect of such prayers was to send a message 'to members of the audience who are non-adherents that "they are outsiders, not full members of the political community"'. Yet, Chief Justice Rehnquist, writing for the minority, objected to the tone of the majority ruling, which bristled 'with hostility to all things religious in public life', while the Justices declined to rule on a lower court decision which had allowed the same school district to hold student-led prayers at graduation ceremonies.[3]

The problem of the relationship between religious communities and public authority in the United States is always complicated by the tensions between the self-image of America as a religious, indeed overwhelmingly Christian, country and an equally tenacious commitment to inclusiveness: minorities of all kinds must not just be but must also feel themselves to be a fully integrated component of a diverse and complex society. In the United States, it is wiser to think in terms of relationships being established not between Church and State but between churches and states. There is no single culturally dominant church (as there is in France and was for a long time in England), while in terms of the civil power there is no unitary authority competent to furnish universally valid settlements. The fifty states, the federal authority as represented by Congress, and above all, the multitude of Courts with the Supreme Court as custodian of the Constitution all revolve in an elaborate dance.

Some of the more complex and hesitant steps in that dance were exposed to public scrutiny in the election campaigns of the year 2000, just as they had been – although even more openly – in 1988. Early in the campaigns, both of the principal candidates (Al Gore and the ultimately successful George W. Bush) prudently declared themselves to be born-again Christians, and were careful to attend prayer breakfasts and to appeal to as many religious groups as possible. Bush, the Republican candidate, took advice from the ubiquitous Ralph Reed, formerly the effective mobiliser of the Christian Coalition. While campaigning for the Republican nomination, Bush (wisely or not) made a more direct appeal to the fundamentalist Christian Right by making a much publicised speech at the Bob Jones University in South Carolina. The University (which had awarded a degree to the extremist Protestant leader in Northern Ireland, Ian Paisley) prohibited dating by members of different races and was notoriously anti-Catholic. The future President's visit and speech offended many of his more liberal supporters, and even more of the uncommitted voters who proved to be so important in the election itself: for the rest of his campaign he was careful to moderate his tone. Any aspiring American president must now learn to speak the languages of the Enlightenment as well as of the Reformation, of the Old Testament as well as of the New, of Ignatius Loyola as well as of Luther. Both candidates in 2000 declared themselves as being in favour of educational choice and of charter schools, while Bush had many approving things to say about vouchers as well. Al Gore, even had he been so inclined, could not have afforded to do any such thing, for he would then have alienated his strong supporters in the National Education Association, who revered the memory of Horace Mann. In choosing as his vice presidential running mate Senator Joe Lieberman, the first Jewish citizen to fill that place on the ballot, he appealed more directly to religiously sympathetic but traditionally liberal constituencies. An Orthodox Jew could be relied upon to appeal to those who longed for a return to traditional and decent values, while at the same time reassuring those who feared any erosion of that strong wall of separation between Church and State which Jewish groups had consistently defended. But it was, above all, important to keep a delicate balance. Lieberman hoped to distance his party from some of the less savoury episodes of the Clinton years and confidently proclaimed his faith. But when he appeared to be in danger of advocating too close an identification of religious loyalties with political virtue, anxious voices were raised. He too soon learned to moderate his tone. Again, America was being deliberately projected as a deeply religious country – if no longer exclusively Protestant, then at least Christian, or at least Judaeo-Christian, or at least monotheistic, or at least theistic, or at least deist, or at least … religious. It was at all events unambiguously clear that the Catholic community and its traditions had by now been accommodated in the mainstream of American political, social and economic life. If Catholics had enemies, they were certainly not mainstream Protestants. In the long run, albeit not in the way he would have expected, John Ireland had won the battle. But that very success inevitably raised uncomfortable questions about the role of Catholic schools, of their relationship to the publicly provided educational system, of the justifications for their separate existence, and of their access to public funds.

By the time of Kennedy's installation in the White House in 1961, Catholics throughout the United States had established themselves as a considerable force. They had long constituted the single largest religious denomination and by 1960 represented nearly one-quarter of the population of the United States. But even more significant was the position of Catholics at the very centres of power, wealth and influence. The Catholic population had in the past been marked by a particular character, itself the consequence of patterns of large-scale immigration from Europe and of heroic efforts to preserve in an unfriendly environment national identities and Catholic habits. The Catholic Church was by 1960 quite plainly no longer the church of the immigrants, of the tightly knit ethnic communities concentrated in the inner cities and sustained by a network of 'national parishes'. After World War II, the GI Bill had opened opportunities in higher education to new sectors of the population, and prominent among them were Catholics. Government-funded mortgages enabled many of them to move from the inner city to the suburbs, which were themselves rapidly growing. Americans, and American Catholics prominently among them, were becoming a nation of car drivers, and the building of new highways during the Eisenhower presidency further encouraged the flight to the suburbs.[4] Catholics were becoming more prosperous and suburban – in a phrase, more American, and less easily distinguishable from their Protestant fellow countrymen. As the descendants of previous generations of immigrants moved out from the inner city to the suburbs, in many cases finding themselves well satisfied with the public schools provided by the more prosperous school districts, so their place has been to some extent filled by new waves of immigrants, of predominantly Hispanic origin and unaccustomed to paying for schooling. The demand for Catholic schools became less insistent, and the justifications for them less clear. By the mid-1980s, only the Episcopalians and Presbyterians had a membership with a higher proportion of households enjoying an annual income of more than $40,000. The ghetto Church of the nineteenth and earlier twentieth century had faded into a nostalgic past. In the early 1920s, for example, two-thirds of the children of Polish immigrants attended Polish parochial schools: but no longer.[5]

The growing scale and confidence of an enlarging Catholic school system were reflected in the development of high schools. The earliest Catholic schools had, for obvious reasons, been elementary and parochial. Such high schools as had been built were for the most part established by the religious orders and had a strongly academic character: indeed, in many cases such establishments long offered both a high school and a college education under one roof. High schools were, in contrast, not generally available for the immigrant groups which historically constituted the bulk of the population of the Catholic elementary schools. The first impetus towards the development of a more popular and less expensive version of the Catholic high school came from the Baltimore plenary council of 1884, which encouraged the creation of diocesan high schools, designed to meet the needs of a group of parishes. But in the early 1920s there were still only thirty-five such high schools: the years of significant growth lay between 1925 and 1945. Although by 1962, 344 diocesan high schools had been successfully established, even then only about one-third of Catholic students attended Catholic high schools, compared with about one-half of all Catholic students attending elementary schools. This imbalance in provision between the elementary and secondary sectors helped to perpetuate the markedly academic character of the Catholic high school, and doubtless contributed to its reputation for academic success.[6]

Until 1965, Catholic schools of all kinds had consistently and confidently grown in size and importance. An enrolment in 1880 of 405,000 had risen past 2.5 million by 1930, to 3.1 million in 1950, and peaked in 1965 at 5.5 million. These five and a half million students were taught in thirteen thousand schools, and accounted for 12% of the total school (K-12) population of the country. There then followed a precipitous and unanticipated decline: between 1965 and 1990 Catholic schools lost fully one-half of their student numbers, and in the latter year therefore accounted for only 5.46% of the total school population.[7] Moreover, and mainly as a result of the opening of many non-Catholic private schools designed to serve the needs of a fundamentalist Protestant community increasingly dissatisfied with the prejudices of the 'Godless' public schools, the Catholic share of the private education market itself declined. In 1965, students in Catholic schools formed 87% of the non-public school population: the corresponding figure in 1984 had fallen to 64% (and, as will appear, has since declined further). This decline was caused by the interaction of a number of contributory factors. The one most difficult to quantify, namely, a collapse (real or imagined) of confidence in the necessity and value of separate schools for Catholics, is discussed below. Obviously linked to this was the major shift of the Catholic population from the inner city – where for obvious reasons the existing Catholic schools were located – to the more prosperous suburbs, where such schools had not been implanted and the public system was itself viewed as satisfactory by many Catholic families. Reinforcing such tendencies was an overall decline in at least the measurable aspects of loyalty to Catholic traditions and religious habits. Over the last thirty years of the last century, active membership of the Roman Catholic Church fell significantly. Although this decline was less steep than that in the membership of the traditional Protestant churches (witness, for example, 44% for the Episcopalians), it was counterbalanced by an increase of 96% for the Mormons, 211% for the Assemblies of God, and an arresting 863% for the Church of God in Christ. Meanwhile, the proportion of the population adhering to the Islamic faith had during the same years advanced to 3.5%, making it comparable in scale to Presbyterianism. The general continuities in the American commitment to religious causes and attitudes, to which reference has already been made, obviously mask profound changes in specific religious loyalties, which themselves affect the debate on government relations. Roman Catholics must now be recognised as but one among the many faith-based groups.[8]

Between 1963 and 1974, the proportion of those claiming membership of the Roman Catholic Church who attended church regularly dropped from three-quarters to one-half, while the percentage going to confession fell from 37% to 17%. Some commentators attribute such abrupt changes to the upheaval in Catholic attitudes and loyalties initiated by the Second Vatican

Council convened by Pope John XXIII in 1962, and in particular to the emphasis laid in some of its pronouncements upon the importance of coming to terms with the modern world, or upon the defence of religious freedom in general terms as a natural right to be extended to the adherents of all faiths (and of none). Traditionalists were even more disconcerted by such innovations as the vernacular versions of the traditional Mass, or the perceived devaluation of ceremony and ritual. The unwillingness of a significant part of the Catholic population in America to accept the rulings of Pope Paul VI on contraception created further tensions.[9] Between 1966 and 1978, fully ten thousand men left the priesthood, while the number of seminarians, or priests in training, declined by over 70% in the twenty years between 1964 and 1984.[10] Between 1966 and 1980, the number of women religious (nuns and sisters of all kinds) dropped by 30%. In the three years immediately after the convening of Vatican II, 4332 women in America left their religious orders but, curiously perhaps, even more new recruits joined: the number of nuns and sisters therefore peaked at 181,421 in 1966, but had fallen to 126,517 by 1980.[11] The overall picture is, therefore, one in which, over the second half of the last century and against a national background of sustained or enhanced public concern with religious issues and observances, institutional Catholicism declined sharply. One index of this unquestionable decline in the institutional strength and visibility of Roman Catholicism lies in the ratio of active priests to the Catholic population as a whole: by 2005 this ratio will be only half of what it had been in the mid-1960s.[12] This is not, of course, to suggest that there was a neatly corresponding decline in the personal (crudely distinguished from the official) loyalties of most Catholics.

The liberalising in the 1960s of the official attitudes of Rome towards the modern world and to other Christian denominations, the blending into the mainstream of American life of traditionally Catholic and immigrant communities, the enlarging prosperity and suburbanisation of many traditionally Catholic families, the economically threatening decline in the number of religious sisters and brothers willing to work for a pittance in Catholic schools were all factors which contributed to the decline in the number of Catholic schools in the later twentieth century. The hesitant aspirations to provide a place in a Catholic school for every Catholic child – the ideal of John Hughes but not of John Ireland – began to look not only unrealistic but also anachronistic. The formal efforts of some bishops to resist the sociological and ideological tendencies of the age had little practical effect, even although in the years after World War II fifty-five of the one hundred and four dioceses had statutes requiring children of Catholic families to attend Catholic schools whenever that was practicable.[13] In the twenty years between 1964 and 1984, when the future seemed most bleak, 40% of high schools and 27% of elementary schools disappeared from the Catholic scene.[14] By 1985, between fifty and one hundred Catholic schools were being closed each year. More recently, the picture has become more nuanced as the rate of decline has been arrested, if not in some ways reversed. Nevertheless, a further 435 Catholic schools closed between 1990 and 1994. Diocesan investment even in the schools that survived was sharply reduced: in 1990, the archdiocese of New York reduced by one-half the amount of subsidy paid for the support of 160 of its 243 schools. The situation is further complicated by the uneven distribution of such reductions, for the most part reflecting movement within the Catholic population from one part of the country to another and the arrival of new immigrants. The loss of schools has been especially severe in the North-east, with the archdiocese of New York suffering most.[15] However, these figures for overall reductions do allow for the opening of new schools in suburban areas, and in the last decade of the century, as will be shown when the current situation is analysed later in this chapter, the decline has been to some extent checked.

In the 1960s, however, and in the years which followed, Catholic schools confronted a major crisis. The members of the religious orders, and especially of the female Congregations, on whom the schools had depended for so much of their teaching, left in large numbers. Catholic families became more prosperous and moved to the suburbs. The ties between ethnic and religious identities were loosened. The mood of Vatican II encouraged contemporary Catholics to develop a more open and engaged attitude to the world of which they were a significant part. The authority of a hierarchical church was weakened by a fresh emphasis on the autonomy of the individual conscience. The aspirations of the 1884 Baltimore Council had in any case never been realised: the ideal of a Catholic school for every Catholic child had never been achievable, and for many Catholics now seemed undesirable. The crisis in numbers and funding was accompanied by a crisis of confidence as well. Such shifts of sentiment are accurately reflected in the publications of the period – several of which bore titles making clear the preferences of the author – which attracted a good deal of general attention. In 1964, Mary Perkins Ryan published *Are Parochial Schools the Answer?* and addressed precisely these questions. There could be better and less expensive ways of preserving the Catholic faith in America and, in the absence of any real hope of substantial support from public funds, there appeared to be no way in which the large existing system of schools could be preserved, and still less, fundamentally adapted to match the increasing mobility of the Catholic population.

In the following year, the debate about the place of Catholics in American society and intellectual life was widened. Observers had already recorded a significant change in the attitudes of the Catholic community towards the schools to which historically it had owed so much. Nostalgic loyalties to a distinctive tradition – marked by a suspicious although historically justified isolationism, by a populist and unquestioning piety, by an emphasis on puritanical virtue rather than intellectual rigour, by a dependence on teachers imbued with a monastic spirit – had already begun to erode. Gary Wills evoked this new spirit in his characterisation of Catholic education in *Bare Ruined Choirs*.[16] The old order was crumbling, and needed to be replaced:

> *That time of year thou mayst in me behold*
> *When yellow leaves, or none, or few, do hang*
> *Upon those boughs which shake against the cold,*
> *Bare ruined choirs, where late the sweet birds sang.*

Andrew Greeley was later to characterise this period as 'a golden twilight'. A popular musical affectionately satirising the archaic attitudes of the teaching nuns – *Do Black Patent Leather Shoes Really Reflect Up?* – enjoyed a considerable Broadway success. In 1965, Mgr Jon Tracy Ellis published an influential article ('American Catholics and the Intellectual Life') deploring the philistine prejudices of many Catholics, and not least of Catholic educators, the lamentable weakness of Catholic higher education, and the lowbrow isolationism of many Catholic schools. For a while, it seemed that the schools would find themselves without friends, and that the successors of the bishops who had raised funds and earned reputations as energetic builders of schools and churches would find other uses for the diminishing resources at their disposal. But in 1967, the National Council of Catholic Bishops responded with the unambiguously titled 'Catholic Schools are Indispensable', following it five years later with a more reflective call to action, 'To Teach as Jesus Did'. It seemed that Catholic schools, however hard pressed over the coming years, were, after all, not about to disappear.

Discussions about the role of Catholic schools, as of the reasons for which they might (or might not) receive support from public funds, must always take account of the striking fact that the majority of the children of Catholic families do now attend public schools: over 80% in the case of elementary, and over 85% for secondary schools.[17] Nor, as will appear in the discussion of the character of the American Catholic school, is it the case that all the students in all the schools are Catholics or come from Catholic families. In the year 1997-98, 2,648,859 students were enrolled in these schools: 1,995,649 in primary, 13,932 in middle schools, and 633,818 in secondary. Of the 8223 schools, the great majority (6897) are primary, 1219 are secondary and 107 are classified as middle. Some 152,260 teachers (full-time equivalent numbers) are employed in the schools. Attention has already been directed to the decline in numbers since the peak years of the 1960s. In geographical terms, the decline has been very uneven: of the six regions in which the schools are grouped, three have recently registered a decline and three (led by the South-east) an increase.[18] In the decade between 1985 and 1995, 120 new elementary and 14 new secondary schools were opened.[19] The National Catholic Education Association reported in 1998 that 170 new schools had been opened in the previous ten years (although the total number of schools had, of course, declined), and that overall enrolment had risen for six consecutive years. Closer examination of the figures, however, reveals that across the full ten-year period, overall enrolment fell by 1.5%, secondary by 9.2% and K-8 by 3.2%. The only sector which had grown was, in fact, the pre-school, which registered a massive increase of 123%. What must be of greatest significance to the wider discussion of the relationships of the private sector of education to the public system and to public funding is the shifting proportions of the provision within the private sector itself. In 1970, private schools enrolled 11.1% of the total number of K-12 students across the whole country; in 1990, that percentage had fallen only slightly to 10.7%. However, in the earlier year, the Roman Catholic share within that slice of 11.1% was 9.1%, with only 2.0% remaining for other providers of all kinds. Twenty years later, the corresponding proportions (again of the total school population) were 6.0% and 4.7%.[20] Within the non-public sector, the relative decline of the Catholic school population is, therefore, being all but matched by an increase in the enrolments by other groups, and notably by fundamentalist Christians. At the beginning of the twenty-first century, the Catholic schools do, nevertheless, remain the largest single group of private schools in the United States.

Whether those schools constitute 'a system' is, of course, a significantly different question. In some important senses they obviously do, and not least because of their incorporation in a vast international network of Catholic schools, working within a framework of doctrine and practice as established by Rome. Although clear general principles are set by the Vatican, extensive local variations in their application reflect widely different social and political circumstances, and often incorporate formal arrangements made with the civil powers through Concordats and similar instruments. For reasons already explored, there could be no such universal arrangements in the United States, where all essential powers in matters of education belong to each of the states, and not to Washington. At the same time, and notably as a result of a growing intervention since the middle of the last century by federal powers in educational matters, questions bearing upon the relationship between federal funding and religiously affiliated schools have been propelled towards the top of the public agenda. The resolution of such questions lies ultimately within the brief of the Supreme Court, which (as was argued in chapter 8) finds great difficulty in formulating universal and consistent principles to govern Church/State relations. Such factors obviously inhibit the evolution of any sharply delimited 'system' of Catholic schools, with an unambiguously defined place in public life (of the kind which, for example, they now enjoy in France). But although there may be no national Catholic system, there are influential coordinating agencies. These have been of particular importance for the Church in the United States, where – even although the Cardinal Archbishop of New York has over time come to enjoy an informally pre-eminent authority among his fellow bishops – there is no primate. The canonical body representing the bishops, on the model required by Vatican II, is the the National Conference of Catholic Bishops (NCCB), existing alongside the United States Catholic Conference (USCC), which fulfils a more consultative and political role, and includes representatives of priests and lay people. Each of these bodies (formed in the 1960s from the National Catholic Welfare Council, which had itself existed since 1919) has committees and other groups concerned with educational questions. More influential upon the daily life of the schools is the National Catholic Education Association. The NCEA, which was founded in 1904, has headquarters at the heart of Washington, DC, with a very wide membership and a series of specialist advisory and coordinating services.

All such national bodies insist that, as a necessary corollary of the Roman Catholic understanding of the nature of the Church, final responsibility for education within his diocese rests with the bishop of the place. The 175 dioceses are the linked but largely autonomous components of a loosely articulated system. Only the diocesan bishop can authorise the use of the term 'Catholic' in the title of a school, and his has always been the dominant voice in determining whether and where schools might be built, and under whose auspices they might be conducted. All dioceses now have school boards or committees, and a professional Superintendent of Schools. The degree of control exercised varies greatly: in some large dioceses, an impressive hierarchy of support and of control exists – not, however, to be compared in scale and complexity with the bureaucracies that flourish within the public system itself. In others, the supervision is light and schools are left very much to their own devices. Such differences often, but by no means invariably, reflect differences in the scale of the local exercise or in the geographical distribution of schools. Even in those dioceses where there is some urge towards centralisation, there are quite narrow limits on the control which can be exercised by the diocese. Catholic schools in America fall into three broad categories: those which are maintained by a parish or a small group of neighbouring parishes, those which are provided by the diocese for a wider constituency (the 'central' schools'), and those which belong to the so-called 'private' group, nearly all founded and to some extent still owned and maintained by the religious orders. The great majority of elementary schools are of the parochial variety, whereas among the secondary schools, 42% are classified as private. In some major cities nearly all the Catholic high schools are in this sense private. The median payment for tuition for the elementary schools is $1499, and $4100 for secondary: within the secondary category there is a wide range of fees, reflecting wide differences of type and of academic quality. Diocesan authority over the private schools is considerably weaker than that exercised over the parochial and central schools. The contrast with the French system, marked by a high degree of control and a clear bilateral relationship with a unitary State, is sharp and illuminating.[21]

To what extent has 'the Catholic character' of these schools survived or been modified by the changes which marked the latter half of the twentieth century? The greatest single change has probably been in the composition of the teaching force. Of the 150,000 teachers employed in the schools, only

7.8% are now members of religious orders; within that 7.8%, 6.2% are women. Some 91% of all the teachers in Catholic elementary schools are women and 53% of those in secondary schools, compared with 84% and 51% in public schools. As 94% of all Catholic schools are now coeducational, the problems of dependence on a largely female workforce are reduced. Teachers in Catholic schools work for an appreciably lower salary (and fewer retirement and other benefits) than their contemporaries in the public schools. In 1994, the average salary for a teacher in a Catholic elementary school was $18,000, compared with $33,000 in the public system. Such a differential presupposes a commitment to teaching largely uninfluenced by financial considerations. Many of these teachers are either young (and for that reason relatively inexpensive) or married women, returning to teaching (or becoming teachers for the first time in their lives), preferring for a variety of reasons to teach in Catholic schools while adding a supplement to an already established family income. Among the school principals, however, 52% in secondary schools and 51.3% in elementary are still members of religious orders. Principals and senior teachers and administrators who are not members of religious orders, and notably those teaching in the so-called private Catholic schools, are prepared carefully for their tasks, and inducted into the style and principles on which the religious order supervising the schools was and is based. Of the general body of the teachers, nearly 90% describe themselves as Catholic. Within that figure there are regional and other variations: in secondary schools in the South-west, for example, 22.8% of the teachers are recorded as non-Catholic. Nevertheless, the current proportions suggest that in America there is an adequate supply of Catholic teachers to teach in Catholic schools, the identity of which for that reason seems relatively less threatened.[22]

If most teachers in Catholic schools are, with whatever degree of intensity, Catholics, so are most students in most schools. The global national figures do, nevertheless, mask wide variations – not only between one region and another but, even more strikingly, in the same city between neighbouring schools. Moreover, significant changes over time (in popular attitudes as in the demographic constitution of the schools) must raise questions of the resilience and relevance of the Catholic traditions of education. In 1970, fewer than 3% of students came from families that did not regard themselves as Catholic. That proportion had by 1980 quadrupled to 11%, and appears – for the moment at least – to have levelled off at around 13.6%.[23] Three-quarters of the principals responding in a survey conducted during the 1990s asserted that religion was not a factor in deciding which students to admit.[24] Some 24.4% of the students come from minorities, and within that total 8.1% are black and 10.4% Hispanic. The place of these Catholic schools in American society has, as has been noted, been profoundly affected by the shifting demographic balance of the country: as the descendants of the older waves of immigrants move into the suburbs, so their place is to some extent taken by newer immigrants, many of whom are, however, settling in quite different parts of the country. These new immigrants come from Mexico, Cuba, Haiti and Puerto Rico. One-quarter of the Catholic population of the United States is now Spanish speaking, and that proportion rises to two-thirds in Florida, Texas and New Mexico.[25]

In what ways does this multitude of heterogeneous Catholic schools differ from the public schools – which are, it must be remembered, attended by the great majority of the children of Catholic families? The most recent and comprehensive study of the character of the schools was completed towards the end of the last century by Bryk and his colleagues at the University of Chicago. That impressive analysis was the result of ten years' work, drawing on existing databases, a series of questionnaires, and intensive case studies of seven schools. From this array of evidence, the study moved forward into a discussion of contexts and causes, grounded in the proposition that – for whatever reasons – Catholic schools did seem generally more successful in raising the achievements of many students, and not least those from disadvantaged backgrounds. This interpretation of a great deal of evidence was, of course, to command a key position in the lively debate on the contribution which the schools might – if granted further public financial support – be able to make to resolving an urgent American problem. Disentangling the causes, or even establishing the definitions, of the distinctiveness of the American Catholic school is no easy task. Opinions are certain to differ on the importance, for example, of an 'inspirational ideology', manifest for some observers in the commitment of teachers, their willingness to work for lower salaries or to devote personal time and energy to their tasks. Advocates of systems of schooling based on choice are likely to attribute the perceived success of the schools to their freedom from bureaucratic shackles.

Bryk and his collaborators elected to identify five factors which contributed significantly to the success of the schools which they had studied. First came the focus on a delimited academic curriculum, a concentration on what are popularly regarded as the basics, and a belief that a challenging curriculum of this kind (unashamedly traditional, if you will) should be offered to all students and not only those deemed by teachers or administrators to be headed for a college education. Of comparable significance was the commitment of the staff to a generous definition of their own responsibilities towards students: teaching involved rich human relationships, and the influence of good teachers expands far beyond the limits of the classroom and the completion of instructional tasks. Associated with such a concept of the teacher's role was a prevailing vision of the school itself as a learning community. Such a school gained, fourthly, by being small. Large schools, unless designed and administered with great skill and sensitivity, tend to be impersonal and cumbersome. Finally, the governance structures were relatively simple. There were fewer layers of bureaucracy, and less restrictive regulation than in the contemporary public school and the larger system-wide organisations of which it was a part.[26] More sceptical analysts are inclined to suggest that a large measure of the success of the schools must be attributed to less benign or idealistic factors. As Catholic families, like most but not all American families, have prospered and moved up the economic scale and out of the poor inner cities, so they have acquired a capacity to exercise greater choice in the disposition of their incomes. In spite of energetically promoted campaigns to serve the disadvantaged populations (as in the Big Shoulders scheme in Chicago), Catholic schools for the poor are indeed disappearing and the Church may be drifting from its evangelical mission.[27] At the same time, more prosperous suburbanites are less inclined to send their own children to the Catholic schools than were their own parents or grandparents. Conversely, some non-Catholic families (although there seems little hard evidence for this probability) may well choose to send their children to some of the more prestigious and costly private Catholic high schools. One severe critic has gone further than this in asserting that the favour currently bestowed by public opinion on previously disdained Catholic schools is essentially a product of the political climate. Since the publication in 1983 of *A Nation at Risk*, it has become universally fashionable to heap blame for all the ills of America on the weaknesses of its public schools. The promotion of Catholic schools – although not, of course, necessarily by those responsible for them – is an integral part of this denigration of public schools and the systems which sustain them. For Robert Baker, the apparent success of the Catholic schools must be interpreted in this context, and their academic achievements attributed to their growing elitism. Moreover, this scholar alleged, the achievements of those schools had been improperly exaggerated: they may have made a modest difference for the most disadvantaged students, but that is all. The doyen of the studies of Catholic education promptly and indignantly protested that in reality most of the admitted changes in the recruitment to Catholic high schools (the alleged 'eliting') took place *after* the 1980 studies of the achievements of those schools. Moreover, so sweepingly uncharitable a reading of the motives and achievements of the schools must be counterbalanced by the evidence of the continuing mission of the Catholic schools to the inner city and, even more, by a disaggregation of what is meant by 'Catholic schools'. It is entirely reasonable to suppose that many of the best known private Catholic high schools do consolidate their achievements and reputation by carefully selecting their students, by teaching them rigorously, by rejecting the unsuitable, and by charging high tuition fees to fund their efforts. But what is true of such schools may not apply to the much more typical parochial elementary schools.[28] The most recent research does, however, clearly imply that Catholic schools in America now stand at a crossroads, a point at which fundamental questions are raised about their identity and purposes. They do not as a general rule serve, in the sense in which they once plainly did, the poor and the disadvantaged.

> *It appears that the high quality and the increasingly high cost of*
> *education in Catholic schools is causing students with average to scarce*
> *economic resources to go elsewhere for their schooling. With each passing*
> *year, there are fewer students attending Catholic schools, and those who*
> *do attend are increasingly non-White, non-Catholic, nonreligious, and*
> *yet from homes of high socioeconomic status. ... This current state of*
> *affairs is a 180-degree turnaround from all previous decades in the*
> *twentieth century. In those times, the schools were affordable, and*
> *consequently attended by students from all social classes. Of course, in*
> *those times past, the schools were also all-White, all-Catholic and*
> *consensually more religious.[29]*

Rising costs and profound changes in the constituencies making use of
Catholic schools are the necessary background to the current debates about
the various voucher schemes which have been actively developed in recent
years. Catholic leaders who are anxious to maintain the mission of their
Church to the poor and the disadvantaged are attracted to them as a means
of refurbishing that economically threatened mission. Middle-class families
who would, for some of the more obvious consumerist reasons, wish to make
use of the schools would welcome the relief which vouchers might, under
certain conditions, offer. The early years of the present century are likely to
prove decisive in redefining the shape of future Church and State relations in
the field of education, and in clarifying the interpretations of the First
Amendment. The example of Ohio will now prove to be especially
illuminating, and even more so when deployed against the background of the
presidential election of the year 2000. George W. Bush made great play
during the election campaign of the importance of faith-based initiatives, and
specifically of the use of voluntary organisations in the delivery of social
services of all kinds. Some of the euphoric enthusiasm for such proposals,
linked to an ill-defined 'compassionate conservatism', soon evaporated as
supporters of the Christian Right realised that such government support
would probably have to be extended to 'faith-based' organisations of all
kinds, including non-Christian groups or (even more controversially)
Scientologists. Organisations like Americans United for the Separation of
Church and State had even more fundamental reservations, and were fearful
of the obvious dangers of evangelisation and discrimination. Legislation was
nevertheless introduced in 2001 to facilitate such developments, although the
promised federal initiative on vouchers seemed less likely to mature. The
initiative for the public funding of religious and other private schools may
therefore continue to rest with the states. The state of Ohio has since 1995
developed a voucher scheme for the city of Cleveland, designed to rescue
students (and especially students from poor and black neighbourhoods) from
the manifest inadequacies of the public system. Such schemes clearly have
the capacity to appeal to a wide variety of legitimate interest groups,
including those who adopt a libertarian view of the power of markets, blue
collar workers with ambitions for the education of their families, and strong

constituencies within the non-white population who have long been outraged by the inadequacies of what has been available for them.

The Cleveland scheme, mirrored to some extent by experiments in Milwaukee, has heavily depended on the cooperation of the Catholic schools, many of which seized the opportunity of escaping from the trap into which their ever increasing poverty was forcing them. Of the 56 private schools which cooperated in the Cleveland scheme, 46 had clearly defined denominational affiliations, and of these, the overwhelming majority were and are Catholic. Moreover, in the year 1999-2000, no fewer than 96% of the students receiving vouchers were enrolled in sectarian schools. In agreeing to be part of this now well-established scheme, the schools nevertheless were required to agree that they 'may not discriminate on the basis of race, religion, or ethnic background' in admitting students. Such requirements raise immediate and interesting comparisons with the requirements in France, and contrasts with those in England. The scheme itself seems, at least on the surface, to represent a direct public investment in religious schools, although its defenders naturally claim that it represents no more than a sensible extension of the long accepted child benefit theory. It has been consistently challenged by groups dedicated to a strict interpretation of the First Amendment, including those who see a direct threat to civil liberties and those who defend (from a variety of motives) the integrity of the public system sanctified by Horace Mann. The plan has been rejected by the state courts and (although only by a 2:1 vote) by a federal court of appeal as being a direct violation of the First Amendment, and in the autumn of 2001, the Supreme Court finally declared its willingness to take the case: it began to hear oral evidence in February 2002. This new case (Zelman v. Simmons-Harris) will bring to the top of the public agenda all the issues with which this book is concerned, but which even now are unlikely to be finally resolved by a Court which continues to be deeply divided. The tragic events of 11 September 2001 have added a painfully new urgency to the public discussion of the relationships between religion, politics, culture and education. Questions about the future relationship of Catholic schools to the State and to public funding are inevitably now part of a much wider and infinitely more complex picture than when *Everson* was first indecisively decided.[30]

Notes

[1] Underkuffler, 2001.

[2] *The Economist*, 27 March 1997; *Kappan*, February 2000, pp. 425-432 and September 2000, p. 50; *New York Times Magazine*, 7 December 1997, for those statistics.

[3] *The Economist*, 24 June 2000; *Kappan*, October 2000, pp. 175-176.

[4] Morris, 1997, p. 225.

[5] Youniss et al, 2000, p. 194.

[6] Fass, 1989, pp. 193-196; Carper & Hunt, 1993, pp. 140-141.

[7] Bryk et al, 1993, pp. 32-33.

[8] *New York Times Magazine*, 7 December 1997, citing Starke.

[9] *Humanae Vitae*, 1968.

[10] Youniss et al, 2000, p. 209.

[11] Dolan, 1992, p. 438.

[12] Morris, 1997, p. 317.

[13] Hunt & Carper, 1992, p. 142.

[14] *New York Times*, 25 February 1984.

[15] McLaughlin et al, 1996, p. 186.

[16] Wills, 1971.

[17] Doerr & Menendez, 1991, p. 23; Baker & Riordan, 1998, p. 17.

[18] NCEA, 1997-98.

[19] Youniss et al, 2000, p. 16.

[20] Doerr & Menendez, 1991, pp. 23, 49.

[21] *Kappan*, October 1999, p. 106.

[22] Schaub, 2000.

[23] *Kappan*, October 1999, p. 110.

[24] Bryk et al, 1993, p. 129.

[25] Dolan, 1992, p. 427.

[26] Bryk et al, 1993, p. 16.

[27] O'Keefe, 1996, p. 181.

[28] Baker & Riordan, 1998; and see the reply by Andrew Greeley in *Kappan*, September 1998.

[29] Riordan, 2000, p. 49.

[30] Harris, 2000, pp. 68-69; Witte, 2000; Peterson et al, 1999; *New York Times*, 24 January 2001; United States Court of Appeal for the Sixth Circuit, 11 December 2000.

CHAPTER 12

Three Countries:
Catholic schools in France today

The decade spanning the years 1984 and 1994 was of critical importance in redefining the relationship of the State in France to the Catholic primary and secondary schools of that country. The year 1984 registered the high water mark of the advance of 'liberalism', as that volatile principle was coming to be admired and practised in what the French are pleased to call the Anglo-Saxon countries. Among the millions in France who then took to the streets there were many who were devout defenders of the rights of the Church, of the centrality of religion in the whole of the educational project, and who were therefore content to place themselves in that long tradition which was suspicious of the all-embracing claims of a secular and Jacobin state. Among those to whom the religious core of the issue was of supreme importance, most were doubtless more comfortable with the gentler precepts of Montalambert than with the authoritarian bigotry of Maurras or the implacable hostility to the Republic displayed by the enemies of Colonel Dreyfus. Roman Catholicism in France had indeed changed fundamentally during the lifetime of the Fourth and Fifth Republics: there was no longer any conflict between its precepts, especially as redefined during Vatican II, and loyalty to the French State. Many Roman Catholic parents, as will appear, preferred a specifically and traditionally Catholic education for their children. But many more parents, equally content to march with the UNAPEL and its allies, were more immediately interested in preserving some alterative to the state system, and in enjoying the flexibility offered by the coexistence of two school systems. They marched to Verdi's rousing chorus in praise of liberty, and not to the rhythm of hymns. Both groups of parents were persuaded that, since the residual conflicts of the nineteenth century had faded, they should not be expected to pay the full costs of such an alternative schooling. Debré rather than Combes was the Prime Minister they admired. Thus, 1984 represented the triumph of the liberal principle: it elevated the local interest above the national, valued the family rather than the collective, and celebrated the values of civil society – as represented on this occasion by the Church, perceived as a voluntary association operating under the Law of 1901. The overt appeal was to *liberté* as one of the three dogmatic keywords of 1789. Mitterrand's electoral hopes for a unified and secular (*laïque*) national educational system had been frustrated.

By 1994 however, the balance of sentiment had shifted in dramatic ways: in that year, a sustained effort – pursued, of course, against the wishes of the same and apparently indestructible President – to provide significantly greater support for the private schools provoked yet another rash of street demonstrations. This time, as will be argued later, it was to be the principle of *égalité* that would triumph. But in the immediate aftermath of 1984 the cause of Catholic schooling had seemed secure. After three years of tangled debate and noisy but peaceful demonstrations, even the politicians seemed exhausted. Savary and his Prime Minster, brusquely abandoned by their President, slipped from the scene. Laurent Fabius, the youthful model of a more modern and digestible form of socialism, became Prime Minister. The education portfolio was committed to Jean-Pierre Chevènement – a tough Republican of impeccable left-wing credentials who was to make something of a habit of resigning from governments when he disliked their policies. For the moment, however, the most urgent tactical requirement was to cool tempers and allow a breathing space. Chevènement was deeply committed to the values of the 'School of the Republic', and to preserving its purity. In that sense, he had no wish to see a distinctive Catholic tradition uncomfortably accommodated within it. The contractual principles embedded in the Debré Law should, therefore, be respected: although the State could by contract allow the Church as a legally recognised association to undertake certain defined tasks of public utility, an unambiguous separation of the realms of Church and State must be scrupulously preserved. He therefore proposed that certain 'simple and practical measures' should now be introduced to assist the effective operation of existing contracts. Concessions should be made to and by both sides, as they had defined themselves in the previous three years. These measures were announced in August 1984. The CNAL and its allies were somewhat appeased by the restraints now placed on the operation of the Guermeur Law. Public funds should be more strictly controlled, and the State would no longer pay for new teaching appointments in Catholic schools without careful review. The operation of the *carte scolaire*, the 'education map' which determined the distribution and allocation of school places and resources, would in future be subject to more state control, and less open to interpretation or exploitation by the private (that is, Catholic) schools. Teachers in those schools were now to be nominated by the Rector, the public official responsible for the management of the local educational system, and not by the Catholic authorities themselves. The UNAPEL and its allies, on the other hand, were reassured by guarantees that teachers in Catholic schools were not to be incorporated within the ranks of the teachers in the public system, that the 'simple contract' as established in 1959 would be preserved indefinitely, and that the funds due to their schools (the troublesome *forfait*) would in future be paid promptly and in full, by the local as well as by the central authorities. In effect, the 1959 Law had been restored and clarified.

In the quinquennial elections for the National Assembly held in 1986, the Socialists were defeated and the President (whose term of office was at that time for seven years) was therefore obliged to invite Jacques Chirac to become Prime Minister. This was the first, but not the last, period of cohabitation during the Fifth Republic – a period, that is, when a politically partisan President would find himself working in uneasy alliance with a Ministry whose political loyalties and aspirations were opposed to his own. Fortunately perhaps, Chirac and his Minister of Education, Monory, had no wish to reignite the fires of controversy which had enveloped the Catholic schools question. In any case, they were fully occupied with the problems generated by the unsuccessful attempt to introduce reforms in higher education. In March 1986, Monory went so far as to describe the private school question as 'closed' (classé).[1] Two years later, after completing his first seven-year term as President, Mitterrand was elected for a second term, and promptly exercised his constitutional right to call a parliamentary election. This time, his own (albeit fractious and divided) party was successful, and in the next five years there were three successive Socialist Prime Ministers. For all but the last of these years, however, the Minister of National Education was Lionel Jospin, later to become Prime Minister himself – but under a right-wing President. Jospin was of Protestant descent, sometimes accused of displaying characteristically Jansenist attitudes, but in fact not holding strong religious opinions. His plans for reforms were extensive, but did not include any aspirations to reopen the vexed private school question. His critics nevertheless had good reason for complaining that he was unfriendly towards the Catholic schools. He certainly gave no sign of financial generosity towards them, and did nothing to encourage the local authorities (especially the communes) to fulfil their obligations to pay the forfait. On the contrary, the Prefects were instructed to take action against any local authorities which appeared to have paid too much to the Catholic schools![2] The financial issue was now becoming a major source of dissatisfaction to the Catholic authorities and to parents. Although the arrangements as originally proposed in 1959 were relatively straightforward, they had been seriously complicated by the decentralising legislation of the 1980s. That legislation (within the framework of which, it will be recalled, Savary had hoped to place the revised arrangements for the Catholic schools) had delegated from Paris to the local authorities much of the responsibility for educational funding. For their normal running costs (although never for the salaries of the teachers) and for some capital expenditure the public lycées were now dependent on the regions, the collèges on the departments, and the primary schools on the communes. Many of these local authorities continued to be dilatory or evasive in meeting their presumed obligations towards the Catholic schools – arguing that, since many of these schools served several communes, it was often the responsibility of districts other than their own to contribute to such charges. The reluctance of the Minister to intervene in such cases contributed to the financial problems of the schools and to the growing unease of the Catholic lobby, which had shown the full extent of its strength in 1983 and 1984.

During the last year of the Socialist Government under the premiership of Pierre Beregovoy, the responsibilities of the Minister of Education were assumed by Jack Lang, the flamboyant Minister of Culture. With a parliamentary election imminent (in 1993) and a presidential election only two years after that, Lang was anxious to pacify the advocates of the private schools and to resolve a number of problems. He negotiated skilfully with Père Max Cloupet, who had succeeded Guiberteau (now promoted by the Archbishop to be Rector of the Institut Catholique – the Catholic university institute in Paris) as Secretary General for Catholic Education. Some critics suspected that the good Father had been led up the garden path and, given the probability of a change of government in the near future, should have held out for a better deal. An agreement was at last reached on the calculation and payment of sums due to the Church for the maintenance if its schools. At the same time, the Church was relieved of some financial burdens by the incorporation of its own future teachers in the new national system of teacher training. Students intending to teach in Catholic secondary schools could now attend the IUFM (the university institute of teacher preparation) on the same basis as their contemporaries seeking careers in the public schools. Like them, they entered a competition at the end of the common first year of their postgraduate training, although they would then (if successful) be admitted to study at public expense for the CAFEP (a qualification specific to the private school) rather than for its public school equivalent, the CAPES. Primary school teachers would continue to attend Catholic training centres, which were, however, now to be fully funded by the State within the framework of the IUFM. Although many Catholic teachers or intending teachers welcomed these changes, others were predictably suspicious of what might look like a first step towards their full conversion into public servants – the *fonctionnarisation* so dreaded by Cardinal Lustiger in 1984. The SNEC-CFTC, faithfully pursuing its anti-integrationist policy, unsuccessfully appealed to the Conseil d'Etat against these new arrangements.[3] While these so-called Lang-Cloupet accords were being negotiated, the Secretary General in November 1992 observed (perhaps unwisely) that 'There is no longer any problem between Catholic education and the Government'.[4] In spite of such a cheerful interpretation of current Socialist policies, many private school advocates (and not a few politicians) hoped that the legislative elections of 1993 would produce a change in political control, and lead to a significantly better financial deal for the Catholic schools.

Those elections led to another period of cohabitation, with Edouard Balladur of the Rassemblement pour la République (RPR) leading the centre right government under the watchful eye of a Socialist President. The controversial and provocative François Bayrou of the Union for French Democracy (UDF), an *agrégé* and author of a life of Henry IV, became Minister of National Education. The coalition of the RPR and the UDF had secured the largest parliamentary majority since 1815 and the pressure from their supporters to address some of the long-standing grievances of the supporters of Catholic schools proved irresistible. The mood was very different from that prevailing in the first cohabitation of 1986-88, and the parliamentary majority more substantial. The underlying problem of the 1980s was, therefore, at last directly addressed. Since the reforms of that decade had committed vast new financial responsibilities for education to the localities (regions, departments, communes) those local authorities, it was urged, must now be allowed to extend financial help to Catholic as well as to public schools. Under the prevailing arrangements, the Catholic schools were suffering from a very obvious disadvantage. The Falloux Law of 1850, parts of which were still in force, limited to 10% of the total budget the assistance which 'the collectivities' (local authorities) could contribute to the funding of private schools. The framers of the Debré Law of 1959 had, of course, not foreseen the shift from central to local funding which would follow twenty years later. It was argued that local authorities should therefore now be permitted to contribute more realistic sums to the costs of Catholic schools, including assistance towards the provision of new buildings. The repeal of the inhibiting clause of the Falloux Law was therefore vigorously promoted, although Mitterrand manoeuvred to achieve a delay in passing legislation on this subject by refusing a request for an extraordinary session of Parliament in the summer of 1983. A law was nevertheless finally adopted by Parliament on 15 December 1993, and the Christmas holiday intervened.

It was now the turn of the champions of the principles of *laïcité* to take to the streets in order to oppose any strengthening of the Catholic school system. It was, of course, ironical that they should now do so in defence of that same Falloux Law which had in 1850 registered a considerable victory for the clerical party. Something of the enthusiasm shown in the initial opposition to the law of 1959 was now rekindled. On 13 January 1994, the Conseil Constitutionnel ruled that the proposed law was in fact invalid on the grounds that it violated the fundamental principle of *égalité*. Since local authorities would behave differently in different parts of France, and Catholic schools would therefore receive more support in some areas than in others, all Frenchmen would not be receiving equal treatment in a Republic proclaimed to be 'one and indivisible'. The law must therefore be struck down. Three days later, on a wet and cold Sunday, in an effort to consolidate this apparent victory, the CNAL and its allies proceeded with their plans for a massive demonstration in Paris. An estimated 600,000 demonstrators this time took to the streets. Over eighty organisations were represented, led by the big battalions of the FEN and of the FSU (Fédération syndicale unitaire) – a new union grouping which had recently broken away from the hitherto dominant union. Chevènement and Mauroy both joined the march, as did two thousand Freemasons, reaffirming their historic commitment to the School of the Republic and to the memory of their heroes, Ferry and Combes. One of the banners appealed directly to the legends of the 1880s: 'Come Back Jules!' A Brittany mayor led a delegation of seventy from a commune with a total population of seven hundred. He expressed the local resentment, within a predominantly Catholic region, provoked by the efforts of Paris to make his community pay for the support of Catholic schooling: two hundred pupils attended the local public school, while thirty-five were enrolled in a Catholic establishment. In the canton of Josselin, on the other hand, there were thirteen Catholic schools and only one public school: this hardly represented any genuine choice. The years 1984 and 1994, in their very different ways, proved that the old antagonisms were still alive. Any attempt to disturb the delicate and vulnerable compromise of 1959 was still certain to destabilise any government.[5]

For the immediate future, however, the compromises engineered by the Socialist politicians Chevènement and Lang survived. It did not, of course, follow that all difficulties of a financial and administrative order evaporated overnight: many of them had been displaced and dispersed to the local scene, and for the rest of the century there were no more great national demonstrations reviving the slogans of the nineteenth century. The massive cost of supporting Catholic education had apparently now been accepted by the State – always defined in France as the central government and not the local collectivities, even although the latter drew most of their financial resources from the Parisian coffers. In 1996, one calculation suggested that the annual bill for teachers' salaries alone was thirty-one billion francs: the equivalent at the time of £3,100 million or $4,650 million. This figure did not include expenditure on Catholic higher education, or agricultural education, or the additional 4.5 billion francs paid, mostly for the support of non-teaching staff, as part of the State's contribution to the troublesome *forfait*. Nor did it include various social security payments paid by the State for several categories of employee. Above all, it took no account of the growing, and apparently unmeasured, proportion of the costs of Church establishments borne by the local authorities under locally determined agreements. Many primary schools had chosen to continue to shelter under the umbrella of the 1959 *contrat simple* simply because its less restrictive terms often enabled them to negotiate very favourable settlements with local authorities, especially in areas where Catholic loyalties were strong. The sober and careful national newspaper, *Le Monde*, estimated that, taking these many overlapping categories into account and adding such supplementary costs as helping to maintain historic buildings belonging to the Church, no less that 12% of the total derived from all tax revenues was in fact applied to purposes linked with the mission of the Roman Catholic Church in France. Its correspondent noted the comparison with the 8-10% accruing to religious bodies in Germany from the payment of the Church Tax in that country.[6]

Nearly all (one authority cites 99.5%) Catholic schools in France are now operating formally under a public contract to provide specified educational services to the public – either, as has just been noted, under the *contrat simple* or under the more comprehensive (and apparently generous) *contrat d'association*.[7] Within metropolitan France, 1,926,398 pupils attend Catholic schools under contract: 834,609 in the primary sector, and 1,091,789 in the secondary.[8] These primary and secondary pupils are at present enrolled in a total of 8237 establishments: 5250 primary schools, 1636 *collèges* (lower secondary schools), 823 general *lycées*, and 528 vocational *lycées*. Of these upper secondary schools, nearly 400 also offer courses beyond the *baccalauréat*, many of them preparing older students for entry to the prestigious *Grandes Ecoles*, or teaching for an advanced technical qualification (the BTS). These 2 million students are taught by 129,775 teachers, 40,845 in primary schools, and 88,930 in secondary. These schools also employ 40,000 administrators, heads of schools and others (full-time equivalent figures). The scale and significance of Catholic education continues to vary widely across the highly distinctive regions of France. The three Academies (educational districts) of Nantes, Rennes and Lille account for over 30% of the total number of students in Catholic schools through metropolitan France, whereas Limoges enrols less than 0.5% of that total. These wide disparities are now and will continue to be reflected in debates about the future of Catholic schooling in France, and help to explain why national issues are likely to be less important and controversial than the regional and local. In the Academies of highest Catholic concentration identified above, over 50% of all secondary school students are enrolled in Catholic schools. In Brittany, over 40% of all students (primary as well as secondary) attend Catholic schools.[9] Even within Academies where there is a smaller proportionate concentration of pupils in Catholic schools, local anomalies can lead to tensions, especially at times of financial stringency. In the diocese of Lyons, for example, twelve villages are served only by Catholic schools. Throughout France as a whole, Catholic schools supported by public funds enrol 15.5% of all primary pupils, and no less than 19.5% of secondary. Nevertheless, across the closing years of the century there was a small but significant decline in enrolment in the schools under contract. Primary enrolments between 1994 and 2000 fell by 1.89% and secondary by 2.77%. There continues to be a wide variation in the size and importance of the schools. Many establishments differ from their public school neighbours in enrolling, albeit in distinct units, the whole range of pupils from the age of 3 to that of 22. St Michel de Picpus in Paris, for example, has some 700 pupils in its primary sector, 950 in the *collège* and 950 in the *lycée*, as well as substantial numbers (essentially, in terms of international comparisons, already within higher education) in the more senior sections preparing for the entrance examinations to the *Grandes Ecoles* and for the higher technical qualifications mentioned earlier.

In spite of the large subsidies now paid to enable Catholic schools to meet some of the national and local needs in education, it is still necessary for them to charge fees: not, of course, formally for tuition but as contributions to those expenses which, by however lax an interpretation of the doctrine of the separation of Church and State, cannot legitimately be assigned to public funds. The payment of fees, even in cases where generous and flexible scholarship provision is made, naturally affects directly the admissions policy of any school. Critics argue that it enables such schools to be socially and economically selective, whatever the pure Republican doctrine of the 1959 Law might require. The fees paid vary widely, not only across districts but also among schools of different types. In Paris, typical costs could be FF3700 for primary and FF9000 for upper secondary, whereas in Nantes the charges could be as low as FF600. Such variations make it hazardous to draw general conclusions about the character of Catholic schools in France.

One revealing index of the volume of public support for those schools is furnished by the size of the membership of the UNAPEL – the national confederation whose headquarters are strategically lodged alongside those of the Enseignement Catholique and a host of associated organisations, in the rue St Jacques in Paris. The UNAPEL brings together all the local organisations of parents, mobilised since the 1930s and more especially the 1950s in the local APEL – L'Association des Parents des Elèves des Ecoles Libres. These active local groups, exercising considerable influence over the conduct of the schools, describe themselves as supporters of the 'free' school, rather than of Catholic institutions as such, and their relationship to the formally constituted church bodies is often, as in 1984, complex. In France – in this respect quite unlike several other countries – the identification of the independent school predominantly with the Catholic Church is of particular significance. Eight hundred thousand families belong to the UNAPEL, and their interests are carefully protected by the efficient dissemination of relevant information and advice, the mobilisation of pressure groups (parliamentary, local, regional, public relations) and the monthly distribution of *La Famille Educatrice*. The relationship of French society to the Roman Catholic Church is marked by its own subtleties and ironies, having something in common with the relationship of English society to the established Church of England. The deep-seated Gallican tradition, appealing to such heroes of French culture as Bossuet, tends to emphasise the indigenous nature of that Church and its ideological identification with the nation. Distinctions between Catholics who are 'believers' and those who are 'practising' are a commonplace in everyday discourse. The Church has for many decades, but especially since the end of the Second World War, been preoccupied with the phenomenon of 'dechristianisation'. There is an important sense in which France remains culturally Catholic but theologically non-Christian. Even the humanist and agnostic President Mitterrand valued his special relationship to the French Church. Napoleon had astutely characterised Catholicism as the religion of the majority of Frenchmen. Eighty per cent of French children are baptised, although regular attendance at Mass has dropped to about 10%, and only 6% for those under the age of 35. On the other hand, the unexpected and spectacular success of the International Youth Day in Paris in August 1997 reminded those who might have preferred to suppose otherwise that the Church in France still made a considerable appeal to younger people. Nevertheless, a strong current of anticlerical opinion continues to flow through France. There were, for example, vehement protests in 1996 when the Pope made the fifth of his visits to France, this time to celebrate the fifteenth centenary of the baptism of Clovis and the conversion of France to the Catholic faith. In Tours there was a campaign of 'debaptism', mounted by those who insisted on the removal of their names from the baptism registers and resented being counted as Catholics simply because of the traditional and largely social preferences of their parents. The Freemasons, yet again, made their own voices heard and even President Chirac judged it prudent to moderate his own initial enthusiasm for celebrating an event designed to reassert the authentic identity of traditional France.[10]

It is, therefore, unsurprising that astute observers should have detected two distinct tendencies within UNAPEL and among those parents and families who choose, at some modest financial sacrifice, to make use of the Catholic rather than of the public system of schooling in contemporary France.[11] Nor is there necessarily any hostility, or even awkward inconsistency, between these two bodies of opinion. Careful analyses in the 1990s demonstrated that many families making use of the Catholic system were essentially attracted by the performance of the schools, their success in achieving good academic results, and by the opportunity which they offered of a relatively inexpensive alternative to a public system which often seemed bureaucratically rigid and unresponsive to parental preferences. In one sample of such parents, no less than 37% had made use of the private system for one or more of their children at some point and for some period of time. Percentages, although in themselves impressive, showing only the number of pupils enrolled in Catholic schools at any *one* time (as reported earlier) are therefore misleadingly low. They tend to underreport the degree of general support for the existence of the Catholic schools, and imperfectly reflect parental motives in choosing them. There are many families who might be characterised as *clients de passage*, or (less elegantly) as zappers.[12]

The frontier between public and private education, or indeed between secular and religious, is very much more permeable in France than in many other countries. All observers agree that there is a great deal of movement between the two, even if precise figures are hard to establish: one recent comment suggests that at least half of all French families make use of both systems at some point. Moreover, well-advertised problems affecting the fully public sector tend to encourage migration, permanent or temporary, into what is naturally perceived as a safer (and possibly more disciplined) environment. A recent estimate suggests that the movement of students from public to private was, in one year, double that of the transfers in the opposite direction.[13] Other observers have, however, chosen to stress the importance of a hard core of families who quite deliberately choose a Catholic education simply because it is Catholic, and argue that those who cross and recross the public/private frontier represent only a minority.[14] There is little doubt that during the 1980s there was a strong parental reaction against what were denounced as the dangerously innovative practices associated with the ministry of Alain Savary, and that many families did indeed prefer the safer and more traditional pedagogy associated with the private Catholic schools. Although such schools were, of course, required by the terms of their contract with the State to observe the national curriculum programmes, they were under no obligation to adopt the latest pedagogical fashions.[15] An understanding of the importance of the parent as a consumer exercising educational choices in a modified market environment was well developed at the time by Robert Ballion.[16] The shifting balance of parental presences must vary (although it seems that the necessary regional studies have not yet been undertaken) from school to school and, even more significantly, from region to region. A religious motivation determining the choice of a school may prove to be more significant in districts where Catholic schools serve only a minority of the population (as in Limoges) than in those Academies – like Nantes or Rennes – where a Catholic school is probably the most accessible and obvious choice for many families. There are, moreover, likely to be considerable differences even within the same geographical area. The Congregations are certain to be in principle more highly committed to the provision of an education which, while legally open to all comers, remains unambiguously Catholic. In 1998, there were still 28 religious orders for men and 156 for women, responsible for 2500 educational establishments (of a total Catholic provision of nearly 9000).[17] Although there had been a precipitous decline in the number of members of religious orders working in these schools still formally maintained by the teaching orders, determined efforts continue to be made to ensure that the directors of those establishments, when they are lay people, are fully aware of and committed to the distinctive style associated with the religious order, as manifested in the *caractère propre*. Catholic schools in France will continue to balance the principle of religious engagement with that of openness to a public defined in liberal terms. Even in cases where such *ouverture* might not be a natural preference, the Debré Law of 1959, since it sat within the framework of the recently adopted Constitution of 1958, required such *laïque* openness, and forbade the exercise of religious discrimination against any pupil.

The 1959 Law was perfectly explicit on this point, and the necessary willingness of the Catholic authorities to observe its requirements and continue to enjoy public funding had by the end of the century profoundly changed the character of education in Catholic schools. Friends and enemies were likely to agree that they had become, in a phrase, much less Roman Catholic and more like public schools with a mild Catholic flavour. The tension between serving the public purposes of a lay Republic and responding to the evangelical mission of a church was not resolved: or rather, it was managed in different ways in different institutions at different times. The Law may indeed have been clear enough in theory, but distinctions between that which was publicly funded and therefore subject to state regulation and that which was privately sponsored and part of the context rather than the content of schooling were in practice much more difficult to maintain. The schools obviously cannot require adherence to any religious belief, or insist on attendance at Mass and other religious ceremonies. Nor could public funds be used to finance the teaching of the catechism – although the situation was and is less clear with regard to the teaching of 'religious culture', or of comparative religion. The Law was emphatic:

> In private establishments which have accepted one of the contracts described below, the teaching (enseignement) placed under the regime of the contract is subject to the control of the State: the establishment, while preserving its own character (caractère propre) must provide this teaching in total respect of freedom of conscience. All children, without distinction of origin, opinion or belief, have access to it. [18]

Nor was it easy for the Catholic schools and the authorities which governed them to steer a prudent course in their admissions policies between exercising forms of social and economic (rather than religious) discrimination and admitting students without any regard to the ability of their families to pay the appropriate fees. Critics have consistently objected that the Church has in reality applied inappropriate social criteria in deciding which pupils to admit, and which potentially difficult young people to exclude. But there is no reason to doubt the sincerity of those within the Catholic system who regret that children from disadvantaged families are often excluded. A declared willingness to create schools in economically deprived areas has been frustrated not only by the necessity of charging some fees but also by the requirement that schools should normally have operated successfully for some five years before they could receive state funding. Cloupet made precisely this point at the national meeting of the Enseignement Catholique in 1993, stressing that the necessity of state control of the schools under contract had by then been fully accepted, but yet again drawing attention to the perverse effects of the Falloux Law of 1850. Local authorities which would have been content to assist Catholic schools more generously were being prevented from doing so: they still are. After the failure to remove that obstacle in 1994, Catholic education was for several years left relatively undisturbed. Even the return of a Socialist government in 1997 (after President Chirac's miscalculation in calling an early parliamentary election) did not lead to any revival of the anti-Catholic movement. The now weakened FEN and the FSU, for the moment at least, were preoccupied with more urgent concerns. Lionel Jospin as Prime Minister remembered only too well the disturbances of an earlier period. His provocative Minister of Education, Claude Allègre, inherited or manufactured too many other problems to have time for the now quiescent religious issue. His unpopularity led in March 2000 to his replacement by the buoyant Jack Lang, who had already demonstrated his willingness and ability to keep tempers cool. Tensions did, of course, persist: many of the teachers within the publicly funded Catholic system envied the financial privileges of their colleagues in the secular schools, notably in such matters as retirement benefits. Five thousand of them took to the streets on 7 October 2000 while thirty thousand signed a petition seeking fuller incorporation in the state system: most teachers in Catholic schools then went on strike for a day in the following May.[19] The future of the Catholic schools was not an issue in the campaigns before the presidential election in May 2002. Much had indeed changed since May 1981.

During these years of relative calm, the bishops and the various organisations responsible for Catholic education, after nearly four years of discussion, completed their task of providing a generally agreed new administrative and legal framework for their work in the *Statut de l'Enseignement Catholique* (1996). This document steers a difficult course between the values of openness in a publicly funded system and the distinctiveness of a religiously based education. References to *l'ensemble de l'Enseignement Catholique français* stress the coherence and consistency of that totality. Such an emphasis, of course, represents a very different understanding from that implied by the contractual model of the 1959 Law, in which discrete agreements are concluded between the State and each individual establishment. The episcopate and the Enseignement Catholique were now, in fact, very close to promoting the concept of the *université bis* as a nation-wide systematic alternative to the public system, coordinated from number 277 in the rue St Jacques. That system is carefully designed at every hierarchical level: for the school itself, the department and the diocese, the Academy, the region, and the nation. The document also endorses a stronger emphasis on the importance of the supervision (the *tutelle*) of the local bishop, in canon law responsible for the integrity of the education provided in any establishment within his jurisdiction which wishes to call itself Catholic, whether or not conducted by one of the Congregations. The vision of Catholic education in France is now that of the Second Vatican Council, as expressed in the 1965 encyclical, *Gravissimum Educationis*. It has a significant public service to perform, and the rights of parents to choose a Catholic (or any other religiously distinctive) form of schooling for their own children entails the acceptance by the State of a duty to provide funds too enable such choices to be given real effect. The 'establishment of Catholic education' has now become the 'Catholic establishment of education', existing alongside those public establishments which also have a worthy part to play in the provision of education for the whole citizenry. Its religious duty is to display but never to impose a faith: *exposer* but not *imposer*.

Much of the pressure in French society for maintaining a separate Catholic school system had arisen from resentment at the monopolistic claims of a secular State. Against that monopoly (as epitomised by Napoleon's *Université*) the Church aspired to protect a monopoly of its own, taking advantage of political opportunities to extend its power. This extension of the power of the Church was, in turn, bitterly resented by the anticlerical party, fully mobilised at the time of the Dreyfus affair and securing a spectacular victory in the separation of Church and State in 1905. The groups devoted to the cause of Roman Catholic education, and notably the Congregations, had naturally enough been happy under the *ancien régime* to enjoy the protection of the Bourbon State. They had similarly been content to profit from the favour and patronage of Charles X or, for a while, of Napoleon III. But these were tricky allies and, under the inspiration of Montalambert and Lammenais, wiser counsels had prevailed. The claims for Catholic education became appeals to the principles of liberty, as was dramatically demonstrated in 1984. Nor could that liberty be confined to Catholics: similar rights could no longer be denied to Protestants, to Jews or (an issue of growing importance in France today) to Muslims. Catholic schools in France now live within the framework of their own *Statut* but also in the environment defined by Rome in the recent declaration of the Congregation for Catholic Education. Its letter of June 1998, *The Catholic School on the Threshold of the Third Millennium* (L'Ecole Catholique au Seuil du Troisième Millénaire), characterises Catholic education as a service of *public* utility, with a special responsibility towards the poor. It also marks the continuing shift away from the assertion of the institutional claims of the Church towards an emphasis on the rights of families and of individuals, whatever their faith, and on the principle of subsidiarity. Superior powers, like the State, should undertake only those tasks which other entities may not better fulfil for themselves.

> *The correct relationship between the State and every school – not only the Catholic school – is to be understood not so much in terms of institutional relations as in terms of the right of the individual to receive an adequate education based on free choice.* [20]

In France, as in much of Europe, Church and State questions are being redefined in, if not superseded by, the language of choice, individual freedom and the market.

Notes

[1] Battut et al, 1995, pp. 207-210.

[2] Lequiller, 1992, pp. 76, 81.

[3] Judge et al, 1994; Battut et al, 1995, p. 210; *Le Monde*, 20 May 1993.

[4] Battut et al, 1995, p. 267.

[5] *Le Monde*, 15 and 18 January 1994.

[6] *Le Monde*, 11 May 1996.

[7] Le Bret & Baulic, 1989, p. 42.

[8] The figures given here relate only to primary and secondary schools, and not to agricultural education. They are derived from the statistics updated annually by the Enseignement Catholique and published on the Internet (http://www. Scolanet.org) and in the series, *Enseignement Catholique Actualités*.

[9] *Le Monde de l'Education*, August 2000, p. 8.

[10] *The Economist*, 30 August 1997; Cholvy, 1991.

[11] Battut et al, 1995, p. 149.

[12] Lequiller, 1992, p. 12; Langouët & Léger, 1994; *Le Monde de l'Education*, October 1991.

[13] *Le Monde de l'Education*, February 2001, p. 27 and May 2001, p. 22.

[14] *Le Monde*, 11 May 1996.

[15] Prost, 1992, p. 173.

[16] Ballion, 1982.

[17] Le Bret & Baulic, 1989, p. 119.

[18] Article 2.

[19] *Le Monde de l'Education*, May and June 2001.

[20] p. 16.

CHAPTER 13

Three Countries:
Catholic schools in England today

After completing his work on the 1944 Act, which survived as the structural basis of the English educational system for the rest of the century, Rab Butler remained for nearly forty years at the centre of English political and public life. Throughout those decades, the major questions affecting the relationships between Church (or rather churches) and State in Britain continued to be resolved in the corridors of power in Whitehall and Westminster. Butler's last substantive political speech was made in 1980 in the House of Lords. It was, unsurprisingly, something of a period piece, delivered in the year after the arrival at 10 Downing Street of Margaret Thatcher, Britain's first woman Prime Minister and a former (if somewhat disillusioned) Secretary of State for Education.[1] The timing was apposite, for that significant event marked in many ways the end of the long years of relatively calm consensus. In economic affairs, Butskellism (the liberal, mildly statist amalgam captured by the conflation of the surnames of Butler himself and of the Labour leader, Gaitskell) was now formally discredited. In the world of education, the old civilities of a partnership embracing the LEAs, the churches and central government (for which Thatcher had shown scant respect during her dynamic years as Secretary of State for Education between 1970 and 1974) were about to be placed under severe strain. The new Conservative Government signalled the death of Butler's key principles in the field of educational policy. One early manifestation of this new and less open-handed style was the Conservative determination to restrict the rights of families to be given free public transport to the denominational schools of their choice. LEAs had generally interpreted their discretionary right to provide such transport in generous terms, and any restriction of such privileges would plainly have major implications for the viability of the denominational schools.

Butler in 1980 was no longer at the centre of public life, as he had retired from the House of Commons shortly after the victory of Harold Wilson's Labour Party in the general election of 1964. In 1965, he become a life peer and, as Master of Trinity College, Cambridge, returned to the heart of his family's historic position in English life. He had by then held office as Chancellor of the Exchequer (a position which had enabled him to support the enlargement of grants for denominational schools), Leader of the Commons, Home Secretary and Foreign Secretary but had twice failed to secure the highest office of all. Fifteen years after his political retirement, in defending for the last time the principles of partnership which had underpinned the 1944 settlement with the churches, he was supported by the doyen of the Catholic peers, the Duke of Norfolk. The Government's own proposals were defeated by 216 to 112 votes.[2] But the years of peace were at an end, and the years of Conservative rule from 1979 to 1997 were to impose a great strain – especially after the general election victory of 1987 – on Church and State relations. The Catholic schools were especially affected by these new pressures which, moderated as they undoubtedly were by the Labour victory of 1997, still define the relationships in England of the denominational, and especially Catholic, schools to the State.

Across the three decades before these major changes in ideology and policy (in some ways mirrored and anticipated by shifts in Labour party policy signalled by Prime Minister Callaghan's speech at Ruskin College, Oxford in October 1976), the traditions of consultation and cooperation had been followed with remarkable consistency, and no small success. In the aftermath of the Butler Act and the end of World War II, there was a general, if sometimes reluctant, acceptance that the partnership of Church and State was an inescapable fact of life, and that without active and publicly funded cooperation, the educational system could never move forward. In that sense, the painful lessons of the first half of the century had been well learned. By 1975, the percentage grant paid towards the capital costs of voluntary schools had risen from Butler's original 50% to 85%, where it was to remain for the rest of the century. The partnership between government, LEAs and the voluntary bodies had been consolidated by an awareness of the urgency and scale of the tasks to be accomplished after 1945, and by a steady lowering of the temperature of the religious debate. Church affiliations were now less passionately defended, and Christian leaders drew closer together in lamenting the overall decline in religious observance and in the pervasively Christian character of national life.[3] One of the most bitterly resented features of the classical dual system, the single school district where the Established Church enjoyed a virtual monopoly of provision, evaporated as small schools were closed or amalgamated or absorbed into the LEA system. Of the four thousand single school districts still existing in 1944, only a few hundred survived by 1959.[4] When the capital grant for church schools was in that latter year significantly increased to 75%, there was little or no protest from the heirs of those who had in 1902 denounced the iniquity of 'Rome on the Rates'. Indeed, free church leaders now seemed more disposed to see Christian schooling (especially if it were in a mild Anglican form and Nonconformists were represented on the governing bodies of such schools) as building a serviceable bulwark against the creeping advance of secularism:

> *It is certain that the year 1959 has marked a definite change in the*
> *nature of the education problem. ... Christians of every church*

recognised with great anxiety that increasing numbers of children are growing up with no real contact with a church of any kind. ... Fifty years ago the situation was not nearly so grave as it is today ... it could reasonably be hoped that non-sectarian Christian teaching in day-school would be followed by active linking with a worshipping community through home, Sunday School or Church. That is no longer true. The Roman Catholics and the Anglicans are quite justified in being anxious about the education of their own and other children, and Free Churchmen must face the situation as it now is.[5]

In the years after 1945, the churches, but especially the Roman Catholics, engaged in a vigorous building programme, made triply necessary by the raising to fourteen of the school-leaving age in 1947, the long-delayed reorganisation of schools along lines long ago commended by Tawney and Hadow and which the 1936 Act was intended to facilitate, and the inevitable damage to and neglect of school buildings throughout the 1939-45 War. Although the Church of England chose to keep many more voluntary aided schools than either Butler or Temple had anticipated, many Anglican schools did – as they had assumed – become controlled, and thereupon ceased to be a financial burden upon their parent Church. But since the Catholics, by contrast, had totally and consistently rejected the controlled option, they were, therefore, still left with a substantial financial problem. It was pressure from them which led to a progressive raising of the level of government subsidy for capital costs. Such costs were elevated by the new building regulations of the post-war years, designed essentially to improve the standards of provision in all publicly provided or supported schools. Between 1945 and 1968, the costs of Catholic building projects were double those of the Anglicans, in spite of the fact that they at first provided fewer schools and had fewer financial resources of their own. Pressure for a more generous measure of government support therefore came primarily from the Catholic community, while some Anglicans even opposed any such variation of the 1944 settlement.[6]

The Catholic campaign began as early as 1949, when a House of Commons debate nevertheless made it clear that nobody by then wished to resurrect religious controversy. The problem was, once again, essentially one of logistics, and the main arenas of debate therefore continued to be Parliament and the Ministry. The Catholic bishops, led successively by Cardinals Griffin and Godfrey, showed great restraint in pressing their case, much of which was presented on their behalf by Bishop Beck (later Archbishop of Liverpool). The Catholic vote was still of great importance, especially in cities like Leeds and Liverpool, and the Labour Government in 1950-51, sustained in office for a while by only the smallest of Commons majorities, attempted to woo it with promises which were promptly and prudently balanced by proposals made by Churchill (Prime Minister again in 1951) and his Chancellor of the Exchequer, Butler himself. Some relief was granted in 1953 by technical amendments in the regulations, and eventually in 1959 (when Macmillan was Premier) the capital grant was raised to 75% for all new voluntary aided secondary schools.[7]

Although by 1959 the relative size of the voluntary sector as a whole had diminished, the balance within it between the Anglican and Roman Catholic components had once again shifted significantly. Even more significant, given the less autonomous and distinctive character of controlled schools, was the fact that all the Catholic schools (with a negligible and anomalous exception) were aided, and that the bishops had actively encouraged campaigns specifically intended to open more Catholic secondary schools to receive Catholic pupils from their own primary schools. In 1959, 77.3% (compared with an equivalent 69.6% in 1938 and 48% in 1903) of all school places in England and Wales were located in fully maintained LEA (so-called county) schools. Some 12.8% of the overall total of places available nationally in 1959 were furnished by the Church of England, and 7.6% by the Catholics. But of the 12.8% of Anglican places, slightly less than half were in aided schools whereas, of course, all the Catholic places were in aided schools. By 1959, therefore, there were more places in Roman Catholic voluntary aided schools (7.6% of the total national provision) than in their Anglican counterparts (6.1%). This shifting balance permanently affected the shape of the debate about the future of all the church schools.[8]

The embedding of the voluntary schools in the public sector of education, and the enlarging engagement of the Catholics in the provision of aided secondary schools, secured that – whether in principle they liked it or not – the LEAs in most parts of England and the (two) Churches were now locked into a partnership. None of them would welcome a repetition of the circumstances of the 1890s or of the years between the two Wars, when the inability of the Churches to fund the reorganisation of their own schools acted as an effective brake on educational progress. In areas where there was now both a large concentration of the Catholic population and a weighty investment in the expensive complexities of secondary education, such inherently desirable cooperation became essential. Since the administrative areas of LEAs and dioceses rarely coincided, achieving such effective cooperation was, however, rarely simple: the Archdiocese of Liverpool, for example, included four hundred Catholic schools, the support and management of which depended on continuous cooperation with eight separate LEAs.[9] At the same time, the intimate links of schools with parishes were now less essential than they had been when the whole of the voluntary investment had been in elementary education: both the diocese and the LEA were now entangled in multilateral negotiation and development. The planned integration of the voluntary, and especially the Catholic, provision with that of the LEA as a whole therefore became the central issue, linked, of course, to key questions of funding and the equitable distribution of resources: the themes of debate were now even more clearly logistic rather than doctrinal. In a sermon, delivered in the presence of Harold Wilson (then

Labour Prime Minister and a Liverpool MP), Cardinal Heenan (Archbishop of Westminster from 1963), proclaimed:

Legislation on Church schools is no longer a controversial issue between religious denominations or political parties.[10]

Controversy in the 1960s focused instead on the social and political issues in which education is always enmeshed, and in those years, especially on the battles raging around the reorganisation of secondary schools on comprehensive lines. Although the Butler Act was silent on this contentious matter, after 1945 the general assumption within all the main political parties had been that the universalisation of secondary education would proceed on the lines assumed to be appropriate by Tawney and later made more explicit in the Hadow, Spens and Norwood reports. Although all children should indeed move from elementary (now rebaptised as primary) schools to secondary education at about the age of eleven, they should not all receive the same kind of secondary education nor attend the same institutions. The grammar school (about which many in the Labour Party remained deeply ambivalent) would continue to provide an academic education for a talented minority, recruited on the basis not of their parental status but of their natural and innate talent. For the majority, however, an education more appropriate to the nurturing of technical skills or general employability would be provided. These oversimplifications had, of course, always been challenged, but never more openly than in the party campaign leading to the election of a Labour Government in 1964. The determination of the Government to press all LEAs to move quickly towards a comprehensive and inclusive form of secondary education raised formidable problems for the voluntary partners of those same LEAs. How, in the absence of a renewed flow of funding, could they respond to these new and expensive demands? No wonder the Cardinal reassured the Prime Minister that there need be no kind of political or religious opposition to increasing state support for voluntary schools.

In this same year of 1965, Bishop Beck – while continuing as the official Catholic spokesman on educational matters – became Archbishop of Liverpool, where of course particular problems had always to be faced. He was assisted in his negotiations at both regional and national levels by the generally favourable attitude of Catholic leaders and thinkers to the general principles of comprehensive education: the more idealistic emphases of those principles harmonised well with Catholic ideas of social justice, and of service to the whole community and to the poor. Even before the Labour victory of 1964, eleven Catholic comprehensive schools had been founded. And even the generally prickly question of the direct grant schools was dealt with pacifically by the Catholics. These grammar schools (fully one-third of which were Catholic) occupied a special, and deeply valued, place in the English educational system. Formally, they were independent schools, many of a high academic quality, which offered a considerable number of free places for able pupils and received generous central government grants as well as support from LEAs. Many of them, like Manchester Grammar School and other establishments in the North, were academically prestigious without, it was argued, being socially selective. At the same time, many of them did include a considerable number of fee payers. The Catholic direct grant schools were, however, in many ways distinctive, and closer in style and quality to many of the county grammar schools. They had never been perceived as places of particular privilege: the Donnison Commission, set up by the Labour Government to integrate these schools within the emerging comprehensive system, noted that 86% of all places in these Catholic schools were free. When, during the second Labour Government of these years, the direct grant was abolished, forty-eight of the fifty-one Catholic schools became voluntary aided. The three which did not were in Liverpool, which (as always) had problems of its own.[11]

Where problems of reorganisation did arise, they were often the consequence of a determined defence of existing schools by those loyal to them and to what they had provided. Any major reorganisation threatens existing institutions. Such shifts of attitude within the Catholic community, and the associated divisions between bishops and lay people, were to be salient again in the 1990s. The problems of reorganisation within major cities, and on this occasion notably in London where there was a heavy concentration of both Catholic and Anglican voluntary schools, proved to be especially intractable. But nothing could be achieved without some further relaxation of the limits placed on government funding for church schools. The Secretary of State for Education therefore proposed in 1966 that the percentage grant for capital projects might be raised to 80%, and this provision was without controversy included in the Education Act of the following year. With each percentage step on the road to fuller funding (85% in 1975, 90% proposed in 2001) the church schools became ever more fully committed to and dependent upon their partnership with the State.[12] In his autobiography published in 1971, Cardinal Heenan described this progression as 'giving what Catholics called, neither contemptuously nor ungraciously, instalments of justice'.[13]

The necessity of maintaining, alongside the local and diocesan negotiations with the LEAs, constant pressure on central government – which determined at one and the same time the level of the grant towards capital costs, the total sum available for building in the voluntary sector (effectively, by now, Catholic and Anglican), and the division of that total among the LEAs – led to a slow but ultimately significant increase in the influence of the central agencies of the Catholic Church in England. Much ground had been covered, and impressive victories won, since the bishops of the 1930s had asserted their independence of their nominal archiepiscopal leader and even objected to his independent consultation of the Catholic Education Council. The Association of Diocesan Commissioners of Education was founded in 1949 in an attempt to coordinate all applications to the government for funds and to introduce some measure of professional coherence across the various dioceses. The Catholic Education Council itself enjoyed very limited powers, and until 1949 had no full-time secretary. Bishop Beck as its effective chairman demonstrated the advantages of a more sustained approach to government. But the Council remained a fragmentary organisation until its complete overhaul in 1991, from which it then emerged as the Catholic Education Service, with (eventually) four forums representing the Diocesan Commissioners, the Catholic teachers' groups, the specialists in religious education, and those concerned with higher and further education. Most significantly, it was reconstituted as an agency of the Bishops' Conference and therefore became more closely integrated with the formal structures of power and responsibility within the Church. It was then to prove a vocal and effective organisation in the spirited debates about the balance of Church and State powers in the last decade of the century.

The growing interest and power of the hierarchy in matters of national educational policy created certain tensions across the decades when the Catholic Church, nationally as well as internationally, was experiencing deep changes in demography and ideology, and therefore in its social and political relationships. The pontificate of John XXIII (from 1958 until 1963) and the Second Vatican Council which he convened fundamentally challenged some of the cherished beliefs, and doubtless prejudices, of clergy and laity alike. In particular, of course, they generated a new awareness of the importance of the laity, now becoming – as a consequence of rising educational standards and the upward social mobility of the traditional Catholic population – much more influential in England (as in the United States). A new spirit of critical enquiry led, in both these anglophone societies, to an unprecedented questioning of the traditional priorities accorded to maintaining distinctive and separate Catholic educational institutions. In 1966, one critic argued that:

> *There are some historical grounds for believing that a common school, in which the children of Christians of various kinds together with the children of 'pagans' are educated side by side, would be a means of breaking out of the cultural ghetto constructed by and for Catholics since the sixteenth century.[14]*

Even more sharply, the dependably provocative Oxford don, Terry Eagleton, objected that:

> *Most people who have gone through the process of Catholic education and emerged with any salvaged awareness won't need to be told that there is something badly wrong with our schools.[15]*

While these may have been isolated voices of Catholic dissent, the growing confidence of the laity, now authenticated by the pronouncements of the Vatican Council, was of wide significance in these same years and prepared the ground for later controversy.

The shifting balance between clerical and professional groups, on the one hand, and the power and influence of a previously docile laity was more widely reflected in the contemporary movement, which has since lost none of its momentum, towards giving parents and families a more decisive voice in the management of schools. Although the Taylor Committee, reporting in 1977 and convened by the Government to address this very theme, had been instructed (after pressure from the Catholic episcopal lobby) to exclude from its remit any consideration of the voluntary aided schools, the matter could not be indefinitely ignored.[16] Of more direct significance for relations between the laity and the Catholic hierarchy was the shifting demography of these years. In 1930, the Catholic population of Great Britain was approaching two and a half million; in 1960, it was approaching five million; and by 1990, it was over five and a half million, and therefore formed some 10% of the total population.[17] The number of baptisms, which between 1960 and 1990 fell from 1.2 million to eight hundred thousand, did not, however, match these increases. This was an ageing and apparently less observantly devout generation than many of its predecessors. Within it, the Irish constituency was still of central importance: between one-fifth and one-quarter of the Catholic population were either first or second generation Irish, and another one-third were Irish by more distant descent.[18] For this and other reasons the affinities of the Catholic population with the Labour Party remained strong. In spite of the massive efforts made by the Catholic community and the matching injections of public funds, it has been estimated that even in the mid-1960s (when the Catholic school population reached its peak), only some 60% of the Catholic population in fact had access to Catholic schools.[19] At the same time, and with results of obviously political and social significance, the impressive investment in building new secondary schools meant that the percentage of the total relevant population attending Catholic secondary schools rose from 2.9% in 1949 through 7.9% in 1969 to approach 10% in 1988.[20] The raising yet again in the 1970s of the school-leaving age, this time to sixteen, generated a peak enrolment in Catholic schools of nearly one million. Pressure on the resources of the Church was correspondingly severe, and in 1975 – the year before Shirley Williams became the first Roman Catholic to preside over the education ministry – a Labour Government (doubtless attentive to the interests of many of those who had voted it into power) raised the building grant to 85%, where it remained for the rest of the century. Although there was thereafter a sharp decline of nearly one-quarter in absolute numbers of pupils in the Catholic schools, with 329 of them closing between 1978 and 1993, demographic change meant that the percentage of Roman Catholic (baptised) pupils actually entering Catholic schools across this period rose significantly from 55% to 72%. Equally significant in the longer run, as background to the growing debate about the distinctive Catholic identity of these schools, was the increase in the proportion of non-Catholic pupils being admitted to these schools. Within secondary schools, for example, this proportion rose from a negligible 3.2% in 1980 to 16% in 1993.[21] Catholic secondary schools, with standards incomparably higher than they had enjoyed thirty years earlier, were now available for all Catholic children who wanted them and who had attended Catholic primary schools. The Catholic community had finally shed its alien and immigrant character, had successfully penetrated the middle classes, and in effect become what one scholar has characterised as a 'domesticated denomination'.[22] For how long, and under what terms and conditions, would it continue to value the distinctively Catholic character of schools which had been created in different circumstances and for different social and religious purposes?

Such questions were given a new and sharp edge by the revolution in attitudes and public policy encapsulated in the victory of Margaret Thatcher and the Conservatives in the general election of 1979. Educational (and indeed social) policy in the 1980s was characterised by a disillusionment with the alleged progressivism of earlier decades, by an acid distrust of the entrenched powers of professionals as 'providers' of public services, by an emphasis on the powers and rights of 'consumers' (notably of parents), by a strong commitment to the beneficence of the market, by a distrust of the historic influence of so-called intermediate powers, of which the LEAs were a spectacular example. Parents as consumers of educational services should therefore be free, as far as could be rendered practicable, to choose among different providers of educational services. It followed inexorably that such 'providers' (schools and their controlling bodies) should be given as much competitive freedom as possible and that as much information as possible should be made available to allow prudent market choices to be made. Such information should be hard and objective, and therefore reliably based on a system for the rigorous and consistent national testing of the achievements of pupils and of individual schools. Such testing could obviously be meaningful only if all schools were working towards commonly agreed (or imposed) standards and targets, which in turn required a clear definition of the content of a universal national curriculum. This cluster of principles and practices may, therefore, be appropriately described as an educational equivalent of monetarism. In such a coherent and consistent ideological system, there was room only for the promulgation of clear national objectives, public testing and publication of achievements, competition among schools, with a high degree of managerial autonomy accorded to those same schools. There was less room for diversity and fundamental variety, and also little space for large and (allegedly) bureaucratic bodies – such as local authorities or indeed the Churches – to interfere with the operation of a market dominated by a central government in strategic control and schools and parents operating in essentially local markets. New conflicts between 'Church' and 'State', as organised national entities, would therefore inevitably arise.

It would, of course, be dangerously misleading to suggest that this climatic change in the 1980s was ever as monolithic as the preceding summary suggests, or that it was without historical justification as a critical response to the structural weaknesses observed in previous years, or indeed, that it was a sudden and wholly unprecedented shift of opinion and policy. It is common, and correct, to draw attention to the speech made at Ruskin College, Oxford in October 1976 by the Labour Prime Minister, James Callaghan, as a clear example of the growing disillusionment with the achievements of British education and of the sharpening anxiety about the consequences of such failures for the economic competitiveness of the nation. The Great Debate orchestrated by the Labour Government and which followed that significant speech demonstrated only too well the range of contemporary disillusionment. It was, nevertheless, the shift in power and attitude in the corridors of Westminster and Whitehall that injected a new urgency into the reforms initiated by the Conservative victory of 1979 and accelerated by the installation two years later of Keith Joseph as Secretary of State. A marked legislative impetus was given to these reforms by the third successive electoral victory of the Conservatives under the leadership of Mrs Thatcher in 1987. Kenneth Baker then assumed national responsibility for education and in the following year, the Education Reform Act of 1988 was inscribed on the statute book. This wide-ranging Act, together with its Labour successor exactly ten years later, implicitly redefined the relations of Church and State in England. That was not of course in any sense the main intention of these Acts: on the contrary, politicians were anxious to avoid any such distractions from their main purposes and had no wish to rekindle antique controversies. But these two Acts did, nevertheless, change the landscape of those relations in ways which at the beginning of a new century are now being slowly and hesitantly explored.

The key issues are now interlocked in complex ways. The raising of the capital grant for voluntary aided schools to 85% in 1975, and the generally amiable relationships in the 1970s between the Churches, the LEAs and central government, meant that financial questions were no longer as dominant as they had constantly been for the past one hundred and thirty years. Demographic change, reinforced by reorientations in national policy, although not initiated with any intention of varying the religious settlement, now shifted the themes of debate towards more fundamental issues of control, the systemic coherence (or atomisation) of the voluntary sectors, the admissions and staffing policies of schools and, as a corollary, the denominational character and purposes of those establishments. Policy changes of the 1980s ensured that there should for the first time in British history be a national curriculum. What should be the Catholic response to that? The abolition of Her Majesty's Inspectorate, relationships with which had been carefully circumscribed and nurtured since the 1840s, led to its replacement by a more strongly evaluative set of functions (incorporated within the Office for Standards in Education [OFSTED]). What would be the Catholic response to that? The deliberate loosening of LEA controls over admissions, the principle that funding should follow pupils, that individual schools should be able to recruit more freely and from a wider pool of applicants, thrust schools into a competitive situation. What might be the Catholic response to that? The delegation of extensive financial and managerial responsibility to every school and to its governing body would now allow schools to deploy their own resources more flexibly and, albeit within national guidelines carefully imposed, to evolve their own policies and styles. What could be the Catholic response to that? Above all, the 1988 Act allowed, and detailed government policies actively encouraged, schools to move away altogether from local authority control and involvement, and to become grant-maintained schools (a category invented in the Act). A voluntary school could, therefore, by choosing this seductively new status, receive a 100% grant towards its capital expenditure as well as other generous financial inducements, thereafter define its own functions and policies, and in doing so not only relinquish engagement with 'its' LEA but also cease to be part of an integrated diocesan pattern of denominational education. What was the Catholic response to that?[23]

It would seem self-evident that the traditional apologia for a Catholic school, as one in which Catholic children were taught by Catholic teachers, would include the unspoken subtext of there also being a recognisable Catholic curriculum. In fact, once the centrally important matter of religious instruction had been disposed of, traditional definitions of such a curriculum had been vague and unsatisfactory. There had been much talk of Catholic (or, of course, Anglican or simply Christian) values and attitudes 'permeating' a curriculum, or indeed the whole atmosphere, of a school. This is doubtless why the formula of Catholic teachers teaching Catholic children would continue to be so serviceable. In fact, of course, until 1944, the Catholic maintained school (the non-provided school in receipt of public grants) did not formally control its own 'secular' curriculum: although the Act of 1944 did concede such a right, one Catholic scholar has argued that it had never been in any meaningful way exercised.[24] One attempt to do so, in the significantly chosen year of 1980, seemed to result only in a statement of imprecise aspirations. Yet, of course, the Catholic Church (or, it could well be argued, any intermediate body in a liberal society) would be bound to harbour serious reservations about government control of the content of education: even if the requirements of the National Curriculum, although burdensome, might not be immediately offensive, what if a more overtly anti-Christian or anti-religious government were ever to come to power? In the event, the Roman Catholic bishops could do little more than protest, as they duly did in 1987, that schools had:

> *enjoyed the right to determine the complete school curriculum in the light*
> *of their understanding that the educational progress should serve and*
> *nurture the whole person. The proposed Bill takes away that right. ...*
> *In practice this means that the Secretary of State and his advisers have*
> *the last word on what shall be taught in Catholic schools, even if this*
> *conflicts with the ideals and practices of Catholic education. ... Secular*

authorities with no professional competence in the matter ... have
ultimate control of the curriculum in Church schools.[25]

In more general terms, the Catholic bishops (under the leadership in educational matters of Bishop David Konstant, and in unison with their Anglican cousins) lamented their exclusion from the process of policy-making and consultation. Partnership, an Anglican leader complained in 1990, 'seemed to have slipped out of the Government vocabulary'.[26]

When confronted with some of the harsher manifestations of the doctrines of the market and of competition, bishops made more authoritative statements in reaffirming the importance of a theological appreciation of the nature of 'the common good'. As there developed (under John Major after 1990 as well as during the Thatcher years) a progressive hardening of the government belief in competition among individual schools, so Christian leaders responded by emphasising what they perceived to be more religious and humane values.

We do not in principle oppose increased independence and self-
management for schools. However the GM option is more than this. It
intensifies financial and curricular inequalities between schools and
creates new inequalities. It also supposes that schools derive their
strength from their own autonomy, without any sense of having a wider
responsibility (the common good).[27]

Such competition, overtly promoted by the publication of league tables showing the comparative results of named schools, was sharpened – and had indeed been made possible – by the decline in the size of the population of secondary school age. The number of pupils in secondary schools dropped from 3,866,000 in 1980 to 3,070,000 in 1988 and then (after a temporary rise in 1990) down in 1996 to 3,010,000. Over the same period, the total number of secondary schools of all types fell from 5506 to 4572: in those that remained, there were many, however unevenly distributed, empty places – and unfilled desks now, of course, entailed an immediate loss of funds.[28] The closing of 329 Catholic schools between 1978 and 1993 has already been noted. Growing uncertainty and covert or overt competition among schools led to the 1986 requirements that they should articulate and publish their admissions criteria. As the Roman Catholic birth rate also declined, some Catholic schools came under financial pressure to admit pupils who were not, and made no claim to be, Catholic by tradition or in loyalties. The relative success of voluntary schools in the published league tables of school performance naturally reinforced the tendency for some of those schools to remould their admission criteria, and so maintain the quality of their achievements as well as their appeal to success-minded parents. The conflict of commitments and of principles surrounding admissions policies was understandably much more immediate and acute than vaguer anxieties about the curriculum. For perhaps the first time in England since the days of William Ullathorne, Catholic leaders had to address seriously questions about the true mission and purposes of their schools. By 1994, the percentage of non-Catholics admitted to those schools had risen to nearly 13%.[29]

The reasons for this change are not easily disentangled. Faced with the brutal alternative of irreversible decline or closure, some schools doubtless admitted non-Catholic pupils whose parents had some general preference for a school with a religious base, or favoured one which was thought to promote a more traditional and disciplined approach to learning, or were seeking one which was competitively successful in terms of published results, or managed to harbour a volatile mixture of all three motives. Some research suggests that, having admitted pupils of other Christian or non-Christian faiths (or of none), a number of schools then failed to make any adequate provision for them. Others took the opportunity of selecting pupils on the grounds of ability or general acceptability. Others, however, preferred to risk survival by jealously preserving a distinctive Catholic character, excluding wherever possible all pupils whose families were not Catholic. Even within one diocese or city, variations of practice remain wide. In a small, yet interesting, number of cases, special arrangements were made with Anglicans to provide joint schools. Although such 'ecumenical' schools, reflecting some of the spirit of Vatican II, certainly had some enthusiastic and committed supporters, the prevailing motives, at least for Catholic leaders, seem to have been pragmatic rather than principled. In at least one case, an anticipated change in the conditions of the market led in 2002 to a withdrawal from such cooperation.[30] All these fluid uncertainties (about the composition of the student and teaching bodies, about the nature of a Catholic curriculum, about an ecumenical preference) led one student of the Catholic schools in the last two decades of the century to claim that these once distinctive schools had in an essential sense lost their way, and to lament that episcopal preoccupations with maintaining a decent share of resources and of the markets in educational provision had deflected attention away from resolving more fundamental questions of purpose. It certainly proved impracticable, at a time of falling numbers and in widely differing local circumstances, to impose any general rule: in 1986, the Catholic authorities suggested, but could do little more, that a total of 15% in Catholic schools might represent a reasonable maximum number for non-Catholic pupils.[31]

In Birmingham, however, it was calculated that by 1992 as many half of the pupils in Catholic schools did not come from Catholic backgrounds: for some, as will appear, these changes offered a welcome challenge, but to others they constituted the greatest of all threats. They fear that Catholic schools will become indistinguishable from other maintained schools, and that the roots which have nourished their continuing support from non-public funds would soon wither. Equally significant, both in terms of reflecting the realities of a rapidly changing situation and in forcing attention onto questions of identity, were the changes in the staffing of Catholic schools in England. As in other countries, a major influence on the evolving character of the schools had been the precipitous decline in the numbers of the professed Religious (Sisters, Brothers and priests) teaching in the schools. In the remoter past, their vocational commitment to engage in the missionary work of teaching for little or no reward had been the economic mainstay of the schools. Even after their virtual disappearance, it might have been supposed or hoped that teachers for Catholic schools would be recruited from Catholic teacher training colleges. But this ideal had, in fact, never been realised, and receded even further as the number of such Catholic colleges declined from fifteen in 1975 to five in 1997. In any case, after 1972 the progressive diversification of the colleges (Catholic or not) into other educational functions broke such continuities as had existed in the lives of those Catholics who progressed as students from Catholic schools into Catholic colleges and then proceeded to teach in Catholic schools. By the 1990s, at least 80% of teachers being recruited to Catholic schools had not attended Catholic colleges for their training, while at the same time many graduates of the Catholic colleges went on to teach in non-Catholic schools, or in increasing numbers to join other professions. By the mid-1990s, the religious orders provided only 1% of the teachers in Catholic schools, while over 28% of the teachers (compared with 22% in 1978) were not Roman Catholics. Within the secondary sector, less than 1% belonged to an order, and 57% of the teachers were Catholics, while 42% were not.[32]

The tensions provoked by these dramatic mutations in demography and in public attitudes were well illustrated by the complex events at St Philip's Sixth Form College in Birmingham, where there had been systematic changes in the formal nature of educational establishments and, of much greater significance, in the ethnic and religious composition of the local population.[33] St Philip's had been a boys' grammar school, before being reorganised as a sixth form college drawing most of its pupils from the contributory Catholic feeder schools which provided for the 11-16 age group. The college was owned and conducted as a voluntary aided institution by the Oratorians, who, gravely concerned at the decline of the Catholic population of the college and its effects on its Catholic character, determined to close it. The defenders of the college as it had recently evolved believed that the variety and diversity of the establishment represented, in the contemporary circumstances of Birmingham, a successful essay in integration and the cultivation of tolerance. The Oratorians relented to the extent of being prepared, while maintaining formal ownership, to hand over the college to be administered by the diocese. Their anxieties nevertheless persisted, especially as by 1992 the student composition of the college had become 32% Catholic, 15% other Christian, 18% Muslim, 9% Sikh, 5% Buddhist, and 13% with no known affiliation. The situation was further complicated by the fact that responsibility for funding and to some extent for regulating the college passed in 1992 from the LEA to a new central (not local) body, the Further Education and Funding Council. The FEFC initiated a major enquiry, in the course of which attention was directed to the anomalies embedded in current arrangements and policies, and even ventured to suggest that the time was ripe for an overall review of voluntary aided status. The college has since been closed.[34]

Sharp differences of opinion have, therefore, emerged within the Catholic community about the policies to be pursued, and in particular about reconciling the interests and ideals of the Church as a whole with the aspirations of particular Catholic schools and communities: the New Conservatism was obviously more sympathetic to the preferences of churches and communities and parents than to the holistic principles of a nationally organised Church, constituting an unwelcome intermediate authority. In 1991, the bishops proclaimed:

> We are concerned that the emergence of a more pronounced market as a divisive force in education means that the partnership between Church and State has begun to change both locally and nationally.[35]

Nor could the Catholic bishops continue to count upon the kind of ready support from Catholics as a whole that they enjoyed in 1944 and in later efforts to influence national policy: neither in the House of Commons nor in the House of Lords, and in spite of the fact that the bishops wrote to every Catholic MP, was there any support for the substantial objections which the hierarchy had urged against the 1988 Act.[36] Even before the dangerous innovations (as Catholics perceived them) of the 1988 Act, the Archbishop of Westminster himself was plunged into serious disputes with his own flock in the matter of school reorganisation. The supporters of the Cardinal Vaughan School in London disliked the plans for reorganisation which the diocese had agreed with the LEA, believing that the creation of a sixth form college would seriously damage the character of the school which they (as parents, governors and teachers) valued. They therefore refused to cooperate, and in June 1987, the Archbishop in effect dismissed two of the Foundation governors, arguing that it was their duty to apply the policies adopted by the Trustees and therefore to give a higher priority to the policies of the archdiocese than to their own institutional preferences. The governors of the school thereupon sought, but lost, a judicial review. However, in a later and unrelated case, the House of Lords doubted the correctness of this ruling by a lower court, and allowed an appeal against the earlier decision, which was then overturned. The school subsequently applied for and secured grant-maintained status: as did the Oratory School in London, where there were similar objections to the reorganisation plans and to which Tony Blair (the Labour leader and later Prime Minister) later sent his own son – in spite of the fact that he was not himself a Catholic and much to the consternation of his left wing critics.[37]

It was, of course, the deeply contested issue of grant-maintained status that sharpened such divisions, and brought to an end the long period of cooperation between the Church(es) and what Gerald Grace has well described as the liberal pluralist State.[38] Grant-maintained status was obviously, in the circumstances outlined above, bound to be attractive to a number of Catholic schools. The financial arrangements were generous, while the school, as a self-governing institution receiving funds only from a remote central authority, would be relatively free from both diocesan and LEA restraints. There was, moreover, a suspicion that the Department of Education and Science had been deliberately slow in recent times in granting approval of capital grants for voluntary school building, doubtless in a concerted attempt to promote the grant-maintained cause. It was estimated that between 1988 and 1992 nearly thirty such bids were rejected on the grounds that there were spare places in the county schools.[39] The temptations for voluntary schools, struggling to meet the demand for places, to move away from LEA involvement into grant-maintained status were therefore very real. Such a move also implied some loosening at least of the links between such a school and its parent diocese and of the partnership with other Catholic schools that such links involved. Although by canon law any school depended upon the bishop for the right to claim the title of 'Catholic', it was rare for disagreements to reach that level of intensity. But what if a former voluntary school, built in part from the contributions of the faithful, chose to admit a majority of non-Catholics, or to apply selective admissions criteria which would exclude poorer or less talented members of the Catholic community, or which damaged other Catholic schools? As with schools which had in the past been reluctant to cooperate with diocesan reorganisation plans, the bishops were understandably uneasy at what might lead to a disintegration of the whole system of Catholic schooling. At the outset, Cardinal Hume had sought but failed to entrench the right of the Trustees to veto any proposal for a Catholic school to become grant-maintained, even if the necessary parental support had been secured for such a move.[40] When in 1993 responsibility for funding the direct grant schools was transferred to a new government agency, the bishops objected that they were given no representation on that body.[41] John Major's ambition was that eventually all schools should become grant maintained and 'freed' from LEA control: his proposals in 1995, two years before his shattering electoral defeat, would have made it much simpler for church schools in particular to make that significant transition. The Churches angrily objected that there had been no consultation about so fundamental a change in policy, and forged a new alliance with the LEAs. The Director of the Catholic Education Service observed:

> *One of the reasons for rejecting the 'fast-track' proposals was that they would have isolated Church schools from others in the maintained sector, those controlled by local authorities. The latter's powers have been considerably weakened by legislation over the past decade, but we have retained our generally good relationships with them. ... The LEA associations have emphasised the value of our partnership with increasing warmth as their own powers have diminished.[42]*

No doubt they had: this was a far cry from the bitterness of 1902, or even the tensions of 1944. One local authority leader who had in easier times dismissed church schools as 'independent schools on the rates' had by 1996 changed his tune.[43] By 1997, the bishops were insisting even more clearly on the priority of 'the common good' over individual or institutional self-interest.

In that year, which also marked the decisive electoral defeat of the Conservatives and the beginning of Tony Blair's incumbency as Prime Minister, 2190 of the total of 21,879 maintained primary and secondary schools in England alone were designated as Roman Catholic, representing 10% of the total number of schools and also of pupils. By January 1998, 60 of those primary schools and 94 of the secondary schools had chosen the grant-maintained path. This, given the strenuous efforts of the Government to make this new status attractive, represented a relatively modest total of 7%. More significant, however, are the differences between the primary and the secondary sectors: it was in the latter that competition among schools was most intense, and seemed certain to grow. Although only one in thirty of the Catholic primary schools ceased to be voluntary schools closely associated with both LEA and diocese, one in four of the secondary schools found it prudent or necessary to accept the more favourable financial deal. This, of course, represented a massive threat to the integrity and coherence of the Catholic school system itself.[44] Change might have been even more dramatic if the political situation in the mid-1990s had been more stable and predictable. In these years, the Labour Party was redefining its policies and principles, and (to use the fashionable term) rebranding itself as 'New Labour'. Although New Labour would prove to be more sympathetic to notions of the market, more sceptical about the virtues of public monopoly, more open to diversification in the educational system than Old Labour, it had repeatedly committed itself to abolishing or reforming the status of the grant-maintained school and, albeit with uneven enthusiasm, to restoring something of the authority and prestige of the LEA. There were at the same time few signs of the survival of any traditional Labour hostility to denominational schools as such. When in 1991 Tessa Blackstone, as a Labour Party spokesperson in the House of Lords, publicly speculated on the desirability of all maintained schools becoming secular, other Labour peers hastened to make it clear that such a revolution was no part of official Labour policy.[45]

As, under the remorseless pressure of deep disagreements about the future relationship of Britain to Europe, the Conservative Party disintegrated, the details of Labour policy on the future of Church/State relations remained vague. Evidently, this was no longer perceived as an issue of any great significance. It was not clear how, if indeed at all, the grant-maintained schools were to be reintegrated within the general system. In 1993, the politician responsible for the Labour Party portfolio on education had written to the Churches giving them a clear warning that a Labour government:

> *will undoubtedly wish to restore the important partnership between central government, local government and the Churches which underpinned the 1944 Act. However it would be unrealistic ... to attempt simply to put the clock back to 1944. It cannot be assumed that church schools that have felt the need to give up their voluntary-aided status in return for 100 per cent funding would have, or would even wish to have, voluntary-aided status restored. [46]*

The clear implication was that they would, therefore, be obliged to become controlled schools, and that was an option which had, of course, always been rejected by the Catholics. The Catholic bishops were agitated. The Labour Party – surprisingly, given the care with which it was polishing its electoral arguments and systematically preparing for a delayed return to power – apparently gave little serious thought to how its objectives were in fact to be achieved without stirring up a hornets' nest of religious objections and without alienating the traditional Catholic vote. It would, perhaps, have been difficult to clarify a policy when the leader of the Party himself chose to send one of his own children to a Roman Catholic grant-maintained school. The proposals made in the Labour Party official publication, *Diversity and Excellence* (October 1995) served only to prolong confusion and uncertainty. The central proposal, to reappear unrefined even after the Labour Party victory, was that the existing and now anomalous pattern should be replaced by a threefold categorisation of schools as 'community' (in effect, a more appropriate title for the former county schools), 'voluntary' (a totally undefined conflation of the controlled and aided categories), and 'foundation'. The last, for which no clear theoretical defence was offered, was plainly designed to offer some consolation to former county schools which had (imprudently, it might now appear) become grant maintained and for which the voluntary status was obviously inappropriate. It was eventually to prove of some use as a, perhaps ephemeral, safety net for such schools and for some denominational schools as well. The assumption, obviously, was that the denominational schools which had been grant maintained should now become voluntary again. But what in detail could that now mean? To the Catholics in particular, preoccupied with crucial matters such as the control of admissions and the composition of governing bodies, such vagueness was bound to be deeply threatening. But, nothing effectively was done to assuage their doubts, or even to clarify the proposals.

In May 1997, the reformed Labour Party was returned to power with a startlingly handsome majority and now faced no substantial obstacle to applying its new policies. Partly as a result of the massive effort to win wide electoral support, those policies differed much less than might have been expected from the market-based policies of the Conservatives. There was to be no return to an ideological commitment to the pure comprehensive school, no attempt to reverse the policies of rigorous and comparative testing based upon a national curriculum, no wholesale restoration of the power of the LEAs. In July, the government White Paper sought to deflect attention away from inconvenient disputes about 'structure' (that is, the contested organisation of secondary schools) towards issues of 'standards'.[47] Nothing was added to what had already been said about the proposed new categories of schools, and the anxieties of the denominationalists were, therefore, in no way reduced. In the intervening months there had been, for a Government anxious to avoid unnecessary and distracting troubles, surprisingly little consultation with the Churches and other pressure groups, who would have had much to contribute to an acceptable clarification of what remained dangerously vague proposals. The complacent and unjustifiable assumption that all voluntary schools were essentially the same was, therefore, bound to be challenged with increasing impatience as legislation was hurried forward. By August 1997, a breaking point seemed dangerously near. The Catholic press proclaimed that 'Bishops Will Fight for Our Schools' and anticipated the toughest battle since 1944. Bishop David Konstant, as Chairman of the CES, accused the Government of 'driving a coach and horses through the whole of the dual system' and lamented that:

> To many of those with influence in our postmodernist, multi-cultural
> State, it matters not one jot if the schools' teachers and pastoral carers
> are Atheists, Druids or Satanists.[48]

Anglicans and Catholics now united to press for the clear recognition of the two original categories of voluntary school, on which Butler and Temple had wisely agreed before 1944. A Government which seemed somewhat disconcerted by this burst of indignation quietly agreed that, in effect and with the minor but potentially significant addition of the foundation school (in which the Catholics were not at all interested), the world should return to its pre-1988 state. But the confidence of the Churches had been severely shaken by the almost casual way in which the foundations of a hallowed settlement had been threatened.

The Blair Government, as good communitarians and sponsors of the Third Way in politics, were attracted by many forms of public–private partnership. They were at the same time anxious in an increasingly diverse society to include educational provision for groups, notably the Muslims, which had hitherto been excluded. A Green Paper in February 2001 was soon followed by a White Paper in which a significant extension of faith-based provision was now proposed, together with increased financial resources and the tempting (to some) promise of 90% support for the costs of such schooling.[49] In the short interval between the two official publications, the Church of England proclaimed its willingness to cooperate in such an ambitious venture, doubtless detecting in it a rare opportunity of recovering some of its rapidly diminishing influence in public life.[50] Other Christian groups, including the Salvation Army, hastened to declare an interest in taking part in such an extension of state aid. The White Paper had, however, stated clearly that the Government would wish any such new schools to be 'inclusive'. Whereas the Anglicans could, of course, have no difficulty with such a requirement, the Roman Catholics – alert as they always had been to any threats to Catholic identity – expressed grave misgivings. In a statement issued by the Director of the Catholic Education Service on 19 March 2002, proposals that anyone other than the governors and trustees of a Church school should control admissions were dismissed as 'nonsense'. Quotas reserved for pupils of other faiths could lead to Catholic children being deprived of places. Suggestions that Muslims should emulate the success of Catholic schools by setting up their own schools were, on the other hand, welcomed. The historic rationale of the place of Catholic schools within a publicly funded educational system had, nevertheless, now been irreversibly widened by new policies and, above all, by the increasingly powerful demands of other faith groups for a share of public money and support. Some of the implications of these developments will be explored in the next and final chapter.

At the beginning of the twenty-first century, Catholic schools enjoying state funding, however uncertain about their longer-term future and destabilised by the recent erosion of a historic consensus, make a major contribution to public education.[51] Of the 21,550 maintained schools in England (only) and as recorded in January 2001, 63% are (in the terms of the 1998 Act) community schools, the lineal descendants of the county schools of 1944 and the 'provided schools' of 1902. Just under 4% – most of them former grant-maintained schools which had under the 1944 Act been county or controlled schools – are now reclassified as foundation schools. Only one Catholic school chose this status. The remaining 33% of schools in England are formally in the voluntary sector, 20% as aided (including, of course, virtually all the Catholic establishments) and 13% controlled. Not all these controlled schools necessarily have denominational or, indeed, any religious affiliations: of the same overall national total of 21,150 schools, 70% are described as having 'no religious character'. Among the denominations, the major provider in strictly numerical terms is still the Church of England (with 4700 schools) but, as has been repeatedly emphasised in these pages, many of those schools (2031 to be exact) are controlled. As controlled schools, in many ways they stand close to the community category, and indeed, many former Anglican schools had long since been fully integrated within the LEA provision, and have a diminished or negligible denominational character. On the other hand, all the Catholic schools (with yet again one or two tiny anomalies) are voluntary aided. At the beginning of the twenty-first century, therefore, the Catholics have the largest number of fully denominational schools: 2102, compared with 2031 for the Established Church. Catholic schools, therefore, form 10% of the total number of all schools in England, and educate just under 10% of the total school population of 7,483,780. They have a significantly larger number of secondary schools than the Anglicans and, since such schools tend to be larger, the Anglican aided schools account for only 6% of the total school population. At no time, of course, could the Catholic school question have been treated in isolation from that of other faith groups: indeed, they originally owed their place within the public system to the previous existence of the Anglican school settlement, and to the anomalies which that privileged position had entailed. In 2001, there were still 28 Methodist schools (although only three of them aided), 74 other Christian schools (some of them jointly provided by more than one denomination), 31 Jewish and – of potentially great significance – two Muslim schools and two Sikh. One of the 'other' Christian schools is owned by the Seventh Day Adventists. The recognition of these new schools will soon offer to the strong Catholic position in England at least as many complex and novel challenges as the incorporation within the public system of the Roman Catholic schools had in an earlier century created for Anglicans, Nonconformists and secularists.

Notes

[1] The volatile title of the Cabinet Minister responsible for education reflects the growing importance of that office in political life, as well as, more recently, changing beliefs about how it should relate to other responsibilities, for example, for publicly funded science, employment or training. In 1944, of course, the President of the Board of Education became the Minister of Education, in 1964 the Secretary of State for Education and Science, in 1992 for Education, in 1994 for Education and Employment, in 2001 for Education and Skills.

[2] Howard, 1987, pp. 360-361; Arthur, 1995a, p. 101.

[3] Parsons, 1993.

[4] Murphy, 1971, p. 121.

[5] Free Church Federal Council Education Policy Committees, 1959, I, quoted in Murphy, 1971, pp. 121-122.

[6] Cruickshank, 1963, p. 173.

[7] Arthur, 1995a, pp. 31-32.

[8] Derived from the table in Cruickshank, 1963, p. 191.

[9] Arthur, 1995a, p. 96.

[10] *Education*, 5 March 1965.

[11] The Public Schools Commission (1970) Second Report, vol. 1, p. 51. London: Her Majesty's Stationery Office.

[12] Benn & Simon, 1970, pp. 278-283; Fenwick, 1976, p. 140; Murphy, 1971, p. 122; Arthur, 1995a, pp. 95, 96, 101.

[13] Heenan, 1971, p. 265. Heenan became the eighth Archbishop of Westminster in 1967.

[14] Cameron, 1966, p. 111.

[15] Arthur, 1995a, p. 99; Grace (2002), pp. 27-28.

[16] Chadwick, 1997, p. 49.

[17] Butler & Butler, 2000, p. 562.

[18] Arthur, 1995a, p. 90.

[19] McLaughlin et al, 1996, p. 6.

[20] Arthur, 1995a, p. 103.

[21] Hypher, 1996, p. 223.

[22] Hornsby-Smith, 1987, p. 204; Hickman (1995).

[23] Grace, 2001.

[24] Arthur, 1995a, pp. 111-112.

[25] Maclure, 1988, pp. 20-21, citing Bishops' Conference of England and Wales, 1988, p. 11.

[26] Chadwick, 1997, p. 47.

[27] Catholic Education Service (1992) *A Response to the White Paper*.

[28] MacKinnon & Statham, 1999.

[29] Arthur, 1995a, p. 101.

[30] Hypher, 1996, p. 216; Chadwick, 1994. The example referred to is in Oxford.

[31] Arthur, 1995a, p. 113.

[32] Catholic Education Service: Report for 1995; Arthur, 1995a, pp. 113, 190, 198.

[33] Hewer, 2001, pp. 516-517.

[34] Murray, 1996, pp. 239-245.

[35] *Catholic Herald*, 21 June 1991.

[36] Arthur, 1995a, p. 117.

[37] Ibid., p. 180.

[38] Grace, 2001.

[39] *Times Educational Supplement*, 7 February 1992.

[40] *The Times*, 13 January 1988; Chadwick, 1997; Arthur, 1995a, p. 115.

[41] *The Times*, 13 January 1988.

[42] *The Tablet*, 18 May 1996.

[43] Chadwick, 1997, p. 66.

[44] The outcome for Anglican schools was significantly different, as many more of these schools were, of course, controlled and not aided, and therefore already in receipt of a full 100% grant for capital building works and all repairs. In any case, the diocesan management of the Anglican schools had traditionally been more relaxed than that of the Catholics. Nevertheless, 162 of their schools (more than for the Catholics) became grant-maintained in these years. These figures are derived from the official statistics, published in 1998.

[45] *Hansard*, House of Lords, vol. 526, col. 254, cited in Arthur, 1995a, p. 210.

[46] *Church Times*, 29 April 1994.

[47] 'Excellence in Schools', cmd. 3681. London: The Stationery Office.

[48] *Catholic Herald*, 19 August 1997.

[49] Department for Education and Skills, 2001a.

[50] Church Schools Review Group, 2001 (The Dearing Report).

[51] The figures which follow are derived from the Department for Education and Skills (2001b) *Statistics of Education*, Tables 21, 22a, 22b, 23a, 23b and 24.

CHAPTER 14

Contrasts and Cautions

This book has attempted to hold together within a unifying framework the comparative history of three quite different traditions. The shared terms 'State' and 'Catholic', running like two vivid threads through the whole tapestry, have in fact proved to be much less monochrome than might have been expected. The account given of their interweaving across the three societies therefore often dissolves into three idiosyncratic narratives, between which the contrasts are often more salient and illuminating than are any comparisons or cross-references. The first part of this final chapter will first explore those contrasts and distinguishing differences. But the work should not stop there. Beneath the three constituent narratives run certain unmistakably common themes. It would be overambitious to claim that there are clear 'lessons to be learned' and which can be articulated as prescriptions for future policy. But it is possible to discern some signposts, and to frame some clear cautions. Such conclusions might be especially important at a time when there is good deal of public talk, but not enough sustained and well-informed discussion, about the likely consequences of an extension of faith-based schooling and of public funding for it. To such a discussion, and viewed as an extended case study, the experience of one denomination in three contrasting countries over the past two centuries is indeed relevant. If history and comparative studies had absolutely no 'lessons to teach' or warnings to suggest, they would hardly be worthy of serious study.

Ireland and Mann

John Ireland was chosen to lead the short procession of six representative characters moving across the earlier pages of this book simply because – perhaps more than any of the five who follow him – he relates through his life and background to all three of the countries under review. He was born in Ireland, then under British rule, and into a family which was forced by economic necessity and the policies of an unsympathetic Protestant establishment to migrate to the United States. In that missionary country, he was directly influenced by French-speaking Catholic clergy rooted in their European origins and who secured for him an education and training for the priesthood in France, by the classical culture of which he was permanently affected and impressed. In America itself, he worked to clarify and defend the special (yet rigorously orthodox) character of American Catholicism. The supreme task for him was to secure the universal reconciliation of devotion to Rome with patriotic loyalty to the Republic. Education should, therefore, serve to produce good Americans as well as good Catholics. And since America was, from the earliest years of the Republic, destined to develop as a multiethnic and multicultural nation, he was opposed to any system of schooling which could serve to perpetuate the diverse and divisive cultures of the immigrants from old Europe. Catholics, he argued, should therefore, wherever practicable, attend the common schools, and those schools should be hospitable to them and respectful of their religion and traditions. 'The free school of America! Withered be the hand raised in sign of its destruction!'[1]

In fact, the evolution of the ideas and practices associated with Horace Mann rendered that ideal inaccessible. Mann himself argued and campaigned, often in terms congenial to Ireland, for a school which would be non-sectarian and yet clearly marked by strong moral as well as civic values. In a country which was, and remains, both deeply religious and distinguished by a rich diversity of denominations and sects, it was imperative to maintain and proclaim the centrality of a religion marked by a simple adherence to the principles of the Christian gospel and a belief in a supreme and transcendent being. For many of Mann's own contemporaries, such a formula represented a profoundly unsatisfying and syncretistic reduction of distinctive Christian doctrines and a dilution of the evangelical message. In time, however, and confronted with the mounting threat of an increasingly secular ideology, most Protestants closed ranks in defence of a common school which would be Christian while remaining unwelcoming to the indigestible Catholics. The dilemma for those Catholics and their leaders was compounded by their immigrant status, and by the widespread suspicion which they aroused. Separate schools for Catholics became an imperative for these new communities, with little or no support at any time from public funds. Eventually, the survival of their own separate schools would come to depend on an augmentation of such funds. Archbishop Ireland was, in principle, defeated.

Combes and Guizot

John Ireland had, for a short while, been encouraged by Rome to preach his characteristically American message to the French. For a few optimistic months it seemed just possible that the old Gallic antagonisms between an anticlerical Republic and a monarchist and authoritarian Church would be buried. Such hopes were pulverised by the bitter arguments enveloping the Dreyfus affair, as Emile Combes was carried to high office on a wave of resentment against the power of Church and priests. The Catholic education establishment, which had survived all the successive vicissitudes of the nineteenth century, was now frontally attacked by Combes and his allies, and a separation of State and Churches formally decreed. The schism was perpetuated in society and in politics. A relatively pacific advocate of the separation of Church and State had argued:

> *Those who abdicate their rights as persons and subject themselves to a religious power have no right to teach. The State has the right to preserve youth from their influence. Monastic society and democratic society are incompatible.*

A less moderate Catholic youth in 1928 attacked the statue of Emile Combes with a hammer and was shot for his pains. A century sooner, a period of (often uneasy) cooperation between public education and the Catholics had been initiated by Guizot, the Protestant Anglophile, whose ideal form of government was a constitutional monarchy in which extremes of politics or sentiment would be avoided. At the same time, he consolidated the Napoleonic concept of a statist form of education, in which a centralised State would provide the national framework and the impetus for a publicly funded system, in which the Church would be granted a considerable yet never predominant part. At the beginning of the twentieth century, Guizot's attempt to reconcile the work and interests of the State with those of the Catholic Church in France was, for half a century, abandoned.

Morant and Ullathorne

Robert Morant, after his oriental adventure, spent the rest of his life working as a civil servant in London. Although his sense of order was as powerful as that of Guizot, if not of Napoleon, he was well aware of the limitations imposed by English habits and constitutional arrangements and learned to work through the established institutions and elected politicians. With all the polished skill of a high bureaucrat, he used one problem to solve another, exploiting the difficulties of the Churches in maintaining their schools in order to effect a moderate rationalisation of the untidy patterns of educational provision and control. His work, in spite of the public protests it provoked, ensured that the resolution of questions related to government support for faith-based schools would for the century which followed be contained within the parliamentary context. The Catholics, even more than the Anglicans, desperately needed such government money but, even more than the Anglicans, nursed deep anxieties about the compromises which were attached to such financial support, and the loss of autonomy and identity which they threatened. No Catholic leader articulated these doubts more clearly and bluntly than William Ullathorne – a member of an Old Catholic family who in his lifetime saw the Roman Catholic community in England multiplied and permanently changed by the influx of Irish immigrants. Grants became even more indispensable and were, on an increasing scale, sought and accepted. William Ullathorne had been in principle defeated.

◆◆◆◆◆

Of the three contemporaries flourishing at the turn of the nineteenth and twentieth centuries with whom this book began, Ireland might well be described as embodying one clear – although never uncontested – understanding of what it meant in the last decade of the nineteenth century to be a loyal American Catholic, with a commitment to public education and the exaltation of the Roman faith. His contemporary, Combes, also educated in a French seminary, was characteristically Gallic in belonging unambiguously to one of the 'two Frances' into which his society was divided. Morant was the principal architect of a system which secured the funding of religious schools while attempting to relate them to a pattern of local coordination. In all three countries, then, the terms of the twentieth century debate on the relationship between public and Catholic education were firmly set at the turn of the nineteenth and twentieth centuries, and that vigorous debate was then to be energetically pursued in three arenas, similarly typical of the three nations.

The Courts

For the United States, the key issues were revolved, and may one day even be resolved, in the courts of the land, and notably within the Supreme Court itself. The seizing of independence from British rule – and indeed, in many cases the foundation and settlement of the pre-existent colonies – necessarily involved a rejection of English forms of ecclesiastical establishment. In so far as America had a sacred text, it was the Declaration of Independence supplemented by the Constitution itself.[2] What exactly that would imply for the relations of the State and religion in the field of education remained obscure and was not always clarified by jurisprudential exegesis.

The United States, unlike Britain and France, is built on the rock-like principle of the separation of powers, and the Constitution (and notably the First Amendment) referred exclusively to the powers and duties of the federal government, and not directly to those of the constituent states. All powers not formally delegated to that federal authority remained the intact prerogative of the states themselves. With notable exceptions, for much of the nineteenth century the State and Church question which troubled European nations remained dormant across the Atlantic. Catholic schools were developed alongside an inhospitable public system, and sometimes received without serious challenge a measure of public subsidy. The active engagement of the courts was a pronounced feature of the twentieth rather than of the nineteenth century, and especially of the period after 1945. The 'wall of separation' which for Thomas Jefferson had been a serviceable metaphor was now canonised as a doctrine, and became an abiding and controversial theme in public and judicial debate. The major issues under dispute naturally found their tortuous way to the Supreme Court. A striking feature of the decisions of that Court is the apparently unbridgeable split of opinions among the wise Justices themselves, who have often divided five to four. Direct subsidy to Catholic (and other religious) schools must, it is now agreed, be legally forbidden – prohibited just as emphatically as it has always been allowed in England, as well as in France before the anticlerical laws of the late nineteenth century and since the Gaullist volte-face represented by the 1959 Law. But indirect support is another matter altogether, clearly allowable under some circumstances, at least since the landmark Everson judgment in which (confusingly again) the arguments of the Court pointed in one direction, and its conclusions in quite another. A revival of interest – especially since the presidential election of 2000 – in faith-based initiatives propels to the top of the agenda the question whether publicly funded vouchers should be used to support families wanting their children to attend Catholic schools. That matter is unresolved as these pages are written, and may well remain so long after they are read. The decisions of the Court will reflect any changes in its own membership as well as, in more subtle and nuanced ways, underlying shifts of public opinion. Any such shifts of opinion will be profoundly affected by longer-term reactions to the events of September 2001, and by the evolving debate about the nature of a healthy relationship between religion and civil society in the liberal democratic state.

The Streets

In France, only rarely are major policy disagreements resolved in the courts. In the hexagon, and especially in Paris, such matters are more likely to be settled by revolutionary convulsion, or by massive street demonstrations and a display of public indignation. It seems sometimes to be simpler to change the government, or even the form of the regime, than to adjust a policy. Adjudication and compromise have little appeal. A remarkable feature of the French system and method of government is the survival of a resilient cluster of administrative principles and of public expectations across a sequence of sharp and sometimes unpredictable changes in the form of government. Across the years included in the studies in these pages, France enjoyed or endured the Bourbon monarchy of the *ancien régime*, revolutionary improvisations, the First Republic, the Directory, the Consulate, the First Napoleonic Empire, a restored Bourbon monarchy, the Orléanist monarchy of Louis Philippe, the Second Republic, the Second Empire, and then – punctuated by revolution or coup d'état – three more Republics, interrupted by the aberration of Vichy. And yet, a cluster of widely held axioms persisted throughout this turbulence: France was a nation one and indivisible, Catholicism was the religion of the majority of Frenchmen, the State had an overarching responsibility for a range of public services (and especially education), schools were created and sustained by that State to transmit French culture and to inculcate the values and practices of patriotism and civic duty. Prestigious educational institutions might alter their names with every change in the form of government, and yet their continuous identity – as for the *Université* itself – survived.[3] The hands on the levers might change but the engines of state rolled on. An observer is left with the powerful impression that institutions which had been abolished in fact sometimes disappeared underground for a while, to surface again in more propitious times. After 1789, all the familiar institutions – the law, the professions, the Gallican Church, the universities and the educational system – disappeared, or so it seemed. Priests emigrated, sometimes to reappear in Yorkshire to minister to the remnants of the Catholic community in England, and sometimes in America to keep alight the candles of the old faith. But with the sceptical and opportunist Napoleon, the Church was effectively restored as a compliant partner of the State, and much of primary education was left in its safely traditional keeping. In the elite realm of secondary education, the University was now to reign, even if revolutionary events on the streets gave the Church an ephemeral control of it. Guizot, by no means an open enemy of the Church, nevertheless ensured that after the disturbing events of 1830 the State should seize overall control of the school system, and of its teachers and programmes of study. A succeeding regime, duly initiated by revolution and demonstration, shifted the educational balance back towards the Church by recognising its freedom to provide secondary as well as primary schools. Twenty years later, however, a disastrous war and a brutal revolution and counter-revolution in Paris were the prologue to a series of anticlerical laws, severely clipping the educational powers of the Church.

The short-lived attempt at reconciliation, with which Archbishop Ireland himself was so closely associated, was drowned in the public storms of the Dreyfus affair, in the aftermath of which the most draconian of all laws against Catholics and their formal place in public life was imposed on a resentful Church. The collapse of the Third Republic and the creation of the puppet Vichy Government introduced a short period when government tried, but with indifferent success, to repair some of the damage which had been inflicted on the Church and its schools. The liberation of France led to a hasty reversal of policy towards the Catholic schools, and a determination to return to the sacred principles of Ferry and of Combes. The constitution which inaugurated the new post-war regime was the first, but not the last, to enshrine the principle that the French Republic was *laïque*. As the nation struggled to meet the enlarging educational needs of the whole population, the Catholic schools were left suspended in a financial limbo. Only rebellion on the streets of Algiers and popular protests on those of Paris would make possible the return to power of de Gaulle. The new President was convinced that the regeneration of France could, as a matter of practical politics and logistics, be achieved only with the cooperation of the Catholic schools: the dilemma was not unlike that presented in England after 1870, in 1902, in the 1920s and 1930s, and (above all, of course) after 1944. In 1959, against massive objections and monster petitions, de Gaulle therefore pressed through a new law. Catholic schools could now accept from the State contracts enabling them to deliver a public service while also requiring that the basic laws of the Republic be observed. Catholic schools under contract must therefore observe the universal norms and standards of the public educational system, and may not discriminate against non-Catholics in deciding which pupils to admit to their many schools. A precarious balance had at last been achieved: any attempt to tilt it in favour of either the Catholic or the *laïque* interest would hereafter be resisted by the descent into the streets of thousands of citizens.

Attempts to limit the independence of the Catholic schools were in this way defeated in 1984; efforts to augment their public funding were by the same means frustrated in 1994. For the moment, the scene may now appear peaceful, and at the time of writing the current Minister of National Education (Jack Lang) obviously has no intention of rekindling old and distracting disputes. But the fault lines running across the system are now moving, and future disputes (for they are certain to arise) may well be deeply influenced by changes in the religious demography of the country. Although Jews and Protestants have, of course, long enjoyed alongside the Catholic majority the same advantages and obligations conferred by a formal contract with the State, the number of schools involved has been small and no awkward problems of admission or identity arise to disturb a convenient consensus. Islam is now, however, in numerical terms the second religion of France and has been the occasion in recent years of threatening tensions within the public system. It seems highly probable that, at some future date, a demand (as in England) for state support for some Muslim schools will be articulated. At that point, the streets may once again become the familiar arena for confrontation and settlement.

The Corridors

In England, on the other hand, only a handful of questions about church schools have ever been ventilated in the courts of law, while the days of popular marches and special trains crowded with protestors against 'Rome on the rates' are long gone. In England, the heart of debate and decisions has been in the small area surrounding the Palace of Westminster, with its lobbies and the bureaucratic warrens of Whitehall and its satellites. This is no doubt the method of dealing with conflict which Guizot, who shared John Ireland's distaste for popular tumult, would have preferred for his own country. The earliest subsidies to church schools (meaning at first the schools of the Church of England and Protestant Nonconformists) were made by Parliament under procedures approved by it. In response to political pressures heightened by the extension of the parliamentary vote to Catholics, this limited generosity was soon to be extended to the urban schools supported by the Roman Catholics. The first legislative marathon unrolled in

1870, when the rudimentary foundations for a dual system were laid. The longest legislative procedure of them all followed in 1902, and was accompanied by the elaborate manoeuvres of civil servants, with Morant outflanking Sadler and other rivals for office and influence. The foundations of the dual system were now strengthened and adjusted, with a fresh emphasis laid on the alignment of Anglican, Catholic and other denominational schooling with the ever enlarging provision being made by the newly established and elected local education authorities. The legislature was the scene for determined but unsuccessful attempts in the next few years to reverse the settlement which Morant had achieved. The corridors of London, of course, continued to be of central importance, but were increasingly complemented and complicated by those in county and city halls and their offices. Many of the political and bureaucratic tussles were now to take place in the shires and boroughs of England, and to be deeply influenced by local circumstances. The political importance of Catholics was concentrated, although never exclusively, in a number of major industrial cities, and in the hands of their elected representatives, local or national.

Archbishops and ministers shuttled restlessly to and fro in negotiating the settlement of 1944, incorporated within an Education Act of a significance which transcends quarrels about the historic 'partnership' of Church and State. Nevertheless, yet again, the major reshaping of the national educational system could simply not have been achieved (as de Gaulle recognised in France) without a partnership with the Churches, and therefore without an increase of public funding for the denominational schools. The Act introduced a lengthy period of peace and accommodation, with steadily rising levels of public funding for Catholic and all other faith-based schools – a protracted calm rudely shattered by the very different and sharply abrasive mood of the 1980s. Catholic and Anglican bishops felt that they were now being excluded from a world in which the competitive imperatives of the market were held to override the traditionally Christian values of a society built on the kind of virtuous consensus which Rab Butler had sponsored. If Whitehall was to define the content of the curriculum, and if competition among schools was to replace an evangelical mission, what place in national society would there be for Catholic schools? A Prime Minster who, ignoring the protests of traditionalists within his own party, sent his own children to state-supported Catholic schools might, however, be expected to be more sympathetic, and so it proved. In spite of some inexplicably clumsy and avoidable early misunderstandings, the 1998 Act (the last important piece of legislation of the last century in this field) restored the essential outlines of the status quo. Indeed, the White Paper presented to Parliament in 2001 went further in holding out a promise of a broad extension of the arrangements for the support of faith-based schools, with higher levels of public funding and a new emphasis on the requirement that faith-based schools should be 'inclusive'. The precise role of Catholic schools within such a new dispensation remains for the moment very unclear.

As in both the United States and France, the future relationship of Catholic schools to the State now merges into larger and even more complex issues, as older and tougher distinctions between religious and secular groups fade into the mists. It remains to be seen how much of this new debate will, as it would certainly have done in the past, be developed within a parliamentary context.

•••••

The State

Ireland and Mann – the Catholic and the Unitarian sympathiser – both lived within the same frame of reference, and in spite of their obvious differences shared much more than a common language. Combes and Guizot – the Freemason and the Protestant separated both by ideology and by seventy years of eventful history – in the same way shared defining assumptions about society and culture, as well as the language which Ireland admired so much. Morant and Ullathorne – the reforming Anglican and the dogmatic Romanist – inherited the same history and shared many unspoken assumptions about the nature of Englishness. For each of these three apparently ill-assorted pairs, the resonances of terms like 'Church' and 'State' were significantly different, and distinctive. Some, but not of course all, of those distinctive differences are mirrored in the characteristically national means of resolving disputes and of defining nationally specific boundaries between Church and State: means which in the shorthand consistently employed in these pages are labelled as courts, streets and corridors. The unavoidable question, therefore, must be: can the comparative history with which this book has been concerned be best understood as three versions of the same story, or as three essentially different narratives? Each nation, as has been repeatedly demonstrated, worked with locally specific notions of the nature and purposes and functions of the State. For the Americans, federal authority was contractually constituted in order to bind together diverse states and variant traditions. Education, for most of the period under review (but steadily less so after about 1950), remained essentially a responsibility of the local community, and to some extent of the families and churches which composed that same community. The State (of course, in the special American sense of that term) furnished a regulatory framework and encouraged local initiative. Washington, until international competition became a dominant theme if not an obsession of federal policy, should do little more than provide the most general kind of rhetorical encouragement of educational effort, with an occasional and specific injection of stimulating funds. No national Ministry of Education or its equivalent existed before the presidency of Jimmy Carter. The only task which had previously been assigned to an embryonic national agency had been the unintrusive collection of harmless statistics. The courts, and archetypically the Supreme Court, sat above local preoccupations in order to arbitrate and adjudicate, to clarify and interpret the Constitution and the intentions of its framers, and – again, especially after the middle of the last century – to build and defend a wall to separate the powers and duties of government from those of religious bodies and other voluntary groups. With one brief and inglorious exception, no serious effort was made to limit the rights of parents to have their children educated as they chose and in schools which they favoured – provided always that those same parents were prepared to pay in order to exercise such rights, and that public money was not perverted into the support of any kind of sectarian education.

For Combes, Guizot and their fellow countrymen, by contrast, the State was the active guarantor of the republican (or bourgeois Orléanist) virtues and of the triple principles of 1789. Since the Republic always is one and indivisible, education must serve above all to cultivate unity, coherence, and patriotism – even if the nature of the State to be served and revered itself changes dramatically as political dynasties and regimes rotate. The State had in consequence both a right and a duty to regulate and to proscribe, and to administer from Paris a centralised system (moderated but not changed fundamentally by the reforms of the 1980s). A powerful and omnipresent Ministry of National Education (under various names) flourished throughout the last two centuries, sometimes cloaked in the panoply of the *Université* and of its Grand Master. At the same time, the Catholic Church in most circumstances preserved a considerable measure of its autonomy and venerable authority in educational matters. Sometimes accepted (with more or less warmth) as a necessary partner in the work of educating the public, at other times it was bitterly resented as an offensive challenge to the monopoly of a genuinely *laïque* system of public education

For the contemporaries and (even more strikingly) the predecessors of Ullathorne and Morant, the State was to be viewed with no small suspicion, whereas (until very late in the nineteenth century) no effective and accountable forms of government at the local level existed even on paper. England was the last of the three countries in which government (national or local) was willing to accept even a minimal form of direct responsibility for education and for the provision of schools. In England, therefore, a state-supported network of church-related schools existed long before a state-provided system was even contemplated by anyone other than a handful of continental-minded reformers. The natural provider of a modestly defined public education was the Church of England by law established (in Erastian terms, the spiritual and cultural embodiment of the nation state). Catholics and other minority groups were, with some reluctance, slowly admitted to share those tasks and the public resources that were increasingly linked with them.

Catholics

If the core meanings of the monosyllabic 'State' slip and slide as the Atlantic or the Channel is crossed, so also does the nature of the Catholic community to which the civil power must somehow relate. One of the original reasons for choosing Roman Catholics as the subject of this particular case study – an analysis of relationships between faiths and governments in three states – was that Catholicism is marked by a greater degree of uniformity across all societies than can be detected in any other form of the Christian faith, or indeed, in any other religion. Catholicism should therefore be expected to provide a conveniently stable constant in any cross-national study. Protestants of all varieties, by contrast, have little international organisation, and even less doctrinal uniformity. Although the Orthodox churches share a set of distinctive common traditions and styles of worship, they would never be described as speaking with one voice or accepting the suzerainty of one patriarch. It is one of the acknowledged strengths of Islam that it embraces a great variety of theological subdivisions and geographical diversities. Buddhists and Hindus have no recognised international organisation and possess neither the will nor the means to impose uniformity or consistency. By contrast, Catholics are bound together by an elaborate system of belief and discipline, by a common liturgy, by strong and interconnected international organisations (such as the religious orders), by a widely accepted appreciation of the nature of a Catholic education, and above all by the authority of the Supreme Pontiff and an elaborately bureaucratic machinery of management.[4] But this real and substantial unity cloaks a surprising degree of variety. Italian Catholics are not just copies of Dutch Catholics. The Americanists discussed in a previous chapter had a special, but assertively loyal, understanding of the ways in which they differed from the Europeans. In France, the Gallican tradition kept alive a long-established tradition of wary suspicion of Rome and the ultramontanes. In England, the Catholics who had sheltered a simple but deep faith across centuries of disdain and persecution were sometimes embarrassed by the Italianate novelties of new converts from Anglo-Catholicism or the exotic exaggerations of the Irish immigrants in the sprawling conurbations of the North.

Such differences directly affected the ways in which Catholics have over time related to the State in all three countries, as well as influencing the policies and stratagems adopted to secure government recognition or support. Moreover, in each of the three countries, the defining characteristics of the Catholic population have themselves changed significantly in the course of the two hundred years surveyed in these pages. For much of that time, the Catholic Church in the United States was a church for immigrants who needed all the help they could get in overcoming nativist prejudices against them. The national parish and its associated school offered a shelter in which cultural roots could be nourished, and instruction given in the vernacular. The dispute between those who saw all this as a necessary but temporary stage on the path to full incorporation in American life and culture and those who saw it as inherently desirable was a recurring theme in the development of American Catholicism and of the educational institutions associated with it. The schools for these new Catholic communities were not the schools which Horace Mann had tirelessly promoted. But during the last century, and at an accelerating pace, American Catholics moved steadily into the mainstream of national life, achieving social and economic success, joining the middle classes in the suburbs. The election of John Fitzgerald Kennedy to the presidency in 1960 is commonly and correctly seen as the most impressive manifestation of this profound change. More recently, the nature of the Catholic population has been further modified by the influx of new and largely Hispanic immigrants. The expectation of contemporary American Catholics (in terms of the kind of education they want and for which they might anticipate support from public funds) is now quite different – different, that is to say, both from what it had been, and different too from what it is in other countries.

Nothing could be more striking than the contrast between the situation of American Catholics and the historic position of Roman Catholics in France. Although French Catholics were, at several points in their history, attacked or vilified, not for a moment could they have been treated as marginal. Catholicism and the French monarchical State were closely entwined, and even the Revolution of 1789 could not break all the imprinted habits of thought and of feeling. The rise of the Huguenots and the ferocity of the Wars of Religion broke the symmetrical monopoly of *une foi, une loi, un roi*. Although the Edict of Nantes conceded that within one France two faiths could be accommodated, within a century it was revoked by a king reputed to have boasted that *L'Etat, c'est moi* and determined to identify loyalty with religious fidelity: to be French was to be Catholic.[5] After the aberrations of the years of revolution, Napoleon's Concordat reaffirmed this traditional identification. There was then (and perhaps even is today) a sense in which to be French is also to be Catholic by default, just as to be English is (as Hooker affirmed) to be Anglican. A Frenchman might be an atheist, but he was a Catholic atheist. The occasionally comic wrangles over the commemoration in 1997 of the fifteenth centenary of the baptism of Clovis revived all the ancient sentiments, as well as rekindling the animosities which had smouldered since the Enlightenment. The country of Clovis was also the land of Voltaire. The Revolution and the anticlerical movements of the nineteenth century did indeed split France into two and deepened the schism in the educational system, now producing *les deux jeunesses*. But Catholicism in France, revered or hated, was inescapable. Under the *ancien regime*, virtually all the schools had been Catholic, as they had never been in America and had not been in England since the Reformation. Catholic education was not just part of the mainstream: it was the mainstream. Of course, after 1789 things were never the same again and the *Université* and all that it represented proved to be a powerful and generally victorious rival. Yet, the Church continued to dominate primary education for much of the nineteenth century, and clung to a significant share of secondary education as well. From time to time, indeed, its position was actually strengthened, as it was by the *loi Falloux*. Even after the work of Guizot, the frontiers of public and private were blurred and the influence of the clergy over the public schools system was as pervasive as it was resented. Catholics preserved their own schools for moral and spiritual rather than pedagogic reasons: few citizens then doubted the quality of the education provided by the Ministry of National Education, but devout Catholics rejected the secularism and anticlericalism associated with it in the minds of their bishops and political leaders. Marshal Pétain's nostalgic restoration of the Old France and its values was emotionally linked to the revival of Catholic privileges, which proved an uncertain blessing for the schools. But, once again, those schools – if only because of their overall number and concentration in certain regions – could not be ignored. Within fifteen years of the collapse of Vichy, de Gaulle's government felt obliged to strike a new bargain with the Catholic educational establishment. Without its help, reform would continue to be frustrated. But the 1959 Law changed the character of Catholic education in France. Catholic schools under contract to the State (and that means most of them) were now directly subject to the educational laws of the Republic, and would no longer be able (even if they wished) to serve a specifically Catholic constituency. The schools evolved to constitute a second and alternative sector of publicly funded education, requiring only a modest financial contribution from families. As confidence in an expanding and changing public education system declined, so the schools offered an attractive (and not necessarily permanent) alternative to families-as-consumers, and their religious mission was and is obscured. Without the intimate and instinctive association of Catholicism with Frenchness, such a development would have been unthinkable. The status of Catholic schools in France is therefore closer to that of Anglican than of Catholic schools in England.

The marginalised situation of the Catholics in England stands out in sharp contrast to their centrality in France, after as well as before the Revolution of 1789. The Reformation in England was grounded in an identification of Church and State as two aspects of the same regal unity and (in the eyes of the prevailing establishment) the Archbishops of Canterbury and York were the legal and lineal descendants of their medieval predecessors. Roman Catholics were not only heretics but rebels as well, and therefore more dangerous than even the wilder Protestant Nonconformist dissenters. They were for that reason to be stripped of all civil rights and excluded from the political community. Roman Catholicism could survive only if its adherents were undetected and silent. Even when a modest measure of relief was extended to them, the Recusants were obliged to live like mice in the woodwork. Their schools were correspondingly invisible, and families who could afford to do so sent their children abroad to be educated. All that was changed by Emancipation and, even more powerfully, by the arrival of the Irish in successive waves of immigration. An affordable Catholic education was now as important for these new and poor citizens as it had been for the Poles settling in Chicago, or the Germans in Minnesota. Even so, it is hard to suppose that Catholics would have received state funding for their schools if the same privilege had not already been conferred on the Established Church, whose right to such support was held to be natural and beyond dispute. There were no 'public' schools in England, only denominational (and overwhelmingly Anglican) schools which could not plausibly be represented as the right and proper places for the education of Catholic children. Government grants were extended to the Catholics simply because it became impracticable to deny them or to refuse such modest concessions as the reading of the Bible in the Douai rather than the King James version. The argument for this extension of the grant arrangements already in force was accepted even more readily as the Catholic community was still small. No one anticipated that, by the last of the years of the last century, there would be as many Catholics as Anglicans in denominationally specific schools. The Catholic community in England drew its political strength, to which its success in extracting government grants was so obviously related, from a unique mixture of the power of the Old Catholic aristocracy and the weight of their parliamentary votes as the franchise was progressively extended beyond the middle classes.

Cautions

The State did not take the same form in all three countries, while in each of them the Catholic community differed in multiple ways. It is, therefore, clear that no glib comparisons may legitimately be drawn nor rules of universal application distilled. Lessons, if indeed there prove to be any, cannot be simple or immediately transferable. Yet, there are some underlying continuities and commonalities of great importance – both to an understanding of the past, and to the elucidation of the likely consequences of present and future developments in all three countries. These are presented as cautionary notes, of which the first is negative. There is nothing automatic or self-explanatory or self-justifying about the extension of public support to private denominational schools. In every single case examined here, such an extension of support has been the product of local and national conditions and of the circumstances of the day. It is not acceptable to argue that because an arrangement 'works' in one country and is there accepted as both morally and politically appropriate, it should therefore be transferred elsewhere with little further thought.[6] History as much as geography changes the conditions. Catholics in England received grants because Anglicans already did. Catholic schools in France were treated punitively when they were identified as directly hostile to the Republic, but more generously when their participation was deemed to be indispensable to a restructuring of the national educational system. Although it is agreed that Catholic schools in America cannot directly receive government subsidy, pupils in those same schools are denied financial support in some circumstances and granted it in others because the Justices cannot agree on an interpretation of the First Amendment. Circumstances alter cases.

None of the three nations now wishes to prohibit varying forms of non-public education, or to deny to families the right to educate their younger members in ways compatible with their own values or religious loyalties. There must, of course, always be at least some debate about the conditions to be universally applied, ranging from a simple observance of health and safety rules, through certain moral safeguards, to more detailed prescriptions about the content of studies or the qualifications of teachers. But there is now, and has been for many decades, a reluctance in democratic societies to limit by law the practice of home schooling, or its obvious extension into teaching provided by parents choosing to act as a group. The attempt to create a monopoly for public schools provided directly or indirectly by the State was, as has been shown, short-lived in the United States and intermittent in France. The issues in all three countries have always been sharply focused on money, on the appropriateness of public subsidy and the conditions to be attached to it. The acceptability of public funding for denominational schools is now general in France and England but still disputed in America. In the two (and other) countries in which it is generally accepted, it is the conditions to be imposed (as well as the level of subsidy) which will for the indefinite future continue to be debated. It emerges from this comparative study that, once conditions have been accepted, they will subsequently be adapted in ways rarely anticipated at the time of the original compromise. The English attempt to insist upon the reading of the Authorised Version of the Bible soon had to be abandoned, even though great importance was at first attached to this requirement. School Inspectors belonging to denominations accepting government grants, once perceived as an essential safeguard, disappeared within thirty years. The level of subsidy, at first restrained (for quite different reasons) by the insistence of both donors and recipients, rose to levels that would once have been quite unacceptable – and in England may now move to at least 90% of capital costs and 100% of recurring expenses. In America (even although direct subsidies to religious schools are outlawed), the circuitous methods of applying public funds for the benefit of students have been subject to constant review and adjustment by the courts. In France, successive administrations have varied the conditions governing the appointment of teachers, the formal relationship of those teachers to the public service, and the means of preserving the *caractère propre* of the Catholic establishments under contract to the State. The conditions of grant will always vary over time, and have unpredictable (and in the eyes of many) undesirable consequences.

Equally unpredictable is the extent to which grants originally intended for and strictly limited to named denominations are subsequently extended in ways which, again, no one had anticipated and few would have welcomed. An early English example of such a development, of considerable interest in the context of this book, is the extension of subsidies – first intended for the Established Church in particular and an acceptable group of Nonconformists – to Roman Catholics and, much less controversially, to Jews. The most striking contemporary example, raising issues of fundamental importance beginning to surface only as this book is written, is the extension of such grants to the other faiths now playing an important part in British society, and especially to Muslims. This same issue is unlikely to be indefinitely sidestepped in France. Examples from the United States are, for the obvious reason that direct subsidy is not allowed, inevitably less striking. But it is noteworthy that, when they belatedly realised that government bounties would not be confined to the groups to which they themselves belonged, advocates for the extension of faith-based activities (including schooling) lost much of their initial enthusiasm for this project favoured by President-elect Bush.

The importance of these cautionary principles – the non-transferability of national experiences, the unpredictability of the ways in which initial conditions attached to subsidy will be varied over time, the impossibility of limiting or even knowing in advance the nature of the groups to which similar subsidy will eventually be extended – becomes even more clear when applied to the major contemporary issues affecting the relationship of the State to faith-based schools. In the United States, the key issue is, and will probably continue to be, that of vouchers, in their various forms. The arguments for them, whether presented as an alleviation of the crippling problems of the Black community in the inner cities or as an extension of choice for middle-class families, are, of course, powerful. A decision, or series of decisions, by the Supreme Court to favour such a development will have the certain consequence of not only strengthening the Catholic schools but also of opening the gates for public subsidies to support schools maintained by all kinds of groups, religious and other. The splintering fragmentation to which that would lead seems, against the background of this comparative and historical study, highly undesirable. It would certainly represent an irreversible defeat for the principles of the American public school.

The situation in France seems at once less threatening and more complex. There, the more obtrusive issue seems at present to be the relationship of the substantial Muslim community to the *laïque* public school which the State still champions. The story of the *foulard*, while formally tangential to this study, is in fact illuminated by it.[7] The first response of the devoted advocates of the French version of the public school was that they were determined to resist an intrusion into that school of any religious practices which they regarded as potentially divisive. The wearing by Muslim girls of the distinctive headscarf was at first questioned and in several widely reported cases rejected by the authorities for precisely this reason. For the moment at least, tempers seem to have cooled. In other societies (and notably England), the obvious response of a community which felt that its own values and practices were being rejected would be to seek to establish many schools of their own, and to secure for them the same standards of state funding as Christian and Jewish schools already enjoyed. Any such demand would be certain to raise the temperature of the debate, and to bring directly into question the settlement already concluded with the Catholics, but never accepted with any enthusiasm by the inheritors of the republican tradition. For the moment, Muslims seem unlikely to seek such contracts with the State, if only because this would require them to apply criteria for admission and for the conduct of their schools which would be unacceptable. A more likely and desirable outcome may therefore be the continuation of the effort by the responsible authorities to make the public schools at least as hospitable to Muslims as they have long been to many Catholics. The previous history of France reviewed in these pages further suggests that the Catholic authorities will be wise to resist, on whatever grounds they can defend, any extension of the present arrangements favouring their schools. A disturbance of the present delicate balance would have alarming consequences for them, and for the calm of French political life.

In England, on the other hand, there is obviously no intention whatsoever of maintaining either the present balance between community and voluntary schools or the equilibrium within the religious sector itself: on the contrary, and as has been explored earlier, the stated intention of the Labour Government led by Tony Blair is that there should be a marked increase in the provision of voluntary faith-based schools. Such a policy fits neatly with the Government's continuing distrust of LEAs and its well-advertised preference for a great diversity of schools operating under different rules and developing a specific character. Considerable sums have been provisionally set aside to stimulate the creation of new, as well as the expansion of existing, faith-based schools. This time (and exceptionally) the pressures for such increases in the percentage share of the costs of such schools and in the total number of schools allowed has come not from the Roman Catholics but from faith groups other than Christian, and from the normally reticent Anglicans. It is the latter who seem most likely to be able and willing to respond convincingly to the repeated emphasis in government statements on the importance of inclusivity. A speech confirming this policy of expansion and inclusion was made by the Secretary of State for Education and Skills to the governing body of the Church of England on the same day that it received yet another gloomy report on the national decline in church attendance.[8] It remains highly probable that, when and if the impetus for further expansion is established, other faith groups – including the evangelical Christians – will wish in their turn to take advantage of these new policies. This has constantly been the pattern in the past. Several worried critics, by no means all of them committed to a secular form of education, have already pointed out the divisive dangers of a further fragmentation and a splitting of a unified school system along religious and racial lines. Such concerns were tragically sharpened when the terrorist attack on the World Trade Center in New York on 11 September 2001 brought to the surface the full extent of the distrust which many Muslims throughout the world entertain for post-Christian Western culture. The longer-term consequences of encouraging different religions and denominations to favour and protect their own schools can, as this study has shown, never be anticipated. Within half a century, a British government could well be confronted with a plethora of such applications for assistance, some of them originating from groups whose very existence raises problems for a democratic society. Attempts to regulate such a development, and to distinguish between religions of which the State approves and those of which it does not, will then plunge government into precisely that excessive entanglement with religion against which the Supreme Court of the United States has so sternly warned. England stands at a critical point in the development of relations between the State and faith-based schools and, for once, the lessons of history and of comparative studies are all too clear.

The policy options available in all three (and, of course, in many other) countries may be mapped along a continuum. At one extreme stands Prohibition, the enforcement of draconian laws against any forms of schooling except those provided and controlled by the State. This is a policy option now universally rejected, although two of the three countries scrutinised in this study (and especially France) have at one time or another been attracted by it. At some distance and pointing towards a more liberal set of policies stands Separation, nurturing respect for religion in its many forms and guaranteeing the rights of families to choose the schools they want and are prepared to pay for, but firmly rejecting any state involvement, financial or otherwise. Next comes a range of options loosely grouped as Accommodation. Various forms of this option are now operative in all three countries, with France (now) and England (always) distancing themselves from any clear advocacy of Separation. Finally, and standing beyond the policies of Accommodation, are those pressing towards Expansion. These policies, of which the British Government is the most vigorous exponent, stand at the opposite extreme from Prohibition. They presuppose the enthusiasm of the State to commit more and more of its educational responsibilities to private and semi-private groups of all kinds, and notably to create as many faith-based schools as possible, each paying at least lip-service to the principles of inclusivity, but each developing its own style and culture. To summarise therefore: America currently moves somewhere between Extension and Accommodation, and France stands at and for Accommodation while leaning nostalgically towards Separation, while England presses towards Extension.

The argument derived from the cautionary principles of this chapter is, when oversimplified, that historical and comparative studies suggest that America would be wise to stand where it is, and lean towards Separation, and that France will prudently maintain the present position, while an English government would be wise to reverse its present Extensionist leanings. In the United States, it is this very set of choices that will shortly be clarified by the

Supreme Court. If France is to preserve the present equilibrium, it will develop generous policies which, without offending the basic principles of *laïcité*, will ensure that members of its newer populations will not be or feel rejected by the public system. It is in England that the situation seems likely to be most tense. The argument that Muslims and others should now enjoy the same privileges as other faith-based groups seems on grounds of simple equity alone at present irresistible. A policy of Separation which would reduce all faiths to equal misery is inaccessible, and no government seems likely to take it seriously. It would, however, be practicable to restrain rather than enlarge government grants and to discourage rather than actively encourage new initiatives, while responding as sensitively as possible to the demands of the minority communities. The present 'balance' is clearly unacceptable. If the consequences of further fragmentation are to be avoided, then it follows that Catholics and Anglicans – while remaining good Accommodationists – will recognise that Christian charity requires them to abstain from any further expansionist claims and indeed to propose some reduction in their present share of the voluntary sector. Anglicans might, for example, elect to yield some of their present schools to the Muslim community, members of which already favour and are welcomed in many of them. Equally bold and generous adjustments will be needed within the mainstream primary and secondary schools themselves. They will need and no doubt wish to evolve an increasingly open policy towards the teaching of religion, and a determination to achieve that degree of inclusivity on which the peaceful survival of British society will depend. John Ireland might well have succeeded if the schools promoted by Horace Mann had not become aggressively Protestant.

Others will, it is to be hoped, draw different conclusions from the narratives and analyses deployed in these pages. But no one is likely to doubt the importance and urgency of the questions raised, or the value of those contributions towards their resolution which can be derived from comparative and historical studies.

Notes

[1] This chapter draws almost exclusively on the arguments of previous pages, and only additional references are given. This quotation occurs at the beginning of chapter 2 and the next quotation on p. 33.

[2] See Maier, 1997.

[3] Judge et al, 1994, p. 39.

[4] Reese, 1996.

[5] Judge, 1969.

[6] For an exposition of this argument, and one of the most scholarly and persuasive statements of the case for government support for faith-based organisations see Glenn (2000).

[7] This is a theme of major significance to an appreciation of the relationship of religion and the public school in France, which at many points illuminates 'the Catholic question' and has influenced the writing of previous chapters. It can be touched only briefly here and deserves to be better understood in anglophone countries. Some sense of the range of recent discussion is given in Allieu (1996), Altschull (1995), Barbier (1995), Baubérot (1990), Coq (1994), Etienne, (1989), Gaspard & Khosrokhvar (1995), Harscher (1996), Keppel (1991), Mayeur (1997), Nouaillhat (1999) and Poulat (1987).

[8] *The Times*, 15 November 2001; *Church Times*, 16 November 2001.

Bibliography

The United States

Ahlstrom, S.E. (1975) *A Religious History of the American People*. New Haven: Yale University Press.

Baker, D.P. & Riordan, C. (1998) The 'Eliting' of the Common American Catholic School and the National Educational Crisis, *Kappan*, 80, pp. 16-23.

Bradley, G.W. (1987) *Church-State Relations in America*. New York: Greenwood Press.

Bryk, A.S.. Lee, V.E. & Holland, P.B. (1993) *Catholic Schools and the Common Good*. Cambridge, MA: Harvard University Press.

Bryson, J. & Houston, S. (1990) *The Supreme Court and Public Funds for Religious Schools*. Jefferson, NC: McFarland & Co.

Buetow, H. (1970) *Of Singular Benefit: the story of U.S. Catholic education*. New York: Macmillan.

Butler, J. (1990) *Awash in a Sea of Faith: Christianizing the American people*. Cambridge, MA: Harvard University Press.

Carper, J.C. & Hunt, T.C. (Eds) (1984) *Religious Schooling in America*. Birmingham, AL: Religious Education Press.

Carper, J.C. & Hunt, T.C. (1993) *Religious Schooling in the United States K-12: a source book*. New York: Garland.

Carter, S.L. (1993) *The Culture of Disbelief: how American law and politics trivialize religious devotion*. New York: Basic Books.

Carter, S. (2000) *God's Name in Vain: the wrongs and rights of religion in politics*. New York: Basic Books.

Cherny, R.W. (1985) *A Righteous Cause: the life of William Jennings Bryan*. New York: Little, Brown.

Chubb, J.E. & Moe, T.E. (1990) *Politics, Markets, and American Schools*. Washington, DC: Brookings Institution.

Clune, W.T. & Witte, J.F. (1990) *Choice and Control in American Education*. Philadelphia: Falmer Press.

Cogley, J. (1973) *Catholic America*. New York: Dial Press.

Coleman, J.S. & Hoffer, T. (1987) *Public and Private High Schools: the impact of community*. New York: Basic Books.

Coleman, J.S., Hoffer, T. & Kilgore, S.B. (1982) *High School Achievement: public, Catholic and private high schools compared*. New York: Basic Books.

Convey, J. (1992) *Catholic Schools Make a Difference: twenty-five years of research.* Washington, DC: National Catholic Education Association.

Cremin, L.A. (1957) *The Republic and the School: Horace Mann on the education of free men.* New York: Teachers College Press.

Culver, R.B. (1929) *Horace Mann and Religion in the Massachusetts Public Schools.* New Haven: Yale University Press.

Curry, T.J. (1986) *The First Freedom: Church and State in America to the passage of the First Amendment.* New York: Oxford University Press.

Diamond, S. (1989) *Spiritual Warfare: the politics of the Christian Right.* Boston: South End Press.

Doerr, E. & Menendez, A.R. (1991) *Church Schools and Public Money.* Buffalo, NY: Prometheus Books.

Dolan, J.P. (1992) *The American Catholic Experience: a history from colonial times to the present.* Notre Dame, IN: University of Notre Dame Press.

Doyle, D. (1980) Public Policy and Private Education, *Kappan*, 62, pp. 16-19.

Draheman, D.L. (1991) *Church-State Constitutional Issues: making sense of the Establishment Clause.* New York: Greenwood Press.

Fass, P.S. (1989) *Outside In: minorities and the transformation of American education.* New York: Oxford University Press.

Fellman, D. (1969) *The Supreme Court and Education.* New York: Teachers College Press.

Finke, R. & Starke, R. (1992) *The Churching of America 1776-1996.* New Brunswick: Rutgers University Press.

Formicola, J. & Morken, H. (Eds) (1997) *Everson Revisited: religion, education and law at the crossroads.* Lanham: Rowman & Littlefield.

Gaddy, B.B., Hall, T.W. & Marzand, R.J. (1996) *School Wars: resolving our conflicts over religion and values.* San Francisco: Jossey-Bass.

Gallup, G. & Castelli, J. (1989) *The People's Religion: American faith in the 90s.* New York: Macmillan.

Gleason, P. (1987) *Keeping the Faith: American Catholicism past and present.* Notre Dame, IN: University of Notre Dame.

Glenn, C.L. (1988) *The Myth of the Common School.* Amherst: University of Massachusetts Press.

Glenn, C.L. (2000) *The Ambiguous Embrace: government and faith-based schools and social agencies.* Princeton: Princeton University Press.

Good, T. & Braden, J. (2000) *The Great School Debate: choice, vouchers and charters.* Mahwah: Erlbaum.

Graham, H.D. (1984) *The Uncertain Triumph: federal education policy in the Kennedy and Johnson years.* Chapel Hill: University of North Carolina Press.

Greeley, A.M. (1982) *Catholic Schools and Minority Students.* New Brunswick: Transaction Books.

Greeley, A.M., McCready, W.C. & McCourt. K. (1976) *Catholic Schools in a Declining Church.* Kansas City: Sheed & Ward.

Gutmann, A. (1987) *Democratic Education.* Princeton: Princeton University Press.

Harris, J.C. (2000) The Funding Dilemma Facing Catholic Elementary and Secondary Schools, in J. Youniss & J. Convey (Eds) *Catholic Schools at the Crossroads*. New York: Teachers College Press.

Howe, Mark de W. (1965) *The Garden and the Wilderness: religion and government in American constitutional history*. Chicago: University of Chicago Press.

Hunt, T.C. & Carper, J.C. (Eds) (1992) *Religion and Schooling in Contemporary America: confronting our cultural pluralism*. New York: Garland.

Ireland, J. (1890) State Schools and Parish Schools – is union between them impossible? *NEA Journal of Proceedings and Addresses, Session 1980*. Topeka: Kansas Publishing House.

Jorgensen, L.P. (1987) *The State and Non-Public Schools*. Columbia: University of Missouri Press.

Kaestle, C.F. (1983) *Pillars of the Republic: common schools and American society, 1780-1860*. New York: Hill & Wang.

Kantowicz, E.R. (1983) *Corporation Sole: Cardinal Mundelein and Chicago Catholicism*. Notre Dame: Notre Dame University Press.

Koenig, H.G. (1980) *A History of the Parishes of the Archdiocese of Chicago*. Chicago: Archdiocese of Chicago.

Larson, E.J. (1985) *Trial and Error: the American controversy over creation and evolution*. New York: Oxford University Press.

Lazerson, M. (1977) Understanding American Catholic History, *History of Education Quarterly*, 17, pp. 297-317.

Levy, L. (1994) *The Establishment Clause: religion and the First Amendment*. New York: Macmillan.

Maier, P. (1997) *American Scripture: how America declared its independence from Britain*. New York: Knopf.

McCarthy, R.M., Skillen, J.W. & Harper, W.A. (1985) *Disestablishment a Second Time: genuine pluralism for American schools*. Grand Rapids, MI: Christian University Press.

McCluskey, N.G. (1964) *Catholic Education in America: a documentary history*. New York: Teachers College Press.

McGreevy, J.T. (1998) *Parish Boundaries: the Catholic encounter with race in the twentieth century urban North*. Chicago: University of Chicago Press.

Messerli, J. (1972) *Horace Mann: a biography*. New York: Alfred A. Knopf.

Morris, C.R. (1997) *American Catholics: the saints and sinners who built America's most powerful Church*. New York: Times Books.

National Catholic Education Association (1983) *The Catholic High School: a national portrait*. Washington, DC: NCEA.

National Catholic Education Association (1998) *United States Catholic Elementary and Secondary Schools: the annual statistical report on schools, enrollment and staffing 1997-98*. Washington, DC: NCEA.

Neuhaus, R.J. (1984) *The Naked Public Square: religion and democracy in America*. Grand Rapids, MI: Eerdmans.

Nord, W.R. (1995) *Religion and American Education*. Chapel Hill: University of North Carolina Press.

O'Connell, M.R. (1985) *John Ireland and the American Catholic Church*. Minnesota: Minnesota Historical Press.

O'Keefe, J. (1996) No Margin, No Mission, in T. McLaughlin, J. O'Keefe & B. O'Keefe (Eds) *The Contemporary Catholic School: context, identity and diversity*. London: Falmer Press.

Paterson, F.R.A. (2000) Building a Conservative Base: teaching history and civics in voucher-supported schools, *Kappan*, 82, pp. 150-155.

Perry, M.J. (1997) *Religion in Politics: constitutional and moral perspectives*. New York: Oxford University Press.

Peshkin, A. (1986) *God's Choice: the total world of a fundamentalist Christian school*. Chicago: University of Chicago Press.

Peterson, P., Howell, W. & Greene, J.P. (1999) *An Evaluation of the Cleveland Voucher Scheme after Two Years*. Cambridge, MA: Harvard University Press.

Ravitch, D. (1973) *The Great School Wars: New York City, 1805-1973*. New York: Basic Books.

Ravitch, D. (1981) *The Troubled Crusade: American education 1945-1980*. New York: Basic Books.

Reese, T.J. (1989) *Archbishop: inside the power structure of the American Catholic Church*. San Francisco: Harper & Row.

Reese, T.J. (1992) *A Flock of Shepherds: the National Conference of Catholic Bishops*. Kansas City: Sheed & Ward.

Reese, T.J. (1996) *Inside the Vatican: the politics and organisation of the Catholic Church*. Cambridge, MA: Harvard University Press.

Riordan, C. (2000) Trends in Student Demography in Catholic Secondary Schools, in J. Youniss & J. Convey (Eds) *Catholic Schools at the Crossroads*. New York: Teachers College Press.

Ryan, M.P. (1964) *Are Catholic Schools the Answer?* New York: Holt, Rinehart & Winston.

Sanders, J.W. (1977a) Nineteenth Century Boston Catholics and the School Question, *Working Paper Series No. 2*. Notre Dame: Cushwa Center.

Sanders, J.W. (1977b) *The Education of an Urban Minority: Catholics in Chicago 1833-1965*. New York: Oxford University Press.

Schaub, M. (2000) A Faculty at the Crossroads: a profile of American Catholic school teachers, in J. Youniss & J. Convey (Eds) *Catholic Schools at the Crossroads*. New York: Teachers College Press.

Sorauf, F.J. (1976) *The Wall of Separation: the constitutional politics of Church and State*. Princeton: Princeton University Press.

Stevens, M.L. (2002) *Kingdom of Children: culture and controversy in the homeschooling movement*. New Haven: Yale University Press.

Tyack, D. (1987) *Law and the Shaping of Public Education 1784-1954*. Madison: University of Wisconsin Press.

Tyack, D. & Hanson, E. (1982) *Managers of Virtue: a history of leadership in American public education 1820-1980*. New York: Basic Books.

Underkuffler, L.S. (2001) Public Funding for Religious Schools: difficulties and dangers in a pluralistic society, *Oxford Review of Education*, 27, pp. 577-592.

Vitullo-Martin, T. & Cooper, B. (1987) *Separation of Church and Child: the constitution and federal aid to religious schools*. Indianapolis: Hudson Institute.

Walsh, T. (1996) *Parish School: American Catholic parochial education from colonial times to the present*. New York: Crossroads/Herder.

Wills, G. (1971) *Bare Ruined Choirs*. Garden City, NY: Doubleday.

Wills, G. (1990) *Under God: religion and American politics*. New York: Simon & Schuster.

Wilson, J.F. (1986, 1987) *Church and State in America*, 2 vols. Westport: Greenwood.

Witte, J.F. (2000) *The Market Approach to Education: an analysis of America's first voucher program*. Princeton: Princeton University Press.

Youniss, J. & Convey, J. (Eds) (2000) *Catholic Schools at the Crossroads*. New York: Teachers College Press.

Youniss, J., Convey, J.J. & McLellan, J.A. (Eds) (2000) *The Catholic Character of Catholic Schools*. Notre Dame: University of Notre Dame Press.

France

Allieu, N. (1996) *Laïcité et culture religieuse à l'école*. Paris: ESF.

Altschull, E. (1995) *Le voile contre l'école*. Paris: Le Seuil.

Atkin, N. (1991) *Church and Schools in Vichy France*. New York: Garland.

Ballion, R. (1982) *Les consommateurs d'école*. Paris: Stock.

Barbier, M. (1995) *La laïcité*. Paris: Le Harmattan.

Basdevant-Gaudemer, B. (1988) *Le jeu concordataire dans la France du XIX⁰ siècle*. Paris: Presses Universitaires de France.

Battut, J., Join-Lambert, C. & Vandermeersch, E. (1995) *1984: La guerre scolaire a bien eu lieu*. Paris: Desclée de Brouwer.

Baubérot, J. (1990) *Vers un nouveau pacte laïque?* Paris: Le Seuil.

Baubérot, J., Gauthier, G., Legrand, L. & Ognier, P. (1994) *Histore de la laïcité*. Besançon: Centre Régional de Documentation Pédagogique de Franche-Comté.

Baumier, A. (1999) Le privé, privé de religion, *Le Monde de l'Education*, 270, pp. 42-43.

Boucher, G. (1996) *Laïcité et enseignement: formation des enseignants*. Paris: Armand Colin.

Bourdoncle, P. & Moitel, P. (1978) *Aumôneries de l'enseignement public*. Paris: Editions du Cerf.

Brodin, J-D. (1994) *L'Affaire*. Paris: Fayard-Juillard.

Burke, P. (1990) *The French Historical Revolution: the Annales School 1929-89*. Cambridge: Polity Press.

Cahm, E. (1994) *L'Affaire Dreyfus*. Paris: Livre de Poche.

Charlot, J. (1994) *La politique en France*. Paris: Livre de Poche.

Chauvin, C. (1999) *Lammenais*. Paris: Desclée de Brouwer.

Chevallier, P. (1983) *La séparation de l'église et de l'état: Jules Ferry et Leon XIII*. Paris: Fayard.

Cholvy, G. (1991) *La religion en France de la fin du XVIII° siècle à nos jours*. Paris: Hachette.

Cholvy, G. & Chaline, N.J. (1995) *L'enseignement catholique en France au XIX° et XX° siècles*. Paris: Editons du Cerf.

Cholvy, G. & Hilaire, Y.M. (1986) *Histoire religieuse de la France contemporaine 1830-1939*. Toulouse: Privat.

Coq, G. (1994) *Laïcité et République, le lien nécessaire*. Paris: Editions du Félin.

Dabousville, P. ('1979) *Foi et culture dans l'Eglise aujourd'hui*. Paris: Fayard.

Duhamel, E. (1997) *La Ve République*. Paris: le Seuil.

Etienne, B. (1989) *La France et l'Islam*. Paris: Hachette.

Etienne, B. (Ed.) (1991) *L'Islam en France*. Paris: Centre National de Recherche Scientifique.

Freyssinet-Dominjon, J. (1994) *Publiqe ou Catholique?* Paris: Nathan.

Gaillard, J-M. (1989) *Jules Ferry*. Paris: Faillard.

Gaspard, F. & Khosrokhvar, F. (1995) *Le foulard et la République*. Paris: La Découverte.

Gelly, V. (1996) *François Bayrou*. Paris: Bartillat.

George, J. & Thorel, A.M. (1995) *L'enseignement privé en France*. Paris: Dalloz.

Gildea, R. (1996) *France since 1945*. Oxford: Oxford University Press.

Halls, W.D. (1981) *The Youth of Vichy France*. Oxford: Clarendon Press.

Handourtzel, R. (1997) *Vichy et l'école, 1940-1944*. Paris: Noêsis.

Harscher, G. (1996) *La Laïcité*. Paris: Presses Universitaires de France.

Hewlett, N. (1998) *Modern French Politics: analysing conflict and consensus since 1945*. Cambridge: Polity Press.

Johnson, D. (1963) *Guizot: aspects of French history 1789-1871*. London: Routledge & Kegan Paul.

Judge, H. (1969) Louis XIV and the Church, in J.C. Rule (Ed.) *Louis XIV and the Craft of Kingship*. Columbus: Ohio State University Press.

Keppel, G. (1991) *Les banlieues de l'Islam: naissance d'une religion en France*. Paris: Le Seuil.

Langouët, G. & Léger, A. (1994) *Ecole publique ou école privé? Trajectoires et réussites scolaires*. Paris: Fabert.

Larkin, M. (1974) *Church and State after the Dreyfus Affair: the separation issue in France*. London: Macmillan.

Launay, M. (1988) *L'église et l'école en France XIX° et XX° siècles*. Paris: Desclée de Brouwer.

Le Bret, M.M. & Baulic, H. (1989) *Choisir une école catholique*. Paris: Centurion.

Leclerc, G. (1995) *La bataille de l'école: quinze siècles d'histoire et trois ans de combat*. Paris: Denoël.

Le Goff, J. (1991) *Histoire de la France religieuse vol. 3: Du roi très chrétien à la laïcité républicaine*. Paris: Le Seuil.

Lelièvre, C. (1991) *Jules Ferry: La République Educatrice*. Paris: Hachette.

Lequiller, P. (1992) *La guerre scolaire n'aura pas lieu*. Paris: Criterion.

Maudoit, A.M. & Maudoit, S. (1984) *La France contre la France – la séparation de l'église et de l'état*. Paris: Plon.

Mayeur, J-M. (1991) *La séparation des églises et de l'état*. Paris: Editions Ouvrières.

Mayeur, J-M. (1997) *La question laïque: XIXᵉ et XXᵉ siècles*. Paris: Fayard.

Mendras, H. with Cole, A. (1995) *Social Change in Modern France*. Cambridge: Cambridge University Press.

Merle, G. (1991) *Emile Combes*. Paris: Fayard.

Messner, F. (Ed.) (1995) *La culture réligieuse à l'école*. Paris: Editions du Cerf.

Nettlebeck, C.W. (1998) The Eldest Daughter of the *Trente Glorieuses*: Catholicism and national identity in postwar France, *Modern and Contemporary France*, 6, pp. 445-462.

Nique, C. (1990a) *Comment l'éducation devint une affaire d'Etat, 1815-1840*. Paris: Nathan.

Nique, C. & Lelièvre, C. (1990b) *Histoire Biographique de l'Enseignement en France*. Paris: Retz.

Niveau, M. (1996) *Les politiques de l'école: entre le mensonge et l'ignorance*. Paris: ESF.

Nouaillhat, R. (1999) *Enseigner les religions au collège et au lycée*. Besançon: Editions de l'Atelier CNDP-CRDP de Franche-Comté.

Ozouf, M. (1982) *L'école, l'église et la République 1871-1914*. Paris: Editions Cana.

Pelletier, D. (1997) *Les catholiques en France depuis 1815*. Paris: La Découverte.

Plenel, E. (1997) *La République inachevée, l'état et l'école en France*. Paris: Stock (reédition).

Poulat, E. (1987) *Liberté-Laïcité: les guerres des deux France et le principe de la modernité*. Paris: Cujas-Le Cerf.

Prost, A. (1992) *Education, société et politiques*. Paris: le Seuil.

Rémond, R. (1965) *La vie politique en France*. Paris: Colin.

Rémond, R. (1985) *L'anticlericalisme en France, de 1815 à nos jours*. Bruxelles: Editions Complète.

Risse, J. (1994) *Le Petit Père Combes*. Paris: L'Harmattan.

Savary, A. (1985) *En toute liberté*. Paris: Hachette.

Schlick, J. (Ed.) (1975) *Eglises et Etat en Alsace et en Moselle*. Strasbourg: CERDIC Publications.

Swerry, J-M. (1995) *Aumôneries catholiques dans l'enseignement public*. Paris: Editions du Cerf.

Tallett, F. & Atkin, N. (1991) *Religion, Society and Politics in France since 1789*. London: Hambledon.

Toulemonde, L. (1995) Le nouveau visage du Privé, *Le Monde de l'Education*, 226, pp. 26-30.

Visse, J-P. (1995) *La question scolaire 1975-1984, évolution et permanence*. Paris: Presses Universitaires de Septentrion.

Weber, E. (1991) *Ma France: mythes, culture, politiques*. Paris: Fayard.

Weill, G. (1909) *Histoire du catholicisme libéral en France 1828-1908*. Paris: Alcan.

Wright, G. (1987) *France in Modern* Times, 4th edn. New York: W.W. Norton.

England

Addison, P. (1975) *The Road to 1945: British politics and the Second World War.* London: Jonathan Cape.

Akenson, D.H. (1973) *Education and Enmity: the control of schooling in Northern Ireland 1920-1950.* Newton Abbot: David & Charles.

Allen, B.M. (1934) *Sir Robert Morant.* London: Macmillan.

Anderson, R.D. (1995) *Education and the Scottish People.* Oxford: Clarendon Press.

Andrews, L. (1976) *The Education Act of 1918.* London: Routledge & Kegan Paul.

Arthur, J. (1995a) *The Ebbing Tide: policy and principles of Catholic education.* Leominster: Gracewing.

Arthur, J. (1995b) Government Education Policy and Catholic Voluntary Aided Schools, *Oxford Review of Education,* 21, pp. 447-456.

Ashraf, S.A. & Hirst, P. (Eds) (1994) *Religion and Education: Islamic and Christian approaches.* Cambridge: Islamic Academy.

Badham, P. (Ed.) (1989) *Religion, State and Society in Modern Britain.* Lampeter: Edward Mellen Press.

Barber, M. (1994) *The Making of the 1944 Education Act.* London: Cassell.

Barker, P. (Ed.) (1984) *Founders of the Welfare State.* London: Heinemann.

Barker, R. (1972) *Education and Politics 1900-1951: a study of the Labour Party.* Oxford: Oxford University Press.

Beales, A.C.F. (1950) The Struggle for the Schools, in G.A. Beck (Ed.) *The English Catholics, 1850-1950.* London: Burnes Oates.

Beales, A.C.F. (1963) *Education under Penalty.* London: London University Press.

Beck, G.A. (Ed.) (1950) *The English Catholics, 1850-1950.* London: Burnes Oates.

Beck, G.A. (1955) *The Case for Catholic Schools.* London: Catholic Education Council.

Bell, G.K.A. (1952, 3rd edn) *Randall Davidson.* London: Oxford University Press.

Benn, C. & Simon, B. (1970) *Half Way There.* London: McGraw Hill.

Bossy, J. (1975) *The English Catholic Community, 1570-1850.* London: Darton, Longman and Todd.

Butler, C. (1926) *The Life and Times of Bishop Ullathorne 1806-1881.* London: Burns Oates & Washbourne.

Butler, D. & Butler, G. (2000) *Twentieth Century Political Facts.* London: Macmillan.

Butler, R.A. (1971) *The Art of the Possible.* London: Hamish Hamilton.

Cameron, J. (1966) *Images of Authority.* London: Compass Books.

Catholic Education Service (1997) *Partners in Mission.* London: Catholic Education Service.

Chadwick, P. (1994) *Schools of Reconciliation: issues in Roman Catholic-Anglican education.* London: Cassell.

Chadwick, P. (1997) *Shifting Alliances: Church and State in English education*. London: Cassell.

Chapman, R. ((1961) *Father Faber*. London: Burns Oates.

Church Schools Review Group (2001) *The Way Ahead: Church of England schools in the new millennium*. London: Church House Publishing.

Conroy, J. (1999) *Catholic Education: inside/out-outside/in*. Leamington Spa: Lindisfarne Books.

Conroy, J. (2001) A Very Scottish Affair: Catholic education and the State, *Oxford Review of Education*, 27, pp. 543-558.

Cruickshank, M. (1963) *Church and State in English Education: 1870 to the present day*. London: Macmillan.

Davies, J. (1994) L'Art du Possible, *Recusant History*, October.

Department for Education and Skills (2001a) *Schools Achieving Success*. London: The Stationery Office.

Department for Education and Skills (2001b) *Statistics of Education: Schools in England 2001*. London: The Stationery Office.

Eaglesham, E.J.R. (1967) *The Foundations of Twentieth Century Education in England*. London: Routledge & Kegan Paul.

Egan, J. (1988) *Opting Out: Catholic Schools today*. Leominster: Fowler Wright Books.

Evennett, H.O. (1944) *The Catholic Schools of England and Wales*. Cambridge: Cambridge University Press.

Fenwick, I.G.K. (1976) *The Comprehensive School 1944-1970*. London: Methuen.

Fisher, H.A.L. (1918) *Educational Reform*. London: Oxford University Press.

Fisher, H.A.L. (1940) *An Unfinished Autobiography*. London: Oxford University Press.

Fitz, J., Halpin, D. & Power, S. (1993) *Grant Maintained Schools: education in the market place*. London: Kogan Page.

Fothergill, B. (1963) *Nicholas Wiseman*. London: Faber & Faber.

Francis, L.J. (1983) The Logic of Education, Theology and the Church School, *Oxford Review of Education*, 9, pp. 147-162.

Gay, J.D. (Ed.) (1982) *The Debate about Church Schools in the Oxford Diocese*. Abingdon: Culham College Institute.

Gay, J. & Greenough, J. (2000) *The Geographical Distribution of Church Schools in England*. Abingdon: Culham College Institute.

Gosden, P.H.J.H. (1976) *Education in the Second World War*. London: Methuen.

Grace, G. (2001) The State and Catholic Schooling in England and Wales: politics, ideology and mission integrity, *Oxford Review of Education*, 27, pp. 489-500.

Grace, G. (2002) *Catholic Schools: mission, markets and morality*. London: Routledge Falmer.

Green, S.J.D. (2000) The 1944 Education Act: a Church-State perspective, in J.P. Parry & S. Taylor (Eds) *Parliament and the Church 1529-1960*. Edinburgh: Edinburgh University Press.

Grier, L. (1952) *Achievement in Education: the work of M.E. Sadler 1885-1935*. London: Constable.

Halsey, A.H. & Webb, J. (2000) *Twentieth Century Social Trends*. London: Macmillan.

Hastings, A. (1991) *Church and State: the English experience*. Exeter: University of Exeter Press.

Heenan, J. (1944) *Cardinal Hinsley*. London: Burns Oates.

Heenan, J. (1971) *Not the Whole Truth*. London: Hodder & Stoughton.

Henson, H.H. (1939) *The Church of England*. Cambridge: Cambridge University Press.

Hewer, C.J. (2001) Schools for Muslims, *Oxford Review of Education*, 27, pp. 515-528.

Hickman, M. (1995) *Religion, Class and Identity: the state, the Catholic church, and the education of the Irish in Britain*. Aldershot: Avebury.

R. Hooker (1981) 'Of the Laws of Ecclesiastical Polity', in P.E. Stanwood (Ed.) *the Folger Library Edition of the Works of Richard Hooker*. Cambridge, MA: The Bellknap Press of Harvard University Pess.

Holland, M.G. (1987) *The British Catholic Press and the Educational Controversy 1847-1865*. New York: Garland.

Hollowell, J.H. (1901) *What Nonconformists Stand For*. London: Free Church Library.

Hornsby-Smith, M.P. (1978) *Catholic Education: the unobtrusive partner*. London: Sheed & Ward.

Hornsby-Smith, M.P. (1987) *Roman Catholicism in England and Wales*. Cambridge: Cambridge University Press.

Hornsby-Smith, M.P. (1999) *Catholics in England 1950-2000: historical and sociological perspectives*. London: Cassell.

Howard, A. (1987) *RAB: the life of R.A. Butler*. London: Jonathan Cape.

Hypher, P.A. (1996) Catholic Schools and Other Faiths, in T. McLaughlin, J. O'Keefe & B. O'Keefe (Eds) *The Contemporary Catholic School: context, identity and diversity*. London: Falmer Press.

Jackman, S.W. (1977) *Nicholas Cardinal Wiseman: a Victorian prelate and his writings*. Charlottesville: Five Lamps Press.

Jeffereys, K. (1984) R.A. Butler, the Board of Education and the 1944 Education Act, *History*, 69, 297, pp. 415-431.

Jeffereys, K. (Ed.) (1987) *Labour and the Wartime Coalition: from the diary of James Chuter Ede*. London: Historians Press.

Judge, H. (1984a) R.L. Morant, in P. Barker (Ed.) (1984) *Founders of the Welfare State*. London: Heinemann.

Judge, H. (1984b) *A Generation of Schooling*. Oxford: Oxford University Press.

Judge, H. (2001) Faith-based Schools and State Funding, *Oxford Review of Education*, 27, pp. 463-474.

Kent, J. (1992) *William Temple: Church, State and society in Britain 1880-1959*. Cambridge: Cambridge University Press.

Labour Party (1995) *Diversity and Excellence*. London: The Labour Party.

Landon, M. (1973) *Anna and the King of Siam*. Bath: Chivers.

Leese, J. (1950) *Personalities and Power in English Education*. Leeds: E.J. Arnold.

Lemosse, M. (1996) *Education et Religion dans les Iles Britanniques: Dieu à l'Ecole, Dieu et l'Ecole*, vol. 13 no. 2. Nice: Cycnos.

Lewis, P. (1994) *Islamic Britain: politics and identity among British Muslims*. London: I.B. Tanner.

Lockhart, J.G. (1949) *Cosmo Gordon Lang*. London: Hodder & Stoughton.

Mackinnon, D. & Statham, J. (1999) *Education in the UK: facts and figures*, 3rd edn. London: Hodder & Stoughton.

McLelland, V.A. (1962) *Cardinal Manning: his public life and influence*. London: Oxford University Press.

McLelland, V.A. & Hodgetts, M. (Eds) (1999) *From Without the Flaminian Gate: one hundred and fifty years of Roman Catholicism in England and Wales 1850-2000*. London: Darton, Longman & Todd.

Maclure, J.S. (1968) *Educational Documents, England and Wales 1818-1968*. London: Methuen.

Maclure, J.S. (1988) *Education Reformed: a guide to the Education Reform Act 1988*. Sevenoaks: Hodder & Stoughton.

Moloney, T. (1985) *Westminster, Whitehall and the Vatican: the role of Cardinal Hinsley 1925-1943*. Tunbridge Wells: Burns & Oates.

Morley, J. (1908) *Life of William Ewart Gladstone*. London: Edward Lloyd.

Morris, A.J.A. (1972) *C.P. Trevelyan 1870-1958: portrait of a radical*. Belfast: Blackstaff Press.

Murphy, J. (1971) *Church, State and Schools in Britain 1800-1970*. London: Routledge & Kegan Paul.

Murphy, J. (1972) *The Education Act 1870*. Newton Abbot: David & Charles.

Murray, V. (1996) Other Faiths in Catholic Schools, in T. McLaughlin, J. O'Keefe & B. O'Keefe (Eds) *The Contemporary Catholic School: context, identity and diversity*. London: Falmer Press.

Norman, E.R. (1984) *The English Catholic Church in the Nineteenth Century*. Oxford: Clarendon Press.

Nugent, A. & Hewitt, T. (1996) *The Voluntary Controlled Schools*. London: The National Society.

O'Keefe, B. (1986) *Faith, Culture and the Dual System*. London: Falmer Press.

Ogg, D. (1947) *Herbert Fisher – a short biography*. London: Edward Arnold.

Parsons, G. (Ed.) (1993, 1994) *The Growth of Religious Diversity: Britain from 1945*. 2 vols. London: Open University & Routledge.

Parry, J.P. & Taylor, S. (Eds) *Parliament and the Church 1529-1960*. Edinburgh: Edinburgh University Press.

Paz, D.G. (1992) *Popular Anti-Catholicism in Mid-Victorian England*. Stanford: Stanford University Press.

Percy, Lord Eustace (1930) *Education at the Crossroads*. London: Evans Brothers.

Percy, Lord Eustace (1958) *Some Memories*. London: Eyre & Spottiswoode.

Rodgers, R. (1955) *Rodgers and Hammerstein's* The King and I. New York: Chappell.

Schiefen, R.J. (1984) *Nicholas Wiseman and the Transformation of English Catholicism.* Sheperdstown, WV: Peatmoss Press.

Simon, B. (1974) *The Politics of Educational Reform 1920-1940.* London: Lawrence & Wishart.

Temple, W. (1942) *Christianity and the Social Order.* London: Penguin.

Timmins, N. (1995) *The Five Giants: a biography of the welfare state.* London: Harper Collins.

Trevelyan, C.P. (1921) *From Liberalism to Labour.* London: George Allen & Unwin.

Trevelyan, C.P. (1924) *The Broad Road in Education.* London: The Labour Party.

Trevelyan, C.P. (c1927) *Education When Labour Rules Again.* London: The Labour Party.

Tropp, A. (1957) *The School Teachers: the growth of the teaching profession in England and Wales from 1800 to the present day.* London: Heinemann.

Ullathorne, W.B. (1857) *Notes on the Education Question.* London: Richardson & Son.

Ullathorne, W. (1995) *The Devil is a Jackass.* ed. by Leo Madigan. Leomimster: Gracewing.

Walford, G. (Ed.) (1996) *School Choice and the Quasi Market.* Wallingford: Triangle Books.

Walford, G. (2000) *Policy and Politics in Education: sponsored grant maintained schools and religious diversity.* Aldershot: Ashgate.

Ward, Wilfrid (1897) *The Life and Times of Cardinal Wiseman,* 2 vols London: Longmans, Green & Co.

Warlock, D. (1997) What the Butler Did Not See, in Catholic Education Service *Partners in Mission.* London: Catholic Education Service.

Webb, S.J. (1901) *The Education Muddle and the Way Out.* London: Fabian Society.

Winter, J.M. (1974) *Socialism and the Challenge of War: ideas and politics in Britain 1912-1918.* London: Routledge & Kegan Paul.

Wiseman, N. (1850) *An Appeal to the Reason and Good Sense of the English People on the Subject of the Catholic Hierarchy.* London: Thomas Richardson & Son.

Wyatt, D.K. (1969) *The Politics of Reform in Thailand: education in the reign of King Chulalongkorn.* New Haven: Yale University Press.

General

Baubérot, Jean (Ed.) (1994) *Religions et Laïcïté dans l'Europe des Douze.* Paris: Syros.

Bereday, G.Z.F. & Lauwerys, J.A. (Eds) (1966) *Church and State in Education: World Year Book of Education.* London: Evans Brothers.

Boyd, W.L. & Cibulka, J.G. (Eds) (1989) *Private Schools and Public Policy: international perspectives.* Philadelphia: Falmer Press.

Bridges, D.A. (1994) *Education in the Market Place.* London: Falmer Press.

Glenn, C.L. (1989) *Choice of Schools in Six Nations.* Washington, DC: US Department of Education.

Green, A. (1990) *Education and State Formation: the rise of education systems in England, France and the USA*. London: Macmillan.

Hanley, D. (1998) Religion, Politics and Identity: the Catholics of France and Britain, *Modern and Contemporary France*, 6, pp. 375-378.

Judge, H., Lemosse, M., Paine, L. & Sedlak, M. (1994) *The University and the Teachers: France, the United States, England*. Wallingford: Triangle Books.

Julg, Jean (1990) *L'Eglise et les Etats: Histoire des Concordats*. Paris: Nouvelle Cité.

McLaughlin, T., O'Keefe, J. & O'Keefe, B. (Eds) (1996) *The Contemporary Catholic School: context, identity and diversity*. London: Falmer Press.

McLelland, V.A. (1992) *The Catholic School and the European Context* (Aspects of Education Number 46). Hull: University of Hull.

Reese, T.J. (1996) *Inside the Vatican: the politics and organisation of the Catholic Church*. Cambridge, MA: Harvard University Press.

Rémond, R. (1998) *Religion et société en Europe: essai sur la sécularisation des sociétés européens (1789-1998)*. Paris: Le Seuil.

Tallett, F. & Atkin, N. (Eds) (1996) *Catholicism in Britain and France since 1789*. London: Hambledon Press.

Tulasiewicz, W. & Brock, C. (Eds) (1988) *Christianity and Educational Provision in International Perspective*. London: Routledge.

Walford, G. (Ed.) (1989) *Private School in Ten Countries: policy and practice*. London: Routledge & Kegan Paul.

Whitty, G., Power, S. & Halpin, D. (1998) *Devolution and Choice in Education: the school, the state and the market*. Buckingham: Open University Press.

Willaime, J-P. (1990) *Univers scolaire et religieux*. Paris: Editions du Cerf.

Abbreviations

APEL	Association des parents de l'école libre
APLE	Association parlementaire pour la liberté de l'enseignement
CFDT	Confédération française démocratique du travail
CFTC	Cofédération française des travailleurs chrétiens
CNAL	Comité national d'action laïque
CES	Catholic Education Service (London)
CPSC	Catholic Poor Schools Committee
EIP	Etablissement d'intérêt public
FCPE	Fédération des conseils des parents d'élèves des écoles publics
FEN	Fédération de l'Education Nationale
FEP	Fédération de l'enseignement privé
FSU	Fédération syndicale unitaire
NCEA	National Catholic Education Association (Washington, DC)
RPR	Rassemblement pour la République
SC	Supreme Court of the United States of America
SGEN	Syndicat général de l'Education Nationale
SNEC	Syndicat national de l'enseignement chrétien
SPULEN	Service public, unifié et laïque de l'Education Nationale
UDF	Union pour la démocracie française